£9·98

Justice. Its determinants in social interaction

Sociology, law and legal theory Vol. 1

Editorial board

Vilhelm Aubert, *University of Oslo*
Britt-Mari Blegvad, *University of Copenhagen*
Wolfgang Kaupen, *University of Cologne*
Kees Schuyt, *University of Nijmegen*

Justice
Its determinants
in social interaction

Torstein Eckhoff

University of Oslo, Norway

Rotterdam University Press/1974

D7452/8/1

IV

To Trygve and Jens,
who have taught me
that questions of justice
are important

Preface to the English edition

The English edition is, for the most part, a translation of the Norwegian text published in Oslo in 1971 under the title 'Rettferdighet ved utveksling og fordeling av verdier'. Certain paragraphs have been rewritten, however, and some examples have been changed. As well as this, a number of references to works written in Scandinavian languages have been omitted and additional references to works in English included. I am greatly indebted to Anne Treite, who did the original translation and whom I consulted before making alterations. The translation involved considerable work, much of it very exacting, but I should add here that she is in no way responsible for the final version.

Fred R. Berger, William Lambert, George Levinger and Nathalie Rogoff Ramsøy have read parts of the English manuscript and given me much valuable advice.

The Norwegian Research Council for Science and the Humanities provided financial assistance for the translation.

Oslo, 1974   *Torstein Eckhoff*

Preface to the Norwegian edition

In this book I discuss questions which have occupied both social science and philosophy a good deal and I try to benefit from the insights found in both these fields. But on the whole the work is more closely connected with social science, especially sociology and social anthropology, than with philosophy.

The work was begun because I became interested in justice or, rather, in the *arguments* of justice. I set myself the task of investigating what distinguishes this manner of argumentation from others, the conditions under which it is used, and the consequences of its use. This led me to study those forms of human interaction in which there is a 'give and take' of positive or negative values (exchange, restitution, competition, revenge and punishment) or in which resources are allocated among a number of recipients. The main purpose of the work is to contribute to the development of general theories concerning these kinds of interaction. Justice has been allotted its place within this framework – but not such an important place as originally intended nor, perhaps, as important a one as the title may indicate. Epistemological questions of what justice is will not be discussed. Nor will any stand be taken on questions of social policy. My role in this book is to observe – not to take part in – debates concerning such issues.

I believe that it was the form of my children's arguments which first aroused my interest in questions of justice. I express my gratitude for the understanding which they thereby gave me by dedicating the book to them. I am also indebted to many others ; first and foremost to Siri Naess who worked with me for several years and who has tested empirically some of my hypotheses in a study of the attitudes of school children and teachers to allocation issues. Of the many people who have assisted me by collecting material or by reading and criticizing draft manuscripts, I would particularly like to mention Torben Agersnap, Mads Andenaes, Vilhelm Aubert, Agnete Weis Bentzon, Mogens Blegvad, Jan Brøgger, Frede Castberg, Nils Christie, Johan Galtung, Fridtjof

Frank Gundersen, Arne Haugestad, Jo Hov, Jon Johnsen, Leif Terje Løddesøl, Thomas Mathiesen, Nils Moe, Harald Ofstad and Nils Kristian Sundby. I would also like to thank the Institute for Social Research for the inspiration derived from the milieu there, and the Norwegian Council for Science and the Humanities as well as the Anders Jahres Fund for their economic support.

Oslo, 1970   *Torstein Eckhoff*

Contents

PART III. ALLOCATION

Part I. Norms, strategies and reasons

1. Introduction

'Les faits moraux sont des phéno-
mènes comme les autres ; ils consistent en des règles d'action qui se
reconnaissent à certains caractères
distinctifs ; il doit donc être possible
de les observer, de les décrire, de les
classer et de chercher les lois qui les
expliquent.'
Emile Durkheim, *De la division du
travail social,* Préface de la première
édition.

I. RECIPROCATION AND ALLOCATION

An important aspect of many – perhaps all – inter-human relations is
what we can call 'transfer'. By this I refer to a situation where one person
undertakes some action in relation to another to which this latter person attaches a positive or negative value. He gives him, for instance, an
object, takes something from him, helps or consoles him, hurts or
offends him.

The theme of this book turns on certain forms of interaction in which
two or more transfers are interconnected. I operate with two main types
of such combinations : 'reciprocation' and 'allocation'. My aim is to
chart reciprocation and allocation activity occurring in different situations and to discuss some of the factors which contribute towards the
regulation of this activity.

'Reciprocation' means a situation of 'give and take' between two
parties. The point of combination here is to be found in the fact that
one transfer is conditioned by another. If positive values are reciprocated I use the expression 'exchange' (fig. 1) irrespective of what kind of

Figure 1

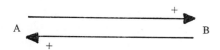

3

positive values are involved. For instance, it is exchange if B buys something from A and pays for it, or if he gets help and support from him and repays with affection and respect. – Another form of reciprocation is present when the parties inflict negative actions on each other. One party harms the other who then reciprocates by revenging

Figure 2

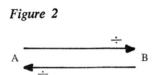

himself or punishing the first party. It can also happen that a negative action gives rise to a later positive action from the same party. For

Figure 3

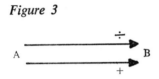

instance, A repairs or pays compensation for damage inflicted on B. The opposite order of sequence can also occur : A has previously given B some assistance or support and therefore feels entitled to inconvenience him or make demands on him. Even though both transfers stem from

Figure 4

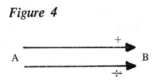

the same party, the term 'reciprocation' is still used in these instances.

As already mentioned, the fact that one transfer is conditioned by another is a common characteristic of reciprocation. I do not indicate any causal relationship with the expression 'conditioned by', but mean rather that transfer No. 1 serves as the reason (or part of the reason) for transfer No. 2, for instance by giving rise to a right or duty to reciprocate, or by making it appropriate or natural to do so. When not otherwise stated, it is assumed that *both* parties consider the transfers

4

to be connected and that both have the same opinion as to what is positive and what negative. But on some occasions I shall include instances where only one party views the transfers as being connected with each other; instances will also be included where, for example, one party regards as a punishment something which the other party has intended as a service.

There can be systems of interaction involving more than two participants where transfers are interconnected in a similar manner. The fact that A gives something to B can, for instance, be a reason for B giving something to C and C something to A. However, I have found it convenient to restrict the 'reciprocation' concept to instances where the situation involves only two parties. These need not necessarily be individuals but may be groups, organizations, states or any other composite whole which is conceived of as an acting unit. Nor do they necessarily have to belong to the same category. One party, for instance, may be an individual and the other a group (or organization) to which the individual may or may not belong.

By *allocation* – which forms the other main set of instances to be dealt with – I refer, among other things, to the process of apportionment which, for example, takes place when mother cuts the cake and gives each child its slice. What binds the individual transfers together in these cases is that the values apportioned are considered to be, or to have been, part of a whole. But transfers which do not have this relationship to each other are also regarded as links in allocation providing the parties involved find it relevant to compare the transferred values. Penalties imposed by courts of law are an instance of this.

The manner in which the participants regard the situation, then, is also a decisive factor here. If there is to be an instance of 'allocation', they must regard the values which are transferred either as parts of one unit or as things which it is relevant to compare. As in the case of reciprocation, it may happen that what one party considers as being a link in allocation, another regards as an isolated transfer. But as a rule I am concerned mainly with those occasions where all participants regard what happens as being allocation.

While reciprocation is defined as a situation existing between two parties, an indefinite number of actors can be involved in an allocation. I refer to the person (or persons) who undertake the actual process of allocation as *distributor*(s) and to those who receive the allocation as *recipients*. Both the distributor and the recipient may be either individuals or composite units.

There are different types of allocation situations. That with which we

5

shall be most concerned is when a single distributor allocates something amongst a certain number of recipients. For instance, the distributor may be a mother or father (or the parents as a single unit) and the recipients may be the children who receive various benefits such as toys,

Figure 5

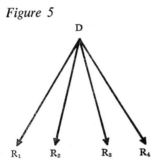

sweets, pocket money, permission to stay up late, praise and encouragement, help and care, love and security, or who are given certain duties to perform such as their homework, or expected to help in the house, or are punished. It is characteristic of the parent/child relationship that during the whole period of upbringing the parents act as permanent distributors of many kinds of benefits and obligations. There are also other permanent and comprehensive D/R relationships; for instance, between the government and the governed, between the management of a firm and its employees, and between the staff of a hospital and its patients etc. But there can also be one-time allocations as when a kind, old gentleman distributes chocolate to some children with whom he has incidentally come into contact.

Sometimes a set of transfers is regarded as a case of allocation even though all or some of these transfers spring from different distributors.

Figure 6

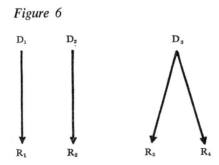

6

Whether there is one or more than one distributor depends on how the situation is perceived. In the application of criminal law, for example, the imposition of sentences can be attributed to the state (fig. 5) or to each individual judge (or court of law) (fig. 6). It can also happen that something is conceived as being an allocation even when the distributor remains unidentified. The line of division between these instances and those where a supernatural Being (i.e. God or Fate) is regarded as the distributor is fluid.

In many cases the same actor is both distributor and recipient : for example when a group of children have collectively been given something and one of the group allocates this between himself and the others. Recipients can also together undertake an allocation without any one of their number being more responsible than any other for the distribution (fig. 7). They reach agreement between themselves or they automatical-

Figure 7

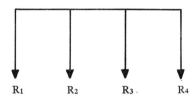

R_1 R_2 R_3 . R_4

ly follow an accepted principle of allocation. Children who share a bag of apples by taking one each and the cinema public which divides time priorities by standing in a queue are examples of such a situation.

Reciprocation and allocation relationships may be interconnected in various ways. One possibility is that two (or more) exchanges are joined

Figure 8

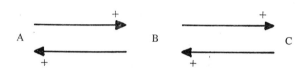

A   B   C

7

(fig. 8). A client (B) in a restaurant, for instance, gives a generous tip to the waiter (A) partly because he has received good service but also partly because he wants to make an impression on the lady (C) he is with and to gain in return her admiration. Another possibility is that two (or more) systems of allocation are connected (fig. 9). For example, there may be an organization (a business enterprise, a government institution etc.) where those in charge allocate the work and other duties and privileges amongst their subordinates while, at the same time, the organization as such acts as distributor to external clients or customers.

Figure 9

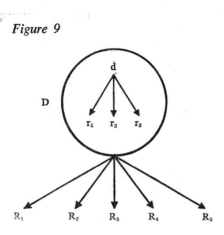

A third possibility, which has great practical importance, is a combination of allocation and reciprocation between distributor and recipients (fig. 10). What the individual recipient receives is often compensation

Figure 10

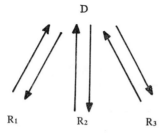

(e.g. wages) for services rendered or punishment for past behaviour. *Both* the mutual relationship in which the individual recipient and the distributor find themselves *and* comparisons between the recipients colour the situation and can mutually influence each other. – Exchange or other forms of reciprocation between recipients may also occur (fig. 11) and can be connected with the allocation when recipients exchange between themselves what they have received from the distributor, or when they compare the outcome of the allocation with exchanges already made (or to be made) of other similar values. Imagined exchange can also enter into the picture as, for instance, when someone expresses satisfaction with what he has received by saying : 'I would not change with you'.

Figure 11

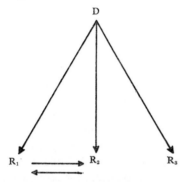

Finally, there is the possibility that an exchange between distributors is connected with their allocations (fig. 12). As an example of this we can take a mother and father who alternately act as distributors to their children. Their ideas differ slightly as to which principles of distribution

Figure 12

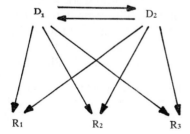

9

should be followed but, to some extent, they adapt to each other. He approaches her ideas of how allocations should be made and she comes nearer to his, and the concessions they thus make are mutually dependent.

II. STRATEGIES AND NORMS

The attempts which will be made in the following chapters to explain patterns in reciprocation and allocation activity rest on the assumption that human beings tend to act strategically and to follow norms. By taking into account both strategies and norms an attempt is made to combine two models of man which have played a central role in the social sciences.

Strategic refers to behaviour which has a purpose and is to some extent planned. The strategist tries to obtain an overall picture of the alternative moves open to action, to weigh the advantages and disadvantages, and to choose the means which seem best suited to promote his goal. When dealing with another person he gives, inter alia, consideration to the manner in which his own actions affect the other person's possible reactions.

The basic assumption underlying economic theory is that people act strategically (in the sense used here). Political scientists have also used strategy models a good deal but as regards human aspirations their assumptions differ from those used by the economists. While economists have operated with a *homo oeconomicus* who strives for economic gain, many political scientists conceive a *homo politicus* who struggles for power.[1] Norm models have long dominated in sociology but the assumption that people act strategically has received greater recognition during the last few years (e.g. *Homans* 1961 and 1962 and *Blau* 1955 and 1964). There are similar trends in the field of anthropology (cf., for example, *Barth* 1966).

Those sociologists and social anthropologists who work with the theory that people act strategically, do not usually commit themselves to definite assumptions as to *what* people strive towards and *what* they try to avoid. Neither will this be done in the present work. I borrow many words and expressions from elementary economics as do Blau, Homans

---

1. The power model is far from being the only one in political science, and its popularity seems to have declined in recent years. A model of political behaviour which is strongly influenced by economic theory has been developed by Buchanan and Tullock (1965).

and others. For instance, I talk about 'costs', 'profits', 'investment', etc., but these words are given a broad interpretation : they refer not only to economic evaluations but also, for example, to such values as affection, security and respect. Nor is it assumed that the strategist is an egoist – he may well have philanthropic goals, so that he considers his activity to be more profitable the more help he is able to give other people.

The strategy model presupposes that people have values of one kind or another. But in its purest form it does not assume that they adhere to any *norms*. There is a striking difference between strategic behaviour and that in which rules of behaviour are followed more or less automatically. To imagine that man is a completely norm-controlled being, therefore, gives a picture which is in sharp contrast to the strategy model.[2] But there is no reason why the two models should not be combined.[3] Human behaviour is both norm-controlled and strategic and there are various connections between strategy, values and norms.

In the first place the use of strategy is often *regulated by norms*. There are norms which forbid strategic behaviour in certain situations or with certain values ('One does not bargain with the truth !'), and norms which exclude any strategic choice by prescribing a certain line of action. But there are also norms which instruct one to behave strategically or indicate which aims and means are to be considered. For instance, parents frequently exhort their children to behave strategically ('Think what will happen if you do that !') or to follow certain lines of strategy ('Be careful !', 'Look before you leap !') or to pay special attention to certain values or certain dangers ('Be careful your brother doesn 't get run over when you take him to kindergarten !'). There are also a great many norms which limit one's choice of strategy. Some have a very wide field of application as, for instance, 'You should not steal' and 'You should not lie', while others are connected with definite trades or professions, fields of activity or situations. For example, we have rules for games and sport, norms for what is fair play, professional ethics, norms for what is acceptable conduct and what is not, etc. Norms limit the strategist's freedom but they can also furnish him with new possibilities. The norm which requires that a promise must be kept, for

2. The contrast between the two types of theories has been stressed by Simon (1957, pp. 196-206).
3. Max Weber did this by taking account of both 'Wert' and 'Zweck' rationality. One of Simon's (1957) main points is that one should try to combine the two models, cf. particularly his remarks (p. 196 et seq.) on 'bounded rationality' (i.e. strategic behaviour within a framework of given norms).

example, makes possible many kinds of business activity which would otherwise be debarred.

Secondly, norms and values can be *used strategically* : when a norm is adopted or enforced this is often done in order to achieve a certain goal. The same holds true of the use made of norms and value judgments in argumentation. The intention may be to influence the other party, e.g., in order to obtain the best possible bargaining conditions or the largest possible proportion of that which is being allocated. Or the reason may be to justify one's own actions to oneself or to others : it is characteristic of the strategic use of arguments that what one says, or omits to say, is determined by the effect one wants to produce. This does not mean that the strategist can never be honest. He may believe what he says but still have considered whether it was opportune or not to say – and if it was opportune to say it in that manner and that situation. But, naturally, not all strategic argument is based on conviction and there are many stages between complete honesty and pure hypocrisy and deception.

In the third place the tendency to act strategically can help to explain *how norms and values come into being, are reshaped and transmitted.* A simple strategy model, often used in explanation, is that people try to obtain pleasure and avoid pain and that they are therefore influenced by systematic rewards and punishment. We find one example of this model in the theory that norms are created when the individual is exposed to continuous social pressure from his surroundings. He is subjected to demands and expectations, he is rewarded for conformity and punished for nonconformity, and gradually acquires other people's norms and values. This model is well suited to explain certain kinds of norm transfer from one person to another, but does not adequately explain how new norms come into being.

But one can also learn without any pressure being brought to bear, for instance through practical experience when dealing with other persons of what is advantageous.[4] By trying different strategies one discovers that in certain situations it is, for example, worthwhile to repay one service with another since there is then a greater chance that something will be given in return another time. And experience which shows that certain behaviour is often profitable can become the basis for the idea that it is *right* to act thus – also on occasions when it does not pay. This learning model is a useful supplement to the previous one because it helps to explain how norms can result directly from inter-

4. Cf. Thibaut and Kelley (1959), especially pp. 24 ff. and pp. 126 ff.

action between persons and how they can change when the conditions of interaction change. We shall be much occupied with this in what follows, particularly in the attempts which are made to explain how principles of justice arise and are perpetuated.

Another important consequence of the fact that people behave strategically, is that the transmission of norms and values – and the prevention of this – can be instrumental in promoting a goal. It is, for example, important for a distributor who wishes to find the optimum distribution to know the value the recipients attach to what they receive. Whether or not a distributor has any interest in publicizing his own norms (e.g. the principle of allocation which he applies) to the recipients can vary. By letting these be known he may manage to have them accepted and thereby avoid conflict. But it is also possible that greater knowledge among recipients increases their inclination to resist and provides them with weapons which they would not otherwise have had. It is important for a recipient attempting to influence a distributor that he knows the latter's norms and values so that he can choose arguments which appeal. In the case of reciprocation as well, it is often pertinent strategy to gain insight into the other party's norms and values, sometimes to let one's own be known, and sometimes to keep them secret. In this manner strategies contribute to channelling the processes of transmission.

III. STANDPOINTS AND REASONS

By *'standpoint'* I mean a position which is taken on how something should or should not be done or as to whether something is true, right, good etc.,[5] and by *'reasons'* I mean something which a person says, writes or thinks *either* in order to reach a standpoint (deliberation, consideration) *or* to justify, defend or attack a standpoint which he himself or another person has taken (argumentation, rationalization).

Assertions used as reasons for a standpoint involve themselves standpoints which in their turn may become objects of argumentation. One who asserts that progressive taxation is unfortunate may, for instance, argue that people would work harder if taxation were not progressive and that this would be all to the good. Here a standpoint is taken both on a question of cause and effect (between taxation and zeal) and on one of value. In the next round reasons can be given for both these

---

5. Philosophers frequently use the expression 'judgment' for what I call a 'standpoint'.

standpoints and in this way long chains of arguments may develop. Sooner or later, however, every chain will come to an end, e.g., when an ultimate position is reached.

Research into standpoints and reasons provides an important source of knowledge of the factors mentioned above. It can be a means of discovering to what it is that people attach positive and negative values, how high they rank the subject in question, whether they consider that values have been transferred and how they experience the situation of interaction in which the transfer takes place. If, for instance, A requests a certain value of B, it is often necessary to look at the reasons in order to find out whether A intends this as a demand for repayment for something he has himself given, or whether it is to punish him, claim compensation, etc. The study of standpoints and reasons, in other words, is an aid towards the *classification* of behaviour into the categories discussed in section I. In addition, it can tell us something about the *norms* and *strategies* regulating interaction situations. The reason given for a claim for reciprocation, for instance, may be that the other party promised to undertake something in return, or that it is in itself right that this be done. Or, an expression of dissatisfaction with an allocation may be based on the argument that others have received more than oneself and that it is only right to share equally. Such arguments may indicate that the participants have accepted the norms referred to and/or that they consider it good strategy to argue with them.

With these points of view in mind it seems appropriate to investigate those standpoints and reasons which *actually occur*. A standpoint cannot be excluded from our field of interest because we hold it to be wrong. Nor can an argument be excluded, simply because we consider it to be incomplete, untenable or dishonest. But incompleteness, untenability and dishonesty are all features of an argumentation which, inter alia, may be relevant in deciding whether strategic reasoning is present and, if so, what kind of strategy has been used.

The fact that attention is directed towards actually given standpoints and reasons does not mean that it is the occurrence of certain words and expressions which is of interest. It is the *meaning* on which attention should be concentrated. In other words, statements must be interpreted and this can give rise to certain problems.

It is sometimes doubtful whether there is any standpoint or reason present at all. Let us take such statements as 'I shut the window because there was a draught', 'I made an after-dinner speech since I sat at the hostess' left hand' or 'I braked because I met another car'. The intention in such cases may be simply to report one's own behaviour and

14

what provoked it. Or the purpose may be to express the standpoint that, under the circumstances, it was *right* to shut the window, make a speech, or brake, and to give reasons in support of this. Certain value premises may be implied by these statements, for instance that a draught is dangerous, that it is polite to make a short speech when one sits at the hostess' left hand, and that one should avoid colliding with other cars.

Even if it is clear that a standpoint has been taken, one cannot assume that something said in connection with this is meant as argumentation. It might be a statement which aims at clarifying the standpoint. Or it may be a statement of the causes which led one to take this standpoint. When a person is asked why he takes this or that standpoint, he might answer : 'because I am an honest person', 'because I am naturally careful', 'because my upbringing was strict', etc. In such cases it is obvious that this person has given no reasons but has only mentioned psychological causes. But what is actually meant can also be doubtful. Let us take as an example the case where a man is asked why he thinks that the person sitting beside the hostess at the dinner table should make a speech, and then gives the reply 'because it is customary'. Generally it would be most appropriate to interpret this as an argument implying that one should do what is customary. But it is also possible that the reference to custom is not made in order to argue that the standpoint is right, but rather to indicate a possible explanation of how one has arrived at this point of view. One of the reasons why we cannot be sure that we have made the correct interpretation in such cases, is that both reasons and causal statements can give an adequate reply to the 'why', and both begin naturally with 'because'. This ambiguity indicates that the difference is not always clear. When, for example, small children come to us with their 'Why's', we sometimes reply with a causal explanation and sometimes with an argument without really considering what it is that the children want answered. *Løchen* (1965 pp. 211 ff.) has pointed out that drawing attention to the psychological factors behind a standpoint, instead of discussing it, can serve as a strategic diversion in interaction situations. I return to this in Chapter 12 section IV.

Interpretation is required not only to find out *whether* there are standpoints and reasons present but also to decide *what* these are. This will be discussed more closely in Chapter 2, which gives a summary of various types of reasons.

It often happens that a person who has adopted a certain standpoint offers several different reasons for it. The deliberations which led up to his decision need not coincide with the arguments with which he defends his point of view. For whom a defence is intended can also result in variations in its presentation. There can, for instance, be differences between what a person thinks to himself, what he says to his wife in the privacy of his own home, what he says confidentially to his friends, and what he writes in the newspaper or says at a public meeting. The reasons he offers publicly may again differ, inter alia, according to his audience on separate occasions. A politician, for example, may well argue one and the same standpoint differently according to whether his speech is made in parliament, at a party-meeting, or when he appears as a delegate at some international conference. It can also happen that the *standpoint* differs from one situation to another.

When standpoints and reasons waver it is easy to insinuate that they (or at any rate some of them) are not honest or genuine. The vacillation can be regarded as evidence of hypocrisy or self-deception, as an attempt to mislead people, or as a sign that the person concerned is a turncoat. This *may*, of course, be the case, but it need not necessarily be so. Let us take as an example someone who on different occasions gives the following reasons for his decision to take part in a scientific congress: (1) 'I have promised to give a lecture there, so I feel it is my duty to go', (2) 'I expect to benefit professionally from the congress', and (3) 'It's good to move around a bit'. These three statements do not contradict one another. They may all be sincere. And it is often difficult to know – also for the person giving the reasons – what is the strongest motive. If all the reasons are sincere, one can perhaps say that each of them is in-complete. But most argumentation is incomplete in the sense that more could have been said. Arguments which refer to the consequences of some action are particularly open to supplementation, because the relevant consequences of an action are legion.

There can be many reasons for adapting argumentation to one's public. Some adaptation is necessary if one is to be understood at all, or if what one says, is to have any appeal. The different circles in which one moves have different concepts, different habits of thought, and different norms and values. Most people allow for this – although to a varying extent. For instance, a point will be differently presented to a child and an adult, argued differently at a Christmas party and in a technical journal, and perhaps differently to sociologists and lawyers. Sometimes this is done deliberately; at others it is unconscious and automatic.

Sometimes a contradictory standpoint is adopted because a new situation arises. *Lysgaard* (1961, p. 12) mentions an instance where a foreman had a rather difficult situation to settle with his men. It was a question of how much work a 'piece' should involve. He approached

16

the workers one at a time, presented them with the problem and, to his great satisfaction, managed to get his solution approved by each of the workers (about 20). However, when the moment arrived for the work to be done and the foreman went over to inspect it turned out that everybody had changed his mind. In his comments on this example, Lysgaard says (pp. 18-19) :

'It is not of such great interest to speculate on what the workers *really* meant – what they said first or what they said last. It is altogether unreasonable in this case to talk about a 'real' meaning, isolated from the relevant context. When one examines this example one quickly becomes more interested in the two situations of social relationship in which the workers consecutively found themselves rather than in the contradictory points of view which they expressed one after the other. One situation in which each workman found himself was *face to face with the foreman*. The other was *face to face with his fellow workers*. The example showed that the workers adopted different attitudes in the two different situations'.

I agree with Lysgaard that there may be instances when it is unreasonable to talk about a 'real' meaning. Even when it *is* reasonable and relevant to talk about a real meaning,[6] it is still interesting to chart the changes in standpoints and presentation of reasons which occur from one situation to another. One can learn from this to what norm pressures a person is exposed and what strategy he adopts in response to them. Lysgaard's example illustrates a special situation to which we shall return in Chapters 11 and 12 where recipients in an allocation system (in this case, the workers) tend to behave differently, collectively and individually.

IV. THE AIMS OF THE WORK

One of the aims of this work is to make a survey of different forms of reciprocation and allocation activity. The material has been taken from many situations occurring in everyday life : from the home, school and work ; from hospitals, prisons and other institutions ; from public ad-

6. Below I shall mention situations where it is relevant to distinguish between degrees of sincerity in standpoints and reasons. To decide what criteria should be employed to judge whether a standpoint is 'sincere' or 'real' naturally presents some problems. But there are several ways of tackling this. One possibility which sometimes recommends itself, is to attach conclusive importance to the stability of the standpoint in question – stability here meaning that it is expressed in many different situations and changes little over time.

ministration, the administration of justice, and politics etc. Most of the examples are based on Norway or other countries with a similar culture, but for illustration some material from more distant cultures has also been used. Where I have found systematic empirical research which is relevant, I have incorporated this into my work, but I have also employed less reliable sources of knowledge, such as my own unsystematic experience and reading. The reliability of the empirical material presented therefore varies a great deal. I mention this now to avoid a qualifying reservation each time one of the many uncertain statements occurs.

In the description of reciprocation and allocation situations special attention is given to the norms and strategies followed. A number of hypotheses are made about the conditions under which certain types of norms and strategies are likely to develop. In drawing up these hypotheses I have, wherever possible, tried to build upon the store of knowledge accumulated in the social sciences. I have, for one thing, drawn extensively on the findings presented in *Berelson & Steiner* (1964). But on many points, earlier research gives little help and I have occasionally ventured some rather bold speculations. I have aimed, however, at providing my assumptions with a content which allows for empirical testing.

The interplay of norms and strategy, touched upon in section II above, occupies a central place in this exposition. Much of what I develop is founded on the assumption that strategy can be a basis for the creation of norms and that norms can be used strategically. Such assumptions serve, inter alia, to explain the development and use of principles of justice.

Norms and strategies are not subject to direct observation. What we observe, and what we draw conclusions from, are partly factual events – e.g., the delivery of an object or the performance of a job – and partly different types of spoken statements. The statements which are of particular interest are those containing standpoints on questions of value and reasons for such standpoints.

The study of how people argue their standpoints in different types of situations and what determines the argumentation patterns, is a field of research which has attracted relatively little attention. I have therefore felt the need to work out a classificatory scheme of reasons and will explain this more fully in Chapter 2. Both there and in the remainder of this work I am most pre-occupied with reasons based on justice.

18

2. Different types of reasons, with special reference to principles of justice

'This process of definition always requires some reflection and care, and is sometimes of considerable difficulty. But there is no case where the difficulty is greater, or the result more disputed, than when we try to define Justice.'
Henry Sidgwick, *The Methods of Ethics*, Book III, Ch. 5.

I. REMARKS ON TERMINOLOGY AND DISPOSITION

If nothing else is said, the term 'standpoint' (or 'position') refers in the following only to positions taken on norms and values, e.g. the conclusion that someone has a right or duty, that something should or must be done, that something is right or wrong, good or evil, valuable or worthless, etc.

I call the state of affairs on which a position is taken the *object of evaluation*. This can, for example, be a decision or other action, an event, process or situation, a rule or an institution, etc.

The elements of reasoning are called 'premises' and 'inferences'. They can be explicitly mentioned or implied. I distinguish between two main types of premises which I call respectively 'value premises' and 'factual premises'.

By *value premises* I refer to statements which contain norms and/or value judgments; by *factual premises* I mean statements referring to mental or physical conditions, events or processes, causal relationships, etc. When it is assumed that a statement follows from one or more other statements, I call this an *inference*.

In the classification of reasons given below, emphasis is placed partly on the way *in which value premises are connected with factual premises* and partly on *the content of value premises*.

When the value premises are connected with the anticipated consequences of the object of evaluation, I say that the reasons are *consequence oriented*. For example: mother says to Peter that he must take cod liver oil, and explains this by saying that it will make him big and strong. The implicit value premise that it is good to be big and strong,

19

is here connected with the assumed consequence of Peter's medicine-taking, i.e. that he will grow big and strong. In *non-consequence oriented* reasons the value premises are connected with existing or past facts, for instance to the objects of evaluation themselves or to the accompanying circumstances or expectations; e.g., mother's standpoint that Peter must take his cod liver oil may be argued by saying 'the doctor has said that you should take it and you must follow his advice'. Various characteristic features of the two main types of reasons are given in section II below.

Irrespective of what the value premises are connected with, the connection can either be *direct* or inferential. In the last-mentioned example where Peter must take his cod liver oil, the connection is direct because the value premise ('you must follow his advice') refers directly to the factual premise ('the doctor has said that you should take it'). If mother had developed her argument by adding 'One should always do what the doctor says', there would have been an inference from the general (one should always do what the doctor says), to the specific (Peter must do so on this occasion). In section III I give a survey of different kinds of general value premises from which inferences can be drawn for both consequence and non-consequence oriented reasons.

One type of value premises which occupies this work a good deal is that based on principles of balance or equality. These principles, which I call *principles of justice,* are discussed in sections IV and V.

In section VI I give a survey of certain relevant characteristics of reasons which have not so far been mentioned. And in section VII I shall have something to say on factors determining the use of various types of reasons.

II. CONSEQUENCE AND NON-CONSEQUENCE ORIENTED REASONS

As already mentioned, what is common to all *consequence oriented reasons* is that they contain assumptions about the consequences of the object of evaluation, and that it is these which are evaluated.

To say that something is a 'consequence' of something else (in the sense that the expression is used here) is the same as stating that there is a *relationship* of *causality* (or probability) between the two phenomena. The assumption that this is the case can be based on day-to-day experience or on scientific research. It can also be based on more or less casual guessing or on belief in the supernatural. What is said about the relationship can differ: Sometimes categorical assertions as to what will happen are advanced, while on other occasions such expressions as 'believe' or 'expect' are used or reference is made to certain possibilities which must be taken into account. Sometimes the degrees of probability are defined precisely, as when a doctor justifies an operation by saying that the likelihood of recovery is 80 % and the risk of the patient dying is only 5 %.

Consequences are always things which, chronologically, *come after* the things they are resulting from. The time interval can be very short as, for instance, when mother says to her small son, 'You mustn't hold your balloon close to the fire. It might explode'. But it can also be very long as, for instance, in the idea of the millennium. In any event, the consequences belong to the future and can only be objects of prediction as long as the qualifying events have not taken place. One therefore has to look forward in order to give consequence oriented reasons for a choice of action which one is in the process of making. But reasoning in terms of consequences does not always have the character of being *future oriented*. It does not have it when one takes a standpoint on something which has happened in the past and has therefore already had consequences. On such an occasion there can be two different kinds of consequence reasons. One can either make a 'subsequent prognosis', i.e. try to put oneself in the past and base one's judgment on what was then reasonable to expect. Or one can – to a greater or lesser extent – take into account what has happened in the meantime, and on the basis of this criticize the actor's mistakes or praise his foresight. Criticism which is based on knowledge acquired after the event is not always justified. For instance, it may be that the actor did not assert that certain consequences must follow but only expressed the opinion that they were likely to occur. His word can thus still be good, even though the turn of events was not what he anticipated. But one is easily exposed to criticism, justified or unjustified, when predictions prove wrong.

The consequences taken for consideration can vary a great deal. They can be few or many, long-term or short-term, simple or complex, certain or uncertain. There is also variation with regard to what in these consequences is conceived as being of *value*. The goal may be to achieve something for oneself. This can be money, power, well-being, good health or anything else. The consequences for another person may also be taken into account, e.g., somebody can do something to help a friend or to hurt an enemy; or it might be the interests of a business enterprise, a political party, a nation or mankind which attract attention. It can also happen that both individual and collective interests come into consideration in the same evaluation. A politician, for example, can

21

attach importance to what benefits his country, and his party, and also to what increases his own chances of being re-elected.

When several different consequences are considered, the values must be in some way *coordinated*. If the consequences are held to be certain and there is a common measure for all values involved, coordination is a simple arithmetical operation : the revenue is aggregated and the expenditure subtracted. But it is frequently not so simple, e.g. because the consequences are not so certain or because one operates with values which are either immeasurable or not comparable. In these cases a common denominator such as 'happiness' or 'wellbeing' may be sought, or priorities may be allotted in some way or other. But it can also happen that one is content to say, 'I have weighed the pros and cons and have reached such and such a conclusion'.

The word 'goal' ('aim', 'purpose', 'end' etc.) is often employed to express the consequences for which one hopes. The goal may be a single event, e.g. to pass an exam or obtain a particular job ; or it can be to increase the supply of a certain value, for example to gain knowledge, earn money or become happier. In the first mentioned case the goal marks the end of one's endeavours while in the last it has more the character of a signpost. If one tries to obtain as much as possible of a value which can indefinitely increase, the realisation of one's goal is a continuous process. Knowledge of a person's goal can tell us something about what consequences he considers relevant and what measure of values or yardstick he uses. But one's knowledge about these things is usually not exhaustive. If, for example, someone says that his aim is to earn money, it is not certain that he will pursue this end at all costs. There could be methods he would avail himself of under no circumstances (e.g. illegal action), and there could be expenditure of a non-economic nature involved (e.g. over-exertion, serious conflicts and unpleasant relations with other people etc.) to which he hesitates to expose himself.

In consequence oriented reasons it is often opportune to take *several alternatives* into consideration. When, for instance, a choice of action is to be made, it may appear insufficient to examine the consequences of only one course of action. Though this may have a predominance of positive consequences, it is possible that other alternatives are even more favourable. One sometimes limits oneself to comparing two possibilities, for instance 'to do' or 'not to do', while on other occasions a very large number of alternatives may be considered. When one compares the consequences of several alternatives, the differences between them usually appear as *differences of degree*. The person who uses consequence oriented reasons therefore tends to use graded scales of value and to express his standpoints in terms of 'better than', 'more favourable than', and 'worse than' – rather than operate with absolute oppositions between 'good' and 'bad' or 'right' and 'wrong'.

The *non-consequence oriented* reasons are of various types.

One important sub-group consists of assertions that past or existing facts have certain *normative consequences*. The opinion, that it is a person's duty to do (or that he 'should' or 'must' do) something or other, is, for instance, argued by saying that 'he promised it', 'was told to do it', that it is 'his fault' that something went wrong, etc. The argument can also assume that the duty is conditioned by the situation ('He should have contacted the fire station when he saw the fire') or conditioned by status ('you must get up for that lady because you are young and she is old'). When it is concluded that someone has a right or a claim to something, or that an action is right or wrong, good or unacceptable, this is often argued in a similar manner.

Reference to the actor's disposition, aims etc. can sometimes be included as steps in such normative reasoning, for instance if there is a question of punishing him or of demanding compensation. It can also happen that a description of a person's state of mind is the *only* reason given for a standpoint taken towards a certain action, – for instance, when action is characterized as being 'innocent', and this is argued by saying that 'he meant well'. Importance can also be attached to the actor's expectations of the possible consequences of his action. The fact that attention is paid to this does not mean that the reasons are consequence oriented. It is one thing to attach importance to the actor's expectations and another to build upon one's own assumptions as to what the consequences of the action will be (or have been). The difference becomes obvious when such expressions as 'he did it with the best intentions' or 'it was well meant' are used to excuse actions which have had unfortunate consequences. However, the division between these two types of reasons is not a sharp one. If, for instance, importance is attached to what the actor *should* have reckoned with, both his subjective assumptions and one's own judgment of the consequences enter into the picture.

Sometimes the object of evaluation itself – and only that – is judged. In such cases it is possible that the reasons consist only of factual premises which serve to support the value premise contained in the standpoint. Someone takes, for instance, the view that 'N.N. is a good person', and this is argued by describing the distinctive traits of N.N.

23

which thus provide a basis for the characterization ('he does everything he can to help others', 'he is honest and loyal' etc.).

A common feature of non-consequence oriented reasons is that they do not have the forward-looking character of consequence oriented reasons. The value premises are associated with facts (events, distinguishing features, conditions, etc.) which belong to the *present* or the *past*. They often (but not always) consist of statements which point out that there are normative connections between such facts. Statements relating to probability or to causal relationships do not occur as often as in consequence reasons. And if anything is said about a causal relationship, it usually refers to the causes of events which *have* taken place (e.g. when damage has been done). Ideas about what the future holds only enter the picture in an indirect manner, for instance when importance is attached to what the perpetrator assumed would be the consequences of his action, in order to judge his objectives.

Another important difference is that they do not have the same tendency to operate with graded scales of value. When an action (event, condition etc.) is to be subsumed under a norm or a statement of value, the conclusion is likely to be an either – or : the action is either covered by the norm, or it is not. The tendency is therefore to operate with a *dichotomy* between right and wrong, guilty or not guilty, etc. (or at the most a trichotomy, for example, between good, neutral and bad). Delicate nuances between different actions can mean that they are each placed on their own side of the dividing line. The standpoints thus easily take on a more absolute character when they are argued in this manner than when they are argued in terms of consequences.

The fact that, in an unadulterated form, the two main types of reasons differ very clearly from each other does not mean that they do not sometimes *form combinations*. Something can be evaluated partly on the basis of its consequences and partly because it is considered good (or bad) in itself. A person who criticizes a system of taxation may, for instance, claim that it has unfortunate effects on productivity and the will to work, and also that it is in itself unjust. In some of these cases it may be natural to say that two different arguments for the same standpoint are involved, but the premises are sometimes so interwoven that no clear distinction can be made.

Whether or not reasons belong to one or other of the types mentioned can sometimes be a matter of interpretation. Let us take as examples reasons which consist of only one simple characteristic (e.g. of an action, an object or a person). Some such characteristics, for instance 'useful', 'damaging', 'appropriate', 'suitable', 'suited' and 'unsuited',

24

point clearly to the fact that it is the consequences which are evaluated ; other characteristics, e.g., 'undeserving', point in the opposite direction ; whilst still others, e.g., 'valuable', 'good', 'bad' and 'unacceptable', are rather ambiguous. With the knowledge one has of the person who has given the reason and the associated conditions one can sometimes guess what is meant. But one must often accept the fact that whether the value premises are connected with the consequences or with the existing facts, or with both, is just not clear.

The two types of reasons described in this section correspond in a way to the two models of man presented in Chapter 1, section II. If reasons could be taken as descriptions of motivation processes, one would describe *strategies* when giving consequence reasons and *norm regulated activity* when giving non-consequence oriented reasons having normative statements as value premises. Both consequence reasons and strategies are characterized by thinking in terms of ends and means. And reasons which consist of statements to the effect that certain actions are right or wrong or conditioned by someone's rights or duties etc. correspond very well to the model of man as a norm-regulated being.

But reasons cannot, without further investigation, be considered as reports on motivation processes. The motive for giving a reason is usually to convince oneself or another of the validity of a standpoint. And that which is considered suitable for convincing does not always coincide with the motivation behind the standpoint. One cannot, for example, take for granted that a person who acts strategically will always advance consequence reasons for his standpoints. It may sometimes be poor strategy to publicize the strategy one uses. And it can be good strategy to use normative arguments which are likely to be effective when you want to convince another person. The converse can be true, i.e., that a norm-motivated standpoint is defended by consequence arguments, for instance because the milieu is such that one knows that this kind of argumentation will receive most attention or because one is attracted by utilitarian ideas and therefore believes that the standpoint will be more convincing when a consequence oriented reason can be found for it.

III. INFERENCES DRAWN FROM RULES AND PRINCIPLES

In section I, I distinguished between value premises connected *directly* with the relevant facts (or consequences) and value premises from which one draws *inferences*. Some reasons have value premises of only

25

the first mentioned type. The examples given in the previous section are mostly of this kind. In this section I shall have something to say on the role inferences play in reasons. Only very simple deductions (i.e. inferences from the general to the more specific) will be discussed. Both value statements and normative statements can serve as bases for inferences, but I shall mainly deal with inferences based on norms.

The words 'rule' and 'principle' will be used in this and what follows to designate norms which are general i.e. which do not only encompass one individual case but a class of cases. If the norm has a relatively specific content I shall call it a 'rule'; if the content is more diffuse, I shall use the expression 'principle'.

Inferences from rules and principles can occur both in consequence oriented and in non-consequence oriented reasons. By combining the two sets of characteristics one obtains four types of reasons (cf. fig. 1). Of these types II and III are the most usual. If the situation is covered

Figure 1

Types of reasons

	Consequence oriented	Non-consequence oriented
Rule oriented	I	II
Not rule oriented	III	IV

by a rule (or principle), it is normally considered a sufficient reason to refer to it. It is not then necessary to say anything about the consequences (unless the rule requires it – see below), but one must show that the rule fits the facts. On the other hand, if no rule (or principle) is applicable, it is usual to turn to consequence oriented reasons. For many purposes, therefore, a useful classification can be made by distinguishing between 'consequence oriented reasons' and 'rule oriented reasons'.

However, reasons which are neither consequence nor rule oriented also occur – for instance, 'the doctor said this and you must follow his advice' (type IV) – and reasons which are both (type I). These last-mentioned types are gone into more closely below. There are several variations of them:

In the first instance, rules or principles can form a *framework* around

26

the evaluation of consequences (fig. 2). By this I mean that they serve as meta-reasons justifying the fact that consequences are taken into account and the way in which this is done. In every-day life it is usually not considered necessary to justify this. But in philosophical discussions it is often done. A philosopher may justify the importance attached to consequences when judging actions by referring to the utilitarian principle :

'An action is morally right if, and only if, it produces at least as much happiness as any other action which the agent could have undertaken in the circumstances in which he was placed.'

Figure 2

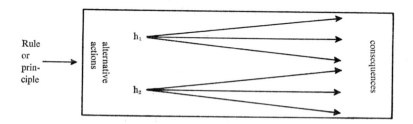

Rules and principles of law can also serve as similar frames of reference. For instance, the law may give the judge limited discretionary power by setting a goal to be reached or by instructing the judge to take into consideration certain consequences of his decision.

Secondly, rules and principles can be the *object* of consequence oriented evaluations, as when a proposed rule of law is evaluated in terms of its expected consequences. Sometimes evaluations of this kind are combined with inferences from the rule. This manner of reasoning is common in moral philosophy where it is often called 'rule-utilitarianism'.[1] Characteristic of rule-utilitarianism is that an action is not evaluated on the basis of its own consequences but on the basis of the consequences of the rule (or principle) under which the action can be classified (Fig. 3). That A should keep his promise to B, for instance, is argued by saying that promises should be kept because general acceptance of this rule has favourable consequences.

1. Cf. Harrod (1936), Mabbott (1939), Harrison (1952-53), Rawls (1955), Hospers (1961 pp. 311 ff., references pp. 342-43), Blegvad (1964), Bedau (1963 pp. 291 ff.), Lyons (1965), and Sobel (1965).

Figure 3

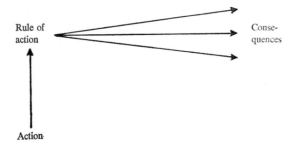

Rule of action

Conse-
quences

Action

Rules and principles may also be drawn upon when evaluating consequences (fig. 4). A father, for instance, urges his son to read industrious-

Figure 4

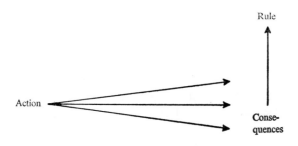

Rule

Action

Conse-
quences

ly to obtain a good exam result, and explains the value of the exam by
saying, 'everyone should acquire a good education'. After this, attention might perhaps be drawn to the gratifying consequences of following this rule, so that we have a combination of the conditions illustrated
in figs. 3 and 4.

Standpoints to rules and principles are certainly not always justified
by consequence considerations. The rules are sometimes rather inferred
from other rules (or principles). There are two main types of such inferences. The one method involves deducing the rule's *content* from
another and more general rule. For example, mother says to Peter that
he must never hit his little sister, arguing this rule by saying, 'One never
hits people who are smaller than oneself!' or 'Boys don't hit girls!'.

The other type of inference involves deducing a rule's *authority* from another rule. For instance, Peter justifies the rule that he should not hit his little sister by saying, 'Mother has said that I mustn't'. The value premise which is taken for granted can here be, for example, the rule that 'One must do as mother says'. In a similar way rules can be backed by statements such as 'The boss has decided this', 'It is according to the law' or 'It is one of God's commandments'. Even though it may not be directly mentioned, it will usually be understood in such instances that one must accept the decisions of these authorities. The authority can also be completely impersonal. A rule is justified, for instance, by saying 'it is customary to do it this way', hence implying that it is right to follow custom.

Reasons of this type sometimes form chains with many links. This is particularly the case where a formal system of rules has been built up step by step, e.g., a country's legal system where the constitution lays down who can make laws and the legislature delegates authority to the executive, which again gives power to its subordinate agencies. Such a hierarchical system of rules can also be found in other big organizations. When an enterprise is organized with the help of such a system of rules, this can in several ways influence the manner in which values are reciprocated and allocated. We shall return to this later.

IV. PRINCIPLES OF JUSTICE

One group of principles has been given special attention in this work. I call them *principles of justice* because I am under the impression that the word 'justice' – both in everyday conversation and in philosophical literature – is often given meanings which come close to those which are used here. But I should like to stress that I do not intend to advance any theory as to the use of the word 'justice' nor to adopt any position on the ontological question 'what is justice ?'. The definitions which I give are stipulated and are motivated by the desire to obtain a set of concepts suitable for discussing the problems tackled in this book.

Since this is the goal, it is not necessary to give any survey of the connection between my categories of justice and those which have been advanced in philosophical literature. However, I should mention that the similarity is greatest to the philosophical tradition springing from *Aristotle's* Nicomachean Ethics (fifth book). Apart from Aristotle himself, I have also received inspiration from, inter alia, *Sidgwick*

29

(1893), *Hart* (1961), *Hospers* (1961) and *Perelman* (1963).[2] My concept of justice has also something in common with concepts used in American sociological literature, for instance *Homans's* (1961) 'distributive justice' and *Gouldner's* (1960) 'norm of reciprocity'.

There are certain *principles of reciprocation and distribution* of values which will be called principles of justice in the following. I will first examine the principles concerned with reciprocation : The central idea in these principles is that there is some degree of reciprocity and balance in relations between parties. I use *retributive justice* as a common term for them. There is a principle of retributive justice for each of the four forms of reciprocation mentioned in Chapter 1 (figs. 1-4) :

1. For an exchange situation the principle 'Good shall be repaid by good' applies. The fact that one party has performed a beneficial service or sacrificed something for the other, may require that the latter do something in return, e.g. perform a counter-service.
2. In a situation where an evil is reciprocated, the principle 'hurt can be repaid by hurt' applies. The fact that one party has offended or injured the other may give the latter the right to avenge himself. The principle may also occur in a 'must' version so that the one who has been hurt is considered not only entitled to avenge himself but duty-bound.
3. In a situation involving restitution the principle 'A wrong shall be righted' applies. When one party has offended or injured another it may be considered his duty to perform a positive act in order to restore balance, e.g., to repair the damage, or make some other form of redress or compensation.
4. The fourth form of reciprocation is characterized by a positive transfer of values followed by a negative transfer. The corresponding principle of justice is that someone who has received a beneficial service must expect certain disadvantages or burdens to be imposed on him in return.

Principles Nr. 1 and 4 have in common that one party becomes the other's 'moral creditor' by the transfer of positive values. But the

2. I am also indebted to Rawls (1971) even if he does deal with problems which are rather different from those discussed in this book. His primary subject is the basic structure of society, not specific allocations with which I am concerned. And he is not occupied with various conceptions of justice but with the concept which 'free and rational persons concerned to further their own interests would accept in an initial position of equality as defining the fundamental terms of their association' (p. 11).

principles each indicate their own method of settlement. According to principle No. 1, the debtor must make the settlement by paying his debt, while according to principle No. 4 it is the creditor who makes the correction. The two principles can be combined in such a manner that the settlements appear as alternatives or perhaps as a cumulative solution. But there are also situations where only the one and not the other principle is considered applicable.

There is a comparable similarity between principles No. 2 and 3. The one party here becomes a 'moral debtor' by inflicting negative values on the other. According to principle No. 3 the debtor himself requites the wrong while according to principle No. 2 it is the creditor who arranges the settlement. These principles can also be combined in various ways.

What is common to the four principles is that they involve the right or duty to one or other form of *retribution*. By this I mean a right or duty which is conditioned by a transfer and which serves as the basis of a new transfer in the opposite direction or with reversed values. The principles are also based on ideas of *equality*, demanding that the exchanged values shall have equal weight if balance is to be restored. The scales held by the Goddess of Justice symbolize this idea. If the scales do not balance, weight must be laid on the side which has become too light, but not more than is necessary to restore equilibrium.

The ideas of balance with which we are concerned are of a *normative* kind. I find it advisable to say this because such words as 'equilibrium' and 'balance' can also be descriptive. They are often used to designate the state of a physical, biological or social system in which opposing forces or processes hold each other in check.[3] It is in this sense that the expression is used when, for instance, we say that there is balance between demand and supply or when we talk about a country's balance of payments. Descriptive concepts of equilibrium can also be applied to the interaction situations with which I am concerned. But 'retributive justice' is not such a concept. It does not serve to describe situations or explain processes but rather to justify demands and duties.

Distributive justice is the term I shall use for those principles of justice which apply to situations of allocation. Their central idea is that recipients should be treated equally. Both retributive and distributive justice, then, are connected with equality. What this involves will be discussed more closely in the next section (V), but I should like to mention at this stage that equal treatment can mean different things. The prin-

---

3. Russett (1966) has given a historical survey of the use of this kind of equilibrium model in the social sciences.

31

ciple sometimes means that the recipients should have (or receive) an equal quantity of the values being allocated, for example equal-sized pieces of cream cake or the same number of months of military service. In other cases relative equality is called for, for example that the relation between labour input and wages, between guilt and punishment, etc., should be the same for all. The same order of priority ('first come, first served') and the same opportunities (e.g., via the drawing of lots) are other forms of equality to which principles of justice can refer.

The expressions 'party', 'recipient' and 'distributor' are used in the same sense when discussing questions of justice, as when reciprocation or allocation conditions are discussed. Both individuals and collective units of any kind can thus be involved. As regards distributive justice, there is no limit to the number of recipients who can be involved; whereas retributive justice always refers to a relationship between two parties. However, I include cases where one of the original parties is replaced by another, for instance because of inheritance, and cases of representations when as, for example, the state exercises retribution on behalf of a victim by convicting the criminal.

Principles of justice are not the only norms applicable in situations of reciprocation and allocation. There are many written and unwritten rules about repayment, compensation and punishment and about different kinds of allocations. Some of these rules closely resemble principles of justice as far as their content is concerned. However, before calling a norm a principle of justice, I require (1) that it be based not on a formal decision (law, regulation, order, etc.) and (2) that its area of application be not limited to special reciprocation or allocation situations. A rule that one must send a Christmas card to everyone from whom one received a card the Christmas before, or a rule requiring the equal distribution of spoil after some kinds of hunting or fishing trips, I do not, for instance, regard as a principle of justice. It is quite another matter that such specific rules are sometimes *justified* by saying that they accord with principles of justice.

Reciprocation and allocation can also occur without any norm regulating the terms. One gives something back, for example, in return for what has been received because one feels an urge to show one's gratitude, or because one reckons that this will increase the chances of getting something another time. The reason for allocating something in a certain manner may also be that this is considered appropriate. For instance, the cloakroom attendant gives a number to each guest, not because this ensures a just distribution but because it is the simplest way in which to retrieve their coats.

Although principles of justice are by no means the only factors which apply, they do play an important role in many reciprocation and allocation situations. They can be internalized so that they directly affect the behaviour of the parties concerned. And whether they are so or not, they can be appealed to as arguments or as a justification.

The expression *conception of justice* here includes both abstract ideas as to what justice demands and concrete conclusions that something or other is just or unjust. By *statements on justice* I refer to statements which express such ideas. The occurrence of the *word* 'justice' is neither a necessary nor a sufficient condition for the presence of a statement on justice. Neither is it sufficient that someone favour equality or retribution. There must be a demand for equality (or retribution) for the sake of the principle – or, if you wish, for the sake of equality itself.

Statements on justice can refer to many different things. The reference can be to actual or conceived *conditions,* for instance to the way in which something is distributed or could be distributed. Or it can be to an arrangement or a rule. A system of taxation or a rule of criminal law can, for instance, be characterized as just or unjust. An *action* (e.g. a decision) or an *omission* can also be just or unjust. A distributor's decision may be characterized as unjust if he acts in defiance of a principle of equality, e.g. if he gives some of the recipients too much or too little or neglects to give at all to someone who should have had something. In the same way, one party in a reciprocal situation can be criticized for being unjust if he does not perform the action he is supposed to or if he demands or takes too much from the other party.

The word 'just' (and words derived from it) is sometimes also used to characterize persons (e.g. 'he is a just arbitrator'). In these cases it is often used in an even wider and vaguer sense than that used here. But there can also be occasions when a 'just' person refers to one who strives to follow principles of balance and equality in his decisions.

Inferences drawn from principles of justice can be considered sufficient arguments. For instance, mother justifies the manner in which she has allocated the cake by saying that she has divided it equally and that this is the fairest way of doing it. This type of reason is non-consequence oriented (cf. section II above). But statements on justice can also occur in consequence oriented reasons. In some cases the stated *aim* of an activity is to promote justice in some field or other. It may, for example, be a just system of voting or a fair distribution of the national income which one tries to promote. In other instances justice has more the character of a *means.* One first claims, for example, that an action, condition or arrangement is just, and if this is contested one defends the principle of justice which one has applied by pointing to its favourable consequences.[4]

Statements of justice and other premises can also be used side by side – for mutual support of the same standpoint or as pro and contra arguments. It may be claimed, for instance, that a punishment is just and that it also has the beneficial effect of deterring the convict and others from committing similar actions in the future. Or it is claimed that the wage which an employer pays, although it is in accordance with the contract, is not fair compensation for the work done.

Because principles of justice are so general and vague, they have a wide and very elastic area of application. They can be drawn upon as supporting arguments for, or form a basis for criticism of, many different kinds of social institutions. And they can be the foundation of new institutions, via the crystallization of specific rules from general principles. These are important traits in the ideology of justice with which we shall have much to do later.

V. THE DIFFERENT PRINCIPLES OF JUSTICE AND THEIR
CONNECTION WITH EACH OTHER

Equality is involved in both retributive and distributive justice. In the previous section I indicated what kind of ideas on equality are implicit in the expression 'balance' and 'equal treatment'. I shall now go into more detail concerning what these expressions entail and what the connections are between the two main types of justice.

As already mentioned, it is characteristic of principles of justice that they are general and vague. However, I exclude from the concept principles of equality which are so general that they are almost meaningless, for example 'what is like, shall be treated alike'. I agree with *Ross* (1958 pp. 269 ff.) that this only means that certain actions must be similar or, in other words, that they must follow certain rules or patterns. The content of these rules is quite undecided as long as 'what is like' is unspecified.[5]

---

4. The question whether 'justice is useful to society' has been discussed and answered in the affirmative by several of the English utilitarians (Hume, Mill, Spencer, Sidgwick etc.), cf. Eckhoff (1963) with references.
5. Many authors include adherence to certain types of rules (e.g. legal regulations) in their concepts of justice. Aristotle (Nicomachean Ethics V, vii) called this *'conventional* justice'. He distinguished between this and *'natural* justice' which coincides better with the concept used here. Similar distinctions

34

The principles which I call principles of justice are somewhat more specific in that they at least give certain indications of *what* shall be like for *whom*.

Let us first look at *distributive justice*. Here there is already some inherent specification since this has to do with equality between recipients in situations in which values are allocated. However, it is an open question to *which* allocations the required equality should apply. There are allocation situations where the principle is not considered relevant. And, if the principle is applied, what is taken into consideration when the judgement is made can vary. On some occasions attention is paid only to what the recipients *receive* from the single allocation process. On other occasions account is also taken of what they already *have* of the relevant value : in other words, it is their accumulations after one or more allocations have taken place which are compared.[6] Variation may also occur with regard to the delimitation of the group of recipients who are to be treated equally, and in the definition of the 'recipient unit'. For instance, when people contribute towards a joint present, should a married couple be regarded as one or two units of allocation ? All these questions are discussed more thoroughly in Chapter 8.

In addition, there are opportunities for variation when it comes to *what* should be the same for the recipients. The most important alternatives are :

1. *Objectively equal amounts to each,* e.g., so that children obtain equally large pieces from a slab of chocolate, all citizens have the same sized bread ration when there is a shortage of food, all men have the same number of months of conscription, or that all parking offenders be given the same fine. The yardstick used here is objective in the sense that individual features of the recipients are not taken into account. Everyone gets the same regardless of their personal circumstances. But that which is considered 'the same' can easily depend upon subjective appraisal, which is often the case when the values are complex. Among other things, there can be a question of whether it is sufficient that all

---

(but partly with other expressions such as 'formal/substantive' or 'conservative/ideal' are to be found inter alia in Sidgwick (in Olafson 1961 p. 11 and pp. 27-28), Perelman (1963 pp. 11 ff.), Rawls (1971, pp. 58-60 and 235-243) and Castberg (1957 p. 74). See also Hart's remarks on the distinctions (1961 pp. 156-157) and Frankena (1966 pp. 4-5).

6. Cf. Oppenheim (1968) who talks about 'equal allocation' when the allotments are of the same size and about 'equal distribution' when attention is paid to making the accumulations equal.

recipients get the same *amount* of values or if it is in addition necessary that they also have the same *kind* of values. The slogan 'equal rights for women' can camouflage much disagreement on that subject. The meaning can be that men and women, all together, should receive equal amounts of life's benefits and opportunities, but that they should not necessarily have the same benefits. Men, for instance, can receive more values from their occupation while women receive more from the home. Or the meaning may be to assert the more radical demand for equality, i.e., that each individual pleasure and each individual opportunity be evenly divided between the sexes.

2. *Subjective equality of transfers.* Allotments need not here be objectively the same size but they must, in some manner, be subjectively equal from the recipients' point of view. It may, for instance, be required that each person receive a sufficiently large allotment to acquire the same satisfaction, or suffer to the same degree, as each of the other recipients. Or perhaps it is claimed that the recipients should be brought to the same level, wherever possible, when account is taken both of what they had previously and what they now obtain of the relevant value. Equal value can also mean that everyone gets what he needs to reach the goal he has set himself : for example, mother helps the children finish making their Christmas presents or father helps them with their homework ; some receive more help than others but all are given equal treatment in the sense that each completes his work. The last possibility I shall mention is that recipients are considered to have rights or duties in relation to the distributor (e.g. based on contracts or on retributive justice) and that equal value is achieved when these rights and duties have been attended to so that each person 'gets his due'. The person who pays his creditors what he owes them, for instance, can be said to treat everyone alike even though he owed one person a large amount and another only a small amount.

3. *Relative equality.* Here importance is attached to a variable characteristic of the recipients or of their performances, for instance how much work they have done or how severe were the crimes they committed. The demand for equality is satisfied if the ratio between the value of the allotment and that of the characteristic is the same for everyone. As an example let us imagine that there is a demand for 'same job, same pay' and that we use the number of items produced as a measure of the work done. If three workers have each produced 3, 4 and 6 items respectively and receive 30, 40 and 60 pence in payment, the claim for

relative equality will have been met because the ratio (10 pence per item) is the same for each of them. This can be expressed by saying that the claim is met when $a^1/p^1 = a^2/p^2 = a^3/p^3 \ldots = a^n/p^n$ (when a represents the individual allotment value and p represents the input value of each recipient). Ideas of relative equality cannot always be cast in numerical terms as they have been in the above example. One may have certain – approximate – conceptions on comparability even though one cannot indicate the size of the values being compared. It might be felt, for example, that R_1 deserves a 'much' higher wage than R_2 because he is 'much' cleverer, and if the latter only receives a 'slightly' fatter pay packet this may be regarded as a violation of the principle of relative equality. Ideas of relative equality are often connected with situations where it is natural to attach importance to what the individual recipient has earned – of good or evil. But they can also occur when other criteria are considered. In connection with export and import regulation it has, for instance, been advanced as a principle of distributive justice that each firm should receive a quota corresponding to a fixed percentage of what it exported or imported during a given base year.

4. *Rank order equality*. A necessary condition for application of this principle is that there be some consecutive order between the recipients with regard to rank, worthiness, seniority, position in a queue, etc. The requirement of equality is that the order of the transfers be the same as that of the recipients. It is the principle sometimes used in allocating time priorities – for instance, that the eldest receive first and the youngest last. On other occasions it is the *size* (or the quality) of allotments which is determined by the sequence – for instance that the eldest get most and the youngest least. There are also instances where the consecutive order is important in both these ways : for example, the position one has in the cinema queue can both influence how quickly one comes in and how good a seat one gets, and whether one gets in at all.

5. *Equal opportunity*. If several people are equally close to receiving a benefit or a duty which is not divisible, the allocation may be based on chance – for example by drawing lots. Everyone then has an equal chance (or opportunity) of receiving the advantage or the burden. Equal opportunities are also spoken of in cases where the realization of opportunity does not depend on chance but on the efforts of the recipients. The government, for example, allocates educational resources in such a manner that everyone has the same opportunity of developing himself.

Of the principles which have been mentioned, that of objective equality (No. 1) and of allocation by chance (No. 5) have in common the point that no *characteristic of the recipient* is considered relevant in deciding what is equal. In the other forms of equality different characteristics of the recipients do receive attention. The most important of these characteristics can be designated as follows :

a. *Need.* The word 'need' is sometimes used to indicate that an individual 'desires' or 'feels the need for' something or other. On other occasions it is used in a sense which has a somewhat normative connotation : one does not attach decisive importance to what the person concerned desires but to what one believes he 'really' needs or to what 'would be good for him'. The word 'need' will be used as a common expression for both these types of criteria.
b. *Fitness.* This refers to the recipients' ability to utilize or take care of the values they receive, to their ability to bear the burdens imposed on them, and to learn from the punishment or rewards they receive, etc.
c. *Desert.* I include under this word situations involving questions of retribution. Rewards or punishment, for instance, are dealt out on the basis of what the recipients are supposed to deserve.
d. *Status.* By a person's 'status' I refer to his inclusion in a category such as, for instance, 'child' or 'adult', 'rich' or 'poor'. The expression 'status' will only be used when the category in question has social relevance in many different connections. The categories can either be rank ordered (e.g. senior/junior) or on the same level (e.g. man/woman). Only in the first case is the above-mentioned principle of rank order equality applicable.
e. *Position.* This refers, for example, to a person's position in a queue or on a waiting list, or to his place at table when the food is sent round.

In Table 1 the different forms of equality (1-5) and the different recipient characteristics to which claims for equality can refer (a-e) are assembled. A cross has been placed by some of those combinations which occur most frequently. But there are also possibilities other than these : for instance, relative equality may be based on need, or rank order equality on either desert or fitness. I should also like to point out that there are no sharp dividing lines between the different characteristics and that some of these can be combined. Both fitness and desert can, for instance, be taken into account in a case of allocation.

38

Table 1. *Principles of equality applied to allocation*

What is to be equal	Relevant characteristics of recipient					
	Need	Fitness	Desert	Status	Position	None
Equal amounts to each						x
Subjective equality	x		x			
Relative equality		x	x			
Rank order equality				x	x	
Equal opportunity	x	x				x

If a judgment is based on *one or other* of the principles of equality mentioned, this is sufficient to classify it as a statement on justice. This applies even though it is uncertain *which* principle is the relevant one. However, it will for many purposes be useful to distinguish between the different sub groups in Table 1.

Finally I should mention that the recipient characteristics referred to (need, fitness, desert, status and position) can be relevant in several different connections: they can be taken into account when deciding what each individual recipient is to have even if the question of distribution is not considered relevant. They can form the basis for principles of distribution to which no ideas of equality are attached. And when there is first a question of equality importance may be attached to them partly in deciding *what* is to be equal (as mentioned above) and partly in deciding *who* is to get equality of treatment. A claim for equality based on status, for example, may partly be a demand for rank order equality between the different categories (e.g. higher wages the higher rank a man has) and partly a demand for equally large allotments to everyone belonging to the same category.

We shall now look at those ideas of equality which are involved in principles of *retributive justice*. We are not here comparing a set of parallel transfers, as in the case of distributive justice, but transfers which take place between two parties in such a manner that both register debit and credit entries. One of the main points is that the parties (or one of them) get what they (he) have *deserved*. But notions will differ as to what must be equal in order to satisfy this claim.

39

It is sometimes required that the transferred values – from an objective point of view – be of the *same size* (and perhaps of the same type). The *lex talionis* principle : 'an eye for an eye, and a tooth for a tooth' is an example of this. Corresponding ideas are to be found with regard to compensation, for instance that values of the same kind and size be returned for those that have been spoilt or damaged. Justice requiring absolute equality is less applicable in exchange situations, something which probably follows from the fact that exchange is seldom profitable for both parties unless the exchanged values are of different kinds.

As mentioned above (under point 1), when it is a condition of distributive justice that equally large allotments be made then the characteristics of the individual recipients are disregarded. But this is not so with retributive justice because here the first transfer comes from one or other of the parties concerned. Importance is attached to something that he has done when it is claimed that he must be paid (or pay) back in kind. As far as this goes, it can be said that a principle of desert is being followed in spite of the fact that the yardstick is objective.

Importance is often, however, also attached to other factors, for instance to how great an effort has been made by the one party, or to what extent it is his fault that he hurt the other, or to the consequences for the other party. The needs, capabilities and opportunities of the parties, their age and sex, rank and position, etc., can be considered relevant factors in the overall evaluation of what they have deserved. The type of equality which is claimed in such instances is usually one or other form of *subjective equality*. Attention is sometimes concentrated on the situation of *one* of the actors so that it becomes almost a question of whether or not his credit and debit items balance. One makes a comparison, for instance, between what he has contributed to the relationship in the form of toil, costs, sacrifice or expectations and what subjective values he has obtained from it. Or one compares what he has contributed in the way of malice, inconsideration or neglect with what he gets back as suffering, humiliation and privation. *Which* of the parties receives most attention can differ. The justice involved in returning evil for evil may, for example, either be judged on the grounds of whether the wronged person gets the revenge to which he is entitled, or – which is more usual in current criminal law philosophy – on the grounds of balancing the offender's moral account with society.

However, it also happens that *both* parties' credit and debit items are considered as being important. Intuitive overall considerations as to whether the system is balanced or not can be decisive in such a situation. But more specific criteria of equality might also be available. One reckons, for instance, that both parties have gained from the transaction (something which often happens in exchange) or that they have both lost on it (for instance, when a wrong is avenged) and claims that the 'net profit' or the 'net loss' be equally large for both parties. Or it is claimed that the ratio between, for instance, expenditure and revenue be the same for both parties. I do not know whether such ways of considering the situation play any role at all in practice. But they have, even so, a certain theoretical interest. The idea that net profits (or losses) be of the same size (or relatively the same size) can also be expressed by saying that what the parties *together* earn (or lose) in the exchange of values be divided equally (or relatively equally) between them. In other words, the notion of equal distribution can be contained in that of balanced reciprocation.

The principles of rank order equality and of equal opportunity which were mentioned above in connection with distributive justice (points 4 and 5) are unlikely to ever serve as independent balance criteria. When uncertainties are exchanged their degree of uncertainty may well be considered but it is most likely that the uncertainty only enters the picture as one of several factors in an overall evaluation. The consecutive order of transfers can be of primary importance : among other things, it decides what takes on the character of requital and this can be conclusive when evaluating where justice lies. It is a normal requirement, for instance, that punishment follow *after* the offence. One cannot be punished for the wrong one perhaps (or certainly) will commit in the future. In an exchange situation attention is also sometimes paid to the consecutive order : the private, for instance, must salute first and the officer then acknowledges the salute. But it is difficult to find cases where consecutive order is the only thing to which importance is attached when judging whether the situation is in balance.

I have now looked separately at each of the two categories of justice and have discussed various common and individual features belonging to them. But both distributive and retributive justice are sometimes connected with the same situation, e.g., when there is such a combination of allocation and reciprocation as mentioned in Chapter 1 (figs. 10-12). A workman complains, for example, that his wage is unfair, partly because he gets less than other people with whom he compares himself and partly because he does not think that he gets as much as his work is worth. Or a person who has been convicted of a criminal offence complains partly that his sentence is too heavy compared with sentences passed on other people and partly that it is out of proportion to his own guilt. On some occasions such mixed conceptions of retribution and distribution merge into an intuitive overall impression that something is just or unjust.

It can also be, however, that the two components are kept separate and that the evaluation of them need not be the same. This applies even if desert is considered relevant both with regard to distribution and retribution. In the example given above, it is possible that the wage earner claims that neither he nor his colleagues receive as much as they really deserve, but that there is relative equality between them. The opposite can also be the case. A person may admit he has got what he has deserved but claims that others receive even better treatment, and that this is unfair.

Later I shall discuss how conceptions of just retribution and distribution can influence each other in situations such as those mentioned above.

VI. SOME VARIABLES

Reasons can vary in many respects. Some of the variations formed the basis of the division into categories made in the previous sections. But there are also variations which will be regarded as differences of degree within these categories, and which partly cut across them. Some of the differences of degree have been mentioned or implied earlier, and we shall often return to them. A survey of the most important is given below.[7]

In the first place the *scope* (in time and space) of the relevant *class of events* which comes in for consideration will vary. For instance, there may be large variations in what one considers relevant to include in a comparison : e.g., should consideration be given to the chocolate John received yesterday when deciding whether it is fair that Peter, and not John, get chocolate today ? How far back in time is it necessary to go ? Is it relevant to also take account of the fact that Peter and John have received things other than only chocolate ? Is it relevant to make a comparison with what the neigbours' children get ? Similar variations are to be found when reciprocal situations are deliberated. Larger or smaller parts of a chain of events – and affairs which lie near or far from each other in time – can be weighed against each other. Concep-

---

7. In this section I talk only about reasons, and in my examples generally use reasons based on justice. But similar variations are to be found in both strategies and norms.

tions of what belong together and what do not, what has been settled and what is still pending, how long one can wait before repayment is made, and how much time can lapse before one's claim becomes obsolete, all these can decide where the line is to be drawn.

Secondly, there are differences when it comes to how specific or (conversely) how *diffuse* reasons can be. The fewer characteristics (of persons, situations, etc.) considered relevant and the less complex and more visible these characteristics are, the more specific I consider the reasons to be. The talion principle 'an eye for an eye, and a tooth for a tooth', for instance, is a more specific reason for correct punishment than the reasons which are usually employed today. Naturally, the various aspects of a decision need not be backed by equally specific reasons. For example, the argument indicating that there should be punishment may be specific while the reason for how punishment should be carried out may be diffuse, or the opposite way round.

In the third place, reasons can, to a greater or lesser degree, be *person oriented*. By this I mean that characteristics of persons, e.g. their desert, need, intentions, age, sex, etc. are taken into account. The degree of person orientation is determined by how large a proportion of the total set of relevant criteria is of this type. As the opposite of person oriented, I use the expression *object oriented*. Strongly *object oriented* reasons are reasons which contain few or no characteristics of persons. The principles of distributive justice that everyone should receive an equal amount or that everyone should have an equal opportunity to something, are extreme examples of object oriented reasoning because no personal characteristics are relevant. All the other principles of distribution mentioned in section V take different recipient characteristics into consideration. But the degree of person orientation shows large variations within each of the categories mentioned there. In the case of relative equality based on desert, for instance, notice is sometimes taken only of the overt action or achievement while on other occasions importance will also (or only) be attached to whether the individual recipient – on the basis of his own capabilities and possibilities – has 'done his best'.

The specific often goes together with the object oriented and the diffuse with the person oriented. But there are, after all, two dimensions involved here and it does not always happen that the two sets of variables go together in this way. On the one hand there are object oriented evaluations based on diffuse criteria : the manner in which examination results are determined at Norwegian universities is an example in question. The evaluation aims at being predominantly ob-

43

ject oriented (the faculty of law, for instance, seeks to insure this by making all written exams anonymous) but the criteria which decide what marks are awarded are often rather diffuse. On the other hand there are person oriented reasons which are relatively specific, for example when attention is only paid to seniority in the promotion of employees.

Person oriented reasons differ between themselves in several ways. Amongst other things, *which* of the individuals' situations is taken into account can vary. When a case of reciprocation is being evaluated, as mentioned earlier, importance may be attached to one or other or both of the parties' situations. And as regards allocations, person orientation can be directed towards the distributor or the recipients.

There can also be variations as to which personal features are considered relevant. Sometimes attention is only (or preferably) paid to a person's behaviour and attitude, etc. in the situation concerned. Significance is attached, for instance, to the costs he has had – by way of work and toil, sacrifice, setbacks and disappointments – or to the benefits he receives from the reciprocation or allocation. Often, however, more permanent characteristics of the person concerned are also (or only) considered, for instance his age, sex, race, rank, wealth, social standing, intelligence, education or ability. When such personal qualities are considered important in the final decision they take on the character of some kind of *capital value* [8] which bears interest. The 'capital' may be something the person concerned has had from birth (for instance, his sex or race) or it can be something which he himself has acquired (e.g., education and expertise).

Importance can be attached to capital values in all forms of reciprocation (exchange, punishment, compensation, etc.) and allocation. The fact that a person has invested a great deal is often an argument in favour of his receiving greater privileges than others. But the capital accumulation can also serve as an argument in favour of his shouldering more duties ('noblesse oblige') or bearing heavier loads.

VII. SOCIAL DETERMINANTS AND EFFECTS OF REASONS

The manner in which people argue their standpoints is certainly, to a great extent, culturally conditioned. But it is also influenced by personal characteristics and by the type of interaction which is taking place. It is particularly the last mentioned connection which will be dis-

8. Homans (1961, pp. 74-75 and pp. 235 ff.) uses the expression 'investment'.

44

cussed below ; my aim is here to present some assumptions concerning the social determinants and effects of reasons.

I will first look at some conditioning factors. These can be divided into three main groups : resources, norms and strategies. The question of what the effects of the reasons might be will be touched upon in connection with the discussion on strategy.

By *resources* I refer to what a person possesses of logical training, knowledge and value preferences, etc. – that is to say, of such material as is used in reasons. Resources vary considerably from person to person. Education and experience, among other things, influence both value orientations and the type and extent of knowledge. Insight into causal relationships, for instance, determines what one can produce of consequence oriented reasons. A doctor, for example, is better equipped to decide what should be done to cure a certain illness than a person who has never studied medicine. A civil engineer is better supplied than others with reasons for making a choice between various materials and construction methods. And some professional groups, for instance, lawyers and priests, are specially trained to master systems of norms which can be used to argue certain types of standpoints.

But everything we know and everything we believe in is not involved in each argument. Selection is made and this is partly governed by norms. In addition to the norms which occur in arguments, there are also *norms for what kind of argument shall be used,* or not used, in different types of situations. Some of these norms are connected with social roles.[9] A judge, for instance, refers to laws, regulations and precedents when giving reasons for his decision. And he does so not only because his education has well equipped him for this kind of argumentation but also because it is expected of him in his capacity as judge. Other kinds of reasons are expected of a doctor. His frame of reference should not be normative but causal. He should not, for instance, ask whose fault it is that someone has fallen ill but try to determine the causes of the illness, how it is likely to develop and what chances there are of recovery. There are also norms which indicate what tasks are most suited to the different professions and trades and therefore which types of premises are most suitable when relevant evaluations have to be made. Many of these norms are so firmly anchored in our culture that we find them self evident. But they are not unchangeable. For instance, conceptions as to what kind of premises it is rational to apply in case of illness have changed with the times. And in many fields

9. Cf. Simon (1957, pp. 200-201).

there is uncertainty or difference of opinions. For example, there are conflicting ideas as to whether medical, legal or moral premises are most relevant when judging juvenile delinquency and addiction to drugs or to alcohol.

There are similar norms in walks of life other than the professional, but in many instances the norms are vague and permit great latitude. For example, it may be considered improper to use certain kinds of arguments, but the limits thus given can be so wide that plenty of room is left for variation. The limits are in some cases rather elastic, in others more absolute. For instance it is quite legitimate to pay attention to one's own economic interests when buying and selling merchandise. It is less acceptable to do so when it is a question of selling the family property or of getting married, choosing friends or voting at a public election. And it is certainly improper to attach importance to one's own economic interests when making a decision in one's capacity as public servant.

It appears from what has been said above, within the limits set by resources and norms, there can be a variety of reasons available for the same standpoint. There is therefore plenty of room for *strategy,* i.e. for taking account of what can be achieved by using one argument rather than another. Strategic action does not necessarily involve conscious deliberation. Experience of what pays can be influential even though one does not think about it nor realize that a choice is made. This can be habit-forming and perhaps also lead to the development of new norms.

In what follows I shall indicate some of the *strategically relevant effects* of reasons, i.e. effects which one tends to try to achieve or avoid.

An effect which one often hopes for is that the person to whom the argument is directed will be *motivated* to undertake a certain action – for instance, to grant an application, accept an offer, follow an order or respect a prohibition. In addition to arguments there are sometimes other means of pressure available to the person who wants to extract something from somebody else. He can, for instance, make use of threats or promises. But the fewer sources of power or exchange values at his disposal, the more important it is to be able to advance a convincing argument for the standpoint that it is right or reasonable – or appropriate from the other person's point of view – that he gets what he wants. He must therefore find arguments which appeal to the other party. He must preferably use value premises which the other party accepts and considers relevant to the situation. But at the same time it is important that he keep within the limits of his own resources and norms in order to make the argument appear tenable.

Reasons can also serve as a means of influencing attitudes, conceptions and habits, for instance by systematically choosing as premises the norms and values which one wants to instil into other people. Such training is widely used by parents to their children and by teachers to their pupils. Court decisions are an example from another field. The fact that rules of law are offered as reasons, does not only contribute to giving greater authority to decisions but also to spreading knowledge and increasing respect for the law. A person who intends to influence other people's norms and values cannot always make use of value premises which the recipient already accepts and considers relevant. But the further he goes from what is already accepted the more difficult his job will be and the more easily will consideration for long term effects come into conflict with the desire to influence present individual action. For instance, parents are sometimes faced with a dilemma when they know that the easiest way to get a child to do what they want is to use arguments which are unfortunate from a long term point of view.

Long term influence does not only extend from the stronger party (parents, teachers, government, etc.) to the weaker (children, pupils, citizens, etc.) as in the examples above. Mutual influence can also be exercised between equals. And in relations between the stronger and the weaker, the latter may exercise effective counter pressure. The weaker often tries, through argumentation and other means, to defend his interests and to safeguard himself against arbitrary treatment and oppression. A demand that the strongest follow principles of justice, for example that he divide equally, reward positive action and not punish more than is deserved, can be an effective means of defence.

Reasons are not only motivating but also *informative*. Among other things they can tell the recipient something about the norms, values and store of knowledge of the person who argues. And this will sometimes provide some possibility of predicting his future decisions or actions. But the inferences which can be drawn are not always reliable because reasons can be insincere and they can shift from one occasion to another. The amount of information reasons provide also differs. A person who often makes decisions of a certain kind is therefore, to some degree, himself master of how predictable he is. What it pays to do can vary, and sometimes conflicting considerations are present. In order to exert long term influence it is, as a rule, necessary that reactions be fairly predictable but not to the extent that control can be avoided.

Reasons do not only give information on what can be expected from the actor but also on what kind of *person* he is. The picture they furnish is sometimes uncorrected and shows, for instance, his greediness, recklessness and selfishness. But care is often taken, when furnishing reasons, to present a picture more in line with the impression that one wants to give. In order to achieve this one must sometimes reduce one's demands. A person who would like to have more than other people of a value which is being allocated but who cannot find an argument for this without exposing his greed, limits himself, for instance, to claiming equal treatment which can be argued in terms of justice. The desire to obtain as much as possible can, in other words, come into conflict with the desire that arguments give a favourable picture of oneself. But often the argument which best suits the latter desire, also shows the greatest likelihood of gaining support with the other party, so that the two considerations point in the same direction.

Finally, the significance which reasons can have for the *later evaluation* of decisions and other actions should be mentioned. He who evaluates an action *need* not, of course, base himself on the actor's own argument. But it is frequently natural to do so, inter alia because this is often considered most fair. What the actor can be criticised or praised for – when one keeps within the limits of his own reasons – depends, to a large extent, upon whether or not the reasons are consequence oriented.[10] When an action is defended by saying that it should lead to this or that favourable result, a good criterion of success or failure is whether this actually happens or not. Criticism based on this foundation is difficult to contradict. After the bridge has collapsed it is no use for the constructor to continue claiming that it was strong enough. On the other hand, results achieved give a solid foundation for credit. There are few people who are more admired than those who manage to accomplish something everyone believed was impossible. And between the complete fiasco and the unbelievably good result there is often a broad spectrum of possible results so that evaluations can be widely graded. When the reason for an action is *not* given in terms of consequences but, for instance, in terms of the action being in accordance with a rule, the situation is different. Criticism can here be based on alleged misinterpretation of the rule or mistaken facts. But this is not so easy to prove, for such mistakes belong to the past and do not have the later confirmation of a mistaken forecast. By using reasons which are not consequence oriented one can, then, protect oneself from unpleasant criticism, but, at the same time, one renounces honour and fame. The most one can achieve is to be looked upon as infallible.

10. This point of view is developed further in Eckhoff and Dahl Jacobsen (1960).

It often happens that all the types of consideration mentioned above – and perhaps others as well – are relevant for the person who gives the reason. He wishes, for example, to influence the other party's action in the present situation and is at the same time interested in influencing his future behaviour or attitudes, in making his own future decisions unpredictable, in giving a favourable picture of himself and in avoiding criticism of his own decision. The choice he makes between the different types of reasons available can be of significance on all these counts. Strategies are therefore often products of many different motives which can partly pull in the same direction and partly counteract each other. They can also be to some extent the object of conscious calculation and to some extent rooted in habits which are followed without reflection.

In later chapters some of the questions here touched upon are discussed in greater detail with special reference to reciprocation and allocation situations.

Part II. Reciprocation

3. Different types of exchange and factors regulating exchange

'A man ought to be a friend to his friend and repay gift with gift. People should meet smiles with smiles and lies with treachery.'
The Hávamál, strophe 42
(Norse poem, probably from heathen times, English edition by D.E. Martin Clarke, Cambridge 1923).

I. THE CONCEPT 'EXCHANGE'

As mentioned in Chapter 1, I talk of 'exchange' when two parties reciprocate positive values with each other. The word 'reciprocate' implies that the relationship between the transfers is conditioned either by a norm or by strategy – so that one transfer can be given as a reason (or as part of the reason) for the other. I am usually concerned with situations where the relationship is *mutual*, i.e. where transfer No. 2 is given because transfer No. 1 has taken place, and No. 1 is given because the expectation is that it will be followed by No. 2. But occasions where only No. 2 is conditioned will also be included. If, on the other hand, No. 1 alone is conditioned, no exchange has taken place but an unsuccessful attempt at it has been made.

The conditional relationship between the transfers can be perceived by one party or by both (and possibly also by detached observers). The distinction between one-sided and mutual perception cuts across the distinction between one-sided and mutually conditional transfer mentioned above. Party A's transfer can be perceived as being conditioned by B's transfer by either A or B or by both. And B's transfer can be perceived as conditioned by A's by A or B or both. When nothing to the contrary is said I am thinking of cases where there is reciprocity in both senses, i.e. where both A and B perceive both transfers as being conditioned by each other.

Conditions can rest upon strategy or norms or upon both of these. A common combination is that transfer No. 2 (the return action) is norm conditioned, and that transfer No. 1 (the first action) is strategically conditioned. There is, for instance, a norm that certain services are repaid, and awareness of this norm can make it appear profitable to

53

perform these services. But both normative and strategic reasons can also be connected to the same transfer, e.g., when I help someone, partly because this is expected of me and partly because I anticipate something in return.

The norms and strategies which bind transfers together are sometimes clear and firm. For example, A delivers goods to B because these have been ordered and he expects to profit from the transaction ; and B pays the cost of the goods because it is his legal duty to do so. But the factors connecting the two transfers are often much vaguer and looser. Take, for instance, the idea that benevolence should be repaid with gratitude. The normative aspect of this is to be seen in expressions such as 'debt of gratitude' and 'I owe him thanks', but this is so loose a conception that one does not, for instance, usually talk about an 'obligation' to show gratitude. Strategical considerations can also be very loose and ambiguous and do not have to be clearly recognized. My requirements for calling a transfer 'conditioned' are, on the whole, very modest.

The bare fact that two actors transfer values to each other is, however, not sufficient. As an example let us take the relationship between medical science and hospital patients : patients can be said to receive values from this science since it provides the foundation for their treatment ; and on their side they transfer values to the science by serving as objects of research and as demonstration material for teaching purposes. But if these services are not perceived as being normatively or strategically conditioned by each other, the relationship falls outside our exchange concept. The word 'exchange' is sometimes used in a wider sense in sociological literature – sometimes so wide a sense that it seems to encompass all cases where two categories of people mutually profit from each other.

In other respects the field of investigation is restricted by some authors to encompass only what they call 'social exchange', economic exchange (e.g. buying and selling) being kept out of the picture.[1] The reason for not following a similar line here is that there is a fluctuating boundary between economic and social exchange and the two are often combined. In addition, it is useful to include economic exchange as a basis for comparison since considerably more research has been done in this field than in that of social exchange. I have, however, no ambition to contribute to development of economic theory.

My concept of exchange, then, is fairly comprehensive and contains

1. Cf. Blau (1964 p. 93) and Goffman (1961 pp. 275 ff.). See on the other hand Homans (1961), Foa (1971) and Turner et al. (1971) who include exchange of economic values in their theories.

situations which, among themselves, show wide variation :

In the first place, many different kinds of *values* can serve as objects of exchange : these can be money, material objects, services (e.g. work, help, support, advice, etc.), display of positive attitudes (e.g. of good-will, gratitude or respect), abstention from causing harm, observance of norms (obedience, loyalty), etc. The first action and the return action can be of the same type (for instance, one renders assistance and receives assistance in return), or they can be of different types. And they can be simple or composed of many different values. In the latter instance neg-ative values can also be incorporated in the final, overall reciprocation. I use the term 'exchange' also in this case, provided that the positive values predominate.

In the second place, the *length of time before an exchange is con-cluded* can vary. The first action and the reciprocal action sometimes coincide, while on other occasions there may be a shorter or longer in-terval between them. If the initiator has assumed that some time will elapse before he gets any return, we can say that he has granted 'credit'. The conditions and consequences of giving credit will occupy us a good deal in the following chapter.

Thirdly, the interaction relationships between two parties can vary in their *duration*. On the one hand we have instances where two persons, who otherwise have no contact with each other, undertake a single ex-change. And on the other hand we have permanent exchange connec-tions where actions are constantly being reciprocated. The relationship between the shopkeeper and his permanent customer, between the em-ployer and employee, between parents and children and between spouses are examples of this. The greater the number of different kinds of val-ues which are reciprocated in such a relationship, the less *specialized* I call it. The exchange relationship between husband and wife, for in-stance, is less specialized than that between the shopkeeper and his customer.

In permanent and unspecialized exchange relations, the line between individual exchanges is often rather arbitrary. To take the relationship between government and citizens as an example, the overall recipro-cation of values can be conceived as one large exchange – where the government's economic, social and cultural services and the security and predictability it provides are considered as repayment for what citizens have contributed in the form of productive work, tax paying, law abi-dance and patriotism, etc. Such overall considerations can be applied to the government's relationship to citizens collectively or to its relationship to the individual citizen. But it is also possible to conceive of more

55

limited exchanges, for example when government appropriations for the construction and maintenance of roads are seen as being a service reciprocated for the tax levied on petrol and cars. Varying opinions of what is just can at times come from differing conception of what is included in the exchange.

In addition to the variations which have now been mentioned, come also those which depend on differences between regulating factors. These are discussed in the following section.

II. FACTORS REGULATING EXCHANGE

By the expression 'factors regulating exchange' I refer to factors that make for regularity and predictability in exchange situations. These can be social norms (i.e. norms which are not purely private but which are shared, or at least known, to several people). Or they can be factual conditions inviting consistent strategies.

Many regulating *norms* help to *promote exchange activity*. This can be done directly by norms which prescribe certain types of exchange. We have, for instance, customs prescribing exchange of presents and we have rules of law requiring public utilities to serve the general public at reasonable rates. More important than these regulations (at any rate in our society) are, however, the normative factors which indirectly promote exchange activity by easing or by ensuring the accomplishment of exchange transactions. Rules and principles which state that certain services require counter-services can have such an effect. There are both specific rules and vaguer principles of this kind. Prominent amongst these is the principle of justice that good merits good. In contrast to the other norms mentioned, this does not refer to any specific type of exchange. It has a general content and an undefined area of application. If the conditions are favourable (see next chapter) it can be applied to any exchange situation. Another complex of norms which helps promote exchange activity, is the principle that agreements shall be kept and the specific rules which regulate the contracting and execution of agreements.

Many norms *regulate the position of parties and rates of exchange.* As *Thibaut* and *Kelley* (1959, see especially p. 61) point out, role norms are often involved here. Awareness of the fact that another person is, for instance, one's spouse, employer, shopkeeper or doctor, releases a set of rather definite conceptions as to what kind of services one can expect from this other person, of what one must give in return, and of how one should conduct oneself in order to get the exchange going – or in order to avoid it. There are also other types of norms which regulate exchange conditions : for example, price control and collective wage agreements. Principles of justice also enter the picture in this connection inasmuch as they require balance between give and take. As will be seen in the following chapter, factors regulating the rate of exchange can sometimes contribute to promotion of exchange activity. But it can also happen that they have the opposite effect, e.g., when low ceiling prices lead to stockpiling.

However, there are also factors which directly aim *hindering or limiting exchange activity.* In social anthropological and sociological literature reference is sometimes made to 'channels of conversion' which limit the possibilities of converting one type of value into another (cf. e.g. *Barth* 1963 pp. 10-12 with references). I use instead the expression *'exchange restrictions'.* In one sense this is a narrower concept because it refers only to such value conversion as is brought about through exchange. From another point of view it is a wider concept since it not only covers prohibition of conversion of one type of value into another, but also prohibition of exchange of the same types of values. Prohibition of exchange can vary in severity – from cases where deviating behaviour rouses only slight disapproval to cases where it can be punished by heavy sanctions. It can also vary in its content : prohibition can mean that certain kinds of values (e.g. land which is considered the property of a family or of a tribe) must on no account be exchanged, or it can mean that exchange is permitted but only with certain and not with other values. Friendship, for instance, may be exchanged with friendship but may not be sold for money. Or the group of people with whom one is allowed to exchange may be restricted, for example in such a manner that values can be disposed of to relatives but not to strangers, to countrymen but not to aliens. And lastly there are cases where only the extent of exchange activity is limited. It may be right, for example, to exchange presents as a token of friendship, but there are limits to how often this should happen and to how large the presents should be.

Finally, let us look at regulation which is *strategically* conditioned. A set of strategic choices has a tendency to lead in the same direction if the value premises and the factual premises are, each time, the same. The situation often comes very close to this in permanent exchange relationships where one party, in regularly recurring, similar situations, is confronted by the same partner. He gradually learns how much he can claim and what he must give if there is to be profitable exchange.

In this way there can be marked regularity in the relationship between permanent exchange partners without it being due to adherence to norms. Sometimes, however, such systematic behaviour tends to create norms.

Strategic factors can sometimes also result in uniform patterns of behaviour in wider circles. It is true that patterns of behaviour are seldom identical, for not all people have the same preferences and opportunities. But there are certain features which most people have in common – among other things, they like to receive something for their efforts – and the more, the better, as long as this does not conflict with any norm. The desire for profit can decide which exchanges take place and which do not. It has also the important consequence that alternative exchange possibilities tend to lead to competition. And because sellers must underbid each other in order to get their commodities sold and buyers must overbid to get hold of the things they want, prices and other exchange conditions are stabilized. I use the term *'market'* to designate a situation where there are alternative possibilities of exchange. This expression is used even when the values exchanged are non-economic. The interplay between competition and exchange conditions is called the *'market mechanism'*.

The main topic of the coming chapter turns on the conditions under which the different types of regulating factors are likely to develop. In the following sections of this chapter I give a descriptive survey of different types of exchange.

The survey calls for systematization. But it is difficult to find a satisfactory typology because there are so many different kinds of exchange objects and so many ways in which these can be combined.[2] I have chosen to devote one section to each of the most important types of exchange objects. However, what is written about them is incomplete since by no means are all the possibilities of exchange with other kinds of values mentioned.

III. MATERIAL THINGS AS OBJECTS OF EXCHANGE

There can be different motives for this kind of exchange activity. Sometimes the usefulness of the objects obtained in exchange is the most im-

2. Turner, Foa and Foa (1971) and Foa (1971) have proposed a classification of exchange objects which is somewhat different from the one presented there. They have also developed a theory concerning the relationships between different kinds of exchange objects.

portant factor. For example, we buy things we need for living and things which can make life more pleasant for us. In other cases, it is the symbolic value which is of greatest importance. Some objects (e.g. money) have a generally accepted and standardized symbolic value while others have symbolic value for only a single person or small circle of people (e.g. sentimental value). And finally there are cases where it is not so much the objects acquired but the exchange transaction itself which gives satisfaction.

We shall first look at exchange where the main motive is to acquire the object. Such exchange is occasionally neither regulated by norms nor by market mechanism, which means that the results of the exchange depend entirely upon the individual's ability to discover suitable exchange partners and to negotiate with them. However, economic transactions in both our own and in other cultures are usually regulated in one way or another.

The most important regulating factors with us are market mechanisms and norms governing agreements. But there are also norms that regulate exchange possibilities and exchange conditions more directly (e.g. anti-trust laws, price control, rationing, etc.). These forms or regulation play an important role when market mechanisms fail, for instance because of monopolies or shortages.

Justice is seldom used as an argument in connection with the buying and selling of goods. A person who manages to obtain a commodity without paying for it may be characterized as 'audacious' or 'dishonest' but rarely as 'unjust'. Nor is a salesman normally reproached for injustice when he asks a price higher than the market value, but is rather called 'shameless' or 'unreasonable'. However, during the Middle Ages when the market system was less developed than it is today, negotiations over what could be considered a 'just price' ('*justum pretium*') played an important role.[3] The word 'just' need not have been used in exactly the same way as here, of course, but many things indicated that – at least during the earliest period – deliberations were frequently concerned with what we would call 'just balance'. According to *Weber* l.c., however, attitudes gradually changed character, in step with developments in trade, and took on more and more the features of economic marketing considerations.

There is also evidence from primitive societies which shows that norms tend to develop around exchange transactions when there is a

---

3. Cf. Weber (1925 p. 500 and pp. 801 ff.), Blaug (1968 pp. 31-32) and Salin (1932) the latter having comprehensive references to other works.

lack of market regulation. By and large these norms are more specific than principles of justice. They often regulate in detail who barters what with whom and on what terms. *Malinowski* (1922 and 1926) has described the different forms of exchange in use among the people of the Trobriand Islands. I shall give a couple of these by way of illustration.

Vegetables and fish were exchanged between villages in the interior and villages at the coast (Malinowski 1922 pp. 187-188 ; 1926 pp. 22ff.). Each man had his permanent exchange partner. When the vegetables were harvested the people from the interior travelled down to the coast with large quantities of vegetables and each of them placed his portion in front of the house of his partner. This was an invitation, which could never be refused, to later return a quantity of fish which, according to fixed norms, was of an equivalent value. As soon as the weather and other circumstances permitted, the fishermen went to sea and informed their partners in the interior of this. These again went down to the coast and when the fishermen returned, the fish which belonged to the former was taken straight from the canoes and carried home to the village in the interior. The vegetable cultivators, then, delivered their goods on credit but did not have to be worried about payment. Malinowski (1922 p. 188 footnote) tells that the fishermen felt their duty so strongly that they attended to it even though they could earn 15-20 times more by pearl diving.

But most fascinating of all was the Trobrianders' 'foreign trade'. Their islands formed, together with many other islands in Melanesia, what Malinowski (1922, cf. especially p. 82 et seq.) calls the 'kula ring'. The islands that were involved were inhabited by peoples with different customs and languages, and there were sometimes long distances between the islands so that canoe trips from one to the other could be rather dangerous. Even so, there was regular communication between them. The motivating force behind these expeditions was a desire to receive 'kula' objects. There were two types of these ; necklaces and bracelets. Malinowski compares them with the British crown jewels : they were ugly, useless things, were seldom or never used (not even for personal adornment) but they were considered excessively valuable. The finest had names and long, eventful histories. But in contrast to the crown jewels they were continuously moving between exchange partners. They wandered from man to man around the whole circular chain of islands – necklaces clockwise, bracelets counter-clockwise. Reciprocation took place between permanent exchange partners. But each kula member could have several partners. When he stood facing the centre of the island circle, he had one or more partners to the left to whom he gave necklaces and from whom he received bracelets, and a partner (or partners) to the right to whom he gave bracelets and from whom he received necklaces. The partner could live on the same island or on an island which was the next link in the kula chain, many miles away. There was always a certain interval between one service and the return service – with overseas kulas this might amount to several months. First came an expedition from island A to B with, for instance, bracelets which each of the participants gave to his kula partner, and some time later came an expedition from B to A with necklaces which were distributed there. The journeys were always surrounded with intense excitement because the recipient did not previously know how many and how fine the value objects which the visitors had with them would be, nor did he know the manner in which the objects would be allocated since each participant often had several partners. Although exchange of the kula objects among the people was considered to be the main purpose of the overseas expeditions, this was by no means the only event. They also took large quantities of goods with them which were partly used as presents and partly disposed of as ordinary trade goods. The trade was always conducted with people other than the kula partner.

The kula system afforded, in this manner, a basis for getting together to trade and for making other cultural contacts. There were two features of the system which particularly made it suitable for creating contact between the islands. In the first place, the great value which was attributed to the kula objects was an incitement to venture on long, dangerous sea journeys. In the second place, the fact that one had a kula partner in the foreign place meant that one had also a friend and protector there because, between kula partners, there was a network of mutual rights and duties. The trust and reliance which existed between partners was underlined by the fact that there was always a waiting period between the one service and its return service and also by the fact that the values were brought and not fetched. The kula system also affected the social status of persons within each individual community. To be a kula member, which was by no means universal, was a privilege and it was also an advantage to have as many partners as possible.

There were several other forms of exchange among the Trobrianders (cf. the summary in Malinowski 1922 pp. 177-191). Some of these had an obvious economic stamp but contributed, even so, to stressing the kind of social relationship existing between the two parties concerned. Others had solely the last-mentioned effect. Transactions might consist of an exchange of objects having no particular value to either of the parties involved, or they might just be the return, after a certain time, of the same thing which had previously been given. What was of importance on these occasions was not the exchange of material values but the exchange transaction itself. In many cases this was fenced in by norms which prescribed when and how and with whom exchange could be made. The transaction in such cases contributed to symbolizing the existing family, neighbour or friend relationship between the parties concerned. But in addition to these prescribed exchanges there could also be many spontaneous ones which seemed to have a greater symbolic than economic significance.

Similar forms of exchange activity take place in many other cultures. Nor are symbolic exchanges unknown with us – although they certainly play a smaller role than with the Trobrianders. We exchange Christmas and birthday presents, offer flowers to our hostess when we are invited to a party. Similarly, presents are exchanged when foreign heads of state and prime ministers pay official visits.

The more spontaneous exchange activity which is to be seen amongst children also takes place more often for the sake of the activity itself than for the purpose of acquiring material gain. *Kolsrud* (1958) describes how his 6-7 year old daughter and some friends spent their time swapping glossy pictures. Occasionally one of the girls was ignored for a whole day because she had been 'naughty', but on the whole the small group was well integrated. Kolsrud writes, among other things, on the purpose of their activity (p. 2) :

'Because of the adult's profane interest in motives, I wanted to know what kind of glossy pictures my daughter tried to collect. She was at that moment very occupied with an angel which Mary possessed. This she got, but it shortly changed hands again. It went to Jane in exchange for a small glossy boy who, everyone agreed, was not very pretty.

My curiosity and care for my own offspring led me a little further. When a small boy with blue trousers was not so pretty as a pink angel with white wings, was not the angel worth, for instance, two such little boys ? Four pairs of eyes looked up in wondering incomprehension and gave me a glimpse of another world, a distant land without quantity, a world where angels and blue boys counted alike.'

Because the actual exchange transaction is in itself attributed a value, this means that the partners receive what I call a *non material bonus* through the exchange. What they give each other in addition to the material objects can, for example, be a sign of friendship or attention, a sign of trust if a respite is granted before the service is returned, a sign that they consider each other as equal individuals because they perform on like-footing, or – if the exchange situation is not symmetrical –

a sign that they accept a ranking system between each other, etc. The partners sometimes perceive that they receive such bonus services and take these into consideration when they involve themselves in the exchange, but they are often not aware of it. The bonus values are frequently of such a kind that they help to bind the partners closer together. This does not, of course, apply in all cases. Pleasure in trying to cheat the other party can also be a bonus value. But generally it seems that permanent exchange relationships have an integrating effect.

Personal ties which develop between exchange partners are particularly important in societies which lack, or have only a poorly developed, government apparatus. When there is no police force, health service or any form of social insurance, one can only turn to friends and relations for help in times of need.

IV. WORK AND OTHER SERVICES AS OBJECTS OF EXCHANGE

In addition to trade in material objects, the buying and selling of labour input and other services is the most important form of economic exchange in our society. Agreements and market mechanism also play a significant role as regulating factors in this field. But the contribution of norms which supplement or correct these regulating mechanisms is more apparent here than in the case of trade in merchandize. Some of these norms are specific rules, for example concerning working hours, holidays and workshop security measures, and the qualifications required for performance of certain kinds of service activities (e.g. as doctor, lawyer or craftsman). But, in addition, ideas of justice are more likely to be applicable than in trade. Claims from individual workers or categories of workers for equal treatment, and claims for balance in relationships between employees and employers, can both occur.

These differences between labour relations and trade are probably due to the fact that conditions governing market formation in the two fields are not the same. I shall return to this in more detail in the next chapter. Considerations of justice have, at any rate, a tendency to be regarded as particularly relevant when no market exists. This can apply, for instance, when services are of such a personal character that they cannot be entrusted to just anyone, or it can apply to services which in a particular situation, are monopolized. Let us take as an example a case from an old American Supreme Court decision.[4] A ship

4. Post v Jones (19 How. 150, 1856) discussed by Cahn (1956 p. 212).

was wrecked on a deserted coastline under very dangerous circumstances. Another ship arrived, but its captain made it a condition of saving the crew that he be allowed to buy the cargo from the grounded ship for a price well below its real value. The shipwrecked captain felt forced to agree but later the shipowners took the case to court in order to get the deal invalidated, and won. The court ruled that the defendant was entitled to reasonable salvage money but not to exploit the situation to make economic gain beyond this. The circumstances being what they were, decisive importance could not be attached to the agreement.

Many working conditions are characterized by the fact that, apart from the work done and the wage paid, several other services are exchanged which are normally neither specified in the labour contract nor subject to legal regulation. For instance, it may be that an employee offers more in the form of care, consideration, responsibility and loyalty than his contract or the law requires of him and that, in return, he is respected, that confidence is placed in him, and that he gets security and opportunity for advancement.[5] How important a role such non-material bonuses play varies, of course, under different types of working conditions. The more permanent and more personal the relationship is, the more important will these supplements usually be and the greater will be the likelihood of principles of justice being applied. These can be of a shorter or more long term nature. The characterization 'unjust' will sometimes be applicable when one of the parties has worked up a 'moral credit balance' during an earlier period and the other party later neglects to honour this when he has the opportunity. We can imagine an old servant who has loyally and with much personal sacrifice served a certain family for many years and who – after having become a fixed part of the inventory and it being too late to think of looking for a new post – does not receive the appreciation (e.g. in the form of gratitude, respect or increased wages) which she has deserved.

Services are sometimes exchanged without there being any agreement or institutional regulation of the relationship between the partners. One example of this – on which *Blau* (1955) has considerable empirical material and which *Homans* (1961) comments upon – is the experienced employee who helps the newcomer or less able colleague and who, in return, receives gratitude and respect. In these instances, too, certain

---

5. On such conditions cf. Barnard (1938, particularly pp. 56-61, 92-95, 139 ff. and 240 ff.) and March and Simon (1958 pp. 83 ff.). The authors mentioned stress the importance of 'equilibrium' in the relationships between the business enterprise and the employed, but their meaning is hardly the same as mine when I talk of 'balance'.

regulating factors can be present. If there are several people who need help and several who can give help, a market may be formed. The person who shows least respect and gratitude to his helpers, for instance, may have to increase his counter-services if he is to get the help he needs at all. And the helper who expects too much risks losing his 'customers', which means that he does not receive the appreciation he desires without first reducing his demands. But market mechanisms are usually very imperfect, partly because the working system often limits choice between different helpers and partly because the cost curve for the person who gives help generally rises very rapidly. To give a little help is often quite pleasant, but a lot can be a nuisance. The helper has therefore no strong motive for trying to attract many 'customers' by reducing his 'price'. In addition to the approximations to market regulation which have been mentioned (and sometimes influenced by these) one often finds rather vague norms for what is 'suitable' behaviour in situations where help is wanted or given. Considerations of justice can also enter the picture. For example, if a person who is helped does nothing in return, this can be characterized as 'unfair' and especially so if he, to the contrary, hurts his helper, for instance by talking behind his back to his superiors in order to be promoted at his expense.

There are many other examples of how help, advice or other services are the subject of informal exchange, for instance between fellow workers, colleagues, business connections, friends, brothers and sisters, husband and wife, parents and children, etc. Services are sometimes repaid by services, sometimes through intimation of a positive attitude to the person in question.

In certain fields there are fixed traditional ideas on what is expected of whom. In the relationship between husband and wife, for example, there are often clear norms for what her duties as wife are and what his are as husband. That there are such norms does not necessarily mean that no exchange occurs. For one thing, the fulfilling of one's status duties can be an object for exchange ('When I take care of my duties, you must take care of yours'). We shall return to this type of exchange in section VI. But exchange of ordinary services can also occur. He helps her, for instance, with some of the 'woman's work' while she, another time, repays him with help. Or they do something – over and above what their status duties require – each in his own field. She pays extra attention, for example, to preparing the food because she has a particularly considerate husband. In all such exchange situations considerations of justice can easily be involved.

In a milieu where fixed rules as to what is a man's job and what a woman's are not accepted, it is often more natural to apply distribution than exchange considerations. The couple are considered as having a number of common tasks which are to be divided between them and principles of distributive justice may be considered relevant. However, there may also be exchange situations here, for example when, for some reason or other, there is a temporary lapse from what the couple consider as being the right allocation : we can take the example of a married student couple who, generally speaking, intend to divide equally between them all work concerned with the house, children and cooking. Even so, she takes over all of this during his exam semester and expects him to repay her next year when she takes her exam.

One form of exchange which occurs in many connections is when a person supports another's *opinion* on condition that the latter support his view or compensate in some other manner. We find examples of this in relationships between husband and wife, between brothers, and between friends. And we also find examples in the business world and political life. When votes are to be cast, for instance, there may be an agreement or tacit understanding that A will vote for B's proposal in one case, in return for which B will vote for A's view in another case (or perhaps receive compensation in some other form). *Buchanan and Tullock* (1965, especially p. 131 et seq. and p. 250 et seq.) undertake a thorough analysis of such exchange transactions. They discuss first and foremost the profit and market questions but also touch upon the moral aspects (p. 270 et seq.). *Torgersen* (1967) who gives a number of examples from Norwegian politics (during the period 1884-1940) writes (Chap. 7,2 p. 7) :

'The Liberals had an organization which seemed to act largely as a kind of political *bank* where one could exchange and trade. The Party was in many ways a union of 'intense minorities', groups which individually had limited but strong interests and were willing, when it came to quite a lot of questions, to vote for anything, in return for similar services, something which explains the Party's dual stamp of ideology and bargaining.'

Another service which is often used as an exchange object is the giving of *information*. Some people choose this as their profession, for instance the journalist, spy, detective and research worker. On the one hand such professional people stand in an exchange relationship to their employers or clients. They receive payment for their work and can achieve in addition honour and esteem if they furnish especially interesting or sensational information. On the other hand they often have to give their sources something in return in order to obtain the information. There can be many kinds of return : money, attention, flattery, promises of discretion, etc. *Skolnick* (1967) gives several examples from police investigation work in an American town : among other things it often happened that the police turned a blind eye to minor offences committed by witnesses if these, in return, were willing to give information that could lead to the detection of other criminals.

Information also serves as an object of exchange in private life. One example is the stranger (in the old days, or today in an isolated community) who has travelled a long distance and who is offered hospitality and paid attention in anticipation of his reciprocating by telling them the latest news from the big, wide world. On other occasions it can be a matter of permanent exchange connections for example between people coming together at the club or at a restaurant. Reporting on his investigation of a gang of youths in Oslo, *Brøgger* (1968, 2, p. 20) writes :

'When a crowd of young people came together in the recreation club, it was obvious that they belonged to different groups. I chose one of these groups for closer study and gradually got into good contact with them. We might sit together for hours without anything special happening, but after a while it became clear that information played some role. We could tell each other things, particularly things which had happened in that neighbourhood, news which rarely had any dramatic impact, but we then knew something together. More formally can we say, then, that *information* was one of the values which was exchanged.'

In such cases it is usually what one has oneself to recount which serves as an exchange for what the others have told. But many kinds of supplementary values can enter the picture, for example the pleasure one gets oneself from telling something, appreciation for having told something interesting, respect for having kept within the bounds the others expect of you, and – perhaps, particularly – the feeling of being part of a group which together knows something.

V. TO REFRAIN FROM CAUSING HARM AS AN OBJECT OF EXCHANGE

There are many examples where A does B a service in order that the latter abstain from harming A (or some other person). This can be an isolated exchange transaction as, for instance, when ransom is paid for a prisoner or a kidnapped child, or when a corrupt policeman or judge is bribed in order that someone evade conviction. Or it can be a permanent exchange connection as, for example, when businessmen in the United States make a regular payment to racketeers, or when farmers in southern Italy provide shelter, food and money to bandits. The 'tax' paid by many seafaring nations to the pirate states of North Africa during the last century in order that their ships could sail unmolested, is also an example of this.

There are many instances of such tributes being paid to supernatural beings who, it was feared, would cause damage, inconvenience or suffering. Men have sacrified to gods and demons and have procured indulgence from the fires of purgatory, etc.

The motive for rendering a service to such powerful exchange partners as mentioned in the examples above is not always to insure oneself against harm. It may also be for the purpose of obtaining help, protection or other services. Sometimes it is partly for one reason, and partly for the other. There were such mixed motives for helping bandits, for instance, among the population of a district in southern Italy which *Brøgger* (1968, I) investigated. Amongst other things, the bandits here had placed a tax on the sale of land and on marriage ceremonies. One of the reasons why people paid up was that they expected to suffer if they did not. But the fact that these bandits provided positive services which were worth paying for, also played a role. They were, inter alia, the only people in the area who could effectively solve a conflict since they had both respect and force to back up their decisions.

The relationship between men and gods varies a great deal. In some places the gods are kind so that sacrifices are usually made to them for the purpose of obtaining benefits. In other places they are capricious and dangerous and the sacrifices offered are generally an attempt to conciliate them.[6] *Monberg* (1966) gives an interesting description of the relationship between the inhabitants of the island of Bellona in the Pacific and the gods they believed in before christianity was introduced. The gods there had many characteristics – both good and bad – in common with humans. But they had the power to accomplish things which humans could not. And it was dangerous not to be on good terms with them. Most of the gods were well disposed to exchange activity. They needed the food and utility articles which humans could give them. As a return service they left men in peace and gave them security and protection. However, there were some gods who were so evil and unpredictable that it was of no use to sacrifice to them. These gods were blamed when people suffered misfortune in spite of the fact that accounts had been satisfactorily settled with other gods.

6. Westermarck II (1908 Chaps. XLVIII-LII) is a mine of information on the various features which different peoples have attributed to their gods, cf. the summary p. 728 where he gives as his opinion that the gods have gradually, through the ages, changed for the better, cf. also p. 610 et seq. for exchange motives for sacrifices.

Of more practical importance – at any rate in our society – than the forms of exchange already mentioned, is the situation when A refrains from harming B on the condition that B avoids harming A. Let us take some children playing on a heap of sand as an example. One of them builds a sandcastle, another makes roads and bridges. One fills his bucket with sand, another plays with cars, etc. In such a situation, a child often expects thoughtfulness from the other children and argues his case with a claim to reciprocation : 'I didn't touch your castle, and it is rotten of you to spoil my road'. Similar examples can be found from a multitude of day-to-day situations where consideration is paid to other people with the expectation that they will be equally considerate towards oneself – during play, at school and at work, in married life and on social occasions, etc.

In many fields there are norms indicating the extent of thoughtfulness one should show for other people. All societies, for instance, have legal or traditional rules which forbid certain damaging or dangerous actions. These specific rules are often supplemented by other vaguer and more general norms which show the amount of consideration and attention which is to be expected in various inter-human situations. The relationship between norms and exchange activity is more or less the same here as in the case of services (cf. above under IV). Obedience to norms can be an object of exchange as can also dispensation from following them ('Since you were let off, so can I be'). These relationships will be discussed more closely in the following section (VI).

But on some occasions exchanges take place requiring other or greater mutual regard and attention than the norms lay down. We have an example of this when two enterprises agree to limit competition, for instance by not underbidding each other or by dividing the market between them. Another example is when a married couple or friends adapt themselves by mutually omitting to say or do things which are permitted by ordinary norms but which, they notice, the other person dislikes.

This kind of exchange probably plays a big part in the process of creating norms. There can be a slow transition from avoiding an action because one knows that the other party prefers it this way and because one expects that he will reciprocate – to avoiding the action because one feels that this is the right thing to do even though one gets nothing in return. In this manner particular norms can come to be accepted, for instance within the individual marriage or within a relationship situation between friends. And if several people take part in similar exchange transactions or if other factors lead to a wider dispersal, the norms gradually receive wider recognition. Sometimes, however, there are factors present which deter such norm formation. Ideological support for the principle of free competition could be an example of this in the case mentioned above where competition was voluntarily restricted between business enterprises. It could lead to a situation where there was no development of general norms limiting competition, but where the enterprises concerned continued to regard the agreements made or their tacit understanding as the only basis for their mutual arrangement.

VI. COMPLIANCE WITH NORMS AS AN OBJECT OF EXCHANGE

There is some element of norm compliance in most exchanges since the parties involved wholly or partly comply with each other's claims or wishes. But usually it is not compliance with norms as such but rather the fact that the desired action takes place (or that the undesired action is avoided) which is the essential feature of the exchange. However, there are also cases where obedience to a norm, as a value in itself – alone or together with other values – can serve as an object of exchange.

The importance of this kind of exchange is emphasized by *Malinowski* (1926) in his studies of the Trobrianders' organization of society. As an example he mentions the mourning ceremonies conducted on the death of a married man. When the widow weeps and wails over the loss of her husband, he writes, (pp. 33-34) this may partly be because she is genuinely mourning his departure and partly be due to religious piety and fear, but it is first and foremost in order to fulfil the duty of expressing sorrow which she is considered to have towards her husband's family. Her obedience to what the norms lay down as being the correct way of mourning is a service rendered on her part to her husband's family and it is repaid with presents as soon as the ceremony is over. Both the performance and the reward are links in the long chain of services and counter services which regulate the relationship between the two families.

In our own culture, too, it is a well known phenomenon that compliance with norms can be regarded as behaviour which merits reward. Let us take the relationship between children and their parents as an example. As long as it is not a matter of course in the family concerned that the child automatically does as mother and father say, obedience will easily take on the character of an exchange value which can be negotiated. The parents say to the child, for instance, that it can have this or that (or be allowed to do this or that) 'if you are a good child' or 'because you have been good'. Or perhaps the child asks for something (or permission to do something) because 'I have been good' (or 'obedient' or 'behaved properly' or 'did what you said').

There are many other examples where obedience and loyalty serve as exchange objects – although they are not so frequently used for bargaining as can be the case between parents and children. For instance, someone who accepts employment in an enterprise not only undertakes to work but also, among other things, to comply with his superiors' instructions. And in the composite exchange situation between government and citizen, obedience and loyalty belong to the services which are expected from the citizen. In informal groupings similar exchanges can also occur, for instance in a gang of youths where the big, strong boys protect the smaller and these, in return, do what the big ones ask of them.

In this manner exchange can form a basis for *power*. This is a point to which *Blau* (1964, especially p. 115 et seq., p. 259 et seq. and p. 312 et seq.) attaches great importance. He emphasizes that subordination is an exchange value available even to those who otherwise have few resources. In certain situations it may be necessary benefits. This is true, for instance, if food is needed to keep life going or protection is needed from imminent danger and subordination or submission are the only available exchange values which satisfy the person who can supply the required benefits. Blau contends that 'With the exception of the special case of coercive force, power has its origin in unilateral exchange transactions' (p. 321). I doubt if this general statement is tenable. But exchange activity plays, at any rate, an important role as a foundation of power.[7]

In addition to these non-symmetrical exchanges (which Blau calls 'unilateral') where one side alone subordinates itself to the other, there are also symmetrical exchange situations where compliance to norms is practised by both sides. There can be some element of such reciprocation in several of the situations which have already been mentioned. But let us first look at some clear cases :

Rights and duties in relationships between equal partners as, for instance, between husband and wife, between friends, colleagues, business connections, etc., are often regulated by norms. These can (as mentioned in sections IV and V), for example, be norms referring to one's

7. Exchange activity can also provide power in a more indirect manner than that mentioned in the text, i.e. when profitable exchange increases a person's resources (e.g. of material goods) and thereby also his possibility of exerting influence, cf. Dahlström (1968 p. 144).

71

duty to perform a service and to be considerate. It may be that these norms are so well established that it seems obvious that they should always be followed. But if this is not the case, compliance can serve as a mutual exchange value. In pure form the exchange can consist of 'I will comply with the norms which favour you if you, in return, respect those that favour me'. In this way both parties gain from their mutual compliance with norms, and thereby become more strongly motivated to comply, so that the norms gradually become more permanently established. Exchange activity, then, can help to build up norms – both, as mentioned in section V, by giving rise to the development of new norms, and, as mentioned here, by strengthening existing norms.

Exchanges of the kind mentioned above can occur both when there are two sets of norms (some binding A and some binding B) and when there is one set of norms which both A and B are bound by and from which both benefit when the other party complies. There are many such rules in the legal system of a country, in the by-laws of associations and organizations, in rules for games, sport and play, in norms for behaviour in informal groups, etc. There are also more general norms which it can be equally profitable for each party in a relationship to have the other obey, for instance the norm that a promise shall be kept.

It often seems only right that a person who has benefited from another person's compliance with certain norms should himself behave in accordance with these norms.[8] In any event a group will react against the member who disregards norms the others consider important to keep. And he who shows a greater degree of conformity than the rest of the group will – other things being equal – achieve higher esteem within the group than the others. *Homans* (1950 and 1961) mentions several empirical investigations [9] which support this assumption and offers the explanation (1961 p. 163) that high esteem is awarded in return for a high degree of norm conformity. It is unlikely that exchange (in the sense in which the term is used here) has taken place in all these cases. But it can certainly sometimes be so. There can also be compound exchanges of conformity for conformity, with esteem as a bonus to the one who has a surplus.

8. Hart (1955) who treats the question from the angle of moral philosophy, presents the following principle (p. 185) : 'When a number of persons conduct any joint enterprise according to rules ... those who have submitted to these restrictions when required have a right to a similar submission from those who have benefited by their submission'. Cf. also Rawls (1971, p. 112 and pp. 342-350) and von Wright (1963, pp. 197-219).
9. Among others the Hawthorne research reported in Roethlisberger and Dickson (1939) and Whyte's (1943) investigation of the Norton Street Gang.

For more marginal members of a group another exchange value can also apply, namely that of being accepted as a member of the group. The person who does not observe the rules of the game risks being excluded. One can also be expelled from an association or frozen out of an informal group because of grave or repeated non-compliance with norms. Newcomers are often subject to the strictest adherence to conformity (cf. *Homans* 1961 pp. 339-340) while old and well established group members can allow themselves certain liberties – because they have investments upon which they can draw.

We have now examined two main types of exchange with norm compliance. We first looked at one-sided situations of subordination where A follows B's norms in return for other values. After this we looked at mutual situations of adjustment between equal partners where A and B exchange by complying with each other's norms or joint norms. But there are also intermediate cases where subordination is not completely one-sided but where the leader must, to some extent, adapt himself to the norms of the subordinate in order to have his own norms accepted or his goals promoted by the subordinate.

It is essential for a leader to allow for this if he is dependent upon continuous support from his followers to maintain his leadership. This is particularly so if his group is engaged not in an activity which requires special skills from its leader but which has social intercourse as its main purpose. In such a case compliance with the group's norms for behaviour during social intercourse will be something which is highly valued. The fact that one of the participants lives up to these norms better than the others, can be the reason why he becomes leader.[10] And even though, to some degree, other claims will be made of him after he has become leader, it is still important for him to live up to these norms if he is not to lose some of his popularity. *Whyte's* Street Corner Society (1943) can also in this connection serve as an example.

In cases where activity has a specific aim and the leadership is comparatively authoritarian, one may still have to take account of the same considerations. *Homans's* description (1962 pp. 50 ff.) of his experiences as commander of a small warship during the war, illustrates this. He writes (p. 57) that he gradually learnt that it is only if the skipper does his best for his men, and they know this, that they do their best for the ship. The skipper must therefore have a feeling for the claims and ex-

10. Cf. Berelson and Steiner (1964 p. 343, 3.1): 'The leadership of the group tends to be vested in the member who most closely conforms to the standards of the group on the matter in question, or who has the most information and skill related to the activities of the group'.

pectations of the crew and sense which of these they consider particularly important to have fulfilled. As an example he mentions that it was of decisive importance to the crew, who often had the greater part of their wages sent home to their families, that the little they were to receive themselves was paid out on pay day. This was often difficult because the wage regulations were complicated and relevant information was sometimes missing. But it was so important to satisfy the men's wishes on this point that it had to be done even though there was the risk of paying out too much so that conflict could arise with one's superiors. Another example was connected with enrollment on training courses. Because the navy was expanding there were always some crew members who were at home participating in these courses, qualifying themselves for promotion. The captain had a fairly free hand when it came to choosing men for these desirable trips home. And it was a big temptation to send away the difficult men and to keep on board those who were considered indispensable. But one could not fall for this temptation. The crew's norm stipulated that journeys home should be given to those who deserved them. And a break with this norm was damaging to morale on board.

It is very likely that similar tendencies are to be found in other subordination situations, for example between worker and employer, child and parent, pupil and teacher, citizen and state, etc. Both empirical investigations [11] and less systematic experience indicate that – in certain situations – it is easier for the leadership to obtain cooperation from their subordinates if they, on their part, show consideration for their subordinates' claims and expectations.

Of course, not all subordinates' norms have the same content. However, norms which are related to the need for confidence and security occur frequently. Among other things, these two claims are usually included :
1. that the leader keep promises he makes to subordinates – especially in those instances where a service or sacrifice has been offered in the confident expectation of the promise being kept ;
2. that the leader does not punish actions which subordinates have not been forewarned will be punishable.

I do not claim that these are norms which only subordinates hold. Quite the contrary, they are very widespread in our culture. The leader has

11. Cf., inter alia, the investigations which Berelson and Steiner (1964 pp. 344-346) mention, where democratically-led working groups seemed to be more effective than those with an authoritarian leadership.

74

normally also accepted them. And he is usually interested in his subordinates having at least *some* faith in his promises and at least *some* possibility of predicting when he will punish them, inter alia, because he will not otherwise be able to influence them through promises of reward or threats of punishment. But the subordinates will often expect more in this direction than it is in the interests of the leadership to let them have. They can, for example, tend to interpret as promises statements which are not meant as such, to expect particularly clear advance warning of what may come to be punishable, and to demand a more unconditional adherence to the above-mentioned norms than is considered opportune. They sometimes find support in the idea that they can expect a strict adherence to the norms mentioned as a counter service for subordinating themselves to the leader's authority and for relying on his promises.

One often finds examples of this in the relationship between parents and children. Mother, for instance, says to the child, 'If you behave well today while your aunt and uncle visit us, you may go to the circus tomorrow'. If the child fulfils his part of the bargain but is not allowed to go to the circus after all, he will readily perceive the denial not only as a breach of promise but also as an injustice. Because the mother has used the promise as a means of securing a service, she has created an exchange situation which strengthens the child's feeling of having a right to demand fulfilment. It frequently happens that much vaguer suggestions than the one mentioned have a similar effect.

Examples can also be taken from the relationship between state and citizen. A citizen is inclined to claim security and predictability in return for his loyalty and law-abiding behaviour. Predictability as regards compliance with the two norms mentioned above is often considered particularly important. There are strong reactions when a new law, for example, makes illegal an action which was not forbidden at the time it was undertaken, or when a law deprives a citizen of privileges which he has made an effort to obtain, trusting in the continuing protection of the law. It is particularly such instances which are referred to when retroactive laws are called unjust.

It is sometimes not a single rule but rather a large complex of laws and inherited ideas which together are the basis of expectations. As an example we can take the power to dispose of property and the freedom of contract which formed a framework around the *laissez-faire* economy. Sheltered by these principles, a set of expectations developed according to which there should be freedom from government interference in the private sector of the economy. Legislation regulating economic activity has disappointed these expectations. This is probably one of the reasons why this legislation has been regarded as unjust by many of those who based their economic activity on liberal principles and who made their contribution to society through productive input and loyalty to the legal system. As we shall see later, complaints over the injustice of regulative measures have also had other foundations. Some of these are connected with problems of allocation.

VII. EXEMPTION FROM NORM COMPLIANCE AND FROM THE REPERCUSSIONS OF NON-COMPLIANCE AS OBJECTS OF EXCHANGE

It is sometimes onerous and a nuisance to have to comply with norms. And even if the norms are not too troublesome, it can be nice to neglect them on occasions.

Part of the pleasure of home life, holidays, informal company with friends, etc. derives from neglecting the rules and conventions which otherwise have to be followed. *Other* demands may perhaps be made upon one in such situations. But some variation can, in itself, be a blessing.

When two or more people together disregard social norms which they would otherwise observe, the situation can take on the character of an exchange. Each person tolerates the unconventional behaviour of the others on condition that he himself is permitted to behave likewise.

It can also happen that exemption from the demands of a norm is exchanged for other values. At work and in other situations of subordination the superior, for example, may turn a blind eye to certain types of norm negligence if his subordinates in return put more effort into their jobs. Regulations which the subordinates regard as a nuisance and foolish and which the leadership does not consider very important are well suited as such objects of exchange. In the article previously mentioned on his experiences as commander of a warship, *Homans* (1962 p. 56) gives as an example the fact that he was not so particular about the crew following navy rules on regulation wear. For instance, he did not think it necessary to insist that they followed the regulation requiring white uniforms to be worn in a sea of oil where everything became filthy within a few minutes. This was one of the many things which helped to give the crew the feeling that their captain did his best for them, and which got them to do their best in return.

Blau (1955) found similar exchange situations in a federal control institution he investigated. He mentions (pp. 169 f.) that the supervisors

76

permitted agents to break many minor rules, and that in return they got the agents to adapt themselves to instructions – even when what the supervisors asked lay outside their official power.

However, turning a blind eye to norm-infringement is an exchange object which can quickly be exhausted in a lasting interaction relationship. If, during a sufficiently long period, a superior overlooks all breaches of a norm, this norm will eventually lose its power, and it will become a matter of course that the superior does not react when the norm is disregarded, and no longer a favour granted from his side. Neither is it so simple to insist upon compliance with a norm in some instances and then ignore it in others. A superior is not usually absolutely free to choose when he shall follow one course and when the other if he wants to avoid being accused of inconsistency. If lenient enforcement is to be practised without friction, at least some attention must normally be paid to the subordinates' ideas as to which trespasses are the more excusable.

To overlook non-compliance or to reduce punishment can also be used as a means of facilitating enforcement. It can serve, for example, as compensation to the sinner who has admitted his guilt or has denounced other people. We find examples of this in the home, in school, institutions and enterprises, and in public maintenance of justice. In the American city where *Skolnick* (1967) investigated the work of the police and courts, it was normal (as mentioned in section IV above) – particularly in cases involving the misuse of narcotics – for the police to permit minor offenders to go free if they denounced the more important law breakers (l.c. chap. 6 especially pp. 125 and 137). When cases were brought to court, negotiations in chambers between the judge and the defence attorney often resulted in a bargain : the judge would promise a mild sentence if the attorney could persuade his client to plead guilty (chap. 9, cf. pp. 12-15). Promises of a lenient sentence were also used by the police to persuade arrested criminals to admit as many earlier, unsolved incidents as possible. In this way, the statistics of cases solved – which meant much for the reputation of the police station – were improved (chap. 8).

Situations which differ from the ones mentioned above are those where dispensation from a norm is allowed. Parents often lay down such norms for their children. They say, for instance, that the children must not do this or that without first asking permission. There are a great many such regulations in a country's legislation. Many different kinds of transactions and activities are forbidden to all citizens other than those having special permission (by licence, concession, certificate, etc.). Permission which is granted on the basis of such regulations is an important exchange object but exchange is often regulated by the law which requires certain conditions to be fulfilled before permission can be given. And even when the conditions are not specifically mentioned in the law, it is understood that – at any rate according to Norwegian practice – the authorities must keep to the spirit of the regulations. The purpose of the regulation is in some cases to ensure that a person who wishes to engage in a certain activity has the necessary qualifications to do so. One must, for instance, be able to drive and have some knowledge of traffic regulations etc. before one can expect a driving licence ; one must have been called to the bar before one is allowed to practise as an advocate, etc. In other cases the aim is (also) to limit the numbers entering a trade or profession or to regulate the use of natural resources.

Industrialization and the spread of bureaucracy in our society over the last hundred years have led to an increased use of such systems of regulation. But in many senses the authorities have a more limited access to forms of permission as a means of exchange than was the case in earlier times. For instance, it is no longer possible to grant privileges as payment for personal services as was the custom in the days of autocratic power. And a person who has received a licence or concession cannot normally transfer this. Some of the causes and results of this trend of development (for which there are parallels in most industrial societies) are discussed in the next chapter.

Finally, there are cases where it is neither a question of permission nor of lenient enforcement but of protection against certain repercussions of the actor's own mistakes. One example is the protection from which employees – both in private and public fields of employ – often benefit. If, for instance, a civil servant working in a ministry commits an error, he may be reprimanded by his superiors. But unless his mistake is very serious, he is normally not held publicly responsible. In the press and in parliament it is referred to as an error of the ministry and the minister must expect censure although he personally is not to be blamed. The fact that the individual civil servant is anonymous to the public when he makes a mistake or neglects his duty is a natural counterpart to the fact that he is also anonymous when he performs a good service. It is therefore appropriate to regard honour and responsibility as corresponding exchange values in the relationship between civil servant and minister ; the civil servant does not accept responsibility in return for which he must renounce any claim to honour. The superior gets the honour – and the right to instruct his subordinate as well – but must, on the other hand, accept responsibility.

Responsibility can also be a factor in exchanges with other values than honour. During wage negotiations, for instance, it may be argued that a certain group of men should receive a higher wage because of their responsible jobs. As regards allocation of authority, it has been argued that some people (e.g. high-ranking military officers) must be given 'an authority which corresponds to their responsibilities'. In such cases it is not always clear what is meant by the expression 'responsibilities'. One possible interpretation is, however, that 'to take responsibility' means the same as 'to be exposed to the consequences of (one's own and other people's) mistakes'. It makes good sense to claim compensation for this.

VIII. EXPRESSION OF POSITIVE ATTITUDES AS AN OBJECT OF EXCHANGE, WITH PARTICULAR REFERENCE TO SHOWING GRATITUDE

Several examples have been given above where display of esteem or respect for the other party, or gratitude for what he has done, can serve as exchange values. Sometimes the main objects of exchange are something else – for instance, reciprocal services or mutual conformity to norms – and the showing of gratitude or respect comes as a bonus value. In other instances this is the only contribution from one party. And it can also happen that the main contribution from both sides consists of, for example, a mutual exchange of respect. Even though they may also exchange other values, e.g., support each other's standpoints and follow each other's norms, mutual respect can be the dominating factor which characterizes their whole relationship.

It is always through outward behaviour that values are transmitted. To believe something deep down inside is not enough. The action, therefore, consists in *showing* gratitude (respect, admiration, etc.), not in *being* grateful (or in *having* respect or admiration). And these two do not always coincide. One can smile and say thank you without meaning anything by it, and one can feel gratitude without showing it. Behaviour often seems most convincing – and is therefore also the best means of payment – when it is genuinely meant. But even when this is not the case and even if the other party knows this, it can have some value. It is usually better to receive thanks which one knows mean nothing, than not to be thanked at all. And it is generally better that people pretend to respect you, than that they openly let it be known that they do not.

The majority of the exchange values mentioned in the previous paragraph can serve both as the original service and as the counter service.

This also applies to display of attitudes such as, for instance, recognition, respect and admiration. An exchange situation can, for example, originate when A helps B and receives respect in return. Or it can originate by B showing respect for A and receiving help in return. But when it comes to *gratitude*, the situation is different. This is a typical means of payment – something one gives because one has received. One cannot show gratitude without having (or pretending to have) something to be thankful for. A sign of gratitude cannot, therefore, appear as the first step in an exchange transaction.[12]

As a means of payment, gratitude has something in common with money. The similarity is not only that both are used as a form of payment, but also that both have a wide field of application and can serve as payment for many different types of values. Gratitude can be an adequate counter service whether one has received material objects, services, consideration, conformity to one's own norms, or exemption from conformity to norms or from responsibility. But neither money nor gratitude are universal means of payment. And their areas of application are usually separate, so that it rarely happens that either of them can be the right choice. The areas of application are, in part, so clearly separated from one another that a mistaken choice of means of payment can be as good as no payment – or worse than none. It is shameless to confine oneself to showing gratitude when money payment is expected, and tactless to offer money when only gratitude is expected.

There is perhaps a somewhat wider choice between gratitude and other values used as payment – for instance, the value of returning a service. But here too freedom of choice is limited. Many different factors can decide what kind of counter service fits best. I shall confine myself to looking at only a couple of these :

The rank relation between parties is probably an important factor. That A now and then helps B and receives no help in return but is paid with gratitude, respect or admiration is a sign that A has greater opportunities for giving help than B – for example, because he is a more able person or more experienced or because he has greater resources. The development of such exchange relationships can therefore be a factor which contributes to creating and maintaining differences in rank. And when such differences are established, it may seem impertinent or at any rate tactless if the person who is considered the inferior tries to change the exchange relationship by himself giving help of the same kind as he has received.

12. Simulated gratitude, however, can be a *means* of initiating an exchange.

It should be noticed that this only applies to services which increase one's prestige to be able to offer. If no prestige is involved and the services are only trivial as, for instance, fetching a snack for one's fellow workers during a break or going an errand for the other boys in the gang, the relationship is the opposite. Then the fact that one performs a service and is not repaid with a service of the same kind is a sign (or confirmation) of lower rank.[13] In these instances one does not achieve admiration and often does not receive even thanks as compensation. But one can perhaps get other kinds of counter services or at least acceptance as a member of the group in return.

It may prove true – not only for the above mentioned exchange objects but also for others – that the more equal the parties consider themselves to be, the more likely it is that they find it suitable to repay with values of the same kind and same degree as they have received. However, this does not mean that equal parties always repay in this manner. Other factors can also be of influence.

Among other things, the motives of the originator are significant. One possibility is that he, from sheer goodwill, has given away something, offered a service etc. Perhaps he likes the other party, or is sorry for him, or is attracted by the pure fact of being able to help someone. On such occasions it is usually most suitable to repay with gratitude. By doing this one intimates that one has noticed the helper's goodwill and recognizes that this was his only motive for helping. If benevolence is paid for with something other than gratitude, this can be taken as a sign that one is suspicious of the goodwill and it can thereby reduce the feeling of satisfaction which derives from being helpful. This does not mean that the person who has received help is prevented from returning the help on another occasion. But he should then preferably let it appear as a new service – for which gratitude can be expected in repayment – not as a counter service for the help he himself received earlier.

Benevolence can, of course, be present even though it is not the only motive for an action, and in such a case it may be appropriate to combine gratitude with another counter service. If, for instance, a very busy artisan has been so kind to do something for me which he really did not have time for, it is then appropriate to pay him for the work – and to show gratitude for the fact that he undertook to do it.

A situation in which a person shows benevolence and receives an indication of gratitude in return, is one which often lies on the edge of

---

13. Cf. the example from the Hawthorne investigation which Homans (1961) comments upon pp. 235-237.

our exchange concept (cf. section I). The person who shows goodwill frequently says – and perhaps genuinely means – that he does not expect any thanks for it. If he gets no thanks he may, even so, be disappointed or annoyed. But even this does not have to be the case. When the other party shows gratitude, however, there is a certain element of exchange in the situation. Even if the feeling of gratitude is completely spontaneous it is based on the prior action, and in the expression of gratitude there is an element of reciprocation.

4. Conditions determining regulation of exchange by retributive justice or by other factors

'... the reciprocities processes ...
mobilize egoistic motivations and
channel them into the maintenance
of the social system.'
Alvin W. Gouldner, The Norm of
Reciprocity, *American Sociological
Review*, 25, p. 173.

I. INTRODUCTION

This chapter is concerned with some of the factors regulating exchange activity. One of these factors is the principle of justice that 'good be repaid by good to the extent that balance is achieved'.[1] My attention is mainly focussed on this. But other regulating factors are also considered, particularly specific rules of exchange, agreements, and market mechanisms. The main problems discussed are these : what determines regulation of exchange ; under which conditions is regulation likely to be based on the principle of justice and under which conditions are other regulating factors more likely to prevail ?

By inquiring into these problems I hope to throw some light on what determines the development, transmission and use of the principle of justice. However, attention is concentrated upon one single class of determinants so that several other variables are not discussed. I take a quick look at these before continuing.

It is sometimes claimed that men are *born* with a sense of justice. What this may consist of is usually not specified. However, it seems fairly clear that whatever is congenital is not the adult's differentiated, detailed conception of that which is just and unjust, but rather certain predispositions which are subjected to social influence. No satisfactory explanation to the questions posed above, therefore, can be found in the hypothesis of an innate sense of justice. Nor do I think it necessary

---

1. When 'the principle of justice' is referred to in this chapter, it is to *this* principle of justice that reference is made.

to operate with any such hypothesis in order to explain the fact that conceptions of justice are formed.

Another way of approaching the problem is to look upon ideologies of justice as being *cultural products*. There can be little doubt that there are culturally-determined differences in conceptions of justice. It is true that some social anthropologists claim that the principle of reciprocation is universal. *Westermarck* (1906-08 II p. 155) says, for example, 'To requite a benefit, or to be grateful to him who bestows it, is probably everywhere, at least under certain circumstances, regarded as a duty', and *Thurnwald* (1932 p. 105) says that 'the principle of reciprocity pervades every relation of primitive life'. These points of view have also found support with sociologists. *Gouldner* (1960 p. 171) says, 'Contrary to some cultural relativists, it can be hypothesized that a norm of reciprocity is universal'. These assumptions are probably plausible provided one does not read too much into them. It may very well be that the idea is current everywhere that good should, in certain cases, be repaid by good. But there is certainly plenty of variation from culture to culture as to which situations the principle is applicable and also as to the more detailed content of the principle.

Material from other cultures has occasionally been used for illustration in this book. But no attempt will be made to give a systematic trans-cultural comparison of conceptions of justice. It would be very interesting to have such a comparison but there are probably few cultures where sufficient information is available. Understandably, we know considerably more about the outward behaviour of people of different cultures than about their ideologies.

Nor do I intend to chart ideologies of justice within our own culture. There is, in fact, plenty of material to draw on here – philosophical literature, fiction, discussions of social and political matters, reports from courts of law and from the legislative history of statutes. It can quickly be ascertained that there is material for many differing conceptions of justice in our cultural heritage. It is probable that this heritage sets certain limits to the types of value premisses which can form a basis for evaluation. But the limits are wide – because the arsenals of our culture are rich and full of inner contradictions. Even if one possessed a complete list of their contents, this would not greatly assist in foreseeing in which kinds of situations conceptions of justice are applicable.

Neither is cultural inheritance sufficient to account for the fact that ideologies of justice are transmitted from one generation to the next. Culture cannot be compared with water in a river, carried forward by

84

its own gravity. There must be people who have a motive for continuing to use it, if it is not to be forgotten. *Homans* (1961 p. 390) expresses this point of view by saying :

'... institutions do not keep going just because they are enshrined in norms, and it seems extraordinary that anyone should ever talk as if they did. They keep going because they have pay-offs, ultimately pay-offs for individuals. Nor is society a perpetual-motion machine, supplying its own fuel. It cannot keep itself going by planting in the young a desire for those goods and only those goods that it happens to be in shape to provide. It must provide goods that men find rewarding not simply because they are sharers in a particular culture but because they are men.'

I will concentrate upon some of the factors which condition the *learning* of conceptions of justice and which *motivate* the use of these. The relationship between these factors and cultural traditions is one of interdependence. The learning is facilitated by the fact that certain patterns of action and thinking are to be found in a culture ; and the fact that cultural material is utilized, helps to preserve it for future generations and to further develop and elaborate it.

Both now and later when I refer to 'learning', I use the word to cover all changes in behaviour which are determined by experience and not only those changes which have their foundation in systematic influence from parents, teachers and other authorities. One of my main points is that the idea that it is one's duty to repay good with good and to do this to the extent that balance is regained can have its source in interaction processes between equally placed individuals. Because exchange activity is based upon reciprocity, it is well suited (as *Gouldner,* 1960 p. 173, stresses) to channel egoistic motives into social norms without the interference of a teacher, who can manipulate rewards and punishment, being necessary. Experience which shows that it has often paid to use certain exchange strategies, may give rise to a feeling that it is *right* to behave in this way even when it *does not* pay. When such norms are established they are sometimes followed automatically, but it also happens that strategy influences not only the formation of norms but also their use.

Strategies and norms vary both with the *person* and the *situation.* Some people are more inclined than others to reason and argue in terms of justice. And conceptions of justice seem to vary a good deal. Even though many differences are due to differing social situations, much is also due to differences between individuals. During childhood, age is obviously a significant factor. *Piaget* (1932) and others have investigated the development of children's conceptions of justice. The results of some of these investigations are referred to later (see section VII of this chapter and also chap. 7). But, for the rest, we know very little about the causes of different attitudes to questions of justice. It is probable that there is some connection with personality traits. Ideas of justice can, amongst other things, serve to maintain one's self-respect. For instance, greed can be disguised by justifying a claim with arguments for justice. Or one's own shortcomings can be hidden from oneself and other people when things do not go as they should by blaming another person's injustice. The tendency to do this is much more prominent in some people than in others.

However, what follows is concerned with characteristics which are common to mankind rather than with differences in personality. Beginning with some elementary assumptions about motivation and learning, I shall go on to discuss which strategies the various forms of exchange activity require and what likelihood there is that these strategies will settle into norms.

II. MOTIVATION AND OBSTACLES TO EXCHANGE

In order to understand the importance of exchange regulations we must know something about what motivates man to exchange and about the ways in which exchange can be executed.

An obvious reason for exchange is that what is received is worth more (subjectively) than what is given. This frequently applies to both parties. For instance, they exchange material goods which they evaluate differently. Or they help each other in situations where assistance is a big advantage to the receiver while the giving of it entails only a small sacrifice. On some occasions the overall gain is increased because the parties receive bonus values. For example, they obtain pleasure from the actual exchange activity or they find security and comfort in having someone with whom they can exchange values.

The words 'gain' and 'profit' here refer – as elsewhere in the book – to the overall increase in value which the party concerned achieves through a transaction. Everything to which he attaches (positive or negative) value is taken into account. Allowance is made for both material and immaterial things and for both egoistic and altruistic motives in evaluating them. The relevant alternative possibilities are also considered. If, for instance, A can get more by exchanging with B than with C, it does not pay for him to exchange with C – even though C, too, would give A more than what he would get out of his goods by consuming them himself. In section VI (on market mechanisms) I deal with some of the problems which arise when alternative possibilities of exchange are present. In section VII (on organizations), distribution from a central agency as an alternative to exchange is discussed.

There can be other motives for exchanging than that of making a gain. A person may be aiming, for example, at the long term effect of the activity rather than at the gain to be obtained from the individual transaction. One example of this is the kind of exchange activity which consists of systematic use of rewards as a means of exerting influence (cf. section IX below). It can also happen that one makes an exchange because a norm decrees that this should be done. Initially, however, I will concentrate on the exchange motive that gain is expected from the individual transaction.

At first glance it would seem that, when both parties consider an exchange to be profitable, this exchange will always take place – if it is physically possible to transfer the values and if the exchange is not forbidden. But it is not so simple. When regulating factors are absent, there are certain conditions which can hinder or impede the accomplishment of exchange. Two kinds of obstacles are discussed below: one of them has to do with lack of confidence, the other with price determining processes.

Let us imagine two parties who, in their relationship to each other, are motivated solely by the thought of personal profit. They feel no responsibility towards each other, do not trust each other, and expect no outside help in enforcing their claims. In this situation it is possible to carry out the exchange if it can be arranged so that each party gives with one hand while receiving with the other. But if such a combination of services and counter-services is not practical, the likelihood of the exchange taking place is much reduced. It would be too great a risk to give *first* when one knows that the other party has absolutely no qualms about receiving the service without returning it. The situation would perhaps be different if the conditions favoured continued exchange connections between the two parties. In this event the one who received a service might find it advantageous to make a counter-service, thus increasing the likelihood of future exchange. But such a line of thought already assumes a certain minimum of mutual trust between the two parties.

The likelihood of advantageous exchange taking place is increased if a party is 'credit-worthy' in the sense that he will meet his role even if he has already received his service. It is, however, not sufficient *to be* credit-worthy, one must also *be regarded as* such. It is of little use that

87

both parties are able and willing to fulfil their obligations if each of them thinks that the other is not trustworthy. The result can then be that neither of them dares to give credit. Nor is the converse sufficient, i.e., that both parties trust each other without there being grounds for this, because then one party can render his service and get no return. If we look at the situation from the point of view of one of the parties concerned, we can say that it is an advantage to have as one's partner a man who fulfils his obligations and whom one knows beforehand will do so, and that it is *also* an advantage when one has the possibility of binding *oneself* in such a way that the other party is convinced that one is bound.

This point is emphasized by *Schelling* (1960, especially p. 22 et seq., 43 et seq. and 121 et seq.) who gives some illuminating examples. One of them is this : a child has been kidnapped. The kidnapper offers to deliver the unharmed child back to its father on condition that the father pays a ransom and does not inform the police. The father will gladly accept these terms if only he can be sure that the kidnapper will honour his part of the agreement. But he is not sure that the child will be returned when the money has been sent. And the kidnapper is not convinced that the father will refrain from going to the police after he has the child safely back. Each knows that he is not trusted by the other. Both want to bind themselves in such a manner that sufficient confidence is built up with the other party. But there is often no way of doing this and the result can then easily be what both of them least want, for instance that the money does not reach its destination, that the child is killed and the kidnapper caught and convicted.

Examples illustrating the same point are also to be found in the relationship between antagonistic nations or power blocks. An arrangement that would be to the advantage of both parties (e.g. joint disarmament) may too readily be impractical because the opposing parties, rightly or wrongly, lack faith in each other. The absence of confidence can mean that each party is afraid to make concessions without having some security that the other party will render a service in return. Even the act of proposing mutual concessions can be deemed inadvisable ; it may be taken as a sign of weakness. – The business of achieving mutually satisfactory arrangements can be thwart with real difficulties as is clearly demonstrated in periods of eased tension (as, for instance, between the Soviet and the West during the 1960's when both parties endeavoured to clear away obstacles). One way of making some progress, which is sometimes applicable, is that the parties approach each other gradually through the help of small and relatively uncommitted steps so that each is able to register the other's reactions to his first step before he takes the next.[2] We can perhaps characterize this proceeding by saying that the exchange transaction is divided into small pieces and is spread over a longer period of time in such a way that the parties achieve something which approaches the principle of giving with one hand while simultaneously taking with the other. Since each individual service involves the risk of only a slight loss, some of the difficulties regarding which party gives credit by yielding first are overcome. Procedures have also been employed which furnish the other party with grounds for confidence in oneself, for instance by providing a hostage or, to take a more modern example, by allowing international control or inspection. But such techniques only partially do away with the obstacles to exchange which lack of confidence creates. And they may increase the cost of exchange.

The second type of hindrance which I will examine is to be found when the parties concerned cannot agree on *how much* each of them should give and take. This may occur even if service and counter-service can be exchanged simultaneously and even if both parties have full confidence in each other. And, paradoxically, the more advantageous the exchange for both parties the more difficult it can be to accomplish it. Because, the greater the total increase in value which A and B achieve by exchanging with each other, the greater will be the difference between the poorest conditions which A, if pressed, can accept and the best conditions which he can hope to get from B. Or, to put it another way : the greater the *common* interest the parties have in undertaking the exchange, the stronger *conflicting* interest they will have when it comes to the price to be paid.[3] The supposition here is that each party is exclusively guided by the desire to promote his own interests so that the wellbeing of the other party (e.g. that he does not feel cheated) is not considered by either of them, and that no market exists for the service concerned so that the two parties must deal with each other if there is to be any transaction at all.

If we also assume that neither party feels itself bound by any norm

2. A policy of this kind was proposed by Osgood (1959) as a strategy for reversing the arms-race between the USA and the Soviet Union.
3. The conflicting interests tend to be aggravated when there is a possibility of future exchange activity between the parties, because the price they agree to the first time can create a precedence for later exchange. The man who is too generous in the first round risks, in other words, devaluing the exchange values he possesses. Cf. Blau (1964) pp. 80-81.

for what is a 'just' or 'reasonable' price, the rate of exchange has to be settled through negotiation. And it may be difficult to reach a solution if both parties are anxious to promote their own interests. Each of them will perhaps start at his extreme vantage point and give ground as slowly as possible, partly because too rapid concessions might be taken as a sign of weakness and be exploited by the other party and partly because it may not be wise to give in on some point while there is still hope of the other party giving way. An additional reason for being hard and stubborn is that threats of withdrawing from the transaction are sometimes the only effective means of bringing pressure to bear. Such threats often seem insincere when it remains in the interests of both parties that the exchange take place. It is therefore not enough to threaten, one must also demonstrate in some way or other that the threat is seriously meant. If one of the parties is more adept than the other at manipulating the possibilities mentioned here, or if he has a greater knowledge of the opposing party's preferences than the latter has of his, it can very well be that he gets a price for his service which moves close to the maximum of what the other contemplates giving. But it is dangerous to be too hard a negotiator. This may endanger the whole transaction. For instance, it may be that neither of the two parties dares to make any concession for fear of appearing weak, and that they both so strongly condemn the other party's offer that negotiations reach a stalemate. Or it may be that one party threatens to withdraw completely if the other does not come with a better offer, and that he goes so far in his attempt to make the threat seem realistic that, finally, he cannot avoid putting it into practice.

International politics also provide some good illustrations here. For example, we can imagine a state of opposition between two power blocks. Both are interested in obtaining the greatest possible security against attack from the other side. They begin negotiating an arrangement where block A is to give block B certain security (e.g. by disarming, by accepting certain responsibilities, by permitting inspection, etc.) in return for which B is to furnish similar security for A. This is an exchange where no market is present since neither of the parties is able to secure the values he seeks from any other source. They may have a common interest in reaching an agreement, for instance because they reckon that the risk of war is thereby reduced or because they both, for economic reasons, want to cut down on military expenditure. But they have heavily opposed interests when it comes to the price of the exchange, partly because measures which increase the other party's security (e.g. disarmament) often reduce their own, and partly because other values, for instance power and prestige, may enter the picture as bonus values. Situations of the kind described previously will then be inclined to easily crop up during negotiations. I assume that this aspect of conflict in international relations and the previously mentioned lack of confidence are among the most important causes making it so difficult to reach a compromise which in itself would be in the interests of both parties.

One finds similar situations in many other fields, for instance in business transactions between monopolies and oligopolies, in negotiations between trade unions and employers, and in situations of social intercourse between friends, husband and wife, parents and children, or between others who are mutually dependent upon each other. All such relationships are characterized by the parties' strong common interest in maintaining the exchange connection and by their strongly opposed interests when it comes to how much each should give and take. In the more personal relationships which have been mentioned it is seldom that any overt bargaining over exchange conditions occurs – something which presumably is connected with the fact that non-material bonus values would then be lost. But a silent tug-of-war can still take place in which the parties show varying degrees of reluctance to offer their services. The dilemma which was mentioned earlier can again present itself : the man who is too quick or too generous with his service risks his exchange values being devalued,[4] and he who is too reluctant risks breaking the exchange connection.[5]

4. In this way he harms not only himself but also others who offer the same kind of value, and these latter will sometimes try to exert their influence to prevent anyone from selling too cheaply. One finds examples of this both in business and in more personal exchange situations. For instance, Coleman (1961 pp. 120-22) claims that such factors are present in the relationship between girls and boys in American high schools : the girls have a tendency to look down upon those who 'debase the currency' by having sexual intercourse with a boy before he has expended a sufficient number of dates on her.
5. The Theory of Games has made a valuable contribution towards illuminating the questions discussed above, cf. Luce and Raiffa (1957 chaps. 5 and 6), Rapoport (1960 p. 166 et seq.) and – first and foremost – Schelling (1960). Schelling defines as a separate category those games where the participants have partly joint and partly opposed interests. I shall return later to some of Schelling's viewpoints on this type of game. These 'mixed motive games' are distinct on the one hand from constant sum (or zero sum) games where the participants' interests are directly opposed to each other and on the other hand from cooperative games where the participants' interests coincide completely. The difficulties of arriving at a compromise, of which I have given

Apart from the danger of spoiling the opportunities for exchange, a tug-of-war over exchange conditions is a burden in itself. And the fact that claims are emphasized and threats are made can lead to the loss of subjective bonus values from the exchange (e.g. mutual sympathy or trust). The net gain from exchanges which do take place can therefore be less than it would have been if the conditions had been regulated.

Both lack of confidence and difficulties in price determining can be eliminated by regulating factors. *Confidence* comes, among other things, when the parties feel bound (and know that the other is bound) by norms requiring that services be reciprocated. The principle of justice as well as specific exchange rules satisfy this demand. Other important confidence-creating factors are the principle that promises be kept and the means available for enforcing certain types of obligations. *Price determination* is in many instances guided by market mechanisms but it may also be prescribed by norms. Among other things, the principle of justice can also in this connection be of some significance when claims for balance indicate how large a counter service should be.

The fact that there are regulating factors present will, then, under certain conditions :
1. increase the likelihood of profitable exchange, and
2. reduce the costs of accomplishing such exchanges.
I assume that these conditions contribute to explaining how norms which regulate exchange activity come into being. A more detailed discussion of this is given in the following section with regard to the principle of justice. Some of the conditions necessary for the creation of other kinds of regulating factors are discussed in later sections.

III. JUSTICE AS REGULATOR OF EXCHANGE

As mentioned in Chap. 2 IV, the repayment of good by good will not be characterized as 'justice' when it is done only because it pays to do so. But the fact that this course of action is advantageous to the actor and/ or other persons in certain types of situations can help to explain that people form the opinion that it is right to be just, and legitimate to demand justice, irrespective of whether this is advantageous in the actual situation or not.

note 5 (cont.)
   examples, are reflected in the problems which game theorists are confronted with in mixed motive games. In spite of repeated attempts, no acceptable mathematical solution, such as has been found for constant sum games in the Minimax principle, has been found for these.

Theoretical support for this assumption can be found partly in learning theory and partly in functional sociology. Both maintain that a course of action which turns out to be advantageous [6] tends to be repeated and preserved. While learning theory stresses the advantages the action has for the *individual* learner, functional theory emphasizes what we can call *collective* advantages. What this means, and what connection there may be between the collectivity and the behaviour of individuals, I shall return to after having looked at some of the individual advantages attached to the use of the principle that good be repaid with good.

First of all, however, it should be stressed that some of the advantages obtained from applying the principle of justice, would also occur if the exchange activity had been regulated in some other manner, for example by specific rules or by agreements and market mechanisms. I shall in later sections (IV et seq.) discuss what favours the use of one rather than another kind of regulation in different types of situations.

One of the advantages which an *individual* may obtain from repaying good by good is that other persons gain confidence in him. If he regularly follows this course of action, and is known to do so, others can safely exchange with him even if this presupposes that he is granted credit. And a person who has contact with *others* who are known to adhere to the principle of justice, can safely exchange with them even when he has to give them credit. In other words, the feasibility of exchange can be increased both by behaving justly oneself and by influencing others to do so. The tendency to repay good with good, and to demand that others do the same, is thereby reinforced provided the exchange activities are advantageous and no alternative basis of confidence is at hand.

As previously mentioned, the principle of justice provides a basis not only for confidence but also for price regulation, since the claim for balance indicates the required type and extent of counter-service. This involves both advantages and disadvantages for those who follow the principle. On the one hand it makes the outcome of the exchange

---

6. In psychological and sociological literature the word 'reward' is often used in the same sense as 'advantage' will be used here. My reason for departing from this usage is that the word 'reward' will be employed in another and narrower sense (which is also quite usual). A 'reward', in the sense the term is used in this book, is a benefit which someone gets from another person who wishes to show appreciation for the former's behaviour (e.g. in order to influence him to behave in the same way another time), cf. in more detail section IX below. What I refer to as 'advantage' (or 'profit') covers both reward and all other positive consequences of behaviour.

more predictable and reduces the costs of bargaining. In addition it eliminates the risk of obtaining particularly poor exchange terms. On the other hand, the person who follows the principle abstains from the possibility of maximizing his profit through successful negotiation, i.e., he protects himself against maximum loss, but renounces the chance of maximum profit.[7] We therefore assume that the greater the need for security and predictability, and the more important it is for both parties that the exchange should take place, the greater is the likelihood of the two parties adhering to the principle of justice. If one of the parties is in a poorer negotiating position than the other, it is most likely that justice will be demanded by, or in favour of, the weaker part. He will usually have everything to win and nothing to lose by the principle of justice being applied.

The regulation of prices which follows from the principle of justice is inexact compared, for instance, with a market price or with statutory price regulation. Both the concept of balance and the measurement of values which are involved in considerations of justice are often ambiguous and controversial. In addition one is usually satisfied with *approximate* balance and characterizes only the obvious deviations as 'unjust'. This lack of precision can, in certain circumstances, be a disadvantage, inter alia because it reduces predictability and increases the possibility of disagreement over exchange terms. But in other instances it can be an advantage to have some latitude. I shall treat this in more detail when the principle of justice is compared with other regulating factors (cf. especially section V of this chapter on differences between agreements and justice).

There is reason to assume that the principle of justice will more easily be accepted the *more permanent* the parties expect their relationship to be. Anticipation of continued exchange activity provides a special motive for making a return-service. It also furnishes a motive for not pressing the exchange price too far in one's own favour since greediness often does not pay in the long run. If one gives too little or asks too much, the other party may break off the connection or obtain his revenge with the next exchange. On the other hand it can also be dangerous to be too modest or to yield too easily. This may be interpreted as a sign of weakness and be exploited on the next occasion and will, in any event, create a precedence which is unfavourable. Since showing either greed or modesty has disadvantages, the intermediate strategy of balance may

---

7. There is therefore an analogy between the principle of justice and the Minimax (or Maximin) principle in game theory. See Rawls (1971) pp. 150 et seq.

be preferred. In addition comes the fact that application of the principle of justice tends to give more bonus values the greater permanency there is in the relationship.

Another characteristic of the principle of justice (which has some connection with its lack of precision) is that it has a wide and comparatively undefined area of application. It can therefore easily be transferred to new situations. If, for instance, two parties want to make an exchange in a field where they have no other indication of what the terms should be, their general ideas of balance will advise them though these may not be regarded as morally binding. Some of *Schelling's* (1960) points of view are of interest in this connection. As mentioned earlier, the exchange situation will normally be a 'mixed-motive game', i.e. a situation where the parties concerned have partly opposed and partly common interests. Both in such games and in games where the parties' interests coincide completely ('co-operative games') Schelling assumes that choice of action is often decided by the alternative which most easily attracts attention. The features which help to attract attention to an alternative can be of different kinds : for example, a round number, a central point, or something which in one way or another is unique. Schelling has undertaken a series of experiments (pp. 54-67) where the subjects were asked to make a choice, for instance as to how a certain sum should be divided between two people, in which place in New York two persons should meet if they have not agreed upon a place beforehand, etc. The subjects were rewarded if two partners made the same decision and it turned out that a majority of them often did so (e.g. to halve the sum, to meet at the information desk in Grand Central Station, etc.) in spite of the fact that they had no opportunity of communicating with each other. Schelling assumes (p. 67 et seq.) that during negotiations similar tendencies also operate, that one alternative will be considered more 'natural' or more 'appropriate' than others. The reason can be, for example, that this alternative has been chosen on earlier comparable occasions (pp. 67-68), that it helps to maintain the status quo (p. 68), that it is proposed by a neutral third party (pp. 62-63, cf. p. 72 and p. 143 et seq.) or that it appears to be a fair solution (pp. 72-73). If some such clue is the only one present, it can be decisive even though neither of the parties has a particularly strong motive for choosing exactly that alternative rather than the others possible. A principle of justice, for instance, can serve as a focal point even if the parties do not consider themselves morally bound by it and are not under any social pressure to follow it. And where there is some element of obligation or pressure present, these and the above-mentioned grounds for following the principle can mutually support each other. Schelling put it this way (pp. 72-73) :

'... we might argue that the moral force of fairness is greatly reinforced by the power of a "fair" result to focus attention, if it fills the vacuum of indeterminacy that would otherwise exist. Similarly, when the pressure of public opinion seems to force the participants to the obviously "fair" or "reasonable" solution, we may exaggerate the pressure or at least misunderstand the way it works on the participants unless we give credit to its power to coordinate the participants' expectations.'

I will now – temporarily – leave individual advantages in order to take a look at *collective* advantages. By 'collective advantages' I mean the consequences of the individuals' actions which are favourable for a collective unit (group, society, etc.) to which the individuals concerned belong. Both a closer definition of the concept and its relevance for the questions we are to treat, present various problems. Before I discuss these, however, I will survey different effects of the application of the principle of justice which may be characterized as 'collective advantages'.

Some collective advantages derive from the fact that the principle of justice makes possible exchange which would not otherwise take place. On the assumption that exchange opportunities are utilized mainly when they favour both parties, increased exchange activity will, as a rule, lead to a better utilization of the group's (society's) total resources. Economic exchange leads to specialization and division of labour and thereby to increased productivity. And exchange of such values as, for instance, personal assistance and advice, respect and sympathy, in many cases involves a considerable overall increase in value because the benefits received can be significantly greater than the burden of giving them.

The fact that exchange which is advantageous to both parties can help to expand the group's (or society's) overall resources, does not apply unconditionally. Certain forms of exchange can harm society, so that – at any rate in the long run – they lead to a loss of resources. Examples of this are to be found when there are shortages of certain objects which run the risk of being monopolized – or at least being unevenly distributed – if distribution is not regulated. Many of the exchange restrictions to be found in different societies serve to restrain this, e.g., rationing and concession laws, rules which lay down that land is not an article of trade but belongs to the family or the clan, etc. There are also other examples of exchange which can be profitable for the parties involved but harmful to society, e.g., corruption, the sale of votes at a public election, etc. And finally there may be instances where exchange is not directly harmful but where the transfer of values is more appropriately undertaken by way of centralized allocation. We shall return to some of these questions in section VII where the effects of organization on exchange activity are discussed.

Whether the principle of justice or other regulating factors are best suited to increase exchange activity – in those instances where such an increase profits the community – depends, among other things, on what kind of values are involved and whether the circumstances are appropriate for the use of agreements and development of markets (cf. sections V and VI below). In certain fields – for instance, as regards the distribution of material objects in a modern society – agreements and market mechanism are vastly superior to justice as exchange stimulating factors.

But the principle of justice is better suited than most other regulating factors to encourage exchange of such non-material values as, for instance, sympathy, respect, trust and norm abidance. When such values are exchanged, this often means that personal ties develop between participants in the exchange. Exchange activity which is based on justice therefore has a tendency to increase integration. It makes for unity and cooperation within the group. One result of this – which *Gouldner* (1960 pp. 176-177) has emphasized – is that the principle of justice can serve as a foundation for the development of new norms and institutions and as a factor supportive of those already existing.

Several of the examples given in the previous chapter illustrate this. I mentioned there, for instance, how mutual assistance (chap. 3, section IV) and mutual consideration for each other (chap. 3, section V) can contribute to developing and strengthening norms prescribing help and consideration. And in Chapter 3, sections VI and VII, reference was made to investigations (among others, Homans 1962 and Blau 1955) which show that exchange with norm conformity and exemption from norm conformity can create better relations and increased effectivity within organizations. Not all exchanges which have these effects are regulated by the principle of justice. Unregulated exchange and exchange which is regulated, for instance by specific traditional rules, can also have integrative effects. But there are many indications that the principle of justice is one of the most important integrating factors, inter alia, with regard to such exchange as is mentioned in Chapter 3, IV and V.

The opportunity to exchange without the services being simultaneously transferred, not only facilitates exchange but also has the particular significance that a network of obligations emerges. As *Gouldner* (1960 pp. 174-175) points out, this can contribute towards securing peace within the group : the *creditor* has a strong motive for maintaining good relations with his debtor until the latter has fulfilled his obligation – at any rate in cases where the obligation cannot be enforced. The *debtor*, for his part, may have many reasons for behaving well towards his creditor : he may be interested in a continued exchange relationship and in new credit ; he can be grateful or feel himself obliged to *show* gratitude, respect or consideration – as a kind of interest payment – until the debt has been repaid. Ideas of justice often apply to such situations. It seems obviously unfair that a person should harm someone who has rendered him assistance. However, to be a debtor can also result in the opposite reactions. It may be unpleasant and give a feeling of inferiority to owe a debt of gratitude to another man. This occasionally leads to acts of aggression. 'The hand that feeds us is in some danger of being bitten' as Emerson has said (The Writings of Ralph Waldo Emerson, Modern Library ed., N.Y. 1940, p. 403). In order to avoid these harmful repercussions it is important that both the granting of credit and the expected 'interest payments' which were mentioned above be kept within certain limits. And it is possible that the principle of justice can here also make some contribution.

The effect the principle of justice has in stabilizing prices because it demands balance between reciprocal services, can also be a harmony-creating factor. In addition it counteracts waste of time and energy expended on negotiation of terms of exchange, and it increases predictability. As mentioned earlier, an individual involved in an exchange relationship may have different ideas as to whether this is an advantage or not. But for the group or society as a whole, the effects are probably mainly favourable.

When the principle of justice is followed this also influences distribution of values within the group (or society). The balance demanded between service and counter-service helps to prevent uninhibited exploitation of the weak. It is therefore a stabilizing factor. This is not the same as saying that the principle helps to create equality. The effects move rather in the direction of maintaining the *status quo* – whether this consists of equality or inequality – because, on the whole, the principle of justice means that the one party should not increase his values to a greater extent than the other through exchange. But there can be some variation in one or the other direction according to what weight is attached to the parties' investments (cf. chap. 2, VI).[8]

8. It should be noted that I am thinking here only of retributive justice between individuals. Certain conceptions of distributive justice and of retributive justice between groups may help to break down existing discrepancies. I shall return later to these questions.

Exchange activity is not only significant for how values *are* distributed, it can also show something of how they *were* distributed. Among other things, the exchange relationship tells us something of the *ranking* between the parties concerned. If the services are of the same kind and size this can be a sign that the parties regard each other as equals, whereas asymmetrical exchange may indicate differences in rank (cf. examples in chap. 3, sections III and VIII). When such exchanges are repeated continuously, this helps to make the rank differences (or the similarities) more visible and to remove uncertainty with regard to them. Rules regulating terms of exchange between specific partners are probably most effective in this respect.[9] There are also conceptions of justice which reflect differences in rank. But ideas of justice are more likely to have the effect of veiling or reducing the significance of existing discrepancies in rank.

Much of what has been said above about possible effects of the principle of justice is based on rather loose speculation. In many instances it is doubtful what the effects are, and it is also uncertain whether the different effects are advantageous or not for the collectivity. In which circumstances, for instance, is a status quo in distribution of values favourable to a society? I will not venture to try and answer these questions. Instead some remarks will be made concerning the *relevance* of hypotheses on collective advantages in explanations of what gives rise to individual attitudes and behaviour.

We cannot, as a matter of course, assume that men have a tendency to behave in such a manner that the overall effect of their activity is advantageous to the collectivity to which they belong. The assumption that there is a connection between the collectivity's well-being and the individuals' behaviour needs a more detailed explanation.[10]

One possible explanation is that there is a *process of selection*. Collectivities (groups, organizations, etc.) sometimes break up. And it could be that those where the behaviour of the members is most advantageous to the collectivity are the ones which have the greatest chance of

---

9. In primitive cultures there are many exchange norms which serve to accentuate rank and status relations, cf. section IV below (note 13). In societies with a stronger central organization the same tasks are largely taken care of in other ways, for example through formal appointment of office holders, rules governing rank and precedence, wage scales, etc.
10. It has been pointed out that one weakness of certain functional theories is that they assume such a connection without explaining what this assumption rests upon, cf. Gouldner (1960), Homans (1962, pp. 22 ff. and 192 ff.) and Carlsson (1962, especially pp. 205-206).

survival. However, it seems to me that this point of view is of doubtful value as a principle of explanation. It is based, at any rate, on assumptions which are difficult to verify empirically.[11]

Another explanation is that there is a *feed-back* encouraging the kind of behaviour which results in collective advantages.[12] If that is the case the feed-back must go via each individual's motivation. There are different ways in which this could come about :

First let us take the possibility that persons who have some insight into what serves the interests of the collectivity and who are motivated to advance these interests are able to successfully influence the other members to behave in an appropriate manner. As a general assumption this seems hardly plausible. There are certainly some special examples where a group or a society has had such wise, good and powerful leaders. But there is no evidence of this being the rule.

Another possibility – which is more likely – is that some of the advantages which we have called 'collective' are also advantageous to certain individuals and that these latter, in their own interest, influence other people to act in such a manner that these advantages are obtained and preserved. We are now back at individual advantage and can use general learning theory to complement functional theory. In addition to the kind of learning which was mentioned earlier, i.e., that one adapts oneself to following the principle of justice because it is often directly beneficial to do so, I assume that there is a two-stage process which consists of someone learning to teach others to follow the principle.

There can hardly be any doubt that such processes occur. The most obvious instance is when two parties confront each other and one of them is interested in getting a counter-service from the other. This party then has a motive for demanding justice and the demand (and the sanctions which may be applied) can act as pressure on the other. It will often be easy to influence the latter since it can to some extent be in his own interest to repay the service and earn the reputation of being a just person. Even if this is not in itself sufficient to motivate repayment, it can make a person more susceptible to pressure from the other party. The fact that most people participate in a multitude of different exchange relationships and that the roles of creditor and debtor constantly change hands, probably helps facilitate this learning process.

---

11. Cf. Homans's criticism (1962) pp. 22 ff., especially p. 27 of 'Darwinistic' functional theories.
12. Selection and feed-back hypotheses do not contradict each other. They can very well supplement each other as explanations.

People not directly involved in the exchange may also exert pressure. For instance, it is possible that experience which has shown that the principle of justice has an integrating effect and helps to create harmony, will motivate people in regular contact with the parties concerned to try to influence these latter to adhere to the principle. It is also possible that the protection from exploitation which the principle of justice affords the weak in society, fosters a tendency in those who feel themselves weak to advocate the principle in instances other than those in which they themselves are involved. There may also be other ways in which collective advantages can affect individuals' motivation. But, of course, we cannot take it for granted that all behaviour patterns which, from the point of view of a detached observer, seem to be favourable for the collectivity will be strengthened through social pressure. It must be investigated for each individual case whether or not the advantages are of such a kind that they provide individuals with motives for trying to influence other people. There are many difficult questions arising in this connection which I do not attempt to answer.

As already mentioned, profit motives and social pressure can both push in the same direction. But they can also pull in opposite directions. For instance, in certain situations it may not be in the interest of one of the parties to follow the principle of justice, but other people want him to do so and try to persuade him. The different factors mentioned above should therefore be combined if one is to have an overall picture of conditions of learning.

The moral quality of the principle of justice is clearest in those cases where the principle is internalized and is adhered to even if it does not pay and even if the actor is not exposed to any kind of social pressure. In these cases there is also increased possibility of transmission of the principle since those who have internalized it may influence other people to follow it even though their own interests are not advanced by exerting such influence. Buth the internalization process needs some source of energy before it can begin to function and also energy to sustain it. The advantage which individuals gain, in certain instances, by themselves adhering to the principle and by influencing others to do so, probably provides the greatest share of this propellant.

IV. SPECIFIC EXCHANGE RULES

As mentioned in chapter 3, section II, exchange activity can be regulated by specific rules which are either traditional or enacted. There are rules which provide that certain exchanges should take place, rules which regulate the conditions of exchange, rules which prohibit certain exchanges, etc.

As regards their content, some of these rules are closely related to the principle of justice. They may – in common with this principle – demand reciprocity and indicate the type and size of the counter-service. The Trobrianders' rule regarding exchange of fish with vegetables (cf. chap. 3, III) can serve as an example : when the man from the interior has placed vegetables outside the hut of his permanent exchange connection at the coast, the latter is obliged to return a quantity of fish equivalent to the value of the vegetables.

The difference – as I have chosen to define the concepts, see chapter 2, section IV – is that a specific rule limits its area of application to a special type of exchange situation while the principle of justice covers a much wider and more indeterminate field. *Conceptions* of justice can be specific. One can very well imagine, for instance, that it would be considered fair that a fisherman who had received vegetables should return fish in exchange. But if this is to be characterized as a 'conception of justice' the judgment must be based on the general principle of reciprocity and balance – and not on a special rule that fish be exchanged for vegetables. It may be difficult to distinguish the one case from the other, for one thing because we do not always know the basis of a judgment. But it should not be necessary to discuss this further.

The specific rules of exchange existing in a society can affect conceptions of justice in various ways. Where exchange is regulated by detailed and widely accepted rules the principle of justice tends to be displaced or pushed into the background. Prohibition of exchange can also limit the application of the principle of justice. The fact that corruption is not allowed, for example, will prevent a person who is applying for a government post (or a licence, etc.) from pleading that he has a just claim to the position because of personal services which he has rendered the man who decides to whom the job shall go. A more indirect effect of society's rules of exchange, taken as a whole, is that they help to mould people's ideas as to the worth of goods and services and thereby also people's conceptions of what constitutes balance.

On the other hand, the principle of justice can influence the development of specific rules. It can serve as a kind of 'normative raw material' which is easily remodelled and used in the construction of individual rules. This can be effected in different ways. In some cases conceptions of justice become gradually more rigid and finally settle into specific rules. In other cases ideas of justice serve as guide-lines when formal rules are drafted.

102

There can also be different kinds of interplay between justice and specific rules. The principle of justice can, for instance, be taken into account when rules are interpreted. It can also strengthen the effectiveness of a rule when the results to which it leads are considered just. This increases the likelihood of the rule being respected and maintained. On the other hand, rules can also be undermined because they are considered unfair. They can be criticized on these grounds and eventually abolished or altered. Or they may slowly disappear or be reformed because they lack sufficient support.

The mutual influence which the principle of justice and specific rules of exchange exert upon each other does not, however, give a sufficient explanation of how such rules develop and are sustained (or disappear). In order to move a little nearer towards finding the causes, we must start with such considerations as were made in the previous section (III). We must ask what it is that motivates people to adhere to rules and to demand that other people do the same. The emphasis, in this section, is on those rules which are based on tradition and enforced by way of informal sanctions. Some of the conditions of formal enactment and enforcement of rules are discussed in section VII below.

Since some rules have a similar content to the principle of justice, they have also similar effects. They promote exchange activity by creating a basis for the granting of credit and by regulating exchange terms. They can further social integration and peace. They can help to maintain the status quo in distribution of values within a society or group, and they can manifest status relations and differences in rank. Some of these effects can also be produced by other exchange regulating factors (for example, agreements and market mechanisms). But the principle of justice and the specific exchange rules prescribing reciprocity have so many features in common that there is reason to group them together when comparing them with other exchange regulations. I shall use the expression 'reciprocity norms' as a common term for them, and raise the following questions :

1. Under which conditions is it more likely that exchange will be regulated by reciprocity norms than by agreements and market mechanisms ?
2. Under which conditions is it likely that reciprocity will be based on specific rules and not on the general principle of justice ?

Different features of the society (or group) where exchange activity is taking place are certainly significant to both questions. Information available from primitive cultures indicates that reciprocity norms there regulate a relatively larger proportion of exchange activity than with us, and that specific rules are particularly important. This is at any rate true with regard to economic exchange. But reciprocity norms also play an important role in primitive societies as factors which promote integration and display status relationships. The economic and social aspects of exchange activity are frequently interwoven. Some of the examples which *Malinowski* gives of this are mentioned in Chapter 3, sections III and VI.[13] Malinowski (1926 p. 41) claims that the Trobrianders' organization of society as a whole 'is based on a very complex give and take, and that in the long run the mutual services balance'. *Marcel Mauss* (1954), who bases his theory on anthropological material from various cultures in Polynesia, Melanesia and North America and on written sources from ancient Roman, Germanic, Indian and Chinese history, considers it to be a general feature of what he calls 'archaic' societies that exchange activity is tied to rules and that many different values (economic, social, political, etc.) are involved in the individual transaction. In a paragraph on ancient Hindu culture, he concludes by saying (pp. 58-59) :

'There is etiquette at every step. It is not the same as a market where a man takes a thing objectively for a price. Nothing is casual here. Contracts, alliances, transmission of goods, bonds created by these transfers – each stage in the process is regulated morally and economically.'

The dominating position of reciprocity norms in many primitive cultures is probably due to the lack of a government apparatus and other formal organizations. For the reasons which were mentioned earlier (under III), it is perhaps easier for norms which are based on reciprocity than for other norms to be accepted when no lawmaking and enforcing authority is present. In addition to this, the absence of central agencies which can afford protection and allocate benefits and obligations increases the individual's need to base himself on permanent exchange connections. The fact that circumstances are not suitable for the enforcement of agreements and development of markets works in the same direction. When this basis for mutual trust and price determination is lacking, there will be more room for the basis that 'one good turn deserves another' and for price regulation founded on conceptions of balance or on rules indicating the relation between service and counter-service.

A certain parallel to primitive societies can be found in some of the informal groups which occur in our own culture, such as street gangs

---

13. Gluckman (1965) pp. 170 ff. and pp. 242 ff. gives similar examples from the Lozi tribe in Zambia and Bohannan (1955 and 1957, chaps. V and VI) from the Tiv tribe in Nigeria.

104

and groups of play-fellows. Several investigations that have been made indicate that the norms which are formed within such groups and which help to consolidate them often conform to a pattern of reciprocity.[14] Reciprocity norms certainly also play a role in organizations but here their significance is relatively subordinate to other regulating factors.

One difference between these informal groups and primitive societies is that the former are not self-sufficient. They are parts of a larger society which provides them with many of their values and norms and which covers a good deal of the members' most vital needs for material subsistence and for security and foresight. This perhaps helps to explain why the principle of reciprocity is not so frequently moulded into specific rules in these unorganized groups as in primitive societies.

The fact that specific exchange rules play such a significant part in primitive societies has probably also something to do with the static character of these societies. It is likely that there are causal connections between these two phenomena which work both ways. On the one hand, the fact that the society is stationary may contribute to the freezing of reciprocity norms into restrictive rules on who exchanges what with whom and under what conditions. On the other hand, the existence of such rules may be one of the features of the society which makes it appear stagnant and which counteracts growth and development.

In those sectors of an industrialized society which are governed by legislation, market mechanisms and binding agreements, there is hardly room for the kind of customary rules referred to. But enacted rules with a similar content sometimes serve as correctives to market mechanisms (price regulation, concessional laws, pay scales, etc.) and they can help to promote useful exchange activity in cases where agreements are inappropriate (e.g. rules on salvage money).

In these fields which are not subject (or only partly so) to the kinds of regulation mentioned, traditional exchange rules reminiscent of those existing in primitive societies are more liable to develop. Conventional Christmas presents, birthday presents, Christmas and New Year cards, visits and return visits, flowers or chocolates to the hostess, etc. can be mentioned as examples. But the general principle of reciprocity plays a much more important role with us than such specific rules. Specific exchange rules are probably of greater significance in relationships with and between children than between adults. This is perhaps because the assimilation of concrete and easily understood forms of reciprocity can

14. Cf. for instance, Kolsrud (1958), Brøgger (1968, 2) and Whyte (1943), mentioned in chap. 3, III, IV and VI. See also comments on Whyte's investigation in Homans (1950, pp. 156 ff. and 1961 pp. 233 ff.).

be a step in the direction of accepting the general and more diffuse principle of reciprocity. Rules of this kind may also be of some significance in relationships between adults who have no close personal contact with each other by prescribing polite gestures or ways of showing that one has 'not forgotten' the other person. But such rules are of less importance in relationships between persons who have a closer personal contact and who exchange more substantial values with one another.

V. AGREEMENTS

The general principle that *a promise be kept* can–whether it has a moral or legal foundation – perform some of the same functions as the principle that 'good be repaid with good'. The fact that people keep their promises and rely upon other people to do likewise provides a foundation for obligations and trust which, among other things, makes exchange possible even if service and counter-service cannot take place simultaneously. The principle that promises be kept is more comprehensive than the principle of reciprocity in that it can be applied to transactions other than exchange. But it is less comprehensive in the sense that it includes no norm for the type or extent of the counter-service. It is true that a promise (or agreement) can be a means of determining the exchange conditions, but the principle that a promise be kept does not in itself indicate what the content of a promise shall be. There may be limits to the kind of promise which is considered binding. But the area over which this principle can operate will normally be wide and indeterminate and there will be plenty of scope for choice.

For this reason, the principle that promises be kept will often be combined with other regulating factors, for instance with market mechanisms, customary or legal rules, or ideas of justice. Such factors may sometimes influence the content of promises or agreements as, for example, when the price in a sales contract is set in accordance with the market value. On other occasions these factors provide a basis for the interpretation, supplementation or evaluation of an agreement which has been entered into. In a marriage, for instance, a multitude of questions connected with the partners' mutual rights and obligations, about which nothing was decided when they agreed to marry, will be regulated partly by traditional norms and partly by rules of law. Demands for proportionality between service and counter-service can operate both ways. They can determine what *is to be* agreed and they can supplement or correct what *is already* agreed.

106

Another possible connection between justice and agreement is that the principle 'good shall be repaid with good' can serve as an additional ground for keeping one's promises. As *Gouldner* (1960 pp. 175-176) points out one often feels under an obligation partly because one is bound by an agreement and partly because one finds it right to reciprocate. For example, as Gouldner says, it could very well be that an employer pays his workers their wages not only because it is stipulated in a contract that he shall do so but also because he feels that the work is worth the pay. Other examples of this combination of reasons are given in Chapter 3, section VI, where it is pointed out that the two bases for obligation are sometimes interwoven in such a manner that trust and honesty take on the character of values which – alone or together with other values – can be objects of exchange. The point of view may be, for example, that 'when I have *relied* upon your promise and adapted myself to it, you must in return *keep* your promise' ; or 'when I have relied on *your* promise, you must in turn rely on *mine*' ; or 'since I have kept *my* promise, you must in return keep *yours*'. The fact that trust and adherence to one's word can serve as exchange values, also means that the principle of reciprocity can promote internalization of the principle that promises should be kept. And the principle that a promise be kept can influence the formation of conceptions of justice. Besides this, the principles may *also* exert mutual influence upon each other in cases where they are not interwoven because any factor which creates trust is likely to affect the development of other grounds for mutual confidence.

Even though the two principles often supplement one another or combine in some other manner, they can also appear as *alternatives.* Some obligations are entirely determined by agreement, some by justice. And in circumstances where both principles are involved, their relative importance can vary. In what follows some assumptions will be made concerning conditions which determine the application of each of the two principles.

One important difference between the ways in which the two principles work is that an obligation can be made more *explicit* and more *exact* when it is stipulated in an agreement than when its sole foundation is the principle of justice. Exactness is in many cases an advantage since it makes for increased predictability. Many of the kinds of commercial activity which are common in our society would not have been possible if one had been prevented from using agreements and had had to base oneself upon the principle of reciprocity. But exactness is neither always desirable nor always possible. For example, it may be undesirable to fix irrevocably the content of an obligation because the partners do not know beforehand what one of them will need or the other be able to provide when the appointed date arrives. These difficulties are aggravated the more permanent and the more complex and diffuse a relationship is. In addition to this is the fact that some exchange values cannot be quantified since we lack any scale of measurement for them and perhaps also feel that they would lose in value if we tried to measure them. Helpfulness, friendship, gratitudes, respect and loyalty are examples of this. Not only the quantification but also the fact that an exchange is made explicit can lead to a loss of such non-material values. For these reasons, personal services and counter-services in relationships between friends or husband and wife, for example, are ill-suited to detailed regulation through agreement.

Another factor, which is closely connected with that already discussed, is that the use of agreements has a tendency to involve *negotiations* over exchange conditions. When negotiations take place the parties concerned may be stimulated to consider the consequences that an agreement will have for them and will in this way become more conscious of where their interests lie. In addition, negotiations frequently concentrate on those aspects of the relationship where the interests of the parties concerned are opposed, so that the clash is accentuated and they are each driven into a position where they must defend their own interests. Such an attitude is often rational in the sense that it helps increase the gain of the individual in the transactions in which he engages. But as already mentioned (section II) it also happens that bargaining for the best possible terms means that no favourable exchange takes place at all. This particularly applies to fields where there is no market mechanism or other factors regulating prices. Both for this and for other reasons (cf. below in section VI) the use of agreements is favoured when there is a market for the values which are exchanged. Where prices are not determined by market mechanisms there is a possibility that agreements are instead supplemented by ideas of justice (cf. above) or that such considerations take over completely from agreements. One matter which favours the latter alternative is that negotiations sometimes have disadvantages other than those mentioned. When the parties are anxious to promote their own individual interests they often miss such non-material bonus values as, for instance, reciprocal good-will and gratitude.

The two factors referred to above, exactness and negotiation, both help to give agreement-regulated exchange a more *business-like* character than that regulated by conceptions of justice. There is also a strain of

108

commercial ideology in conceptions of justice since one expects to get something in return for what one gives.[15] But this feature is less prominent here since bargaining is not stimulated to the same extent and obligations are on the whole less precise. A consequence of the latter is, among other things, that when service and counter-service are constantly being exchanged it is frequently difficult to tell who, at any given moment, is creditor and who is debtor. One is often therefore operating in a border area between business activity and philanthropy when one does something good to repay a good or does something good because one expects it to be repaid.[16] As already pointed out, there are situations which need to be settled in a *more* business-like manner and there are also those where one wants to be *less* business-like, for example where one wants to do something for a friend because he is a friend and without any thought of being repaid. But in many situations in life, the principle of justice representing the middle way between business activity and philanthropy is the most satisfactory.

There are also differences with regard to *possibilities of enforcement*. Obligations determined by agreement will generally be better suited to organized enforcement procedures than obligations based upon conceptions of justice. Agreements can be given a ceremonial or written form which makes for technical advantages when it comes to enforcement. Evidence can more easily be provided and the content of obligations can be defined more precisely. It may also be of some significance that the damage caused through involving an outside enforcing authority is normally greater in the case of obligations determined by the principle of justice than when the obligation is based on an agreement, because the former more often include non-material values. Such values (e.g. gratitude, esteem and good-will) tend, as *Blau* (1964 p. 17) stresses, to disappear or be considerably depreciated if one attempts to enforce them.

An indication that agreements are better suited to be enforced by the threat of force can be found in the fact that most legal systems go a long way towards assisting in their enforcement. Not all systems go equally far. We can find several examples in history of judicial systems which during their early stages of development only assisted in enforcing certain special types of agreements. In many of these cases there has since been gradual development towards accepting the binding force of

15. Cf. the Gospel of St. Luke 6 (-33) : 'And if ye do good to them which do good to you, what thank have ye ? for sinners also do even the same.'
16. Cf. Blau (1964) p. 112 : 'Social exchange, then, is an intermediate case between pure calculation of advantage and pure expression of love'.

promises (or agreements) as a general principle of law with a wide area of application.

In those societies where there is an organized apparatus of enforcement which gives widespread and effective protection through compelling observance to agreed obligations, the importance of agreements to exchange activity tends to be much greater than in societies where these conditions are lacking. Exchange by agreement, especially, tends to displace the traditional systems of exchange with fixed partners which was described earlier (section IV). Agreements which have legal backing have the advantage that they can be entered into without any personal basis for reciprocal trust being necessary. In this way the number of possible exchange connections is multiplied, something which increases the likelihood of achieving favourable exchange terms and provides for the development of market mechanisms which take over the price determining function from specific rules of exchange. It is true that the social security which an extensive system of permanent exchange connections affords (cf. section IV and chap. 3, section III) is not promoted to the same extent by entering into agreements with a varying circle of strangers, but neither is the need so great for this source of security in a society with an effective legal apparatus.

A final difference to be mentioned is that exchange regulated by agreement is more liable to lead to changes in the *distribution of values* among the members of a society or group than that regulated by conceptions of justice. As mentioned in section III, the latter kind of regulation has a tendency to maintain the status quo. When agreement decides the conditions of exchange, discrepancies in preferences, resources and negotiating skill have greater impact. This increases the likelihood of a redistribution of values. Factors which pull in the direction of change and stability respectively, may therefore to some extent determine whether exchange is regulated by agreements or by the principle of justice.

But there does not need to be an either/or. The two regulating factors are often combined, for instance when freedom of contract is limited through the principle of justice. In these cases justice usually serves to protect the weaker party so that a status quo in distribution of values is upheld. The demand that wages and working conditions reached by agreement be just, is an example of this. And even when there is freedom of contract this freedom is not always used. Businessmen, for instance, may have reasons for avoiding consensual specificity. They may feel, as *Macaulay* (1963, p. 64) has shown, that carefully planned arrangements can create undesirable exchange relationships :

110

'Such planning indicates a lack of trust and blunts the demands of friendship, turning a cooperative venture into an antagonistic horsetrade. Yet the greater danger perceived by some businessmen is that one would have to perform his side of the bargain to its letter and thus lose what is called "flexibility". Businessmen may welcome a measure of vagueness in the obligations they assume so that they may negotiate matters in light of the actual circumstances.'

VI. MARKET MECHANISMS

As mentioned in Chapter 3, section II, what distinguishes a market is the presence of alternative opportunities of exchange so that the person who wishes to exchange does not have to do so with one determined partner but can choose between several. On the assumption that the parties concerned are interested in getting the best possible terms, the various possibilities of choice tend to lead to competition. And since sellers must under-bid each other if they are to sell and buyers must over-bid in order to buy, prices are stabilized. As long as there is a sufficiently large number of competitors on both the demand and supply side and none of them represents such a large proportion of the overall demand or supply that his choice alone significantly influences the market situation, we can call the competition 'perfect'. For the individual seller and buyer the market price will then appear as something objectively given. A seller can dispose of as much as he likes at that price, but if he asks a higher price he will sell nothing. In such situations there is usually no norm that the market price should be followed. A man is not criticized for not doing so but he is acting contrary to his own interests. In other words, the perfect market involves purely strategically conditioned price regulation.

Between the completely isolated exchange connection – where neither A nor B have any possibility of exchanging the values concerned with anyone else – and the perfect market, there are many intermediate cases. There may be a monopoly on the one side so that A but not B has a choice. Or perhaps both A and B have various choices open to them but the total number of competitors is so small that a state of oligopoly exists, i.e. a situation where each individual exercises considerable influence on the market price. There may also be norms, agreements or tacit understanding that competition be limited.

There is little room for conceptions of justice when competition is perfect. The market mechanism takes care of price regulation in a manner which does not invite moralizing.[17] Other factors than the prin-

17. Cf. Weber (1954) pp. 191 ff.

111

ciple of justice will, as a rule, also guarantee that the counter-service is made. The use of agreements which can be enforced (cf. below) is one of the conditions of an extended market and a participant may be regarded as less competitive if he does not fulfil his obligations. However, when competition is not perfect the principle of justice can be of great importance. I shall shortly return to this. First we will look at some of the conditions of approximately perfect competition. The main points to be made can be summarized thus :

The more *numerous* and the more *competitively inclined* the market participants are and the easier it is to *compare the merits* of different exchange alternatives, the more perfect competition will be.

The expression 'market participants' refers to all those who have an opportunity of exchanging the same type of objects with one another. If P and Q are the exchange objects, the number of persons who want to exchange P against Q and those who want to exchange Q against P must, in both instances, be large.

The number of persons who have an opportunity to exchange with each other depends partly upon the density of population and on communications and partly on what risk is involved in dealing with people other than those with whom one has close personal contact. The development of trade was accompanied by various efforts to improve these conditions.[18] The old system of market places and fixed market days served, for example, both to overcome difficulties of communication and to provide increased security. 'All of the "public peace" arrangements of the Middle Ages were meant to serve the interests of exchange' claims Weber (1954 p. 196). The centralization of government power in the various countries of Europe during the 16th, 17th and 18th centuries can be seen in the same light. This provided better opportunities for developing communications and for more effective enforcement of the principle that a promise be kept. The fact that burghers largely supported the princes in their struggle against the feudal system was probably because centralization opened up new possibilities for larger and safer markets.

Another factor which greatly widens the circle of possible exchange partners is the existence of a generally accepted symbolic means of exchange. By this I refer to money and other values which can be used to acquire different types of benefits. Because such values can serve as an intermediary between the goods which individuals primarily need, it

18. Cf. Weber (1954) pp. 194-197 with references, and pp. 346-347 on this development.

112

becomes easier to find a suitable exchange partner. A painter who needs a new suit can, for instance, sell a picture on the open market and buy a suit for the money he receives. He does not have to look for a tailor who is interested in exchanging clothing for pictures. Money has also another function which helps to promote the market system in that it is a means of storing values. One can sell today and keep the money for another day when the need is perhaps greater, when the required benefit is more easily available, or when one has accumulated more capital so that greater values can be acquired. In other words, money more readily enables one to exchange present-day goods with future goods and it can form the basis of an organized system of credit which affords greater opportunities of obtaining present-day goods for goods to be delivered in the future. The development of the monetary system was also associated with the growth of state power and has gone hand in hand with the development trends mentioned above.

Even if one of the two exchange objects is money, the number of exchange possibilities can still be small if the other exchange object is scarce and there are few deliverers of it. How rarely a type of exchange object occurs, however, depends upon whether one operates with a wide or narrow conception of what belongs to 'the same type'. And this again depends on the degree of homogeneity, which I will discuss later.

The *competitive attitude* of the market participants depends upon a number of factors which are hereunder briefly indicated. In the first place, it is of some importance how elastic the demand for and the supply of an exchange object are (i.e. how easily these are influenced by price fluctuations). If there is high elasticity this means that much can be achieved with the help of small changes in prices. Other things being equal, this will increase the tendency to compete with prices. Secondly, it is important whether or not any market participant is able to gain so large a proportion of the total supply that he can exercise a decisive influence on prices. If there is such a possibility, instead of perfect competition one may get cut-throat competition where firms sell at a loss in order to eliminate competitors – or just the opposite where, for fear of such a situation, the participants co-operate in fixing prices. There are many other situations which lead to cooperation or tacit acceptance of a joint price policy – and thereby limit or eliminate competition. And finally, normative ties between exchange partners may restrict competition. Because of loyalty or out of consideration for a traditional exchange partner one makes no attempt to transfer to another who might offer better terms.

The third main condition which helps to provide competition is that

113

it is *easy to compare* the gain to be obtained from the different available exchange alternatives. Although there may be many persons in a position to exchange with each other and they may be prepared to compete over prices, such competition is still difficult if it is not possible to ascertain relatively quickly and reliably which offers are the most favourable.

Comparability depends upon how *homogeneous* the two exchange objects are. By homogeneity I mean similarity between different components of an object with regard to such features as decide their value. Money has a very high degree of homogeneity because most people consider one penny to be worth exactly the same as the next. Goods such as sugar, flour and butter of the same quality, and objects which are produced in series such as cars and TV sets of the same year and make, are also examples of relatively homogeneous objects.

One of the characteristics of homogeneous objects is that their quantity (expressed, for instance, in weight, volume, number etc.) can serve as a measure of value. The more heterogeneous objects are, the less reliable are such measurements of value. For example it is immediately apparent that 5 pence is worth more than 4 pence, but whether 5 horses are worth more than 4 other horses cannot be decided unless there is additional information about each individual horse.

In order to state a price exactly, so that this can be easily compared with prices which other persons take when exchanging the same type of objects in the same market, *both* objects which are to be exchanged against each other must be sufficiently homogeneous for their quantity to give a clear picture of their value. The fact that one of the objects is money is therefore not sufficient for the formation of a perfect market. On the other hand there can be competition, without the use of money, which to some extent stabilizes prices – as long as both types of objects are relatively homogeneous. But money is certainly an important factor promoting the formation of markets both for the reason mentioned here and for the reasons discussed earlier.

To what extent a community's objects of exchange become homogeneous, depends upon many circumstances : among other things, production methods play an important role. Industrialization has in some cases resulted in increased standardization and thereby a higher degree of homogeneity while in other cases it has led to wider differentiation.[19] I will not discuss these questions in detail but restrict myself to men-

19. Industrialization is in turn dependent on the market being sufficiently large for profitable sale of industrial products.

114

tioning two (partly related) categories of exchange objects which under any circumstances tend to have a low degree of homogeneity.

One of these consists of *compound* exchange objects. By this I do not refer to the series-produced object which consists of many small parts (e.g. cars), but only to individual compounds. A factory with buildings, machinery, stores, etc. which is sold as one unit, can serve as an example.

The other category consists of *personal* exchange objects. By 'personal' I mean that the object's value depends upon a person's opinion of, his attitude to or expectations from another person. The display of trust, respect and friendship can be taken as an example. This can hardly be evaluated independently of the person from whom it comes. To be respected by another person can both increase one's self-confidence and give rise to hopes of future benefits, but the extent to which this is the case depends a great deal upon who the other person is. It is therefore difficult to imagine perfect competition with such exchange values. But as mentioned in Chapter 3, section IV, there could be some rudiment of competition here which would partially help regulate prices, for example in the case of exchange of advice and information against respect.

Values of this kind are sometimes bonus services to material values. The overall exchange object therefore takes on both a compound and a personal character. As an example we can take a person who continues to shop with his previous shopkeeper or stays with his employer in spite of the fact that he could obtain more favourable economic terms by changing his shopkeeper or his job. One of the reasons for this may be that the established exchange situation gives the greatest total gain – and, in any case, a gain which it is difficult to compare with what one could achieve in other places – when account is taken of the bonus values which are exchanged. He receives, for instance, expressions of trust, sympathy and respect. Or he swaps information on the weather or the 'goings-on' among the neighbours. The more permanent the exchange connection and the more personal the contact between the parties, the greater is the likelihood of non-material bonus values playing a significant role.

Although compound and personal exchange objects tend to go together, there is still good reason to discuss individually the use of the two kinds of exchange objects.

Personal exchanges contribute to satisfying man's need for security, contact and friendship, warmth and affection. Some of these needs can also be met in other ways. On the one hand the police and the administration of law, social insurance and pension schemes have much the same function of creating security in our society as have the personal exchanges in many primitive cultures. But although the need for such exchange activity decreases with the expansion of organized security measures, the latter never quite replace it. On the other hand spontaneous friendliness and care which does not anticipate any return is also an alternative to personal exchange. In one way exchange activity constitutes something in-between organized social security measures and spontaneous action. There will probably always be cases where this middle way is the most satisfactory. But it is difficult to specify the conditions more closely.

The most obvious reason for operating with *compound exchange objects* is that the combination has a greater value than the individual parts taken separately. For example, one usually gets more for a factory if it is sold en bloc than if the buildings, office equipment, machinery, stocks, etc. have to be individually realized. Such items lose much of their value when they can no longer be used together and perhaps not even for the purpose for which they were intended. In addition, many of the values of the enterprise will be completely lost, for instance its good-will with customers, suppliers and authorities and the value which lies in having a trained and coordinated staff of employees.

The explanation may be the same in cases where the compound exchange object consists of personal services. Marriage can be taken as an example if one regards everything that the couple give each other in the form of material goods, labour, help and support, affection and care, trust and confidence as being part of a comprehensive exchange situation between them. Theoretically it should be possible, instead of getting married, to try and acquire the same benefits individually via exchange with many different persons, for instance by employing a housekeeper, by buying sexual satisfaction on the streets, acquiring a confidential friend, taking out health and accident insurance policies, etc. Presumably, some of the values would be lost and others would be depreciated in this manner. It is also possible that some of the individual specialized exchanges would be better. But the fact that marriage continues as an institution, indicates that the combination, by and large, helps increase the gain for both parties.

There cannot, of course, be perfect correlation between the merits of a situation and actual behaviour in the situations we examine here. Lack of insight and foresight create many deviations and the institutionalization of such relationships as, for example, marriage makes for considerable inertia. What was advantageous in the past sometimes decides what is still practised today. But, even so, there are limits to how long an institution which provides no advantages to those involved can remain unchanged.

It follows from what has been said above that the conditions necessary for the formation of markets partly coincide with those necessary for the use of *agreements*. Among other things, development of state power and of monetary systems are of importance in both cases. And when exchange objects have a personalized character, this counteracts both market development and the use of agreements. But the conditions do not correspond completely : for example, only the formation of markets is restricted when exchange objects are compound, not the use of agreements.

In addition to the fact that the conditions partly coincide, the use of agreements also contributes to providing a situation favourable to market formation. This is, inter alia, because agreements serve as a means of stipulating quantities and of elaborating exchange terms so that comparability is increased. But the use of agreements is not sufficient in itself to provide perfect competition. Nor is it necessary to provide for a degree of (imperfect) competition which has some price regulating effect.

For reasons already given, market mechanisms which are perfect, or nearly perfect, have a tendency to supersede the *principle of justice*. On the other hand, the rudimentary approaches to market formation which sometimes occur, for instance when personal services are exchanged (cf. the example given in chap 3, section IV on exchange of advice against respect), constitute no hindrance to the use of considerations of justice. Neither does a market which is imperfect because of limited demand and supply. We find, especially in relations where one party is in a stronger position than the other, as for instance in the relation of an employer to unorganized employees, that conceptions of justice will often be summoned in support of the weaker party. There is also room for justice when exchange, which is normally regulated by the market, is affected by some unforeseen circumstance with which the market is not equipped to deal, for example if some article which has been sold is incidentally damaged while on its way from seller to buyer and there is a difference of opinion as to whether the buyer should still pay the whole sum or not.

The fact that one finds oneself close to the fringes of market mechanisms, as in the example given above, can even promote the development and use of considerations of justice. If one is to decide whether there is equality or not between a service and its counter-service, one must have some idea of the respective values of these services. And

117

evaluation is always based upon one or other form of comparison. The basis for comparison may be experience from earlier production or consumption of such articles as are involved : for example one may have reached the conclusion that an object is worth more than another because it takes longer to produce or because its consumption gives greater pleasure to the consumer. But experience from previous allocations and exchanges which one has participated in or observed, also play an important role. There is a more reliable basis for evaluating terms when the exchange is not completely unique, so that it is possible to make a comparison between what other people get in similar situations and what one could oneself achieve if the exchange were with another person. It is therefore possible that the tendency to base oneself upon the principle of justice – other circumstances being equal – increases with the increased comparability of the exchange objects, until the level is reached where the market mechanism begins to supersede justice.

VII. ORGANIZATIONS

Organizations are not exchange regulating factors in the same sense as the norms and strategies discussed in previous sections. But there is a close connection between a society's organizational development and exchange regulating factors. In addition to this, the occurrence of organization is one of the factors determining what values will become objects of exchange and who is to take part in exchange relationships.

The word 'organization' will here be used synonymously with 'organized activity' and in such a wide sense that it covers activity of very varied types and permanency from, for example, a small group which is organized for the purpose of carrying out a single job to sovereign states and international organizations. An organization in the sense in which I use the word exists when the following conditions are satisfied :
1. several (at least two) persons are engaged in a certain activity, and
2. there is a norm (or a system of norms) designating someone (e.g. the majority or a leader) to decide on the conduct of the activity.[20]
I shall call such norms 'norms of competence' (or 'power conferring

20. This is not the usual definition of 'organization'. But it gives the concept a coverage which corresponds to a rather common usage of the word. According to some definitions an 'organization' must be deliberately established for the purpose of achieving certain goals. If these definitions were strictly adhered to (something which seldom happens) they would lead to many artificial distinctions. Some national states, for instance, have come into being by deliberate decisions, while others have not. And it can often be very difficult to decide whether something has definite goals or not.

norms'), an expression borrowed from legal philosophy (cf. for example, *Ross,* 1958, p. 32, and *Hart,* 1961, pp. 27-41 and pp. 89 ff.). They are meta-norms (norms about norms) because the expression 'decide' implies that the person or persons designated by the norm of competence have the power to make directives or rules (i.e. norms). An organization, then, is (among other things) an instrument for producing formal rules. Persons who are empowered to make rules or give directives can be said to have 'competence' (or 'authority' or 'power').

If an organization is to be effective – and not just a projected or unsuccessful attempt at organization – the participants must respect the norms of competence so that, generally speaking, they adhere to the rules and directives which have their bases in these norms. Respect for the norms may be due to internalization or based on fear of punishment or on a desire for reward. If respect is due to internalization of the competence norm, exercise of power within its limits is considered legitimate.

Power-conferring norms are created in different ways and vary with regard to content and complexity from one organization to another. There are small organizations where the only norm of competence is a simple principle, for example that the oldest or the most qualified or the majority shall decide. The principle does not have to be explicitly formulated or adopted. It is sufficient that the participants automatically follow it, for instance because they have become familiar with it from other activities in which they are engaged. On the other hand, there are organizations (e.g. sovereign states and large commercial enterprises) where norms of competence constitute an extensive and complicated system of rules, often built up hierarchically. For instance, a constitution may confer power on a nation's highest authorities, authorizing them, among other things, to delegate power to subordinate agencies. These, again, can delegate authority to their subordinates etc.

The power which is conferred on the authorities is usually limited. The limits may be constrained or they may be broad. However, it rarely happens that authority is used to its utmost. Normally the participants are allowed to act freely in many situations which the norms confer power to regulate. There is often also room within the social system covered by the organization for development of norms other than the formal ones. And this norm formation is sometimes of such a character that it is natural to talk of informal organizations within the formal, see *Barnard* (1938 pp. 114 ff.).

The fact that organizations can serve as machinery for producing formal norms, makes them effective vehicles of cooperation. Rules created by deliberate decisions can be differentiated and changed more

119

easily than those which develop by themselves.[21] Organization, therefore, gives a social system both increased solidity and greater flexibility. Division of labour and directed coordination of activity can be implemented to a much greater extent than in unorganized groups. Organizations are also more capable of introducing innovations and of expanding, because the power to make rules can also include the power to make new rules of competence. As I have defined the word 'organization', it is not an essential characteristic that its activity should have a specific goal (cf. above, footnote 20). But, for the reasons which have now been given, it is reasonable to assume that organized activity is generally more goal-oriented than is the unorganized, and that expediency often decides which rules shall be made and how these will be interpreted.

Organizations (in my sense of the word) cannot always be traced back to specific decrees of establishment. They sometimes come into existence of their own accord, for instance when, inside an unorganized group, the idea gradually grows that someone must be responsible for making decisions on questions of common interest. And such ideas are often moulded into norms of competence. A primary condition of the emergence of rule-making power is that the participants realize that rules of action can be made by deliberate decision. *Piaget* (1932) has investigated the development of this understanding with children. Through observation and interviews he studied how the rules of a game of marbles were practised and interpreted, and found that the children's conceptions of the rules moved through three stages. The youngest children played with the marbles, each child in his own way, and that it was possible to alter them or dispense with them if the other and who more or less understood the point of the game were inclined to regard the rules as sacred and immutable. But the oldest boys (11-13 years), who were the only ones who had completely mastered the complicated system of rules, looked upon the latter as something over which they had complete control. They realized that the rules differed in different parts of town, that they were made by the children themselves, and that it was possible to alter them or dispense with them if the other players were in agreement. Many of these older boys had a strong judicial interest in interpreting the rules and in forming new ones. The argument which occurred most frequently when one or other of the rules was discussed was whether it helped to make the game more 'just' in the

21. Hart (1961 pp. 89 ff.) explains, in a most convincing manner, these and other advantages connected with the use of norms of competence.

sense that skill and not luck was rewarded. In other words, conceptions of justice and the importance of agreement served as the primary governing principle in forming the rules. Development stopped at this stage because the boys lost interest in the game when they reached about 13 years, and one can hardly say that a 'marbles organization' had been established. But at least the first obstacles to the formation of such an organization had been overcome.

If an organization is to be formed (other than through pure coercion) a minimum of mutual trust must exist between the participants. Several of the confidence-promoting factors discussed in this chapter, therefore, help to advance the development of organizations. As *Gouldner* (1960 pp. 176-177) has emphasized, the principle of justice is a possible starting point for the formation of an organization. It is easier to enter into cooperation with other people when one knows that they are prepared to return something for what they receive. In addition to the fact that the principle of justice can, in this manner, serve as a starting mechanism, it can also serve as normative raw material for the production of rules (cf. section IV), or be a governing principle such as in the investigation of Piaget referred to above. Traditional rules of exchange might also form the start basis of organizations and provide a pattern for formal rule making. But, because their content is specific, they are not so well suited as the open and elastic principle of justice to serve as the foundation of new organizational formation.

As mentioned in section IV, specific rules of exchange sometimes help to accentuate differences in rank by determining the type and extent of services and counter-services on the basis of the rank relations of the parties concerned. In such situations the rules tend to conserve the existing relations. They support forms of organization where rank and authority go together but counteract the allocation of authority on any other grounds – and can therefore impede economic and technical development and social reforms. There are also other reciprocity norms which can prevent or hamper the development of new organizational forms. In the developing countries traditional obligations to relatives and friends often conflict with newly established duties to employers and political authorities. They can also come into conflict with ideals of impartial and impersonal exercise of authority – as, for instance, when a man who has received assistance from a friend in paying his doctor's bill, feels himself obliged to find employment for his friend's son in the government office where he works.[22]

22. Cf. Gouldner (1960 p. 171) from which this example is taken.

The principle that agreements be kept is one of the most important normative foundations for the establishment of new organizations. The better and more safely agreement mechanisms function in a society, the greater are the possibilities of organizational expansion and development. A network of agreements usually forms the basis for the establishment of all larger organizations in Western industrial societies.[23] When, for instance, a new commercial enterprise is to be started, agreements are entered into with capital investors and credit institutions, employees are engaged, machinery and equipment is bought, etc. On the other hand, as already mentioned (section V), the extensive use of agreements depends upon the existence of organization. There must be state agencies to draft rules, settle disputes and ensure enforcement of agreements, and organized means of communication are necessary for the rapid and safe transmission of detailed information. The development of organizations and the use of agreements in a community serve thus to support each other, and they have a tendency to go hand in hand.

There are similar connections between the formation of markets and the development of organizations. As mentioned above (section VI), the growth of organizations is a necessary condition for the development of extensive markets. Such development presupposes a state organization which can give sufficient security to enable strangers to deal with each other. Organized monetary and credit systems, means of communication and enterprises suited to the mass production of standardized goods are also essential. When markets are so far developed that prices of goods and services are stabilized by the market mechanism, this in turn provides for increased predictability and thereby promotes the further development of organizations.

But when organizational development has reached a certain point, it can also have the effect of *reducing* the significance of market mechanisms and partly also of agreements. These trends can coincide with those mentioned above. Developments in Norway over the past 150 years are an example of this : on the one hand, subsistence economy and permanent exchange connections between single individuals have increasingly given way to a monetary economy with marketing of goods and services ; on the other hand, competition has, in many fields, become less perfect or has been completely eliminated because of the development of monopolies and cartels, trade unions and employers' federations, etc.

23. Exceptions occur when new organizations grow out of a parent organization, for example when the government establishes a new directorate or an industrial concern founds a subsidiary company. But even on such occasions agreements are sometimes used.

And some benefits and burdens have been totally withdrawn from individual exchange activity since public authorities have taken over their allocation. Security against want and injury, for example, is now less dependent upon the individual's personal exchange relations with other individuals because these needs are largely covered by the social services, insurance and pension schemes, the police and the law courts, etc. There has been similar development of educational facilities, expansion of communications and trade, etc. Public welfare and service measures are compensated for through increased obligations on the part of the citizens in the form of direct and indirect taxation and in the form of loyalty to an ever more finely-spun network of laws and regulations.

In other words, organizations can, *in part*, serve as a basis for such exchange regulating factors (particularly agreements and market mechanisms) as lead to increased exchange activity. They can, *in part*, serve as vehicles of new forms of exchange, for example by permitting negotiations between composite units instead of between individual persons. And they can *partly* result in exchange activity disappearing and being replaced by centralized allocation of goods and burdens.

Another reason for the displacement of some forms of exchange by organizational expansion, is that they come into conflict with principles of rational and impersonal behaviour which must be followed if large organizations are to operate effectively. There are several written and unwritten exchange prohibitions which serve to protect these principles. For instance, public assignments and appointments, licences and concessions etc. must neither be obtainable for money nor on the basis of kinship or acquaintance; the man who makes decisions on behalf of public authorities must not let himself be bribed or threatened, or should be influenced by feelings of sympathy and antipathy. He should not, for instance, use his authority to pay off a debt of gratitude or to secure himself future advantages. Many of these prohibitions are built into our ideal of the impartial judge and the incorruptible civil servant.

The older forms of exchange which become superfluous or unwanted because of organizational development can in some instances have been regulated by the principle of justice. In these cases the principle loses ground. But, on the other hand, it may gain new areas of application where new forms of exchange arise. Since, in many of these cases, the exchange partners are large collective units – so that the market mechanism is put out of action – ideas of just balance may easily influence prices. We see examples of this in negotiations between employee and employer organizations on wages and working conditions, between the government and farmers' organizations on prices and subsidies, etc. But the question of just distribution based on comparisons between the different trade groups can also be important. I shall later return to the interplay between these two conceptions of justice.

Interplay between retributive and distributive justice may also take place in connection with allocation processes, for instance in the relationship of government to individual citizen. The particular service which a citizen performs, for example when he pays his taxes or does his military service, does not have the direct appearance of a counter-service for something he has received, since allocation of these burdens generally takes place independently of the allocation of government services to citizens. The questions of justice which are most likely to arise, then, will be those associated with distribution. But as a superstructure over, or a supplement to, ideas on distribution there may be a feeling of exchange taking place between the government and the citizen and it may be thought unjust if the citizen receives less than he gives.

The questions of balance between the government and the citizen have their parallel in other – smaller – organizations than the state. Several examples have already been given, especially in Chapter 3, sections VI and VII. The investigations undertaken by *Homans* (1962) and *Blau* (1955) which were referred to there, indicate that the effectiveness of an organization can be increased when the ordinary participant feels he is getting some return for his efforts and loyalty. The investigations also showed that it may be to the advantage of an organization that its network of formal regulations is not too rigid nor enforced too strictly so that some room is left for elasticity in relations between the management and the employees, and thereby also for the vaguer conceptions of justice.

VIII. JUSTICE AS REGULATOR OF EXCHANGE : SUMMARY AND HYPOTHESES

The discussion of specific exchange regulations, agreements, market mechanisms and organizations (in sections IV-VII) has provided material with which to supplement the views given (in section III) on the principle of justice as an exchange regulating factor. I will now try to draw these threads together.

First we should reconsider what goes on when the principle of justice becomes established. As already mentioned, processes of learning take place. But exactly *what* is learnt ?

Certain *attitudes* are a part of what is learnt and one of the characteristics of these attitudes is that they occupy an intermediate position between the businesslike and the philanthropic. One learns to demand something in return for what one has performed – but to be moderate in one's demands as well. One also learns to make a return payment for what one has received – without being forced to do so – and to apply the golden mean to the size of the repayment. This should not be too stingy, but neither is it necessary to overwhelm the other party with generosity. These attitudes can differ in substance from one person to another and from one situation to the next. On some occasions the claim aspect dominates, on others the service. The field covered by these attitudes will also vary. They can affect a large or a small proportion of the total interaction in which an individual is engaged.

One also learns a *scheme of thought,* the main content of which is that 'good be repaid with good to the extent that balance is achieved'. This scheme can be learnt verbally and can be used – for instance, in arguments – without the user having adopted any of the attitudes referred to above. Conversely, the attitudes can be present without any attachment to the scheme. However, if there is no such connection, the principle of justice cannot be regarded as being internalized. One way in which attachment may be established is when the individual first – through experience of different interaction situations – develops the attitudes referred to and then *himself* builds up the scheme of thought as a generalization of his own experience. But in cultures such as our own where it is easy to find patterns of thinking along lines of justice, it is more likely that individuals become acquainted with the scheme through their environment. However this may be, I assume that when a general scheme is available into which attitudes can be fitted, the learning of these attitudes will thereby be promoted.

It is a feature of the scheme that it is both general and elastic : it can cover many variations of the attitudes mentioned above ; it refers to both one's own and other peoples' actions, and there are no definite limits to the kinds of situations to which it can be applied. This is not the same as saying that it has an unlimited area of application. It is unlikely that any person believes that *all* good in *all* situations should be repaid with as much good as will rectify balance. But the general form of the scheme assumes a relatively wide and diverse area of application. Internalization of conceptions of justice therefore presupposes that the attitudes which have been referred to are connected with so many varied types of situations that it makes sense to attach them to the general scheme.

After this stage has been reached, the learning process still continues.

125

One is confronted with new forms of interaction and one gains new experience of the forms of interaction in which one has already participated. The result may be that the area to which the principle of justice is applied (as a rule of behaviour and/or a pattern of argumentation) is extended. I assume that, other things being equal, the fact that the principle of justice is internalized in one field increases the likelihood of its being used in other areas by the individual in question. But this is not the same as saying that the principle tends to have a constantly widening application. There are counteracting forces – to which we shall shortly return – which can effectively block further expansion and perhaps expel the principle from fields where it has previously been applied.

On the basis of what has been said above, combined with the discussion in section III, the following hypotheses (which must be read with the ceteris paribus qualification) can be put forward :

1. The wider, the less ambiguous and the more varied an individual's experience is that advantages result from
   (a) claiming repayment
   (b) making repayment, and
   (c) showing moderation in both these respects,
   the more likely it is that he will internalize the principle of justice and
2. the wider the area of application he is likely to give it.
3. If an individual knows the scheme of thought contained in the principle of justice, the likelihood of his internalizing the principle is increased.
4. If the principle is internalized in one field, the likelihood of it also being given other areas of application by the individual concerned is increased.

The essence of hypotheses nos. 1 and 2 is that the *advantages* achieved by acting in accordance with the principle of justice condition both internalization of the principle and extension of its field of application. I will now examine what kind of advantages are involved and under which conditions they can be achieved.

As stated in section III, the advantages can be of two different kinds. Firstly, exchange activity becomes more profitable because a greater number of advantageous exchanges take place, and because the cost of carrying them through is reduced. Secondly, advantages can be derived from the approval with which one's mode of action is met. For instance, one receives praise and avoids criticism from those who have internalized the principle or who wish action to be taken in accordance with

126

it. An appropriate combination of the two types of advantages is probably most suited to the creation of conceptions of justice. If concern for one's own profit is the sole motive for behaving in a certain manner, this pattern of behaviour can certainly be learnt but following it does not take on the character of a moral principle. Market mechanisms (cf. section VI) can serve as an example of this.

Whether advantages are attached to the use of justice or not, depends among other things on *the type of exchange situation* concerned. This applies to both the two kinds of advantages. It is not always the same features of exchange conditions which determine both whether justice is profitable and whether it receives social approval. But these will largely coincide, for one thing because profitability in many cases depends upon both parties following the principle. The factors which motivate A *to act* in a just manner will in these cases also motivate him *to claim* justice from B, and to disapprove of B's behaviour if it does not accord with the principle.

What kinds of exchange favour the application of justice depends, among other things, upon what need there is for regulation of the exchange activity. With reference to what has been said about this in section III, we can propound the following hypotheses :

5. The more profitable the exchange is for both parties, the more dependent the parties are on acquiring the relevant values through exchange ; and the more difficult it is to arrange for simultaneous give and take the more likely it is that the exchange activity will be regulated by justice.
6. The more enduring the parties expect the exchange connection to be, the greater is the likelihood of regulation by justice.
7. If one party is in a weaker negotiating position than the other, it is most likely that considerations of justice will be applied by and/or to the advantage of the weaker party.

The reservation 'other things being equal' is quite essential here because it makes a great difference whether or not there are *other* exchange regulating factors at work. Because of its elasticity the principle of justice has facile access to new fields but it is also easily pushed into the background by such regulating factors as specific rules, agreements and market mechanisms. The development of these factors is to a large extent dependent upon the existing social conditions. Let us, however, take a society (like our own) where traditional rules of exchange play only a small role and where the technical and organizational conditions necessary for agreements, market formation and production of formal rules

127

are present. The manner in which the various exchange situations are regulated depends in this case, to a great extent, on the kinds of objects exchanged.

In some exchange situations the principle of justice is the *only* regulating factor. This is most likely when the exchange items are such that they cannot be made the object of explicit, exact and enforceable obligations without being considerably reduced in value. As mentioned in section V, agreements and formal rules are poorly suited to regulate such exchange. Rudimentary market mechanisms can, in certain instances, exert some influence but they will not normally be any obstacle to the formation of conceptions of justice. The availability of exchange alternatives which are to some extent comparable may, on the contrary, help to promote such formation (cf. section VI of this chapter).

In those exchange situations which are regulated through agreements or specific rules, the principle of justice can be of importance as a *supplementary* or *corrective factor*. Conceptions of justice can be taken into account when agreements or rules are formed ; they can also serve as supplementary bases of obligation or as guiding lines to be followed when complementing incomplete agreements or rules, and they can serve as a corrective when stipulated conditions are found to be unjust. The hypotheses which were presented earlier are also relevant in these instances, but they must be seen in connection with the following proposition :

8. The more comprehensively exchange conditions are regulated by rules and/or agreements, and the stronger the feeling of obligation attached to these later, the less likely it is that the principle of justice will be of significance as a supplementary or corrective factor.

Market mechanisms are on another plane than agreements and regulations. They give no grounds for rights and duties but rather for uniform strategies. By themselves they afford only incomplete regulation but together with agreements they may regulate the exchange conditions so effectively that no room is left for ideas of justice. A necessary condition is that the situation permits perfect (or near perfect) competition. As mentioned in section VI, this partly depends upon the available means of communication, security measures and a monetary system, partly upon the competitive attitude of the exchange partners, and partly upon the comparability of the alternative opportunities of exchange. For this last reason, composite and personal exchange objects are, among others, unlikely to be the object of perfect competition.

I have tried above to explain the growth of conceptions of justice and other exchange regulating factors on the basis of the views which were developed in section II. These views were :
1. that it is often worth-while for both parties to exchange values with each other, and that this gives them a motive for exchanging,
2. that lack of confidence and problems connected with price-determination can hinder or increase the cost of implementing an exchange, and
3. that exchange regulating factors serve to overcome these obstacles.
Those conceptions of retributive justice which are connected with rewards, however, cannot be explained in this way.

As mentioned in footnote 6, I use the expression 'reward' to designate a benefit given in *appreciation* of something another person has done.

The action (or omission) which is rewarded has sometimes the character of a transfer to the person who gives the reward. A, who has found B's wallet, returns it and receives a certain sum of money in reward. In such an instance we can say that the reward serves as a counter-service for something B has got from A and that, in other words, an exchange has taken place. But this is not always the case. And even when an exchange has taken place it is not always the profit derived from this which motivates the reward.

There are different motives for giving rewards. Sometimes they are given from spontaneous joy or relief. For instance, A has saved my life or found my wallet and I am immediately filled with a desire to do something for him in return. In other instances there may be norms requiring that he be rewarded. These can be specific rules (e.g. legal regulations which stipulate rewards) or vaguer norms (e.g. the principle of justice).

However, I will concentrate upon a reward motive which is of particular importance, viz., the desire to *influence* the other person. The intention may be to influence one single action, as, for instance, when a reward is paid for information leading to the arrest of a dangerous criminal. Sometimes the influence is of a more enduring character as, for example, that exerted by parents or teachers over children. Praise, encouragement and other rewards which are given to children when they behave according to the wishes of their elders or when they do their best to achieve a goal which has been set for them, are effective tools of upbringing and education.

In some of these instances the reward is part of an exchange which can, in itself, be worth-while for the party giving the reward. The pleasure a parent or teacher experiences when a child behaves well or takes special care with his homework, may more than balance the effort entailed in praising the child or giving him money to go to the cinema.

But rewards are used as means of exerting influence even when this is not the case. It is a sufficient condition for the use of the reward method that the parents (teacher etc.) assume this to be an effective means of achieving the goal at which influence is directed – for instance, that the child grow into a capable and honest person. If this goal is attained, one can say that the parents 'get something back' for what they have done – but they do not get it in exchange from the child. The fact that a child acquires certain qualifications is not – in our sense – a 'counter-service' which he (or she) 'gives' his parents.[24] It may be a *factual result* of the rewards, but this is another matter.

The basic motive for giving rewards as a means of long term influence is then not the same as the exchange motive which we used as our point of departure in section II. Neither do the obstacles to exchange which were mentioned there play the same role. Nonetheless, ideas of justice are often associated with rewards. I shall now point to some factors which may help to explain this.

I assume that the person who gives the rewards (let us call him the 'teacher') is normally inclined to let the other party (the 'learner') know that it is *rewards* he is giving and also *what* he is rewarding. Sometimes this is clearly announced beforehand (a reward is promised) and sometimes at the same time the reward is given. There may be many reasons why a person who transfers a benefit to another wants the recipient to understand why the transfer is made. In the case of the teacher, the motive may be that he expects the reward to be more effective when he lets the learner know that : 'you get this because you acted rightly. Do the same next time !'

I will not discuss in detail whether this is a rational policy from the teacher's point of view. Some forms of learning can certainly take place through the systematic use of rewards even though the learner is not aware of the fact that he is being rewarded. Many experiments with both animals and humans confirm this (cf. *Berelson and Steiner* p. 138 and p. 143 et seq.). But it is still possible that teaching is more effective when the learner *realizes* that he is being rewarded and knows *why*. At any rate this is important if one wishes to motivate the learner to actively acquire the knowledge, skill or qualities concerned. – And however this

24. Cf. the definition of 'exchange' in chap. 3, I.

may be, the most important thing for us is that teachers have, in fact, a tendency to behave as described.

This has important consequences for the learner's perception of the situation. He gets to know that such and such actions (or omissions) are good, and that for this reason they are rewarded. If this is repeated sufficiently often he soon forms the opinion that he can *claim* a reward when he acts in this manner. In addition to what he is intended to learn, for instance good behaviour or industrious attention to homework, he also learns that good behaviour or homework well-done leads to rewards. This conception fits very well into the normative scheme that good should be repaid with good. What is learnt in reward situations and learning to use the principle of justice on other kinds of occasions (cf. section III) will, therefore, mutually support each other.

The factors mentioned so far lead to the following proposition :

9. The likelihood of the learner arriving at the conclusion that certain behaviour gives him the right to claim a reward, is greater :
   a. the more often the behaviour concerned has been followed by a positive transfer of values,
   b. the more clearly it has been pointed out to him on these occasions that the transfer is a reward for the action, and
   c. the better acquainted he is with the principle of justice from other situations.

The fact that the learner knows he is being rewarded will also influence the manner in which he perceives his own actions. He learns that the actions which are rewarded are good, and – particularly – that they are good for those who give the rewards. These actions, therefore, will take on the character – if they have not already had it – of *transfers* to the person making the reward. For example, children who work hard at their homework and are rewarded for this by their parents get the impression that they *give* something to their parents through their homework. Development of this feeling of 'giving' goes hand in hand with the idea already referred to of having the right to obtain something in return, and the two help to strengthen each other. In other words, the same factors which give rise to conceptions of justice, contribute to giving a reward situation the character of being an exchange.

We have now looked at the situation from the learner's point of view. But the teacher, too, sometimes feels that the learner has a right to be rewarded. Part of the explanation for this may lie in the fact that the teacher rewards those actions which he himself approves. The idea that they deserve a reward because of their merit is therefore seldom completely foreign to him. It may have been present right from the beginning even though the main purpose behind the rewards was to exert influence. In any event, he can easily be made to accept such ideas if they are asserted by others, for instance by the learner. If several learners have the same teacher the question of distributive justice can also enter the picture and there can be interplay between the two principles of justice. We will return to these questions in Chapter 10, VIII.

In the beginning the teacher is more or less in control of the *size* of the rewards – as he is of whether they will be given at all. But if he has first instituted a certain practice, he becomes easily bound by this. When the other party has the impression that he has a right to claim a reward in certain cases, he will not only feel that he has been treated unfairly when the reward is not made but also when it is too small. And rewards which are accepted in this spirit are not likely to have the intended pedagogic effect.

Certain ideas of proportionality can also be at work. When rewards have first taken on the character of just repayment for good actions, it is only a short step to the assumption that the bigger the effort or sacrifice behind the action, the bigger reward it deserves. 'Rates of reward' which are adopted for certain types of actions therefore tend to serve as norms when questions of rewards for other actions later arise.

Whereas the principle of justice plays a prominent role with regard to rewards, the other exchange regulating factors are of minor importance in this field. Specific rules and agreements certainly do occur but they play a relatively small part in cases where rewards serve as a means of lasting influence. And market mechanisms are usually not at work in these instances of lasting connections between persons who, as a rule, are mutually dependent upon each other (e.g. parents and children or teachers and pupils). The parties have usually no choice between alternative exchange relations and the competition upon which market mechanisms are contingent, cannot then arise.

5. Restitution

'Hence the strong man who disregards morality and takes advantage
of his strength to injure another is
conceived as upsetting this equilibrium, or order of equality, established by morals ; justice then requires
that this moral *status quo* should as
far as possible be restored by the
wrongdoer.'
H. L. A. Hart, *The Concept of Law*
p. 161.

I. INTRODUCTION

The theme of this chapter centres on those forms of reciprocation which
are characterized by a negative transfer being followed by a positive
transfer from the same party (see chap. 1, fig. 3).[1] For instance, A returns something he has taken from B, or restores something he has
previously disturbed, replaces or repares something he has damaged,
retracts accusations, asks forgiveness for something wrong that he has
done, etc. The negative value involved in such reciprocation I call
'damage' (or 'injury') and the positive *'restitution'* (or 'compensation').

As in the case of exchange (see chap. 3, section I) I do not call something 'reciprocation' unless transfer No 2 is normatively or strategically conditioned by transfer No 1. The relationship can, for example, be
that A feels bound to make restitution because he has caused the damage, or that he is afraid of negative reactions from B and offers restitution in order to preserve his good relationship with B or at least to assuage the latter's feelings. Occasionally only one of the parties involved
perceives such a relation between the transfers but I refer mainly to instances where both parties do so.

As mentioned in Chapter 3, section I, it is usual in the case of exchange that the two transfers are perceived as being *mutually* conditioned : A performs a service because he expects a return service and B

---

1. Reciprocation where the transfers occur in the opposite sequence – the positive first and then the negative (chap. 1, fig. 4) – will not be treated.

makes a return for what he has received. But with restitution the conditional element is usually *one-sided*. Restitution is dependent upon the previous negative transfer but the reverse seldom applies. It can happen that some person hurts another *in order to* create an opportunity for making compensation. But this is not usual.

This difference can also be expressed by saying that the link between the two transfers is often established in advance in the case of exchange, while with restitution it is not established until after events have begun to take place. Partly for this reason the two transfers do not have the appearance of constituting a combined unit as do exchange transfers. This is reflected in everyday speech. There are words for many different kinds of exchange relationships (barter, sale, hire, etc.) but not for any of the reciprocal relationships with which we are concerned here. All the expressions which are available (compensation, reparation, return, restoration, redress etc.) refer to the last transfer and not to the combined reciprocal relationship.

Even though in pure cases there are clear-cut differences between exchange and restitution relationships, there are marginal cases which could as well be placed in one category as in the other. For instance, A has taken an object from B and compensates by paying its value. This differs from exchange since payment is made for what has been taken and not for what has been received. But whether a person is 'taking' or 'receiving' is not always clear. Or suppose A has forced B to do something which the latter finds unpleasant but which benefits A. If, later, A gives something to B this may appear to be a counter-service for the service he received so that the relation becomes one of exchange. But it can also have the character of 'making amends', i.e. of restitution.

Restitution sometimes derives from an exchange. For example, one of the parties in the exchange relationship does not fulfil his obligations on time or in the right manner. This break with his commitments may call for restitution. A subsequent settlement can then partly have the character of fulfilment of the exchange obligation and partly of restitution. These two bases of obligation are sometimes regarded as being separate but it happens that they merge. Examples can also be found of exchange relationships originating in existing or anticipated restitution situations (e.g. liability insurance). We shall return to this later.

In the same manner in which I dealt with exchange (see particularly chap. 3, section II and chap. 4), I will concentrate in what follows upon the *regulating factors*. For reasons which are discussed later, agreements and market mechanisms have usually only indirect significance in restitution relationships. On the other hand, norms play a great role.

134

Firstly, there are norms to the effect that one should avoid inflicting injury. Certain actions which are considered damaging or dangerous may be forbidden and there may also be general requirements of care and consideration. Secondly, there are norms which make it a duty to offer restitution and which sometimes also regulate the type and extent of restitution. These two kinds of norms are frequently coupled so that an infringement of a norm prohibiting injury releases the obligation to render restitution. But these norms are not always fused. The obligation to avoid injury may not be linked with any duty to make restitution, and restitution may be prescribed regardless of whether or not the damage inflicted breaks with any norm.

The conditions which promote the development of regulating norms are not the same in the case of restitution as in that of exchange. We found (in chap. 4) that the development of exchange regulations can be explained in terms of their utility to the parties concerned. They help to create trust and to eliminate price problems, so that it is easier to arrange favourable exchange. This gives grounds for assuming that the common interests of the parties engaged in exchange activity are among the most significant driving forces behind the processes of norm formation (see chap. 4, section III et seq.). But when it comes to norms concerning damage and restitution, there are hardly any grounds for such an assumption. It is true that the parties sometimes have a common interest in *avoiding* a train of events where A first injures B and afterwards makes restitution : the end result in many instances is that both are the losers. But the common interest is less obvious if the two steps in the reciprocation relationship, the act of injuring and the making of compensation, are looked at individually. Such a breakdown gives the best picture of the constellation of interests involved – as they appear to the participants. It has already been pointed out that an overall view of this type of reciprocation is not as pertinent as it is to exchange. For this reason norms which prohibit injury and prescribe restitution are treated separately in what follows – but in such a way that note is taken of the relationship between these two types of norms.

II. NORMS WHICH FORBID INJURY

The question of what gives rise to prohibition of injury (and prescription of solicitude and care) was touched upon in Chapter 3, sections V and VI. As was pointed out, norms of this type may develop within the individual interaction relationship, for instance between friends, married couples, parents and children, employers and employees, shopkeepers and their customers, etc. These norms can in part be founded on the exchange activity which occurs between the parties concerned. In the first place, exchange of the type 'I shall refrain from hurting you, if you refrain from hurting me', or 'I will show consideration for your wishes and expectations if you, in return, show consideration for mine' may contribute to establishing or strengthening a common set of norms on mutual respect and loyalty. In the second place, any form of exchange activity which favours both parties will make them jointly interested in keeping on good terms with each other in order that interaction continue undisturbed. And this mutuality of interest promotes the development of norms which forbid infliction of injury.

Many of these norms, however, have a much wider area of application than the individual interaction relationship. In most societies there are general norms against inflicting injury and it is expected that a certain amount of consideration and care be shown towards all one's fellow beings. Points of view based on exchange are not sufficient to explain the growth of such norms. To be sure, similar processes may also occur in interaction systems where there are more than two participants, so that common interest in peaceful and loyal cooperation becomes embedded in norms on mutual solicitude and care – without it being necessary to bring any pressure to bear to achieve this. But the community of interests is not normally so pronounced in these cases as in the case of exchange between two parties. Conflict may easily arise between the individual's interest in retaining as much as possible of his freedom of action and the society's or group's interest in limiting his freedom in order that he should not injure others. It therefore seems likely that the norms discussed here, to a greater extent than exchange norms, have their bases in collective advantages which lead to social pressure.[2]

III. THE BASIS OF RESTITUTION NORMS

If norms forbidding the infliction of injury have become established in some field or other, the likelihood is thereby increased that norms demanding restitution will also emerge. This is partly because injury as-

2. Cf. chap. 4, section III on the relation between individual and collective advantages. See also von Wright's (1963, pp. 202 et seq.) analysis of the questions mentioned here.

sumes another character when it involves breaking with a norm than when this is not the case. In the latter instance it may be due to accident or it may be an intentional but quite legitimate infliction of damage as, for instance, when a shopkeeper attracts a competitor's customers by charging lower prices or when a person applies for, and gets, a job which other people have also sought. Of course, a person can be reproached for having done some harm even though he has not acted contrary to any norm. But when norms have been broken, opportunities for reproach – and perhaps also for self-reproach – become considerably greater. For the person who is hurt, this means that he has someone whom he can hold responsible for what has happened. It will then be a natural reaction for him to claim some form of restitution and to bring pressure to bear to have his claim realized. And for the one who has caused the damage, the act of rendering restitution helps to ease any feeling of guilt he may have.

But the existence of prohibition against injury is neither a sufficient nor a necessary condition for the rendering of compensation nor for the growth of norms prescribing this. It is quite possible that a man who has hurt another regards his own behaviour as reprehensible without feeling obliged to make good the damage. And conversely, restitution may be made, and it may also be considered right that it be made, although no one feels that the person who has caused the damage should be reproached. In order to explain such facts we must look separately at the interests connected with restitution itself.

Normally, restitution is to the advantage of the damaged party while it imposes a burden upon the one who has caused the damage. However, there can be big differences in what compensation costs the latter in terms of money, energy, time and loss of prestige, etc. In some instances an expression of regret which costs nothing will be sufficient while in other cases a considerable sacrifice is called for. It is the offender's subjective perception of the size of the sacrifice which is of importance, and this can be influenced by many factors. Among other things, whether or not he himself has had any advantage in damaging the other party may play a role. It is probably easier for most people to relinquish acquired advantages than to accept the costs of an action from which they gain nothing.

For a person who acts strategically, the costs of making compensation are balanced against what he can get out of it. As already mentioned, it may help him to get rid of his feeling of guilt and it may also give him other advantages. Sometimes, by making restitution, he protects himself from consequences which may be even more unpleasant – for instance, revenge or punishment. Or he can do away with hindrances to future intercourse with the other party. This will seem to be particularly important if there is already an interaction relationship between the two parties which is advantageous to the one who has caused the damage. For example, in order to avoid losing customers it can pay to make good their losses, and it can be wise to ask forgiveness if one happens to offend a person with whom one wants to be on friendly terms.

These advantages are, however, of another kind than those connected with exchange activities. While exchange is often in itself advantageous, because one receives more than one gives, the advantages obtained by making restitution usually only consist in avoiding something which seems even worse – for instance, the other party taking the law into his own hands or severance of the relationship. Restitution can, of course, also be promoted by other motives, e.g., by compassion or sympathy for the person who has been hurt. But, even so, it seems reasonable to assume that restitution – to a greater extent than the completion of an exchange transaction – is conditional on pressure being brought to bear on the party which is to perform the service.

If the pressure comes only from the other party involved, its effectiveness will, inter alia, depend upon the relative strength of the two parties. 'Strength' in this context refers not only to means of power in the narrow sense but also to factors making for dependence, for example when one party disposes of exchange values which the other needs. Even though the damaged party is in possession of sufficient resources to be able to bring effective pressure to bear, he may not be interested in doing so. Perhaps the person who has caused the damage is unable to make amends or it is too troublesome to get anything out of him. It may also be that the injured party is offended so much that he is not satisfied with restitution but prefers to take revenge or to break off the connection. In the following chapters I discuss factors affecting the choice between different reactions on the part of the offended person. Here I will just point out that the possibility of future advantageous interaction is a factor pulling in the direction of restitution. The fact that his counterpart is interested in a continued relationship provides the offended party with a means of exerting pressure, and because he himself is interested in the same thing this gives him a motive for being content with claiming restitution.

If restitution is to be made, it may be an advantage for both parties that the relationship is regulated by norms. By indicating when, what and how much compensation should be afforded, the norms save the parties the trouble of bargaining and manoeuvring. They also help to

138

reduce any uncertainty as to whether or not full restitution has been made. Similarly to what was assumed with regard to exchange (see chap. 4, section III), we therefore find it likely that the greater the need for security and predictability in the relationship between parties, and the more important it is for them to settle accounts so that the affair will not revive, the more likely it is that norms of restitution develop.

The fact that restitution is made and that there are norms which call for this can also affect *people other than the two directly involved.* Here, as in the case of exchange, it is possible that some of these extended effects can involve such advantages to outside persons that these are motivated to influence the offender to offer restitution. It is also possible that pressure is brought to bear on the damaged party, for instance to get him to be satisfied with compensation or to modify his claims.

The importance that norms prescribing restitution may have for outside persons is partly due to their possible effect of preventing damaging actions. As already mentioned, norms which forbid injury and norms prescribing restitution are often so combined that the obligation to make restitution serves as a sanction and gives the prohibition extra strength. And even when there is no ban on the action concerned but only a requirement that restitution be made if anyone gets hurt, the risk which this involves for the actor can encourage care and concern. There is no doubt that restitutional norms *can* have such a preventive effect. But it is uncertain under which conditions and to what extent this is the case. It is also questionable to what extent tendencies to cause damage *should* be counteracted. Too many precautions can be paralysing, nor should concern for other people be so great that useful competition is debarred.

The fact that values are transferred when restitution takes place can also have consequences for others than those directly involved. The possibility of such transfers may increase the security of potential sufferers. On the other hand, it makes for decreased security for those engaged in activities likely to damage other people. If they are more or less the same people who are both exposed to damage and liable to cause damage, these two effects tend to cancel one another out. And even when different groups (or categories) of people are involved, it is not certain that the transfer of risks leads to an increase in the total sum of security in society.

When there are opposing group interests, however, one of the groups may be sufficiently influential to establish as a generally accepted norm that solution to the question of compensation which suits it best. Studies in legal history and comparative law provide many examples of this.

139

A good illustration is to be found in *Erik Anners's* (1960) comparative investigation of rules concerning return of lost property in various medieval societies. The situation studied is one in which an article of property is first stolen (or lost in some other manner) and then sold to a third party who is in good faith. The question then arises whether the original owner can demand the return of the object or whether the buyer should be entitled to keep it (or possibly be obliged to return it but have his expenses covered). Peasants and tradesmen had opposed interests in solving of this question. It was to the advantage of peasants that the original owner had an unconditional right to take back his property wherever he found it. But the interests of tradesmen favoured rules protecting the man acting in good faith, so that the risk of buying from a stranger would be reduced. Anners's investigation indicates that there was a close connection between the way in which the problem was solved and the influence which the farming and trading sections of the population were able to exert on the legislation. In those old Germanic societies where agricultural interests dominated the solution always went in favour of the original owner, while in many of the urban societies of the late Middle Ages which had strong commercial interests, it went in the opposite direction.

All the effects of norms prescribing restitution which have so far been mentioned can influence the distribution of values in a society. By and large the rules probably serve to counteract changes in the existing distribution.[3] Because of their preventive effect it is more likely that people are able to retain the values they already possess. And in those cases where, even so, damage is done, restitution in many cases re-establishes the status quo. This applies, for example, when a person who has tried to get something at the expense of another is forced to return what he has taken. However, when the offender has gained nothing from the action, the original distribution of values will be changed whether the loss is transferred to him or stays with the damaged party. Even when the individual norms appear to preserve the distribution of values it is not certain that the overall effect of a society's system of restitution goes in the same direction. If, for example, certain kinds of damage involve the obligation to make recompense while others do not, and the risks of causing and of being exposed to the different types of damage are unevenly distributed, the system as a whole

---

3. Cf. Hart (1961) pp. 160-161 who attaches great importance to this. See also chap. 4, section III, p. 98, with reference to the preservative effect of the principle that good be repaid with good.

may lead to a redistribution of values. I will not go deeper into this question. Even if we knew more than we do about the effects norms prescribing restitution have on the distribution of values in society, it would still be doubtful whether these effects have any impact on the development of such rules.

The significance of the last effect of restitution norms which I will discuss here is simpler to gauge. As already pointed out these norms can facilitate the reaching of agreement and the maintenance of peaceful relations between parties and can provide the right conditions for future intercourse between them. These peace-making and integrating effects can often be of positive value to other than the parties concerned – first and foremost to their immediate environment but sometimes also to society as a whole. It is reasonable to assume that this can result in social pressure which both supports restitution and limits its claims.

IV. THE ROLE OF THE PRINCIPLES OF JUSTICE

In the previous section the conditions under which norms prescribing restitution are likely to develop were discussed in general terms. However, these norms differ considerably from one another both with regard to their content and to the manner in which they originate. I will not discuss all these variations but restrict myself to saying a few words about the principles of justice which can enter the picture and about the interplay between these principles and other restitutional norms.

The principle of justice which immediately suggests itself in these situations is that 'a wrong should be righted'. This is based on the normative notion (mentioned in chap. 2 IV) that the relationship becomes lop-sided when one party inflicts damage on the other and that therefore the former must make compensation in such a manner and to such an extent that balance is restored. Hardly anyone would apply this point of view to all possible harmful acts. In other words, the principle does not claim that *everything* which is 'wrong' (in the sense that it hurts another) must be put right but rather that some damaging acts disturb the balance in such a way that they call for restitution. The principle has, in common with other principles of justice, a vague content and an indefinite area of application.

On the whole it is reasonable to assume that this principle of justice is most likely to be applied when the offender can be *reproached* for his behaviour, for instance when he has acted in defiance of generally accepted norms on carefulness and consideration for other people. But the principle is sometimes also applied to cases where the offender can not be reproached. We will look at examples of this later. Conversely, there can be instances where one finds grounds for criticism without, for that reason, wanting to involve considerations of justice. It can also happen that *another* principle of justice – namely that an evil may (or should) be repaid with evil – is used instead of or in addition to the principle that a wrong be righted. For instance, what the offender has done may be considered *so* bad that no form of compensation is sufficient, so that revenge or punishment is necessary in order to restore the moral balance.

Another relevant factor is whether the offender has *gained* from his action. If this is the case, conceptions of justice will sometimes find some support *both* in the idea that 'A wrong should be righted' *and* in the idea that 'Good be repaid with good', it being reasoned that if repayment must be made for what one has *received,* repayment should also be made for what one has *taken.* Distributive justice can also enter into the picture. For example, it may seem unfair that someone who has hurt the interests of other people should acquire advantages from which more solicitous persons are debarred.

In cases of restitution, there is similar interplay between the principles of justice and other norms, as in cases of exchange (cf. chap. 4, section IV). On the one hand, conceptions of justice are frequently coloured by traditional and legal rules of compensation which exist in the society concerned. On the other hand, justice can serve as normative raw material for new rules and as a basis for interpretation and evaluation of existing rules. Because of their elasticity, ideas of justice can easily be adapted to new social conditions and contribute to a reshaping of compensation systems.

We find examples of this in the development of the law of torts. Changes which took place in European tort law during the 18th and early 19th centuries were strongly influenced by ideas of justice. These changes, broadly speaking, meant that a multitude of specific rules providing for definite amounts of compensation to be payed for specific types of offences were replaced by the general principle of liability for fault ; according to this, economic loss should be compensated for in all cases where the offender had shown negligence – but only in these cases. Because of its general scope and elastic criteria, the principle was certainly better suited than the older rules to serve as a guide for courts of law which tried to adapt their practices to the changing social conditions. Among the arguments which were used to support the principle, the conception of a 'necessary' or 'natural' connection between fault and liability played an important role. And this conception, at any rate in some instances, was probably rooted in the idea that liability served as a moral counterweight to fault.

During the last 100 years the principle of fault has partly had to give way to new legal precepts. For one thing, liability without fault ('strict liability') has been introduced in many fields where modern techniques have given rise to new risks. In Norway some of these innovations have been introduced through legislation, but the greater part of the change has come about via court decisions. The development that has taken place can perhaps be characterized as an adaptation of the legal system to the changes in production methods and living conditions industrialization has involved and to methods of distributing losses through organized insurance. Also, during the later phase of development ideas of justice have been brought in to support the formation of new rules. One of the main arguments used has been that a person engaged in an activity imposing increased hazards on his surroundings should in return make amends for the damage which results from the activity – even though this activity has been conducted in a fully responsible manner. The fact that the risk-creating activity involved (e.g. with industrial concerns and means of transport) often entails economic gain to the one who engages in it, is also of significance. It makes it possible to combine the idea that something must be given for what has been received with the notion that the act of exposing someone to risk must be compensated for.

V. AGREEMENTS, ORGANIZATIONS AND MARKET MECHANISMS

Both one-sided *promises* and two-sided *agreements* occur in connection with restitution situations. A person who has done or is likely to do some damage may promise to make amends ; or the other party may promise that he will consider the affair settled if he receives compensation. Promises sometimes serve as supplements to restitution norms, for example by guaranteeing that a norm will be respected or by solving some problem which the norm does not settle (e.g. questions concerning the kind and extent of compensation). But promises are also used in cases where there is no restitution norm.

The person who binds himself with a promise usually anticipates getting something in return. It may be a purely factual effect that he seeks to achieve, for instance to pacify his counterpart. But frequently he hopes for a return service from his counterpart and then an *exchange situation* arises – in addition to or instead of the restitution situation. When agreements are entered into on these occasions they mainly serve as a means of establishing and regulating such exchange.

There are many examples of exchanges where the contribution, or a part of the contribution, of one of the parties is that he takes responsibility for damage which has been done or may occur. The seller promises, for example, to cover the buyer's loss if the goods should turn out to be deficient or be retarded or damaged in transit, and in return he can charge a higher price than he would otherwise have demanded. Or A borrows something from B in return for a promise to replace it if it should be damaged or lost. An undertaking to reduce the risk of damage, for instance by taking special safety precautions, also serves in many instances as part of an exchange.

The person who accepts such responsibility can be a potential injurer or someone who because of his close connection to the values concerned has special qualifications for averting damage. But he may also be an outsider. In industrialized societies the various forms of *organized activity* which aim at obviating or redressing damage and covering losses are of particular importance. Some of these activities are conducted on a commercial basis by private companies such as Securicor, the AA and RAC patrols and the insurance companies, some by humanitarian organizations and some by the public service organizations (e.g. the police, health services, social insurance and other social services, etc.). The relationship between these organizations and those who benefit from their services is regulated partly through agreements and partly through laws, by-laws or other organizational regulations. In some cases there is a pronounced exchange relationship between the parties involved. For example, a man pays an annual insurance premium and in return the company takes responsibility for certain losses he may suffer. Or he pays a regular sum to Securicor in return for which they guard his property. In other cases, for example when a charity organization or the government gives assistance, the exchange element is less obvious. But in these cases, too, certain features of exchange can be seen. For instance, it is possible that the party which renders humanitarian aid expects – and does, in fact, receive – gratitude as a counter-service. And in the relationship between government and citizen, the government's actions in preventing and covering damage can be regarded as one link in a comprehensive exchange relationship where other services rendered by the government are also taken into consideration, and where loyalty, work, tax-paying etc. constitute the citizen's counter-service.

The conditions under which agreements are likely to be used and

144

organizations formed are more or less the same here as in other instances. Reference can be made to what was said about this in Chapter 4, sections V and VII. As mentioned there, there is close interplay between increased use of agreements and organizational growth. On the one hand organizational development must have reached a certain level before there can be any widespread use of agreements – there must be finance and credit institutions, good communications, state institutions which can help in enforcing agreements, etc. And on the other hand the development of organizations depends to a large extent on it being possible to make dependable agreements. Agreements are useful aids both in the establishment of organizations and in their current activity. But although increased use of agreements and organizational development have a tendency to go together for some time, organizations can supersede certain types of agreements when they are sufficiently far advanced. State social insurance measures, for instance, may make it unnecessary to secure similar services for oneself through agreements with private persons.

The organizational measures mentioned above are in many ways better suited than restitution norms to creating security. They are a safeguard against many kinds of damage and loss for which no one could otherwise be held responsible. And even when there is a culprit causing the damage, one usually feels safer if a large organization (e.g. an insurance company) is financially responsible. But of course there are limits to what can be expected. Preventive control measures are seldom completely water-tight and if one tried to make them so this might easily result in intolerable restriction of freedom. There is also a limit to what can be achieved through insurance systems. Only economic compensation is rendered, and the losses must be sufficiently alike and occur sufficiently often to make it feasible to calculate statistically how large a premium is necessary to cover the risk involved.

The use of supervision and assistance measures, insurance systems etc. can, in various ways, influence restitution norms and their application. The growth of the insurance business, for example, has led to many changes in the legislation on torts. In some fields liability has been extended on the grounds that those who risk causing damage are able to insure themselves against this risk. In other fields liability has been reduced because those who may be hurt are able to insure themselves. The rules have also, to a certain extent, become more refined and elastic. For instance, Scandinavian legislation leaves it to the discretion of the judge whether a company which has covered a person's losses may claim the whole or a part of the sum involved from the party causing the damage. Both insurance systems and public and private assistance can also have the factual effect that restitution norms lose some of their practical significance. But this is not likely to happen to all such rules. People can hurt and offend each other in many ways against which organized measures provide no protection but where restitution is applicable.

Market mechanisms can never be of the same importance in restitution as in exchange. Exchange markets exist because exchange is advantageous to both parties. For this reason sellers have a motive to underbid each other in order to sell and buyers to overbid in order to buy. No such competitive motive normally exists in connection with damage and restitution since this is a type of reciprocation which most people prefer to avoid.[4] We can therefore exclude the possibility of competitive markets for damage and restitution.

However, *exchange markets* can in various ways have an impact on the practice of restitution. In the first place markets can be formed for the taking over of risks in return for payment. And if the size of the agreed risk premiums is regulated by market mechanisms this may indirectly also be of significance to restitution settlements.

In the second place it is of importance whether the damaged objects can be traded so that they have a definite *sales value*. This can, among other things, determine if it is possible to insure them. It is quite true that one can insure against loss of certain values which are not merchandise, for instance life and health. But on the whole it is easier to establish insurance systems for those objects which have a sales value than for those which do not. Whether or not damaged goods have a sales value is also often taken into account when compensation rules are drafted. Money compensation is usually considered more natural when the goods have a sales value than when they do not. There is also a tendency to let the sales value decide the amount of compensation. There are practical advantages in having such a yardstick to go by. And the principle can easily be justified by the specific conception of justice

---

4. Competition *to avoid* is possible but it cannot help to stabilize 'prices' for doing damage. Such negative competition between potential causers of damage could, for instance, involve attempts to surpass each other in showing consideration and care and in letting it be known that they were loath to render compensation. And potential sufferers could perhaps compete by exceeding each other in announcing the effective manner in which they enforced their claims for compensation and how large these claims were. The result would be that the positions held by the parties became increasingly estranged – rather than that they approached each other as in the case of exchange.

that there should be absolute equality between damage and compensation. Vaguer notions of justice, however, may indicate that importance should also be attached to other conditions, for example how much blame is to be ascribed to each of the parties involved, how well-off they are economically, what possibilities they have of covering themselves through insurance, etc. Technical developments have given added significance to such points of view because in many fields a small mistake or a little carelessness can result in damage of such economic magnitude that it would be unreasonable to expect the offender to make good the entire financial loss. There are several examples in recent Scandinavian legislation indicating that notice has been taken of this, the courts of law being given discretionary authority to fix compensation at a sum lower than the actual economic loss.

6. Different types of reciprocation having negative values, with special reference to revenge

'... it is considered servile to put up
with an insult to oneself or suffer
one's friends to be insulted.'
Aristotle, *Nicomachean Ethics,* IV.
v.6.

I. THE CONCEPTS 'REVENGE', 'PUNISHMENT' AND 'COMPETITION'

The kinds of reciprocation in which both parties inflict harm on each other, differ so much one from the other that little would be achieved by a joint discussion of them. I distinguish between three main types which I call 'revenge', 'punishment' and 'competition' respectively and below I will outline what I mean by these expressions.

Revenge and *punishment* have several common characteristics. Both are reactions (as are some claims for restitution) to behaviour which is considered wrong. They differ from claims for restitution in that harm is inflicted on the wrongdoer, instead of a positive value being demanded of him. But intermediate and mixed cases occur. If, for instance, the offender is forced to give something to the offended party (money or other material values, apologies, concessions etc.) this normally involves a loss for the one and a gain for the other. Also the fact that the other party is made to suffer or loses prestige may in itself be a source of pleasure and afford a feeling of rehabilitation. How such cases are classified depends upon what is felt to be most important – that one person benefits or that the other is hurt. Occasionally, however, the character of both punishment or revenge and restitution is so prominent that it is most natural to say that a combination of the two is present.[1]

Only those reactions which are expressions of disapproval of the

---

1. Instances which differ from these combined cases are those where two clearly separate reactions – one of which has the features of punishment and the other restitution – come in addition to each other. The offender, for instance, is put in prison and must also pay compensation to the person offended.

148

preceding action will be characterized as revenge or punishment.[2] Harm that is caused to another person, for instance in self defence, often does not fulfil this requirement. Mixed motives can occur, of course. If, for instance, a person has received a blow and hits back, this may partly be to defend himself and partly to show that he objects to the behaviour of his opponent. But sometimes it is not clear whether there is any element of disapproval in the action. It happens not infrequently that injury which is intended as an expression of disapproval by the person who causes it is not interpreted as such by the other party – or the other way round. Disapproval can vary in strength from mild aloofness to the strongest condemnation or disgust. It is often caused by the breaking of a norm, but I do not consider this a necessary condition for characterizing the reaction as punishment or revenge.

On the other hand one condition which I do stipulate is that the damage inflicted is intentional. An instance where A disapproves of B's behaviour and tells him so without intending to do him any harm, falls outside my concepts of revenge and punishment. Even though B finds it unpleasant to be corrected and even though A is aware of this, we cannot say that A has punished B as long as the feeling of unpleasantness is only a secondary effect of A's behaviour and not something at which he has explicitly aimed. But if the correction is not only intended as an explanation of proper conduct but also to hurt by censuring him, an element of punishment or revenge is present. Many other examples could be given of reactions which are partly intended as punishment and partly have other purposes. To say that a person intends to harm another does not mean that this necessarily is his *final* goal. Occasionally hurting another person can in itself be satisfying. But frequently it is only (or also) a means of achieving something else, for instance influencing other people's behaviour or gaining respect.

The difference between revenge and punishment – as the words are used here – is that *revenge* has the character of *personal retribution*. It is always related to an offence which either oneself or one's closest friends or relations have been subjected to, and it is supposed to give the offended party some kind of personal satisfaction or rehabilitation. This feature of revenge is reflected in the expressions 'to avenge *oneself*' (or 'to avenge the offended') and 'to be revenged' ; we cannot express ourselves in this way when talking about punishment. Of course *punish-*

2. Revenge and punishment are thus the opposite of *reward* which is characterized by a benefit transferred in appreciation of an action, cf. chap. 4 footnote 6 and section IX.

ment can also be inflicted because the punisher himself has been offended, and it can be based on ideas of retaliation, but it does not have the feature of personal requital that revenge has. It gives more the impression of being a reaction to something which, from an objective point of view, is not right. Closely connected with this is the fact that it is frequently (but not always) an authority that punishes, for instance the state, teacher or parent, and that the purpose of influencing the offender is more often connected with punishment than with revenge. But to exert influence *can* also be a motive in revenge, of which we have a suggestion in the expressions 'I'll teach you!' and 'That'll do you good!'

All sorts of hurt can be used both in revenge and in punishment, for instance loss of life or freedom, physical pain, confiscation of property, causation of grief, disgrace or humiliation, etc. As mentioned earlier, revenge and punishment can be combined with restitution, as when an offender is compelled to make a return service – partly for the sake of compensation and partly in order to hurt him. There can also be a connection with exchange. One can, for example, punish or take revenge by refusing, interrupting or restricting an exchange relationship. For instance, a child may be excluded from a game 'because he was naughty', or an employee may be dismissed from his job because of irregularities or carelessness.

The strategies, norms and arguments involved in the use of revenge are discussed below in section II and what follows, and punishment is treated in the succeeding chapter. However, I would like first to say something about the kinds of reciprocation of negative values which I include in the expression 'competition'.

Competitive acts are characterized by the motive to achieve something at the cost of another person. A gain can be made at someone else's cost when both parties are trying to obtain the same value, for example the same item of property, good-will, job or spouse. Or it may be that both are striving for things which are mutually incompatible.[3] For instance, there may be a life-and-death-struggle when the future security of one party depends upon the destruction of his opponent. Or there may be a conflict between different kinds of interests, e.g., between commercial and anti-pollution interests when a new industrial venture is planned.

3. There is no sharp distinction between these two types of cases. It is sometimes just a matter of taste whether one talks of the 'same' value or of 'different' values which exclude each other. See Galtung (1965 p. 348 with footnote 3) and Heider (1958 pp. 196-97) with reference to Spinoza. Since the distinction is of no importance to the questions treated here, I will not discuss it further.

Pure competition does not usually involve the intention to inflict harm on one's counterpart. The actor may realize that harm will be done but regards this with indifference or as an undesired secondary effect of his action. On exceptional occasions the harm will be intentional. For example, a man who is fighting can aim to make his blow or kick so painful that the other party is immobilized. This is not sufficient to characterize the action as revenge or punishment since no expression of disapproval need be involved. But, of course, there *are* some actions which have all the features of revenge or punishment and, in addition, a motive of competition. For example, a businessman tries to entice a competitor's customers by spreading slander behind his opponent's back. This he does partly because he wants to widen his own circle of clients and partly because his competitor has on an earlier occasion done something he disapproves of and he wants to avenge himself for this.

A competitive action does not have to be a reaction to something which has already taken place – as in the case of revenge and punishment. Competitive actions are taken both by the person who originates the competition and by the party taking counter-measures.[4] There is therefore no such fundamental difference between transfers No 1 and No 2 as in the case of restitution, punishment and revenge. As with exchange, the reciprocation of competitive actions can appear symmetrical in the sense that both parties are on an equal footing. A series of acts of revenge and retaliation can take on the same characteristics when the process is started but the first injury made is distinct. However, the practical difference does not have to be so big since it is often difficult to decide what came first. Lack of symmetry is usually more prominent in punishment situations – for reasons which I shall return to later.

I have already mentioned, when discussing exchange, some forms of competition which are important in practice. In Chapter 4, Section II we looked at the relationship between two parties who are interested in exchanging with each other. When the terms of exchange are not regulated by norms or by market mechanisms and both parties intend to push their own interests, a tug-of-war easily develops between them. Both sides try to get the best terms possible at the other's expense. And the means which are employed to achieve this goal are often such that the tug-of-war seems like a reciprocation of negative values; for instance, threats can be made to withdraw from the exchange if the other party

---

4. Isolated competitive actions also occur which do not result in any counter-measures and do not, therefore, lead to reciprocation.

does not concede one's own demands, or false information can be given in order to make one's own offer appear more generous than it is. In other words, reciprocation of negative values can be a means of achieving a favourable exchange of positive values. But, as we have seen, these means do not always have the desired effects. It can happen that both parties aim too high and no exchange takes place.

Another form of competition connected with exchange is that which was described in the section on market mechanisms (Chap. 4, Section IV). Here the goal is not to get the best possible terms in an individual exchange but rather to maximize overall gain by increasing turn-over. Strategy will then be the exact opposite of what has just been described. Instead of demanding as much as possible for oneself, potential exchange connections are offered the best possible terms – in order to attract them. In this way two different reciprocation relations are combined. By increasing positive transfers in the exchange relationship, one inflicts the injury that is inherent in enticing clients from a competitor, and there is always a chance that he will hit back, for instance by offering even better conditions.

The two forms of competition referred to differ not only in that their strategies are diametrically opposed but also in their long-term effects. Market competition for increased turn-over tends to regulate the terms of exchange in such a manner that there is no room for manoeuvring in individual exchange transactions. In Chapter 4, Section IV factors which promote one of these forms of competition, and therefore counteract the other, are discussed. The normative exchange regulations, among others the principle of justice, which were discussed in Chapter 4, to some extent counteract both forms of competition. In fact much of what has previously been said about the development of various forms of exchange regulation is also relevant when discussing what gives rise to the above-mentioned kinds of competition.

When values are allocated, there can be competition between the recipients, who each want to obtain as much as possible at the expense of the others involved. This is discussed in later chapters. There are also forms of competition which have no connection with either reciprocation or allocation. But we will not be concerned with these.

Some of the evils which people inflict on each other are neither punishment, revenge nor competitive measures. Harm can be caused by pure sadism or maliciousness, the other party having done nothing to which the offender reacts and the latter expecting no gain other than the pleasure of witnessing the discomfort of the other party. Such actions are not an 'answer' to any former action and are therefore not cases

152

of reciprocation. But, of course, they may later be 'answered' if the other party takes revenge or takes steps to have the offender punished, or if he defends himself so that it becomes a competitive situation.

It also happens that the motive for causing pain is to help or protect the other party. For instance, a baby is securely fastened in its pram so that it cannot fall out and hurt itself, the garden gate is shut so that the children cannot rush into the road and be run over, ill-tasting medicine or painful treatment are prescribed for a patient in order that he can be cured, etc. These actions, too, may be a link in different kinds of reciprocal relations. When the other party understands that the benefits he receives more than balance the unpleasantness, an exchange may take place. The relationship between doctor and patient is an example of this. But it may also be that the other party fixes his attention solely on the unpleasantness and, for instance, takes revenge or such counter-action that the situation becomes one of competition.

II. REVENGE-PROMOTING STRATEGIES AND NORMS

Revenge presumably exists in all cultures, but it varies in frequency and in composition. As already mentioned, all sorts of harm can be inflicted in revenge. And the harm done can differ in intensity and scope from the most innocent of children's pranks to the bloodiest vendettas or wars.

It is not necessary to take strategies or norms into account in order to explain that revenge sometimes takes place. It is enough to point out that offences frequently evoke a feeling of indignation and an immediate urge to repay the hurt. The spontaneous desire for revenge may be translated into action even if the actor knows that this will not pay, and without regard for what the norms prescribe. I do not intend to discuss further whether or not it is a general human tendency to react in this way and, if this is the case, what gives rise to this tendency.[5] I am content to presuppose that not all desire for revenge has to be socially or culturally conditioned.

However, there can be no doubt that social and cultural factors are of importance. The great variations one finds in the frequencies and forms of revenge in various societies and milieus give a clear indication

5. Psychological theories on the connection between frustration and aggression are relevant in this connections. See Berelson and Steiner (1964) pp. 267-270 with references.

of this. Here – as in other kinds of reciprocation – I presume that a study of strategies and norms can help to explain these variations. In this section I will discuss which favourable consequences revenge may have for the individual actor and for the society or group to which he belongs. Examples of norms which prescribe the use of revenge will also be given. In the following sections we shall deal with different harmful effects of revenge and with factors which can help to limit or regulate the use of it. Here, as throughout this book, my basic assumption is that strategies contribute towards creating, maintaining and changing norms.

The advantages an individual obtains from avenging himself sometimes depend upon revenge being combined with restitution. For example, A has taken something which belongs to B and B revenges himself by taking something else from A. The bare fact that one's counterpart has suffered will also, in some cases, give pleasure and be experienced as a form of restitution. As we know, revenge can be sweet.

Revenge and competition can also be combined. For instance, let us imagine two people living in a lawless society, each struggling to kill the other. If one succeeds in doing away with the other this can be both revenge for the suffering he has been exposed to and a means of securing his own existence.

But even when revenge is not connected with such immediate advantages, it is possible that the avenger achieves something else. He may command more respect so that in future other people take care not to offend him. Perhaps he, also in other ways, rises in people's esteem and gains in self-respect. The manner in which people react to offences reveals something of their personality. The act of taking revenge can be a means of convincing oneself and others that one is not the kind of person who will put up with just anything but that one is tough and rough, bold and brave, or perhaps sly and crafty. To the person who strives to create or to maintain such a picture of himself, it may seem essential that he try to take revenge when he has been offended – even if he understands that this will be done in vain or that it will be dangerous.

The evaluation of such personality traits as are revealed in the practice of taking revenge depends, to a great extent, on cultural background and milieu. In a gang of youths whose activity constantly brings them into conflict with other gangs or with the neighbours or police, and where aggressiveness and self-assertiveness are idealized, one must be tough and fierce in order to hold one's ground. The same tendencies, on a larger scale, are to be found in gangster and bandit milieus. We have examples both from the past and the present where whole societies have a manner of living and system of values which make it a virtue to repay an injury and where avenging oneself and one's relatives is not only regarded as a right but also as a duty.

This was the situation in the Nordic societies of Viking times as they are depicted in the sagas of the kings of Norway and – first and foremost – in the Icelandic family sagas. The most idealized character traits were manliness, courage and fearlessness. It was a disgrace not to revenge oneself or one's near relatives – at any rate if compensation had not been made. However, it quite often happened that revenge was averted, for instance through the payment of fines for a murder. And willingness to accept such an arrangement was sometimes lauded. But there were limits to the amount of reconciliation that could be shown. For instance, in Chapter 37 of the Norwegian Gulating's Law from the twelfth century, it was stipulated that :

'No one may claim a lawful fine more than three times, whether man or woman, without taking revenge between times.'

Many other cultures have – or have had – similar attitudes to revenge. For instance, norms which make it a duty to take revenge have been found among the Eskimos of northern Canada,[6] in certain American Indian tribes,[7] in Sardinia[8] and in several other places.[9] And even when it is not considered a duty to revenge oneself, it is in many places considered a right – which makes otherwise illegal actions (e.g. murder) legitimate.

How society evaluates different human characteristics not only affects the tendency to avenge oneself but also those methods of revenge which are utilized – for example, whether physical force or magic and witchcraft, intrigue and cunning, economic power, scorn and ridicule etc. are preferred.

We do not know much about what gives rise to ideologies which favour revenge. Obviously it is of importance whether or not there is a state or other organization which can effectively protect the individual person against offence. But this cannot be the sole significant factor since there are many societies without any such organization where the tendency to resort to revenge is not particularly strong. It is probably also significant whether or not the personal characteristics which are

6. Hoebel (1954) pp. 87 ff. and Rasmussen (1927) p. 190 and p. 235.
7. Hoebel (1954) pp. 139-140 on the Comanche Indians and Fock (1972) p. 151 on South American tribes.
8. Bentzon (1967) pp. 3-4.
9. Westermarck (I 1906) pp. 479-82.

expressed in the urge to take revenge have strategic value in other connections. For example, in a society which is constantly menaced by outside enemies or where people have to fight against the forces of nature, hunt dangerous animals, undertake risky trading expeditions, etc. in order to make a living, such features as aggressiveness, contempt for death and self-assertiveness can be advantageous, both for the individual and for the society. Also, in well-organized and affluent societies there may be groups (e.g. a band of gangsters) who get into a situation where they are surrounded by enemies and lead an insecure life. This may help to explain why such characteristics as those mentioned above can be highly valued. The fact that such groups come into being needs, of course, a separate explanation, but we will not discuss this further.

III. HARMFUL EFFECTS OF REVENGE ; NORMS WHICH FORBID OR LIMIT THE USE OF REVENGE

Even when revenge-promoting character traits are advantageous to the collective, it is not certain that revenge itself is so. To be sure, revenge can in some instances serve as a sanction which helps strengthen norms.[10] It is dangerous to throw stones if they can be expected back again. But as a sanction, revenge has many weaknesses. Because self-assertiveness and the desire to return an evil are the chief motivating powers, revenge is seldom used systematically as a method of teaching norms. There may, of course, be some degree of regularity in its use even though this is not intentional. But the tendency will be for the trend to take a direction which is unfavourable to the majority. For example, it is likely that the most powerful and most inconsiderate will benefit at the expense of other people.

Moreover, revenge often provokes counter-revenge and sometimes leads to an escalation of the conflict to feud proportions. This tendency towards aggravated violence is connected with the fact that here we lack those price stabilizing factors which are at work when good is repaid with good. In Chapter 4 I explained the development of these factors by pointing to the fact that exchange is often advantageous to both parties. The parties therefore tend to move closer to each other's demands and perhaps to seek support in norms indicating suitable exchange payment, in order to increase the chances of the exchange taking

10. Durkheim (1964 pp. 87-88) emphasized this point.

place. And if the connection is maintained, the terms which have previously been applied will tend to be indicative in future exchange. Market mechanisms can help to stabilize the terms as well. But the situation is very different when revenge and counter-revenge are reciprocated. Although, on occasions, some pleasure can be obtained from taking revenge, the net gain is likely to be negative for both parties. Partly for this reason, market mechanisms cannot apply as they do in exchange,[11] nor will there be the same inclination to compromise. It can happen that a person who takes revenge shows some moderation, for instance because he hopes that this will make the other party accept his action as fair requital and let things rest as they are. But showing moderation is certainly not always the best way in which to avoid counter-revenge. It often seems better to hit as hard as possible, incapacitating the other party or frightening him from further action. And if both parties have this attitude, continual escalation is likely – as long as the parties hold out.

There are some indications that the danger of escalation is greater, the more violent the form of revenge. The explanation may be that when life is endangered one is not only concerned with revenge but is also involved in a competition for survival. Revenge and competition motives are frequently combined in this manner both in family and tribal feuds and in national wars.

In many instances the damage and danger connected with revenge hit not only the original parties but also their environment. Escalation can mean that more and more people are drawn in on both sides and hostilities may result in a loss of resources which also affects those who are not directly involved. Therefore, people are often interested in preventing or restricting acts of revenge. In what follows I will look at various strategies which are adopted to advance these interests and at norms and institutions to which the strategies give rise.

In the first place social pressure can be exercised to impede such offences as may release avenging actions. The deterrent effect of the threat of revenge is reinforced when not only the actor but also his environment is likely to be affected. Friends and relatives may therefore try to prevent aggressive actions. However, attempts to make the actor more cautious will often have little effect. For the way of life and system of values which make for vindictiveness usually also promote such actions as provoke revenge.

---

11. The points of view advanced in connection with restitution (chap. 5, section V, footnote 4) are also relevant to revenge.

157

Secondly, pressure may be brought to bear upon the offended party to prevent him from taking revenge or to keep his revenge within certain bounds. The most radical attempt in this direction is to be found in the Sermon on the Mount where we are taught that evil should not be repaid with evil but with good :

'And unto him that smiteth thee on the one cheek offer also the other ; and him that taketh away thy cloke forbid not to take thy coat also' (St. Luke, 6, 29).

Norms which express such high ideals have difficulty in moulding behaviour. But norms which apply more moderate restriction to the urge to take revenge are often accepted.

One type of such norms is that setting limits to the kinds of evils one has a right to avenge. An example of such norms and of arrangements made to overcome difficulties in enforcing them is to be found in Deuteronomy 19. It says here that there should be places of refuge for 'Whoso killeth his neighbour ignorantly, whom he hated not in time past' and gives as the reason that 'Lest the avenger of the blood pursue the slayer, while his heart is hot, and overtake him, because the way is long, and slay him ; whereas he *was* not worthy of death, inasmuch as he hated him not in time past.'

There are also norms which limit the evil that may be caused to other people in revenge. For instance, murder may be absolutely prohibited, no exception being made to allow for taking a person's life in revenge. Usually, in societies which have organized coercive power, there are many prohibitions which are absolute in this sense. According to Norwegian law, for example, it is a general principle that prohibited actions do not become legal because they are taken in revenge. However, the criminal code does make a few concessions to the urge to revenge. The court may reduce the punishment when the act is committed in 'justifiable anger'. And as regards assault and defamation, the law gives the judge discretionary power to acquit in cases of retaliation.

Norms of a third type are concerned with the manner of wreaking revenge. There is room for such norms even when society is pervaded by an ideology favouring revenge. In the Icelandic family sagas we find many examples indicating that not all methods of taking revenge were acceptable. To take a person's life was allowed, but the killing should be done with a weapon ; not, for instance, by burning down a person's house with him inside it – as Flosi and his men did to Njál and his sons.[12] And if a man came upon his enemy while he slept, the latter should preferably be woken and given time to defend himself before

12. Bayerschmidt and Hollander (1955) p. 261 et seq.

being attacked.[13] Norms of this kind coincided well with the ideals of manliness and bravery which nourished the vengeance impulse. They were probably not intended to limit the use of revenge, but they may still have had some such effect.

Revenge-regulating norms of the last category to be examined are those which demand balance between offence and revenge. The principle that 'evil may be repaid by evil until balance is restored' belongs to this category. This principle works in both directions inasmuch as it can serve both to justify revenge and to restrict it. As formulated here, the principle gives a *right* to revenge ('evil *may* be repaid ...'). But there is also a version which makes it a *duty* to avenge ('evil *must* be repaid ...'). Whichever of these two versions is adhered to, there is the inherent limitation that only *evils* may or must be repaid and that revenge must not exceed that which is necessary to restore moral balance. The importance attached to the different aspects of the principle will vary. In other respects as well, this principle – like the other principles of justice – is characterized by vagueness and elasticity. There is room for many different conceptions of what constitutes 'evil' and what makes balance. And the area of application in which the principle is allowed is indeterminate.

It can happen that ideas of balance between offence and revenge (or punishment) are specified in more detail as, for instance, in the talionic principle of the Mosaic Commandment 'An eye for an eye and a tooth for a tooth.' [14] Such specification sometimes occurs in application of the general principle of justice and sometimes in independent specific rules (cf. chap. 2, section IV). The relationship between the general principle of justice and specific rules is, by and large, the same here as in the case of exchange (cf. chap. 4, section IV).

The conditions favouring the formation of norms, however, are not the same in the case of revenge as in exchange. Norms which limit the use of revenge do not have the same basis in the common interests of parties as do norms of exchange. To be sure, parties may have a common interest in avoiding future reciprocation of evils, but in the actual

---

13. An example is found in Njál's saga (Bayerschmidt and Hollander, 1955, p. 331) when Njál's relatives Kári and Thorgeir found eight of the men responsible for the fire asleep. Thorgeir asked : 'Would you wish us to wake them ?' and Kári answered : 'You ask as though you had not already made up your mind not to attack men in their sleep and thus commit shameful manslaughter.' Thereupon they shouted at the men and did not attack them before they were armed.
14. Cf. Exodus 22, 23 et seq., Leviticus 24, 17-22 and Deuteronomy 19, 19-21.

revenge situation their interests are diametrically opposed. The effectiveness of revenge norms is therefore dependent to a higher degree than is the case with exchange norms on social pressure or on organized enforcement. Moreover, the effectiveness of normative regulation is reduced because revenge is often taken in a disturbed state of mind and releases emotions in the person who is hurt.

One side of the question of the effectiveness of norms is their impact on potential avengers. Do the norms make potential avengers restrain themselves more than they would otherwise ? Another important aspect is the influence norms may have on other people. For example, will an act of revenge more easily be accepted as justified redress and not give rise to counter-revenge when it falls within what the norms permit than when it is prohibited ? The answers to these two questions are not always the same. It may well be, for example, that norms discourage the avenger from acting unless he has sufficient grounds and discourage him from going too far but that, even so, those on whom the revenge is inflicted do not accept it as justifiable.

It is seldom that revenge is accepted by the victim, but this does happen. Even in societies where escalation of revenge and counter-revenge is common, there are situations where revenge does not incite a counter-action – even when the victim or his relatives are strong enough to retaliate.[15] It is difficult to find an explanation for this other than that the revenge is considered justifiable – either by the victim himself or by so many people in his environment that he is forced to consent.

IV. SPECIAL TECHNIQUES WHICH CAN HELP HINDER OR RESTRICT THE USE OF REVENGE

The limited effectiveness of norms creates a need for special techniques through which revenge activities can be controlled. Such a technique for the handling of a particular problem case is sometimes invented and applied *ad hoc*. But in some cultures there are also institutionalized revenge-preventing devices. It seems natural to distinguish between norms governing the use of such special techniques and those previously mentioned which directly deal with the right to take revenge.

One such technique consists of arranging some form of contest (a physical or verbal fight or duel) where the exchange of blows or offen-

15. Examples are found in Hoebel (1954) pp. 195-196 and p. 204 (Trobrianders) and p. 299 (Caribs) and Fock p. 350 (Mataco-Indians).

ces is regulated by rules. These formalized hostilities give the parties involved an opportunity to demonstrate that they possess those fighting characteristics which are idealized in their society (e.g. courage and bravery). And they can demonstrate this in a manner which is particularly conspicuous – but often much less devastating than uncontrolled revenge. Damage is likely to be less, partly because the actual struggle is subject to control and partly because the risk of counter-revenge and escalation of the conflict is reduced. The outcome is often looked upon as final (e.g. a divine judgment) and not only the winner but also often the loser gains honour from having participated.[16]

Another technique is to leave the taking of revenge to a person other than the one who has suffered. This is certainly not always a suitable way of restricting revenge. Sometimes it has the exact opposite purpose and effect – as, for instance, when a small boy asks his big brother to beat up another boy who has been nasty to him. But in many cases the fact that a third party takes over (on his own initiative or at the request of the offended person or his relatives) makes for moderation and helps prevent counter-actions. This may be because the third person is – or at any rate seems to be – more impartial than the offended person and that there is therefore a better chance of the action being accepted. Or it can be that the third person – alone or in alliance with the offended person – is so powerful that the other party does not dare to put up any opposition. There can also be other reasons why the intervention of a third person helps avert counter-action, for example that he is a close relative of the man on whom the revenge is to be wrought. *Knud Rasmussen* (1927 pp. 174-75) tells of such a case which occurred in an Eskimo community in northern Canada in 1921 : a man of violent and difficult nature had behaved aggressively and threateningly on several occasions. He had killed one of his neighbours and had hurt many others. Since no one felt safe while he was around it was decided that he must die. The neighbours went to his brother, who was the senior member of the family and a highly respected man, and asked him to execute the 'judgment', to which he unwillingly agreed because he considered it his duty. Since he was both a powerful man and the brother of the murderer there was a double guarantee that the execution would not lead to a blood feud.

It is not always possible to get a third person to take over retribution

16. Cf. Langholm (1965) about French duels in the 16th century. Cf. also Hoebel (1954) p. 92 et seq. and p. 307 et seq., Galtung (1965) and Westermarck I (1906) pp. 497-310.

and to have the offended person assent to this. Usually the latter will prefer to take revenge himself. And it may involve the third man both in unpleasantness and risk if he intervenes. If, even so, he does take action he can have widely varied motives for doing this. One possible reason can be that he identifies with the offended person and is annoyed by the aggression to which the latter has been exposed. In such instances retribution keeps its character of revenge even though a third man has set it in motion. But his intervention will be of little help in restricting or terminating the conflict – unless he and the offended party together represent such power that the other party, for this reason, capitulates. Another possibility is that the third person intervenes because he is interested in making peace or in preventing future offences. This is most likely when the third party has authority over the other two and feels responsible for them. For instance, one of the parents interposes himself between quarrelling children and says, for example: 'I agree with you John that what Peter did was wrong. But I shall not allow you to take revenge. I shall deal with him instead.' It might also be that a third person who has no authority over the parties involved intervenes for similar reasons. The intervention can, in this case, lose the character of personal requital which it must have if it is to be termed 'revenge' (cf. section I). Instead it becomes *punishment* – or perhaps a competitive action.

The different forms of punishment and the conditions required before systems of punishment can become institutionalized, will be discussed in some detail in the next chapter. What we are interested in in this connection is only that punishment can sometimes serve to hinder revenge. It may be that the offended person is immediately satisfied when he sees that his counterpart is punished for what he has done. Or it may be that he has been persuaded not to take revenge or has been forbidden to do so and that the punishment makes it easier for him to accept this.

Restitution can also be an alternative to revenge. As already mentioned, an element of restitution can sometimes lie in the fact that the other party is punished, since it gives the offended party some satisfaction. But more straightforward kinds of restitution may also be relevant, for instance the repair of damage which has been done, compensation in the form of money or other values, the return of objects which have been taken, the retraction of accusations or slander, etc. Revenge may be avoided because the person who has done the wrong himself takes the initiative to make redress or because pressure is brought to bear on him to do this. This pressure may come from the offended party

162

or someone who supports him or it may come from the offender's own circle of acquaintances. As mentioned in chapter 5, section III, the fear of revenge is a factor which can be a motive both for offering restitution and for making other people do so. In the long run this can contribute to establishing and strengthening norms and institutions of restitution.

In cultures which lack an organized coercive power, the building up of restitutional systems is often one of the most important steps in the struggle to restrict the use of revenge. In many instances an active and well-planned initiative comes from relatives, friends or neighbours of the parties involved persuading the latter to achieve some settlement by compensation. There are many examples of this in *Hoebel's* (1954) survey of primitive law. Sometimes the settlements are rather dramatic since the threat of a bloody revenge hangs in the air and nobody knows what the outcome will be before the arrangement is concluded. The following account of a settlement by restitution of a murder case in an Indian tribe on the northwest coast of America can serve as an example:

'The Gilutsa'u spokesman called for the compensation gifts, which were brought forward by the maternal uncle of the murderer and placed before the envoy. The latter arose, holding the eagle tail feather over his breast. He looked neither to right nor left, for to have done so would have indicated that he intended to kill for revenge. The tension was very great since the slightest move on his part could have precipitated general bloodshed. While the gifts were being brought in the relatives of the deceased sang one of their mourning songs. When the amount in front of the envoy satisfied him and his clan relatives he sat down. If they had not received sufficient gifts they would have walked out without a word and the negotiations would have had to be continued by the Gilutsa'u the next day. When the amount was paid there was a general entertainment of songs and dramatizations, ending with a feast.'[17]

Accounts given in Njál's saga from Icelandic society of about AD 1000 are also illustrative. This was a society where the tendency to glorify revenge was in constant conflict with attempts to restrict it. There are examples here not only of men who were goaded on to take revenge by their wives, parents or others, and scorned if they did not do so, but also examples where relatives and friends tried to restrain the avenger and to mediate between him and his counterpart in order to reach a settlement. Physical strength, bravery and contempt for death were not the only features which were highly valued. A man could also win respect by showing restraint and moderation in a tense situation or by showing

---

17. Viola Garfield, Tsimshian Clan and Society (University of Washington Publications in Anthropology, Vol. 7 1939) pp. 259-260 (here cited from Hoebel, 1954, pp. 315-16).

skill in negotiation when peace had to be made between disputing parties. The usual way of preventing or stopping acts of revenge was to reach settlement by restitution. Occasionally the parties came to an agreement of their own accord, but usually other people acted as go-betweens. There were both informal mediation and institutionalized forms of legal proceedings and arbitration. The lack of an organized enforcing power made it difficult to get decisions respected and those who acted as mediators or judges in a conflict frequently showed great ingenuity in reaching a result which both parties could accept. At the Assembly where a conflict was to be resolved money was sometimes collected from the people present in order to sufficiently compensate the offended party without putting too much pressure on the offender. The atmosphere at an Assembly when a solution to a difficult affair was being sought was often very tense. Whether a settlement was reached or whether hostilities would break loose often hung by a thread.[18]

When a settlement is arrived at this means, in many cases, that an *exchange* takes place. One party, for instance, surrenders his supposed right to take revenge in return for payment in the form of material values, apologies, guarantees that he will be allowed to live in peace, etc. Sometimes an exchange can include settlement of several mutual offences which are weighed against each other. If the offences have not been equally bad there may also be a question of reinstating balance. We can find examples both from the saga times in Iceland and from other places [19] of conflicts which are solved in this manner. In Njál's saga there are several such settlements as, for instance, the example below (where murder, physical injury, assault, extra-marital pregnancy and illegal felling of timber were weighed against each other) :

18. Cf. e.g. the account in Njál's saga (Bayerschmidt and Hollander, 1955, p. 249 et seq.) of attempts to reach a settlement when Njál's sons had killed Hoskuld Hvitanessgodi. After both parties had been persuaded to accept a settlement and a sum had been fixed in compensation and was ready to be handed over because the arbitrators and many other people had contributed money, everything was spoilt at the last moment. Njál's son Skarphedin and the spokesman for the other side, Flosí, were unable to restrain themselves from exchanging defamatory remarks. The result was that Flosí withdrew from the settlement and took revenge by burning Njál and his family to death in their house, which in turn lead to counter-actions that cost many lives. Njál's son-in-law Kárí did not rest until he had killed 15 of the people who had caused the fire. Two of these – who had fled the country – he followed to the Orkneys and to England in order to be fully revenged.
19. For instance in Sardinia, cf. Bentzon (1967) p. 5.

'After that Hjalti negotiated with Gunnar's adversaries and brought about a settlement. Each side gave a pledge of peace to the other. Thorgeir's wound was offset by the suit for seduction, and Starkad's wound was cancelled out by his cutting wood on Njál's property. Thorgeir's brothers were atoned for with half penalties ; the other half was forfeited because of their attack on Gunnar. Egil's slaying and Tyrfing's suit likewise offset each other. Hjort's slaying was compensated by the slaying of Kol and the Norwegian, and all the others were atoned for with half fines.' (Bayerschmidt and Hollander, p. 143.)

In what has been said above I have several times mentioned that a *third party* [20] frequently plays an active role in efforts to avoid or to limit acts of revenge. There are several types of third party activity. One type consists of pressure brought to bear on the parties by their milieu in order to get them to show indulgence or moderation. A second type is that of representation where the third party acts on behalf of one of the conflicting parties, for instance by avenging him, speaking for him during negotiations, delivering the gifts which are to assuage the other side, etc. And finally we have various kinds of intermediary activity where the third party mediates between the conflicting parties or decides how the conflict is to be resolved.

Third party intervention can be spontaneous. For instance, when two children come into conflict with one another other members of the play group might get involved as spokesmen for one or the other party or as mediators. But third party intervention can also be institutionalized. In different cultures there are a variety of institutions for representation, mediation, arbitration and adjudication, etc. I will not discuss here the various types in existence nor which factors lead to their development.[21] For our purposes it is sufficient to point out that the growth of such institutions is an important step in the endeavour to control peoples' inclination to hurt each other.

Third party institutions can be engaged in many kinds of conflict other than those we are concerned with in this section. In exchange relationships, for instance, disputes over terms and over rights and obligations can be resolved in this manner. But normally the need to engage a third party to help find a solution is not so great when benefits are exchanged as when injuries are reciprocated. This is partly because – for reasons which have already been mentioned – it is usually easier to reach a compromise when benefits are exchanged. Markets can also develop for such exchange – markets work as a kind of impersonal 'third

20. I use the expression 'third party' as a common designation for anyone who is not one of the parties directly involved.
21. Cf. Aubert (1963), Galtung (1965) and Eckhoff (1966, 2).

party' determining which terms are to be followed – thus making it unnecessary for anyone else to intervene. As already pointed out there is no such possibility when injuries are reciprocated; in addition to this comes the escalation and increased violence which makes revenge and counter-revenge particularly dangerous both for the involved parties and their milieus.

Finally, a few words should be said on the significance of agreements and organizations in revenge.

The use of *agreements* can, in certain cases, extend the scope of revenge, for example when friends or allies commit themselves to mutual assistance. On the other hand, agreements are frequently the means of bringing about arrangements which help to regulate, restrict or stop the use of revenge. For instance, the formalization of revenge which takes place in duels is often based on agreement between the parties involved. The same applies to compromises, reached with or without the cooperation of a third party. Generally speaking, the better established the principle that a promise be kept, the easier it is to introduce arrangements preventing revenge and the more likely it will be that these are respected. When agreements can be relied upon, this makes for means of resolving conflicts. A promise that restitution will be made when sufficient capital has been collected or a promise that in future peace will be kept, are examples of provisions which can secure a settlement if, and only if, there is a basis for trust or possibilities of enforcing the claims.

The chances of regulating and restricting revenge are certainly best when *organizations* having a sufficiently effective power apparatus (e.g. national states) exist. Agencies for law making, law enforcement and adjudication can then be established which, by direct prohibition, by offering alternatives (punishment and restitution) and providing for peaceful conflict resolution, in part can counteract offences leading to acts of revenge and also restrain the urge to avenge. This organizational development can also contribute to changing living conditions within the society concerned so that there is no longer any basis for idealizing character traits which make for vindictiveness, e.g. aggressiveness and the urge for self assertion. But on the other hand organizational development can provide a source for new types of conflict, for instance conflicts between states or other organizations. As a consequence of this there may be acts of revenge which are far more destructive than those any individual person could originate.

7. Punishment

'Es gehört zu den Merkwürdigkeiten
in der Geschichte unseres Denkens,
dass die Menschen immer, soweit wir
zurücksehen können, Verbrechen be-
straft haben und dass sie dabei doch,
soweit wir zurücksehen können, dar-
über streiten, wozu sie es eigentlich
tun.'
Franz Exner, *Gerechtigkeit und Richteramt*, p. 6.

I. INTRODUCTION

I will say that 'A punishes B' if, and only if, the following conditions
are fulfilled :
1. A inflicts harm on B
2. as an expression of his disapproval of something B has done
3. intending that B shall perceive it as harm and
4. without the act having the character of personal requital.
This definition serves to separate 'punishment' from 'revenge', 'competition' and 'restitution'. But as mentioned in Chapter 6, Section I, there
are several borderline cases and on occasions one and the same transfer
can be both punishment and something else. Combinations of punishment and restitution and of punishment and revenge often occur in
practice.

Apart from this it can be difficult to judge whether something is
'punishment' in the sense given above since the definition refers to
psychological factors which are not always easy to discern. These difficulties are accentuated when a person who has injured other people
tries to make his motives appear more creditable than they really are.
For example, when he pretends that his revenge is punishment or that
his punishment is therapy.

Punishment can be an isolated event as when, for instance, a man
sees some boys doing something wrong and punishes them for this. But
the tendency to use punishment (or threats of punishment) is more
prominent in enduring interaction relationships, inter alia because interest in – and the possibility of – influencing the other party is then

normally greatest. The desire to influence may come from a concern to improve the other party, as for instance when parents and teachers punish children. Or it may be due to a wish to protect values which the other party intends to violate. For example, a man threatens the neighbours' children with reprisal if they steal his apples. Combinations of these motives are also very common.

If the punishment is to succeed in its intentions, it must be possible to inflict harm with some degree of regularity and without any great risk of the harm being reciprocated. For these reasons, the conditions most favourable to the use of punishment are normally those where the punisher is considerably stronger than the other party. For instance, punishment is frequently applied by the state to its citizens, by parents and teachers to their children, by elder brothers and sisters or playmates to the younger, by the staff of a prison to the inmates, by superiors to their inferiors, and by collective groups to the individual. Of course a person of equal standing or an inferior also has some opportunity to employ punishment in an interaction situation since there may be reactions against which the other party finds it difficult to safeguard himself, for instance ridicule and expressions of disapproval. But, as a rule, the possibilities of inflicting punishment are greater the stronger the position of the punisher in relation to his counterpart.

There are often other means than punishment available for influencing a person. For example, desired behaviour can be rewarded instead of (or in addition to) punishing the undesirable.[1] The use of punishment and reward for the purpose of exerting influence have in common that they are both intended to have an effect on the *strategies* of the other party. Positive consequences are attached to the desired manner of behaviour or negative to the undesired, so that it may become good strategy for the other party to conform to what is expected of him. However, strategy can also be affected by information. Parents who do not want their children to smoke can, for instance – in addition to punishing smoking and rewarding non-smoking – try to convince their children that tobacco is bad for their health. Information which is given in an attempt to influence may be true or false and the influencer may believe in it or not. To make somebody believe that he will be punished (or rewarded) by a supernatural power, is, for instance, a method of exerting influence which is frequently used.

Strategies which are regularly adhered to can, as elaborated in Chapters 1 and 4, be transformed into new *norms*. To begin or strengthen

1. Cf. chap. 4, section IX on rewards.

168

such internalization processes is often the long term purpose of punishing. In such cases it is usual for the threat of punishment to be combined with verbal inculcation of the norm to be taught. Sometimes the person who seeks to influence also utilizes norms which the other party has already accepted. He may try to persuade him that the situation is covered by such a norm by influencing his interpretation of the norm or his perception of the facts. With a child who has accepted the norm that it is right to do as his friends do, information as to how his friends, in fact, behave can be a suitable means of exerting influence.

Whether it is good strategy to employ punishment and when and how this should be done, depends upon many different factors. The effectiveness of punishment as a means of exerting influence must be taken into account and the expected benefits must be compared with the costs involved in the use of punishment. In addition, it is relevant to ask whether similar results can be better or more cheaply arrived at by other means, for instance through rewards, information or normative arguments. All these questions are difficult to answer since one seldom has any basis for reliable cost-benefit calculation. Punishment is not like exchange where profitability can easily be ascertained by comparing the values of what is received and what given. What one may achieve by punishing somebody is something more remote and uncertain than a counter-service, namely that the behaviour of the person punished (or someone else's) is altered in a desired direction. Success is, as a rule, not immediately ascertainable because it normally takes time to change a person's behaviour. Even when sufficient time has passed it may be difficult to judge whether the changed behaviour of an individual is due to the punishment he has received or to something else. And in cases where it can be assumed that punishment has had some influence, there is frequently no definite basis for ascertaining whether more or less would have been achieved via other means of influence.[2]

The situation becomes even more complicated when considerations other than those of exerting influence are taken into account. Among other things, problems connected with punishment may be linked to

2. Some research has been done on the efficacy of the different means of influencing. Among other things the psychological effects of punishment and reward have been studied, cf. Berelson and Steiner (1964) pp. 72-73 and 140 ff. But the research results can at present provide only modest advice in practical situations.

A point of some importance, however, is that systems of punishment assume *surveillance* and may therefore involve greater costs than reward systems which afford the other party motives for themselves giving proof of their behaviour, cf. Thibaut and Kelley (1959) pp. 242-243.

questions concerning other kinds of reciprocation. For instance, if there is an exchange relationship between the parties, the one who is considering punishing the other must take into account the consequences this can have for future exchange between them. Another kind of situation presenting special problems is where both punishment of the offender and claims for compensation can be resorted to. These can sometimes be combined if a transfer from A to B inflicts harm on A while at the same time compensating B. When it has to be decided whether the reactions should be combined in this way or whether they should be kept separate and perhaps one of the alternatives waived, thought must be given both to the influence that will be exerted on the other party and to the advantage of receiving restitution. The fact that offences may be avenged, must also be remembered. When the offender is punished by the State this can serve as a revenge substitute for the offended person and make it easier to dissuade him from avenging himself. This might make punishment strategically justifiable even when the influence it has on the offender is negligible.

The main purpose of this chapter is to examine different types of norms (including the principle of justice) which regulate the use of punishment. The various strategic considerations mentioned above will only be discussed in more detail to the extent that they are assumed to affect the formation of norms. However, before discussing individual types of norms, I would like to look more closely at certain strategic considerations connected with what I shall call 'questions of acceptance'. These are relevant to much of what will later be discussed.

II. ACCEPTANCE OF PUNISHMENT

When I say that a person 'accepts' a punishment (inflicted on himself or another) I mean that (1) he perceives that the evil is intended as punishment and (2) he considers it to be justified. He agrees, in other words, that something wrong has been done which the punisher has reason to react against in the manner and to the extent which he does. Acceptance can be more or less wholehearted. For instance, it may be agreed that there is reason to punish but objections may be raised over the severity of the punishment or over it being carried out by someone who is not entitled to do so.

For many reasons it can be important to the punisher that his action is accepted.

Because he hurts someone, he will frequently need to defend his

170

action both to himself and others. One should not harm another person without having good reason to do so. When the injury is a punishment which, for instance, serves the purpose of improving the person punished, this may be sufficient justification. But sometimes it is doubtful whether or not the injury has this characteristic. And the punisher sometimes needs the support he can get from those accepting his action as protection against guiltfeelings and criticism.

In addition, acceptance may facilitate the infliction of punishment and reduce the risk of counter-action. If the guilty party himself understands that he has done something wrong for which he deserves to be punished, it is possible that he will cooperate actively by admitting what he has done and voluntarily undergoing punishment. And even if he does not go this far, his inclination to resist and to seek revenge will at any rate be less than it would otherwise have been. Other people's acceptance of the punishment can also be of practical value to the punisher. For example, it may make it easier for him to find out who is guilty, to get hold of this person and to punish him, and to find protection if the guilty party later threatens revenge, etc.

Acceptance can also help increase the effect of punishment. If one manages to convince those whom one is hoping to influence that certain actions are wrong and deserve to be punished, it may be possible to activate them to fight against their own and other people's tendencies to behave in this manner. Offences in such cases have a tendency to release both feelings of guilt within the actor and criticism from other people, so that a self-propelling system of additional punishment comes into operation. These effects are especially tied to acceptance of the idea that the offender's action is wrong. But acceptance of the punishment as being justified is also significant. For instance, a man who acknowledges that his own behaviour was bad but believes that he was punished too severely, frequently becomes so engrossed in reproaching the punisher that he forgets to reproach himself.

Although acceptance is important, it is not a *necessary* condition for effective punishment. For example, punishment can be used to influence the behaviour of animals and babies with whom one cannot verbally communicate. In such instances – at least for the first few times the undesirable action is punished – it is not possible to achieve acceptance by the punished party. There are also many examples of terror regimes kept in power by the aid of punishments which only a very small minority of the population accept. But these punishments must be strict if they are to be successful, and a well-developed apparatus of control and enforcement is necessary. Both the cost and the risk become greater for the punisher if his punishment is not accepted. In enduring and varied interaction relationships as, for instance, between parents and children, teacher and pupils, employer and employees, state and citizen, etc., it is particularly risky to use punishment which is unaccepted. This can hinder or render more difficult the exchange of positive values between the parties concerned, and in other ways be a burden on their relationship. On the other hand, it may be difficult for the punisher to obtain acceptance, and his freedom of action would be considerably curtailed if he only used punishment when it was accepted by the person he wished to influence.

I will now discuss what *gives rise to* acceptance. As already pointed out, acceptance implies that the action which is punished is regarded as wrong and deserving of punishment. In addition, the punisher must be considered the right person to react and the punishment itself must be considered proper. Although there are connections between these three conditions, they are treated separately in what follows.

Negative attitudes to certain *actions* may have formed without any person having systematically tried to influence attitudes in that direction. They can have evolved, for instance, from one's own experience that the actions are damaging or they may be rooted in the processes of norm formation which were earlier discussed (see especially chap. 4). But often the party wanting to exert influence must actively encourage the creation or strengthening of negative attitudes vis-à-vis the punished actions if he is to get the punishment accepted. In other words, he must combine the punishment with other means of exerting influence. This becomes more essential the greater the changes he wishes to provoke in existing attitudes and behaviour.

If the persons to be influenced regard him as an authority who has a right to direct them, it may be enough that he forbid the actions. Mother or father can say, for instance, 'you are not allowed to do this' to their children. If something is evaluated as 'bad' or 'wrong' or 'not done' this can also have an impact if the evaluation comes from someone who is regarded as an expert on what is good and bad. The effect of such a statement can be strengthened when reasons are given in support of it. It may be pointed out, for instance, that the consequences can be damaging and reference will perhaps be made to experience which the person to be influenced has himself had. Or the action is classed with actions which the person concerned already regards as wrong. For example, mother says to Peter, 'You mustn't say 'damn' because it's a bad word'. If the person who is exerting influence himself desists from the behaviour he characterizes as wrong, this will also

172

contribute to strengthening his position. At any rate some explanation or other is frequently required if the influencing party himself does what he has forbidden others to do, e.g., an argument such as 'grown-ups can do this, but not children' or 'this is something the state has a right to, but not the ordinary citizen'.

If bad behaviour and punishment often go together, the fact that an action is punished will readily be taken as a sign that it was wrong.[3] Punishers often try to establish this idea. This is partly done verbally, for instance by letting it be known when one punishes that one is doing so because of this or that bad behaviour,[4] and partly through consistency in punishing. When a person gets the impression that bad behaviour, and only this, is punished, he is inclined to draw inferences from the practice of punishing to the character of the punished behaviour. For instance, if a person knows that other people have regularly been punished for certain actions, he will more easily accept that he himself be punished if he behaves in the same way – not only because a common fate is comforting but also because the punishment the others receive indicates that the action is wrong. Conversely, a break in regularity can hinder acceptance. For example, a man who is punished for something he himself and other people have done many times before without being punished, will often feel that he has been wrongly treated.

Even if an action is considered wrong objections may be raised to punishment on the basis that the offender was not *warned* that the action was punishable (cf. p. 74). And a warning is often not considered sufficient unless the offender had the possibility of taking it into account, so that one can say that he himself took the risk. This presupposes, among other things, that the offence was a voluntary action – and not, for example, an accident or something he was forced to.

The warning may have been directed to the individual actor or it can be a general rule with which he has had the opportunity of becoming acquainted. The fact that other people have earlier been punished for the same type of action can also serve as an independent (or supplementary) warning. Verbal threats of punishment and regularity in the practice of punishing can therefore be of significance to acceptance in two different ways. They can, as mentioned above, strengthen the belief that the action concerned is wrong and, in addition, they can serve as a warning that the action will be punished.

3. For such ideas with children, see Kohlberg (1963 and 1964) with references.
4. See chap. 4, section IX for corresponding tendencies with regard to rewards.

Although it may be acknowledged that an action deserves punishment, it is usually not accepted that any person whosoever may *inflict the punishment*. Sometimes the circle of legitimate punishers may be very wide as, for instance, when small informal punishments are involved (reproaches, indulgent smiles, wrinkling of one's nose, etc.). But even such reactions are often only accepted when they come from someone acquainted with the person concerned and not when they come from a stranger. Occasionally the circle is limited to those who belong to the same primary group as the offender (e.g. the same gang of boys) or who share some activity with him (e.g. play, gambling or the execution of a job). It may be accepted, for example, that one's co-players react when the rules of the game are broken but not that an outsider should do so. It is probably the common interest they share in ensuring that norms are kept which constitutes the most important basis of legitimacy in these cases. Usually only the participants, and not the spectators, have sufficiently legitimate interests in enforcing such rules. In addition, exchange considerations may apply. Those who constitute a group or participate in some joint activity may feel that there should be some reciprocity : 'If I punish you now and again, you must be allowed to punish me'. To the marginal members of a group, the fact that they are allowed to participate may also be a benefit for which they pay by accepting punishment from those with a stronger position in the group.

In many instances the circle is further limited so that only one or a few authorities are considered entitled to punish, for example parents, teachers, the boss or the state. There are a variety of reasons why such authorities should have a special position as administers of correction. In the first place they have the means of power (physical strength, economic resources, organizational apparatus etc.) which increase their ability to punish and reduce the danger of counter-action. In the second place, they also often have a particular interest in exercising influence and feel responsible for doing this. Acceptance of the punishment they mete out is probably promoted by both these factors. Power can serve as a means of creating legitimacy because the powerful person has the possibility of teaching his dependants that he has the right to decide and the right to chastize those who disregard his decisions. And this right is more easily accepted when he has an obvious interest in using his power. The wider the sphere of interests and responsibilities the more extensive is the legitimate authority to punish likely to be. For instance, parents are normally considered to have a much more extensive authority to punish their children than are teachers. Parents can interfere in almost anything that a child does, but if a teacher should punish a child for something he has done away from school and which has no normal connection with school both the child himself and other people will usually react to this.

Exchange considerations can be relevant in this kind of situation too. There is not ordinarily any mutual right of punishment as in the instances mentioned above. But there may be asymmetrical exchanges in which the right of one party (the superior) to punish is compensated for by other kinds of values he offers. The subordinate employee, for instance, must expect to be corrected when he makes a mistake but, in return, he will perhaps get training and advice and be relieved of responsibility. In a similar manner, protection which the state affords its citizens can be regarded as a counter-service for the punishment they must accept if they break the law. Because of the exchange viewpoint the tendency to accept punishment is weakened when subordinates do not consider they get any return for submitting to authority.

The power to decide over others (e.g. to forbid certain actions) and the power to punish those who break rules are often vested in the same person, but this is not always the case. In most national states, for example, the powers are divided between legislators and judges. A similar separation of power is to be found in many other organizations. For reasons to which we shall later return, this may in some instances facilitate acceptance.

One feature of *punishment* which can obviously affect acceptance is the amount of harm inflicted. Presumably, the lighter the punishment the easier it is for the offender to accept it. But other people may take a different attitude. Whether they are most disposed to accept lenient or severe punishment can, for one thing, depend on whether they are inclined to regard themselves as being exposed to the risk of being punished or protected by the rules which are enforced by punishment.

Other characteristics of punishment which can affect acceptance are discussed very thoroughly by *Piaget* (1932) in his investigation of children's conceptions of justice. He differentiates between what he calls 'punishment by reciprocity' and 'expiatory punishment'. He believes that the former can be accepted even when it is exchanged between individuals of equal standing, for instance between children in connection with their play. Expiatory punishment, on the other hand, has its bases in authority relationships and is only accepted where there is sufficient respect for the punishing authority.

Piaget's concept of punishment by reciprocity covers, in the first place, cases where someone is excluded from an activity because he has not done what is required of him in connection with this activity. A child, for instance, is barred from a game as punishment for having cheated. Or a child is lent a book by his father on condition that he is careful with it, and the father punishes the child by taking the book back when he discovers that it has been scribbled in. Refusal to share one's meal with someone who has not been willing to fetch it, and refusal to trust a person who has lied are other examples.[5] All these cases can be conceived as instances of exchange where one party has fallen short and is therefore met with the reaction, 'when you don't do your share, I (we) won't do mine (ours)'. Even if such exchange considerations alone are not sufficient to justify the reaction, they can make it easier to accept the reaction as punishment. And punishments of this kind can, for their part, help to establish and reinforce exchange norms. If, however, there is a firmly established notion that certain services are conditional on counter-services, it will no longer be regarded as punishment but as a matter of course that one does not get anything without giving something.

Piaget also includes under the concept 'punishment by reciprocity' cases where the offender is forced to make restitution. For example, someone is forced to give back what he has taken, to repair or replace what he has damaged, ask forgiveness or in some other way make amends to the person he has offended. In such cases there can be an interplay of compensation norms and punishment acceptance. The feeling that some compensation should be made can facilitate acceptance of the idea that, as punishment, the offender be compelled to make reparation. And the punishment can contribute towards stabilization of restitution norms.

Finally, Piaget includes among 'punishment by reciprocity' that penalty which is based on the talionic principle of similarity between the offence and its punishment. As examples he mentions the child who has hit someone and is hit back, and the one who has broken another's toy and has his own toy spoilt. Piaget's reason for assuming that such punishment is easily accepted is that the guilty party is clearly shown why his action was wrong when he receives the same hurt as he himself has inflicted (see loc. cit. pp. 206 and 231). The validity of the assumption seems rather questionable. It may be that talionic punishments, in certain cases, have such an effect, but in general this is rarely so. Anyway, it does not seem natural to class these kinds of punishments with

5. Cf. Piaget's questionnaire pp. 200-202, comments p. 203 and examples pp. 205-206.

those referred to above, which find support in conceptions of exchange and restitution.

By 'expiatory punishment' Piaget refers to the kinds of punishment which *do not have* any of the above-mentioned characteristics. He assumes that expiatory punishment (in contrast to punishment by reciprocity) is accepted only when it is inflicted by an authority. One of his investigations of children's moral development is based on this assumption. In interviews with children (from 6 to 12 years old) he told them a series of fictitious stories about bad things children had done and mentioned various alternative punishments (loc. cit. pp. 199 ff.). They were asked, among other things, which of these punishments they considered most just. The youngest children (6-7 years) tended to advocate expiatory punishments – some of which were very severe. Those in the middle age group (8-10 years) were more inclined to adhere to punishment by reciprocity, and with the oldest (11-12 years) the inclination was clearly in this direction (loc. cit. table p. 208). No statistical analysis is given of the distribution of preferences for the different types of punishments by reciprocity (refusal to participate in exchange, enforced restitution and talionic punishment), but from what Piaget writes (e.g. pp. 215-216) it seems that the talionic principle was most popular in the middle age group (8-10 years). There were also many among the oldest who kept to this but the trend here went more strongly in the direction of other kinds of punishment by reciprocity. Piaget's explanation of these differences between age groups is that children, as they grow older, free themselves from adult authority and become more imbued with such moral conceptions as are developed through mutual contact between individuals of equal status.[6]

The reason why I have treated questions concerning acceptance of punishment at such length is that I consider them to be of primary significance in the formation of norms. Acceptance can serve as a basis for *normative legitimation* of punishment as well as for norms which *restrict the right* to punish. As already mentioned, it may be good strategy for the person who tries to exert influence through punishment, to keep his punishing within bounds so that it will be accepted – at least to a certain extent – by the persons punished and/or by others. And even if strategic considerations alone are not sufficient to make the

6. Other psychologists who have re-examined Piaget's theories have found similar age differences but are not inclined to accept his explanation of the causes, see Johnson (1962) and the survey in Kohlberg (1964) p. 394 et seq. with references.

punisher restrain himself, they can make him more susceptible to pressure in this direction so that he gradually internalizes norms which restrict his right to punish. In the following section a survey is given of various types of norms regulating the use of punishment and of factors promoting the growth of such norms.

III. DIFFERENT TYPES OF NORMS REGULATING THE USE OF PUNISHMENT

I will first discuss norms giving someone a *right* or an *obligation* to punish. Such rights and obligations are often assigned to persons (or organizations) having authority over others. For example, it is frequently believed that parents have both a right and a duty to punish their children, and that the state should ensure that criminals are corrected. In the case of parents and other people considered responsible for the upbringing or education of children, this duty is often justified by saying that, in the long run, it is in their own interest to be punished : 'spare the rod and spoil the child'. In other cases, for instance as regards the state's duty to punish, consideration for the victim or for others exposed to offences is often given as a rationale for punishment. An extreme version of this point of view is found in *Kant's* theory of criminal law. Kant even went so far as to contend that the state had no moral right to pardon a criminal in cases involving crimes of the subjects against one another 'for exemption from punishment ... in such cases means doing the greatest injustice to the subjects' (Reiss, 1970, p. 160).

Several factors can promote the development of such norms. The victim's urge for revenge and the desire for protection experienced by those who feel their interests threatened can converge towards the idea that offenders ought to be punished. And the punisher will often be disposed to conceive himself as duty-bound to punish. He needs a justification for inflicting harm and what else he may have in the way of defence is not always sufficient. That his intentions are good – e.g., improvement of the person who is punished – is of some help but is not enough if there is any doubt as to whether punishment is the best means of achieving this end. It is simpler to keep to what other people say one *should do*. And an obligation to do something affords better justification than the privilege of doing it, because the person who is under an obligation has no choice. The need to be able to justify one's actions is not always equally strong. Other things being equal, the need probably increases with the severity of the punishment and with the degree of sympathy the punisher feels for the punished. This perhaps helps ex-

178

plain why the tendency to feel obliged to punish is particularly strong in national states and in the family.

It can happen that a person who believes he has done something wrong, inflicts an evil *on himself* for this reason, e.g., that he commits suicide, joins the Foreign Legion, enters a monastery or torments himself with self-reproach, etc. Such behaviour can have different motivations. Sometimes the idea is to avoid some other evil which appears to be even worse than what he inflicts upon himself. In other instances it may be his feelings of guilt and shame which find spontaneous expression in the action. In such cases one sometimes says that the person concerned is 'punishing himself'. However, this situation does not fall within the definition given of 'punishment' since only one person is involved. And these actions are seldom regulated by social norms.

What happens more frequently is that the guilty person is considered as being under an obligation to *cooperate* in some way or other when other people initiate corrective measures, for example by draining the poison-cup, paying the fine, going to the headmaster's study, or by letting down his trousers for a whipping. In such cases the duty is often imposed by some authority, for instance by a judge, legislator, teacher or father. The more readily the punishment is accepted, the easier it is to have such requirements accepted and adhered to, and the smaller will be the costs to the punisher. But it is not a necessary condition for acceptance of these obligations that the punishment also be accepted. If the authority's right to decide is sufficiently well established, it may be thought correct to cooperate when commanded, even though one may feel that the punishment is unreasonable or unfair. Loyalty towards the ideology or political system which the authority represents strengthens the tendency to respect its directives and can perhaps lead to active cooperation in excess of what is actually demanded. It has been claimed, for instance, that confessions made during the Moscow Trials of the 1930's were partly motivated by such feelings of loyalty.

There are several different kinds of norms which *restrict the right to punish :* these can set limits to who has the right to punish, to what types of actions may be punished, what kinds of evils may be used as punishment, the size of the punishment and the procedure to be used when inflicting it.

Some of the norms which restrict *who* has the right to punish are informal and often vague. There may be situations, for example, where a person thinks that punishment would fit but feels that 'I shouldn't get mixed up in this since it doesn't concern me'. If, even so, he does interfere the reaction of the person who is punished can be 'I did something wrong, but *you* have no right to punish me'. Such norms can be based on the tendency referred to above to accept punishment only from people one knows or likes or with whom one is associated in some way or other. Or they may be based on the idea that punishment of that special kind or for that special wrong can only be carried out by a certain authority, for instance by parents or teachers. By definition, power of authorities to punish does not belong to everyone. It is always limited by norms and the limits are usually more clearly defined than in the instances given above.

In national states and other large organizations authority is often formalized through enacted rules determining who can decide what. This both contributes to securing the foundations of authority and to clarifying the delimitations. In many cases there is also some specialization. In the judicial penal system, for example, the legislator, the courts, the prosecution, police and prison authorities each have their own particular function. Specialization means, among other things, that no one has sole responsibility for punishing a person. Persons in authority are therefore less exposed to criticism and self-reproach than they would otherwise be. Specialization thus reduces the cost of punishing. It can also – for reasons to which I will soon return – facilitate acceptance of punishment.

Punishment, as I have defined it, is not necessarily a reaction to norm violation. But it is most used in cases where a norm is infringed. And in some fields there are superior norms limiting the right to punish to cases of norm violation. Earlier, I touched upon some factors which might contribute to the development of such restrictions. In section I of this chapter it was mentioned that the aim of punishment is often to establish or strengthen norms and that punishing for this reason is frequently combined with verbal implantation of the relevant norm. One says, for instance, 'it was wrong of you to behave like that and therefore you must be punished'. When this procedure is followed the person corrected will easily get the impression that punishment is justified *only* for actions which involve breaking norms. The punisher too may be caught up by his own arguments and acquire the same ideas. In addition to this, he may find it advisable to keep within these limits in order to get his punishment accepted (see section II). And strategy which is followed for the sake of acceptance has a tendency to settle into norms.

In many instances there are additional restrictions on the right to punish. It may be required, for example, that the wrong be voluntarily committed and not an accident or an action forced on the wrongdoer,

180

and that the actor be old enough and normal enough to understand that it was wrong. Various other qualifications are also often taken into consideration. Many of these norms can be regarded as manifestations of the tendencies mentioned above to limit punishment to cases where the possibility of influencing the other party and the likelihood of acceptance are greatest.

Not only modifying circumstances connected with the action but also ex post events are sometimes taken into account, for instance in the event that the guilty person shows remorse and tries to improve himself, or makes compensation or wishes to do so. As mentioned in Chapter 5, one way of promoting restitution practices is to exempt persons from punishment if they offer compensation.

The requirement that only violation of norms should be punishable can also be supplemented with additional requirements concerning the rules. For example, it may be claimed that these must be general, that they must be formally enacted by a competent authority, that they must be printed and readily available, that they must have been adopted and preferably also published before the relevant action took place, that they give the information that violation is punishable, etc. Both the U.N. and Council of Europe declarations of human rights[7] make such demands on national penal systems, and in several countries these principles (or some of them) are incorporated in the constitution. Thus, the Norwegian constitution decrees that 'No one can be convicted except according to law' (par. 96) and that 'No law can be given retroactive effect' (par. 97).[8] Similar demands are also sometimes attached to

7. The United Nations' Declaration of Human Rights Art. 11, 2 stipulates, 'No one shall be held guilty of any penal offence on account of any act or omission which did not constitute a penal offence, under national or international law, at the time when it was committed. Nor shall a heavier penalty be imposed than the one that was applicable at the time the penal offence was committed.' Practically identical provisions are found in the International Convention of 1966 on Civil and Political Rights, Art. 15, and in the Council of Europe's Convention on Human Rights, Art. 7.
8. It was during the Age of Enlightenment that principles of this kind came to be accepted in European and American penal law. The French declaration of human rights of 1789 decrees in Art. 8 that : 'Nul ne peut être puni qu'en vertu d'une loi établie et promulgée antérieurement au délit et légalement appliquée'. We find similar resolutions in several of the American human rights declarations and constitutions of the same period. Elaborate argumentation in support of the principles was offered by the German criminologist Anselm von Feuerbach (1775-1833). He formulated the motto 'nullum crimen sine lege nulla poena sine lege poenali', which is frequently quoted, abbreviated as 'nulla poena sine lege'. Cf. Brynolf Honkasalo, Nulla poena sine lege (For-

punishment outside the field of criminal law. *Mathiesen* (1965), for instance, found that attitudes tended in this direction in a prison where he did research. The inmates there felt it was unfair that they should be punished for bad behaviour as long as they had broken no definite regulations (loc. cit., pp. 157-159). And *Selznick* (1969) has found similar attitudes with regard to disciplinary measures in American industry (see p. 113 and pp. 175-76).

When the principles here discussed (or some of them) have become established, they can in several ways increase the possibility of punishment acceptance. Firstly, a special basis is created for regarding actions as wrong when authoritative rules exist which prohibit them and threaten violators with punishment. The tendency to evaluate the actual behaviour negatively is strengthened by the idea that 'the law is the law, and should be kept'. Secondly, rules which threaten punishment and which are publicized in advance, serve as warnings. The person who violates them can be said to have let himself in for something he knew or should have understood would lead to punishment. Thirdly, rules, if they are general, help to maintain conformity with ideals of equality. I will discuss this further in the following chapters where problems of distribution and the tendency to make comparisons are dealt with. And in the fourth place, confidence in a judge's impartiality will be enhanced if he can justify his decisions by referring to general rules (see *Eckhoff* 1965).

Besides it being easier to obtain acceptance of punishment for these reasons, rules can also make it easier *to inflict* punishment. A decision-maker avoids appearing personally responsible for harming another when he is able to show that he is bound by rules.[9]

The norms next to be examined are those restricting the *kinds of punishment* that may be used. Some of these norms set absolute limits: they refer to punishments which – for humanitarian reasons or out of regard for the dignity of man, for example – can under no circumstances be inflicted. What falls in this category is largely culturally determined. Punishments which have been extensively employed in the past and which are still used in some places (for instance, mutilation or torture) are considered absolutely unacceptable to us. On the other hand there

---

note 8 (cont.)
    handlingene ved 17. nordiske juristmøte 1937) and – with regard to the historical and ideological background for the ban on retroactive laws – Bo Palmgren in Scandinavian Studies in Law 1961 p. 95 et seq.
9. This viewpoint is elaborated in Eckhoff and Dahl Jacobsen (1960).

are certainly societies where imprisonment would be regarded as so inhuman that it could not be used.[10]

Further limitations frequently follow from norms imposing special restrictions on the individual punisher. These norms are sometimes determined by a superior authority. For example, it is normal for the legislator to limit the kind of chastisement which may be made use of in prisons, schools, at work, in the home etc. Such limitations may be dictated by reasons of humanity and dignity. As well as this, governmental desire to retain a monopoly of the use of power – or certain types of power – may play a role. Developments in Norwegian legislation over the last century have tended to constrict the right to punish. According to Kristian V's Norwegian Law of 1687, for instance, the 'master in the house' was allowed to chastise 'his children and his servants' with 'a stick or a whip' but not with a weapon. The right to inflict corporal punishment on one's servants (as well as on craftsmen and sailors) was abolished in 1891. Parents or guardians were, however, allowed to use 'moderate physical punishment' on the children in their care until this law was also abolished in 1972.

Informal norms – some having developed within a specific interaction system and others having a wider application – also play an important role. Many of these norms are based on the fact that there are injuries which cannot be inflicted (or benefits which cannot be withdrawn) without endangering the realization of some important goal. Parents who feel responsible for their children's development are reluctant to use punishment which can be harmful or which can impede satisfaction of some vital need. To lock a child into a dark cupboard, let him go to bed without supper, refuse help with his homework, etc. are examples of punishments people avoid using for just such reasons. And if many people believe that certain kinds of punishment are dangerous or have unfortunate effects, norms soon develop which say that such methods of punishment *should never* be employed – without regard for whether or not there is any danger of damage in concrete cases. Special obligations, for example, to keep promises or to pay compensation, can also limit one's freedom of action. Although refusal to comply with such obligations can sometimes be used as a form of punishment, this is not always regarded as legitimate because the duty to keep promises often supersedes the right to punish.

---

10. The difficulties which have beset the Danish authorities in their efforts to introduce prison sentences in Greenland are an indication of such attitudes. See Goldschmidt in Nordisk Tidsskrift for Kriminalvidenskab 1954 p. 144.

The previously mentioned tendency to demand that punishment be tied to rules and that it be predictable, also applies in this field. It is frequently demanded that not only what is punishable but also the type and extent of punishment be fixed beforehand. To some extent, such demands are complied with both in criminal law and in institutionalized penal systems (for example in prisons and schools). However, rules stipulating that only certain definite harms can be used as punishment are sometimes undermined because there may be an element of punishment attached to transfers which primarily have another aim. For example, benefits or burdens are allocated according to what is deserved, so that those who have not behaved correctly receive fewer benefits or more burdens than those who have. Recipients sometimes react to such principles of distribution, and norms may develop which restrict the use of them. I will look at this more closely in the following chapters.

The *amount of punishment* is also often subject to normative restriction, for instance by way of rules specifying maximum and minimum penalties or by normative ideas of proportionality between guilt and punishment. Several factors can assist in explaining the emergence of such norms. Firstly, it is natural to evaluate the severity of punishment in terms of purpose. When the aim behind punishment is to exert influence, criticism can be directed both against sentences which are too mild to have any motivating effect and against those which are unnecessarily severe. And criticism, here as elsewhere, can be moulded into norms. There may, however, be different opinions as to what should be labelled as unnecessarily severe – particularly if one aims at influencing more people than just the offender. As well as (or instead of) considerations of expediency, evaluation of the degree of guilt can be of significance. Most people have ideas not only about what is wrong but also about degrees of wrongfulness. One usually learns to distinguish between degrees of wrong at the same time that one learns to distinguish between right and wrong – since reactions to what is considered 'very bad' differ from reactions to minor wrongs. As we have seen, there is a tendency to regard punishment as being justified only in cases of incorrect or wrong behaviour. And it is only a short step from this position to the contention that punishment should have some relation to the degree of wrong – if one first distinguishes between degrees. In the following sections the kinds of yardsticks used in such cases will be examined and the connections between notions of proportionality and strategic considerations discussed.

Organization can, as previously indicated, affect the practice of punishment in several ways, for instance through the establishment of rule-making and decision-making authorities. *Agreements* play a subordinate role in this field. It can happen that a person gives another the right to punish him, but usually this is only so in cases where the right constitutes part of an exchange transaction. For example, a small boy asks if he may borrow his elder brother's bicycle and says, 'you can beat me up if I damage it'. Or an entrepreneur undertakes to finish a certain job by a certain date and to pay a fine for each day in excess of the required time. In such cases where the right to punish is part of the exchange, *market mechanisms* may enter the picture. In the example of the entrepreneur, for instance, competitive conditions may determine whether or not the clause is included in the contract and what the exact content of the clause will be. And even when punishment has no connection with exchange, the exchange market can be of importance in evaluating both the benefits which are damaged and the benefits withdrawn from the guilty party as punishment. But it should be noted that we are here talking about *exchange* markets. It is difficult to imagine a 'punishment market' which could be 'price-forming' (see chap. 5, note 4 where the same question is discussed with regard to restitution).

IV. PRINCIPLES OF JUSTICE

This section is particularly concerned with the principle of *retributive justice* (see chap. 2, section IV), that injury must (or may) be repaid by injury in such a manner and to such an extent that balance is regained.

As mentioned in Chapter 6 the principle of repaying an injury with an injury can serve as a reason not only for punishment but also for revenge. Here, however, I will confine myself to its application in connection with punishment. The principle can have significance for several of the questions discussed in the previous section : it indicates both *what* can be punished and the *kind* and *amount* of punishment. What has been said in the previous section about factors which promote the development of norms regulating punishment practices is also relevant in explaining how conceptions of justice gain a foothold. But in addition to this comes the close relation between various principles of justice which facilitates the transfer of ideas of justice from one field to another.

Sometimes the principle of retribution is the only norm regulating punishment, but this often works together with other principles or rules – for example, with the principle of justice that those who are to receive punishment be treated alike, or via specific rules of punishment. Later in this section I will look at the different kinds of interplay between norms. But questions concerning equal treatment ('distributive justice') will not be discussed in detail until the following chapters.

The principle of retribution occurs in two versions. In the first, the principle says that an injury *must* be repaid with an injury. The point of view involved here is that requital is necessary in order to reinstate moral balance and that someone (for instance, the government) not only has the right but also the duty to see that this is done. In the second version the principle says that an injury *may* be repaid with an injury. Requital, in other words, is something one has a right but not a duty to ; is not required but is defensible.

It is sometimes hard to distinguish the normative idea of retribution from beliefs in causal connections between wrong actions and unfortunate consequences ('crime doesn't pay', 'honesty is the best policy'). There are many proverbs and sayings which can be interpreted both ways and which show how ideas of causality and requital easily become entangled ('As you sow, so shall you reap', 'A bad penny always comes back'). Such sayings may have their basis in the idea that 'Nature' has the power to repay evil with evil.[11] As suggested by *Heider* (1958, p. 285), we can take this as an indication of the penetrating power of the idea of retribution.

Conceptions of justice can also be interlaced with ideas on causal connections between punishment and improvement. The concept of 'expiation', for instance, is partly connected with ideas of moral balance being restored and partly with notions of the prisoner going through a process which in some way or other will make a better person of him. There is often no clear distinction between these two conceptions.

The idea that it is *necessary* to repay evil with evil in order to restore moral balance has been of particular importance in forming the opinion that the state has a duty to punish criminals. *Kant* (1797) was an ardent protagonist of this idea. He considered it absolutely necessary to punish,

11. Piaget (1932, pp. 250-261) has introduced the expression 'immanent justice' for ideas of an automatic form of justice which results in wrong behaviour being followed by unfortunate consequences without any human interference. He found that such notions were very common among the children (aged 6 to 12 years) whom he interviewed. The inclination to believe in immanent justice was strongest among the youngest and gradually declined as they grew older. Similar investigations in other countries have confirmed that the belief in immanent justice is normal among children, cf. Caruso (1943) and Medinnus (1959) with references. See also Westermarck (1906, I pp. 52-57) on the tendency among primitive peoples to believe that illness and misfortune are caused by sinful behaviour.

regardless of whether or not the punishment had any useful effect. 'For if justice perishes, there is no further point in men living on earth'. (Reiss, 1970, p. 155.) Even if a society were confronted with total dissolution (as, for example, when an island population decided to separate and disperse to other parts of the world), the last murderer who sat in prison should first be executed 'in order that each should receive his deserts and that the people should not bear the guilt of a capital crime through failing to insist on its punishment ; for if they do not do so, they can be regarded as accomplices in the public violation of justice' (Reiss, 1970, p. 156). As was pointed out earlier, the consequences of Kant's point of view that punishment is a moral necessity, led him to protest against the state's privilege of pardoning a criminal. He makes exceptions only in the case of crimes against the sovereign (*crimen laesae maiestatis*). (Reiss, 1970, p. 160). This is presumably because he believes punishment to be a privilege of the offended person. The offence may be forgiven by a sovereign when it has injured only the sovereign himself, but not otherwise.

The idea that requital is essential because 'justice must be done' has played an important role in the philosophy of penal law. It has often been based on religious notions of guilt and atonement, and in this version the idea is still widespread. But viewpoints are seldom formulated so sharply and so uncompromisingly as they are in Kant. Usually some modification of the principle is allowed, for instance that justice be 'tempered with mercy' or that one refrain from punishing when this is obviously useless.

The weaker version of the principle, that an injury *may* be repaid by an injury, can also act as a justification of punishment. But this can hardly be *sufficient* justification, since it is usually held that one should not impose evils on other persons simply because one has the right to do so. A reason is also needed for *availing* oneself of the right – when one is free to abstain from it. This version of the principle of retribution is therefore often combined with arguments of expediency. The reasoning can be, for example, that one has a right to punish because the injury may be requited, and that it is justifiable to make use of the right because of the beneficial effects of punishment. Such beneficial effects can be that punishment serves to educate or improve the offender or to deter him and other people from committing future offences.[12]

In addition to acting as a justification for punishment, the principle of retribution sets *limits* to the right to punish.

12. I will deal with the various types of arguments in more detail in section V.

187

As regards *what* can be punished, there is some restraint in the provision that only *harm* may be repaid with harm. This indicates that behaviour must be bad in some way or other in order for it to be punishable. The requirement can be more closely specified. For instance, it is usual that some of the restrictions on the right to punish which were mentioned above (in section III) are regarded as requirements of justice, e.g. that the action has been voluntary,[13] and that the offender has had prior warning that the action can result in punishment.

Since ideas of balance lie behind the principle that harm must (or may) be repaid by harm, it seems relevant to attach importance to whether or not the guilty party has made compensation. If he has done so, it may be that balance is restored so that the right to punish in this particular instance no longer exists. But a wrong which has been done cannot always be entirely righted by compensation. For example, the action may be conceived as an offence both to the person directly injured and to the authority whose norms were broken, and compensation to the injured person may therefore not be considered sufficient to restore balance.

It is frequently taken for granted that only the person who has done the harm can be punished. At any rate, this is generally so in our society. Collective punishment, for instance, of a class of children at school when the teacher cannot find the guilty pupil often produces the reaction that the teacher was unjust.[14] But the idea that justice can be done by punishing people other than the guilty party has played, and still plays, an important role in many cultures. We find many examples of this idea in

13. The relation between free will, moral responsibility and just punishment has been the object of much discussion in philosophical and legal literature. It is widely felt that only those who have acted of their own free will can be held responsible. And many people consider that the necessary freedom is lacking not only when the action is taken under outer or inner compulsion but also when its causes are fully determined. They believe, therefore, that it is impossible (or difficult) to combine determinism with the notion of just punishment. In my opinion there is no logical contradiction between these points of view but there may well be a psychological difficulty in combining them because it is common to tend to identify cause with compulsion. Common sense experience also seems to show that people become less inclined to criticize the more disposed they are to seek causes. I will not go into more detail on this. For further discussion of these questions see Ofstad (1961) particularly pp. 261 ff., Westermarck (1906) I pp. 320 ff. and Bodenheimer (1967) pp. 175 ff.
14. None of the children Piaget (1932 pp. 231 ff.) examined accepted collective punishment unless exhaustive efforts had been made to find the guilty child, and even then there were many who objected to it.

primitive law (*Westermarck* I 1906, pp. 44 ff.) and in religion, see for instance the Bible's description of the jealous God who 'visits the sins of the father on the children' and its teaching of Jesus's suffering and death as atonement for the sins of mankind. Ibsen has Brand present the relationship between original sin and justice in this manner :

'For I the Lord thy God am a jealous God
And visit the sins of the fathers upon the children
Even unto the third and fourth generation.
The God of Justice watches over us.
He demands retribution.'
(Henrik Ibsen, Brand, translated by Michael Meyer, Anchor Books, N.Y. 1960 p. 118.)

The principle, as I have formulated it, says nothing specific about *who* has the *right to punish*. Sometimes it is assumed that the right belongs only to the person who was injured. But transfer of this right to another person or use of it by someone else on behalf of the injured is often accepted. The idea that some authority or other (e.g. the state) has the sole privilege to punish can be fitted, in various ways, into notions of justice. Authority can be thought of as representing the offended party and can also be considered as being itself offended since its norms have been broken.

Last but not least, the principle of retribution can have significance for the *type and magnitude of punishment*. Advocates of the 'must' version regard the principle as indicating both the minimum and maximum penalty: one should punish sufficiently to restore balance, but no more. But to those who adhere to the 'may' version, it is more natural to regard the principle as indicating only the maximum : it limits the severity of the punishment one has a right to inflict, but there may be reasons for not completely availing oneself of this right. How useful the punishment will be is often taken as another limiting factor. The standpoint then is that the sentence should not be harder than what is just nor more severe than what is expedient.[15]

Ideas have varied a good deal as to what the relationship between crime and punishment must be if balance is to be restored. One answer to this question goes under the name of *'lex talionis'*, which states that the guilty party should have the same kind of hurt inflicted on him that he himself has caused his victim. The most famous formulation of this principle is to be found in Mosaic law :

15. For this point of view, see Exner (1922 pp. 28-29), Hart (1959) and Ofstad (1961 pp. 301-302).

'And if a man cause a blemish in his neighbour, as he hath done, so shall it be done to him ;
Breach for breach, eye for eye, tooth for tooth ...' [16]

As was pointed out in Chapter 6, section III this principle may have helped to restrict blood revenge and it may be that its application has, in some places, been a step in the development from revenge to an organized penal system. However, the principle has also had its advocates in societies where the state has long administered criminal law. *Kant* (1797), for instance, claimed that the talionic principle was the only one which completely satisfied the demands of justice (Reiss, 1970, p. 155). He discussed in detail how it could be applied to different types of crimes. Even where it was difficult to find punishment sufficiently matching the offence (e.g. sex crimes), he did his best to suggest something he believed to be consistent with the principle. Although there have been few as uncompromising as Kant, there are many who have looked upon the talionic form of punishment as the right one for certain types of offences. The notion that a life should be paid for with another life has played a particularly important role in the history of penal law. In types of punishment other than the legal, for instance small punishments exchanged between playfellows, the talionic principle is often adhered to, e.g., when a boy who has been hit hits back and when one who has damaged someone's property has his own spoilt. Such reactions are frequently justified with arguments of retribution,[17] but it is not always clear whether revenge or punishment is involved.

There are many people who are more modest in their claims for balance. They do not expect that punishment be of the same kind as the offence but only that it be equal in *value*. The requirement is often given the negative formulation that the severity of the punishment must not be out of proportion to the severity (or blameworthiness) of the offence. The reason why a negative formulation is preferred may be that the vague value scales with which we operate make it difficult to state positively what kind of punishment is appropriately severe. It is easier to point out clear digressions from what is suitable. Most people in Norway, for instance, would immediately feel that a 6 months' unconditional prison sentence would be much too severe for illegal parking, but much too mild for wilful murder.

16. Leviticus 24, 19-20. See also Exodus 21 and Deuteronomy 19.
17. See section II above on Piaget's investigation of children's attitudes to, inter alia, the justice of talionic punishment.

Notions as to what penalties are suitable for various kinds of offences vary from time to time and place to place.[18] They are influenced by, among other things, penal practices. The tendency to make comparisons and to demand equal treatment – which will be discussed in the following chapters – helps strengthen the significance of a punishment previously been meted out in similar cases as a basis for evaluating what is just punishment. But there are also other factors which can affect evaluation – both of the values the offender has misappropriated and of those taken from him when he is punished. Some indication can, for instance, be obtained from what it costs (in money, time, sacrifice etc.) to produce or replace such values and from how much it is usual to give in exchange for them. It is true that the price one pays when buying something is generally not the same as that one has to pay for having stolen it. But, even so, it does give some indication of how severe the punishment should be. When, for example, a horse costs more than a hen, it seems reasonable that there should be a more severe punishment for stealing a horse than a hen. The evaluation of things which are not normally objects of exchange, for instance life and limb, health, well-being and freedom, can be affected by how great a risk there is normally of losing them (e.g. through illness, want, war or accident) and by how much is done to protect them in the society concerned. This can help determine how they are ranked in relation to each other and in relation to material values. There are many examples from societies where people live dangerous lives and where the importance of owning material objects is great, of theft being more severely sentenced than murder. The evaluation of punishment severity depends on similar factors. The smaller the risk of suffering and the less tolerance there is towards suffering in a society, the more brutal will it appear to use physical torture and mutilation as punishment. And the stronger the feeling that time is in short supply, the shorter prison terms need to be before they appear as a considerable punishment.

There is again great variation with regard to which characteristics of a situation are taken into account when what is fair punishment for an offence is being decided. In the first place, there may be different opinions as to what comprises the relevant *class of events*.[19] In a prison where the inmates' conduct is of significance to the duration of their imprisonment, there is the problem of whether there should be immediate reaction to a certain kind of misbehaviour or whether this misbehaviour

---

18. See Christie (1968) on changes in penal values over time.
19. The concepts used here are defined in Chapter 2, section VI.

should only be taken into account when the time of release is determined. And *if* there is an immediate reaction, it may not be clear whether this is a final settlement or whether something is being saved for the later occasion.

In the second place, there are variations with regard to how specific or diffuse conceptions of justice are. The talionic principle, for instance, is based on very specific conceptions of justice. The amount of punishment is determined on the basis of one, or a few, highly visible and simple characteristics of the offence.[20] It is only necessary to ascertain that a life has been taken, an eye has been hurt or a tooth knocked out for a just punishment to be fixed. On the other hand there are conceptions of justice according to which a variety of factors should be taken into account when punishment is meted out, for instance the motives and temper of the offender, background factors of various kinds, mitigating or aggravating circumstances connected with the misdeed, the type and extent of damage done, etc.

A third important difference is to be found between *object-oriented* and *person-oriented* conceptions of justice. A person-oriented conception takes into account characteristics (personal qualities, motives etc.) of the persons involved. In the case of punishment attention is often focused on the *offender* ; but factors relating to the *victim* may also be considered relevant, for instance his sex and age, whether his behaviour was provocative, etc. The degree of importance attached to personal characteristics and the number of features of the persons involved taken into consideration, can differ widely. It can also happen that punishment is determined on a purely objective basis so that only the external features of the events are adjudged – and in some cases this may be regarded as just.

Person-oriented conceptions of justice differ between themselves with regard to *which* personal features are considered important. Sometimes only those circumstances having a direct bearing on the offence are taken into account, for example the actor's motives and whether he was able to understand what he let himself in for, while in other cases weight is also attached to such enduring features as sex, age, ability, education, profession, social rank and economic standing. The importance attached to certain criteria can vary – for instance, if the victim

20. When it is to be decided whether a situation is punishable or not, supporters of the talionic principle might base themselves on more diffuse criteria. They might, for instance, attach importance to subjective guilt, to the offender's age and soundness of mind, etc.

has high rank, this often makes for severe punishment.[21] On the other hand, it can also happen that features of the victim which are associated with low rank, for example poverty or vulnerability, make the offence seem particularly grave.

Similarly, the rank of the offender can affect the outcome in various ways. Privileges often accompany age and social position. There are many things which are denied to children but not to adults; forbidden to subordinates but not to their superiors. And when a prohibition applies to everyone, reaction is sometimes milder towards the privileged than towards the unprivileged.[22] Various arguments of justice can be found to support such discriminatory treatment. One point of view often advanced is that the higher social rank an offender has, the more serious are the effects of punishment, and that allowance should be made for this when determining the severity of a punishment. It can also be argued that there is a comprehensive exchange relationship between the state and its citizens and that those citizens who are highly esteemed are often 'moral creditors' in this exchange relationship. It may be claimed that though they might have *received* a great deal, they have *given* even more. And it may be thought right to take account of this accumulated credit when fixing punishment.

Ideas connected with exchange, however, can also lead to the opposite conclusion, i.e., that a privileged person is in debt to society, or to fate, because he has received so many of life's benefits. It may be regarded as a reasonable counter-service on his part that he pay strict attention to social norms. In addition to this 'noblesse oblige' point of view comes the 'halo-effect' which leads one to expect a high moral standard from a man of rank. And people may tend to react most strongly to breaches committed by those from whom better things were expected. Conversely, youth, inexperience and poor ability are often regarded as mitigating factors which reduce responsibility.

The fact that there are wide variations in conceptions of justice does not mean that an argument of justice can be found to defend any decision whatsoever. Some variations are culturally conditioned. In our own culture, for instance, there are probably not many people who regard the talionic punishments of Mosaic law as just. Other variations are connected with differences in social situations and in the kinds of punishment involved. For instance, there is a tendency to accept more object-

---

21. Westermarck (1906) I pp. 420-421 and 430-431 gives examples from different cultures.
22. Op. cit. pp. 431-433.

oriented and specific punishments in the case of minor misdeeds (for example, violation of rules at play and in sport) than when more serious offences are involved. The breadth of variation is considerably narrowed when differences determined by culture and situation are not taken into account.

The principles of justice can, in several ways, work together with or have an impact on specific rules of punishment. In the first place, it can serve as a metanorm (i.e. a norm about norms). This is the case when it is considered a requirement of justice that punishment be based on rules which are formally enacted and publicized in such a way that everyone can become familiar with them. Secondly, the principle of justice can influence the making of new rules by serving as a model or as a kind of normative raw material. Thirdly, it can guide interpretation of existing rules and serve as a supplement in fields where rules are lacking or where rules leave certain questions open (for instance, the size of punishment). And last but not least conceptions of justice can form the basis of *criticism* of existing rules and procedures.

V. DIFFERENT KINDS OF REASONS USED FOR AND AGAINST
PUNISHMENT AND THE FACTORS DETERMINING THEM

This section is concerned with all kinds of reasons given for standpoints related to punishment, whether they are arguments for or against punishment as such, or whether they refer to individual decisions or to rules or institutions.

The study of these reasons is of interest from several points of view. In the first place they are a source of knowledge of the strategies and norms related to punishment. To be sure, they are not a completely reliable source and below I will discuss why they sometimes give a distorted picture of the norms and strategies actually applied. Nevertheless they are a rich source of knowledge because reasons are so often given for standpoints which are concerned with punishment. And to be able to utilize this source of knowledge one must know something about the factors determining the use of reasons so that one can avoid the errors. Moreover, what is a source of error when reasons are seen as a means of acquiring knowledge of punishment strategies and norms, can be the key to valuable knowledge when approached from another angle. It can tell us something of the person giving the reason, of the culture to which he belongs, and of the social system in which he operates.

In the general survey given in Chapter 2, section VII, I pointed to

194

three sets of factors helping to determine *whether* reasons will be given and *what kind* of reasons are given. In the first place it is important what *resources* of argument a person has : these are determined by what he possesses of logical training, knowledge, norms and value preferences. In the second place, in some fields there are *norms* for when and what kinds of reasons should be used. But, often, the resources are so extensive and the norms so vague that there is plenty of room for *strategy*. Strategies can influence individual choice of reasons and in the long run can, as mentioned previously, also be habit-making and lead to the growth of norms.

For the person who punishes (and for other people looking at things from his point of view) punishment strategy will to some extent determine argument strategy. When the purpose of punishment is to influence the offender, it seems appropriate to advance arguments which can help to realize this goal. One uses arguments, for instance, as a means of explaining that the action was wrong and must not be repeated. Reproaches and warnings contained in arguments can be intended both for the person punished and for others. And the reasons will be modified according to who the intended addressee is.

The punisher may also wish to address those who feel threatened by punishable offences. For example, he may want to reassure them that their interests are taken care of or to secure their support in imposing the sentence, and therefore will try to convince them that the punishment is suited to protect their interests.

Furthermore, he may need to defend his actions, both to himself and other people. When a person punishes, he consciously causes another person harm – sometimes considerable harm. It is true that the moral principle that one should not hurt another has many exceptions. But because these are conceived as being exceptions to a principal rule, a reason is required for making them. In certain cases it may also be necessary to explain why one *has refrained* from punishing. How important it is to justify one's action can depend upon many factors. Among other things, it can be of some significance whether a heavy or a light punishment is involved, whether or not the right to punish has a solid foundation, whether the decision has been exposed to criticism, whether the responsibility for the decision is shared between several persons or rests on one person alone, etc.

Those who are punished or are liable to threats of punishment may also be keenly interested in the reasons given. To the person who is punished, the premises can be of significance to his self-respect and reputation and to his inclination to accept the decision. And to those who are threatened by punishment, reasons can serve both as a basis for predicting the outcome and as a means of defence. As mentioned in section I, the punisher usually has such resources of power that direct opposition is useless. The only available means of defence in such cases is to argue that there are not sufficient grounds for punishment. Such argumentation can be effective if it is based on reasons which the punisher accepts, e.g., on the kind of considerations which he himself is accustomed to use in support of his decisions. Many factors influence the effectivity of such argumentation, inter alia whether the punisher finds it important to behave consistently and to have his decisions accepted, and whether he has taken steps to eliminate the effect of counter-arguments, for instance by formulating his reasons so vaguely that they are difficult to refute.

The *punisher's* argument strategy can then be affected by his desire to (1) *admonish* and *warn* the punished person and others of like mind, (2) to *reassure* or secure *support* from those who feel themselves exposed to criminal behaviour, (3) to *justify* his own actions, and (4) to *guard against* counter-arguments. These motives do not always pull in the same direction and their relative weights may therefore decide what content the arguments will have.

There are two main types of reasons for punishment. One is that punishment is *useful* because it helps educate or improve the person punished, because it acts as a deterrent for him and others, and because it encourages moral behaviour, etc. The other consists of appeals to *norms* which say that an action is wrong and that it is right or just to punish it. These two types of reasons are often combined, but then usually in such a manner that one of them dominates.

When the purpose is to admonish the offender, the most suitable arguments are usually those of a normative kind. But some arguments based on utility may also suit the purpose, for instance, explanations such as 'I am punishing you because you must learn to behave properly'. On the other hand, there is little point in indicating the effect that a punishment has on *other* people, when admonishing an offender. If, for instance, one says to an offender, 'I am punishing you to scare others away from behaving as you have done', this is more likely to give rise to a feeling of being made scapegoat rather than to seem like a reproach. It may, of course, be useful when other people whom one wants to influence receive a warning that they too will be punished if they behave in a similar manner. But they only need to be told that they will be punished – they do not have to be furnished with the hypothesis that the threat of punishment will scare them.

On the other hand, stressing all possible useful effects of punishment can serve to reassure people who feel threatened by criminal behaviour. To them it can be comforting to hear that punishment is an appropriate way of discouraging both those punished and others from committing misdeeds. Besides giving them a feeling of security, it provides them with a motive for supporting the punishing authorities and for abstaining from taking the law into their own hands.

Utilitarian reasons can also be well suited to meet the punisher's need for justification. They provide especially good defence if he is able to convince both himself and other people that the punishment – in the long run – will benefit the person punished, for instance by educating or inducing him to mend his ways. To claim that punishment is useful to *others* – for example in preventing dangerous and damaging behaviour – is not quite so convincing. Of course, those who adhere to classical utilitarianism will be satisfied if the punishment in general creates more happiness than unhappiness. But one who rejects the idea that the total amount of happiness is all that matters will be inclined to question the fairness of harming one person in order to benefit others. He, too, may feel that the usefulness of punishment has some value as a defence. But he will require a normative supplement – for instance, that the person punished has no reasons for complaint since he behaved wrongly and was forewarned that he would be punished.

The value of a utilitarian justification depends, of course, on how reliable the underlying hypothesis on the effects of the punishments are considered to be. It was pointed out in section I that it is difficult to verify these hypotheses. We have relatively little reliable knowledge of the effects of punishment on the person who receives it and are even more poorly equipped to judge the general effects of threatened punishment.[23] Assumptions as to the effects of punishment are therefore, as a rule, based on belief rather than on knowledge. This can be both a weakness and a source of strength since it makes the standpoints as difficult to refute as to prove.

Among normative reasons, the conception of justice that evil *must* be repaid by evil is particularly suited as a defence for the punisher. If he has internalized this principle he feels that he has no choice when he punishes. He acts as the servant of justice and does what he *must* do. The offender shoulders the whole responsibility, not only for the misdeed but also for the punishment which is regarded as an unavoidable

23. There has been a great deal of discussion as to whether legal punishment has general deterrent, educative and moral effects, see Andenaes (1952, 1966 and 1971) with references.

consequence of the offence committed. Also the weaker version of the principle of justice that evil *may* be repaid by evil can serve as justification. But, as already mentioned, that one has a right to punish will not normally be regarded as *sufficient* reason for punishing, when one is also free to abstain. Additional reasons – based, for example, on such ideas of utility as were discussed above – are therefore required in order to furnish complete justification.

The principle of justice not only gives the right (and sometimes the duty) to punish but also sets limits to that right. These two sides of the principle are so intimately connected that it is difficult to assert one without also accepting the other. From the punisher's point of view, therefore, reasoning based on justice is a two-edged sword. It is well suited to both reproaches and justification but it provides the accused with ample opportunity to produce counter-arguments which the punisher must take seriously. For example, it may be argued that such and such mitigating circumstances are present and that it is therefore not right to punish, or at any rate not to the extent as may have been intended. In addition to arguments of justice based on the principle of balance, distributive justice can also be mobilized as an argument ; that is to say, relative equality with others who have been punished or accused of similar misdeeds can be demanded. Such argumentation, too, can restrict the punisher's freedom of action. I will discuss this in more detail in the following chapters.

Specific rules of punishment can also serve as justification. The responsibility of the punisher is reduced if he can show that he is acting in accordance with rules made by other people or which are traditionally established. This does not completely cover him because there can still be a question of whether it is right to have such rules of punishment and whether these are being interpreted and applied as they should be. Answers to such questions may be given in terms of utility or in terms of justice. But the argumentation will tend to take on a different character when it revolves around rules and institutions than when it is concerned with individual non-institutionalized decisions. There are also considerable differences between the task of making rules and that of applying them and these can affect argumentation in the two situations.

The task of the legislator is to draft and enact general rules dealing with abstract criminal categories. His job is not to inflict punishment on individual persons. This places him at a distance from those who are punished and probably reduces his need to defend what he does. Another important point in this connection is that laws are usually directed towards future actions. The legislator can, therefore, if he has any scruples, say to himself that he has given a warning and that only those disregarding the warning have anything to fear. In addition to the points so far mentioned, the law-giver's general attitude to his activity can be of significance to how he justifies his rules of punishment. If he believes that his main job is to find and formalize norms which already exist, his reasoning will tend to be retrospective. He must try to show that the rules he makes are in agreement with existing practice or moral principles. If, on the other hand, he regards himself as a policy maker endeavouring to advance social interests by influencing people's behaviour, it is likely that he will also apply such ideas to punishment. It is easier for the law-maker than for the person deciding on individual cases to regard as sufficient grounds for punishment the assumption that this punishment will, in general, have socially useful results.

In developed legal systems there is not only a distinction between the making of criminal law and its application in individual cases, but also between different steps in the application procedure and between different groups of officials engaged in law enforcement (police, prosecutors, judges, prison personnel, etc.). Such professional groups tend to develop their own traditional modes of justifying decisions. Strategic considerations may influence the formation of such traditions, but lose much of their significance in individual cases when the tradition is firmly established. Another effect of institutionalization and role-differentiation is that responsibility is divided. Those who are involved have very much the feeling of being just one small cog in a large machine. The need to defend one's own actions thus becomes less pressing but, on the other hand, those involved may need to convince both themselves and other people that the apparatus as a whole has an important function.

Even though an argument is advanced for strategic reasons it may still be honestly and sincerely meant. It is often good strategy to say exactly what one believes. This may – from an objective point of view as well – be true or valid, but it is not always the case. Arguments springing from the need to defend one's behaviour can be full of hypocrisy or based on self delusion as, for instance, when a war of aggression is defended by saying it is just, or when a man who has robbed a homosexual justifies his act by saying that this was a fitting punishment for the victim's immoral behaviour.[24] More moderate forms of self delusion also

---

24. An experienced policeman told me that he has almost never met a robber who has not defended his behaviour in terms of retributive justice. The man who robs a farmer who has come to town with a bulging wallet and has

occur. At the outset, for instance, one may not be quite certain of the validity of one's own arguments but pushes doubts aside and gradually succeeds in convincing oneself that the reasons are sound.

This is probably a factor which plays some role in the process of norm formation. As already pointed out, norms may become accepted because it has turned out to be good strategy to behave in accordance with them. But another basis for acceptance may be that it has been good strategy to use the norm as an argument. It is perhaps doubtful whether what is internalized in these two instances is exactly the same thing. There is frequently a discrepancy between what a person says – even though he may fully believe it – and what he does. But there is at least some connection between verbal attitudes and non-verbal behaviour tendencies.

When it comes to factual premises a kind of similar thing can happen. Doubts about their validity can be pushed aside because this is strategically desirable. And the belief that they square with the facts can gradually become anchored in a conviction which is more or less unaffected by counter-evidence.

Strategic considerations often determine the *choice* between different available arguments. There are many ways of justifying punishment. Even if what is said is honestly meant and even though it appears to afford sufficient justification, it may be that there are also other arguments which *could* have been used but which are kept back or overlooked because their strategic value is less. For this reason it cannot be taken for

note 24 (cont.)
> begun to drink in the company of strangers defends himself, for example, by saying, 'He deserved a rap when he behaved so stupidly'. And the man who uses a prostitute as decoy and robs the person who approaches her, says for example, 'He took my girl and got what was coming to him', or 'He behaved like a swine'.
>
> Aubert (1950) found similar tendencies in his investigation of businessmen's attitudes to violations of price and rationing laws. Such infringements were often defended or excused by alleging that the *authorities* were the real offenders. For example, it was claimed that the price and rationing inspectors were unqualified and bureaucratic, that they cheated or were corrupt, and that the country's tax policy could be compared to theft (see especially pp. 65-67).
>
> The tendencies referred to here can be regarded as modes of reducing the dissonance experienced by a person who has committed acts which are inconsistent with his self-image. Several experimental studies based on Festinger's (1957) theory of cognitive dissonance (e.g. Glass, 1964, and Walster & Prestholdt, 1966) have shown that when a person believes he has harmed someone, he may derogate his victim.

200

granted that the arguments adduced are the only reasons a person has for his standpoint. Nor do they have to be the most important ones. It may very well be, for instance, that a standpoint argued in terms of utility is mainly motivated by ideas of justice – and conversely. This does not mean that the person presenting the argument says something which he does not himself believe. One can feel that punishment is both useful and just – or both useless and unjust. I have discussed in an earlier publication (*Eckhoff*, 1963, pp. 82-84) the tendency to harmonize conceptions of justice and utility in such a way that they point in the same direction.

Whether strategy puts the main emphasis on utility or on justice in arguments concerning punishment, depends on the circumstances. In part it depends – as seen above – on who argues what, i.e., on whether for example it is the punisher or the person exposed to punishment, and whether the standpoint refers to an individual decision, a norm or an institution. And in part it depends upon which strategic considerations are most important to the person concerned. The punisher's preferences, for instance, may depend upon whether he is mainly interested in admonishing the person punished, in reassuring those who feel endangered by criminal behaviour, or in defending his own decisions. But what is good argumentative strategy also greatly depends upon cultural factors. For example, the fact that ideas of justice as reasons for legal punishment were largely superseded in the 19th century by ideas of utility, was certainly tied to a general cultural development. As reasoning in terms of utility generally increased in prestige in the West, it also became better suited to justifying punishment.

Part III. Allocation

8. Allocation and distribution

'I have come to believe that the degree of solution of the problem of distributive justice, or the equitable distribution of the rewards available in a society, is the most important determinant of individual satisfaction and effectiveness and of social peace. So have many philosophers thought, yet it is surprising how few social scientists have given their minds to the problem, though it is readily subject to empirical research.'
George C. Homans in *American Sociological Review*, 1962, p. 270.

I. INTRODUCTION : THE RELATIONSHIP BETWEEN ALLOCATION, DISTRIBUTION AND RECIPROCATION

I use the word 'allocation' to designate the process which takes place when something is dealt out. For example, mother is performing an allocation when she cuts the cake and gives each child a piece. An allocation consists of a set of connected transfers. In this example the transfers originate from the same source (the cake), they are made by the same person (mother) and on the same occasion. However, I talk about allocation processes even when the connections are looser (see Chapter 1, section I).

By 'distribution' I refer to the manner in which a set of elements is grouped. It is in this sense that the word is used in expressions such as age distribution, income distribution and distribution of wealth. There are several connections between the concepts of allocation and distribution. Firstly, distribution can come about through – or be influenced by – allocation processes. For instance, the distribution of cake on the children's plates is a result of what mother undertook when she cut and dealt it out. And the distribution of wealth and income in society is influenced by, among other things, the decisions the authorities take when taxes and social service contributions are fixed. Secondly, ideas on how distribution ought to be can affect allocation processes and their evaluation. For example, mother's desire for a certain distribution

– e.g., that each child gets about the same amount of cake or that Peter gets the largest slice since it is his birthday – determines the way in which she cuts and apportions the cake. And it may be that the children's ideas of how the distribution ought to be decide their evaluation of what mother does. Isolated transfers – and their evaluation – can also be influenced by ideas of distribution. For instance, when an offender is sentenced, care may be taken that the punishment is reasonable compared with punishments others have received on previous occasions.

Interplay between transfer processes and ideas of distribution demands most of our attention in what follows. I am concerned there both with cohesive allocations and with individual transfers, to the extent that questions of distribution are considered relevant. The emphasize is on allocation strategies and norms based on conceptions of distribution. Principles of *distributive justice* – demanding equality in one way or another (cf. chap. 2, sections IV and V) – play a central role among these norms.

There are many connections between allocation and reciprocation. In the first place, what some people regard as reciprocation, others may look upon as allocation. We can imagine, for example, a family situation where the husband washes up and keeps an eye on the children while the wife does some typing for her employer. Some people would find it natural to describe the situation as being one where he 'helps her' with the housework and children while she 'helps him' by earning a supplementary income in support of the family. From this point of view they both help each other and it may be that they look upon their mutual services as an exchange. But for people who do not consider that man and wife each have their definite jobs in married life, it is more natural to view the situation as one of allocation. The point of view adopted can be, for instance, that housework, care of the children and paid employment are common tasks which the couple, in this instance, share between them in the manner described.

In the second place, it can happen that transfers are bound together in such a manner that allocation points of view are applied to some aspects of the events and reciprocation to others. Examples of such combination are given in Chapter 1, section I in the text related to figs. 10-12. I will pay most attention to the combination illustrated in Figure 10 where the allocated values are also links in reciprocation between the distributor and the individual recipients. For instance, in dividing the cake mother allots rather more to John because he has been a help to her and rather less to Peter as punishment for being naughty. When appraising events such as these both reciprocation and allocation viewpoints can be taken into account – as competing points of view or as components in an overall evaluation.

A combination of – or competition between – reciprocation and allocation points of view can also occur in cases where no actual allocation process has taken place but where one or more exchanges affect the distribution of a set of values. A wage agreement between a trade union and an employer for instance, may have the character of an exchange in which claims and counter-claims are adjusted. But, at the same time, the settlement is of significance to income distribution within the community concerned. Ideas of exchange are therefore easily merged with those of allocation.

In other words, the subject of reciprocity was not exhausted in earlier chapters: questions of exchange, restitution, competition and punishment continue to play a part in the discussions of allocation and distribution.

In what follows, an account will first be given of the different kinds of questions connected with allocation and distribution (section II). A survey – largely descriptive – will then be given (sections III et seq.) of the different ways in which these problems are often solved or desired to be solved. The strategies and norms regulating allocation and distribution will not be analysed more closely until the following chapters.

II. DIFFERENT TYPES OF PROBLEMS CONNECTED WITH ALLOCATION
AND DISTRIBUTION

I will begin by examining some problems connected with allocation.

The first question which arises is that of *who is to make the allocation*. Usually this is the one disposing of the values. But if it should be an organization, a decision must be made about to which member of the staff the task will be assigned. Sometimes the person who disposes of the values leaves the job of making the allocation to an outsider or to one of the recipients. For example: a favourite aunt has brought some sweets with her and asks the oldest girl to divide them between herself and the other children. Where the recipients themselves control the values, there can also be alternative procedures – for instance, should they decide jointly how to divide the values or should one person be responsible for this, and if so who?

A second question concerns the *amount of value* to be allocated. Mother must decide, for example, about the total quantity of ice cream, lemonade and jelly she will give the children at the birthday party. And the children will later perhaps make up their minds about how much she *should* have given them.

In addition, there is a question of how the *circle of recipients* should be delineated. In the case of the birthday party it must be decided how many and which children shall be invited. Determination of the *recipient units* may also be problematic, for instance, when there is a choice between giving something to a collective unit and dividing it between its individual members.

We now come to the question of *how much each individual recipient should have* of the values to be allocated. When deciding this, two main types of considerations can be taken into account. Firstly, the situation of the *individual recipient* may be considered relevant. For instance, importance can be attached to how much he needs of the values concerned, whether he is capable of making use of them, whether he has any right to them (for instance, because of a reciprocal relationship with the distributor), etc. Secondly, weight may also be attached to how much the recipients should receive *in relation to each other,* in other words what the distribution should be. Sometimes only the first type of consideration is relevant. As an example we can take a person who has received his salary and who, during the course of the month, spends this in a variety of ways. He pays his rent and electricity bill, buys clothes and food, goes to the cinema and the theatre, etc. In this way he allocates between a series of recipients the money he received in his pay packet. But it is very likely that he attaches no importance whatsoever to how much the recipients get in relation to each other. The fact that he pays £ 15 to his landlord and £ 5 to his tailor is not because the proportion between these two transfers should be 3 to 1, but simply because he owes £ 15 in rent and needs a pair of trousers which cost £ 5. There are also instances where ideas of distribution dominate. For instance, the favourite aunt comes on a visit and has a bag of sweets with her. She considers it of decisive importance that each child receive the same amount. When she bought the sweets she calculated how much a child should have during the course of one afternoon, but this calculation has no relevance in the allocation situation. She may have come to the conclusion that she has bought too little but feels that it is better that everyone get the same inadequate amount rather than that just one person gets enough. Finally, we have instances where both types of consideration are involved. We can, for instance, vary the above example in such a manner that the aunt tries to both satisfy the need of each child and make the distribution more or less equal.

In addition to the issues raised so far – to which the common designation 'substantive' can be given – various questions connected with *procedure* arise. By this I mean questions such as what information should be collected before a decision is made, what opportunity those interested in the allocation should have to argue their own standpoints and to complain if they are dissatisfied, etc. There is often a close connection between procedure and substantive issues. The desire to achieve certain aims or to pay particular attention to certain considerations can influence the choice of procedure. On the other hand, the desire to simplify decision making or to employ a line of action which is not open to criticism may influence the solution of substantive issues. Procedures such as drawing lots or – if two persons are to divide something between them – dividing and choosing, are examples of this.

We now turn to questions of *distribution*. As already mentioned, conceptions of how distribution ought to be can affect both the decisions made during an allocation process and their evaluation. But such questions also arise in other connections, for instance when the distribution of wealth or of political power in a society is evaluated.

A distribution is characterized by the relative size of its parts. All parts may be of equal size or they may have a certain ratio to each other (e.g. John's share being twice as big as Peter's) or to one or another criterion (e.g. wage in relation to working hours). The relation can be a simple proportion or a more complicated mathematical function, or one expressed in vague terms such as 'much more' or 'little more'. Sometimes only a rank order is given, for example that one part be greater or smaller than another.

As mentioned in Chapter 2, Section V there are certain ambiguities involved in characterizing a distribution as 'equal' (or 'unequal') since these terms can refer to different things. What is equal is sometimes the values which each recipient has or receives ; sometimes it is the ratio between the transferred values (e.g. wages) and an applicable criterion (e.g. the number of working hours) ; and sometimes it is the sequence.

The yardsticks used in determining size or rank order also vary. The values can, for instance, be decided by dimension, weight, number of pieces or price or by degree of subjective utility or the extent to which they satisfy a need.

When describing a distribution we are also confronted with the question of how the circle of recipients, the recipient units and the set of values are to be fixed. We examined these problems earlier from the point of view of what an allocation process involved (or should involve). But the questions now appear in a new connection and the answers need not be the same.

209

Firstly, the delimitation of the *circle of recipients* can differ. Some of the recipients in an allocation may not be taken into consideration when the resulting distribution is described or appraised. On the occasion of Peter's birthday party, for instance, it may be that each child finds it apposite to compare what he receives with what the other children get but not with what mother helps herself to. And the opposite may also occur, i.e., that people other than those participating in an allocation process are taken into account, for instance when the employees in a factory make comparisons between themselves and outsiders when evaluating the wage distribution. Something similar applies to *recipient units*. If, for example, a married couple and a bachelor join in giving a present to a common friend, there may be a question of whether the expenditure should be divided equally between three persons or equally between two households. In other words, the issue involved is whether the married couple be regarded as one or as two in relation to the question of distribution (i.e. when their share is fixed). And this question can be solved quite independently of whether they each contribute a little of the share or whether it is all taken from a joint fund.

The *set of values* taken into account when the distribution is described, does not have to be the same as that which has been the object of the allocation process. Some of what has been dealt out may not be reckoned with. Peter feels, for example, that the extra lemonade he received during the party because he had helped mother should not be included when it is judged whether or not the lemonade distribution was fair. On the other hand it can happen that values which originate from different allocations are taken into consideration. It may be argued, for instance, that 'It is just that I get something today, since you got something yesterday' (or '... last week', or '... last year'). Sometimes not only values which originate from earlier transfers but everything that the recipient *already has* (or has had) of these values is taken into account.

In the following section I will give a survey of the various ways in which questions of allocation can be solved. Since many questions arise and there are many ways in which each of them can be resolved, the survey cannot, of course, be exhaustive. For the same reason, classification is difficult. I have chosen to base the main distinction on whether or not characteristics of the recipients are taken into account when determining how much each of them should have. I call the allocation object-oriented when no such characteristics are taken into account. The cases of equal distribution and random selection dealt with in sections III and IV belong to this group. Within the other group – which

210

I refer to as person-oriented allocations – the features of the recipients to which special importance is attached (status, need, fitness, merit etc.) are used as a basis for classification. These cases will be dealt with in section V onwards. One of the disadvantages of this method of classification is that the categories used are not directly comparable. While, for instance, the category 'object-oriented equality' is characterized by the principle of distribution followed, many different distribution principles (or none at all) may be adhered to when there is 'allocation according to need'. However, the classification does have the advantage that it makes use of categories which have frequently been employed in debates concerned with allocation and distribution.

III. OBJECT-ORIENTED EQUALITY

I will discuss here allocations in which the recipients receive shares which are equal according to some objective measure. For instance, a sum of money is divided so that each person receives the same amount in shillings and pence, or the children at a birthday party receive the same sized portion of ice cream and one bottle of lemonade each. Compulsory military service involving like periods of call-up, and an election in which each vote counts the same can also serve as examples.

That an *objective* measure is applied means that no characteristics of the recipients are taken into account when judging what is equal. Once it has been decided what shall be dealt equally among whom, one needs to know no more about the recipients than their number to make this type of allocation. I do not include cases where subjective equality is aimed at, for example by meeting the needs of each recipient equally well. It should be noted that cases where account is taken of what the recipients *already have* of the value to be allocated are not included here. In these instances I say that consideration is allowed for one of the characteristics of the recipients. Incidentally, there are many different ways in which attention can be paid to what the recipients already have.[1]

Objective measures can be of different kinds. Material objects can,

1. Inter alia, two completely different principles of equality can be applied. One possibility is that those who had least beforehand receive so much more than the others that their total *stocks*, after allocation, become as great. For example, mother divides 3 apples between Peter and John. Peter gets one because he already has another, while John gets two. Oppenheim (1968) calls this 'equal distribution' as opposed to 'equal allocation' when the allocated shares are equal.

Another possibility is that the recipients receive equally *in proportion* to for instance, be divided equally according to their money value, or by dimension, weight or number of pieces, or by a rough estimate. Jobs can be allocated so that each person works the same length of time or so that each person produces as much as the next, etc. It may be of some concern to the recipients which of the many possible gauges is applied. The person who works quickly, for example, may be interested in actual work done being the yardstick, while the person who works slowly may prefer the number of hours worked to serve as a basis. And the distributor may pay attention to such factors when deciding which measure to use. I will, however, characterize the allocation as object-oriented even if there is subjectivity involved in the choice between different yardsticks. The only essential characteristic is that the yardstick used makes no reference to recipient characteristics.

The *set of values* which serve as a frame of reference when judging whether the distribution is equal can derive from more than one allocation. As mentioned, only what the recipients *receive* is taken into account ; no attention is paid to what they *already have*. But there may be such connections between two or more allocations that we lump them together when judging whether the recipients have obtained equal shares. It can also happen that what they receive on one occasion is broken up when the distribution is determined or evaluated. For instance, at Peter's birthday party the allocations of ice cream, lemonade and cake may each be separately evaluated. In that event, object-oriented equality is obtained for each of the three items. But it is also possible that different principles of distribution are applied, for example that ice and lemonade are distributed evenly but that everyone can have as much cake as he wishes.

The extent to which the set of values is heterogeneous may determine what kind of measure is used when judging what is equal. The more heterogeneous the set of values, the more diffuse will be the measurement, unless a symbolic means of exchange, such as money, can be used as yardstick. The person who wishes to allocate a heterogeneous set of values so that the recipients get equal shares may find himself in a dilemma. Should he make a broad overall evaluation of what is equal ? Or should he break up the set of values into more homogeneous sub-sets to which he can apply specific measurements of value ?

note 1 (cont.)
what they already have. For instance, free shares are distributed in a shareholders' company and each recipient gets one share for every ten he owns.
I will discuss different variations of these types of distribution in later sections (cf. especially section IX).

212

As an example we can take the farmer who wishes to divide his farm equally between his two sons. If we assume that the property consists of arable land, meadow, forest and heath of varying quality and distance from the farm buildings, it will be extremely difficult to make a satisfactory allocation. An equal division on the basis of economic value is not necessarily a satisfactory solution. If, for instance, it is intended that both shares be equally suited as agricultural land, a long series of factors must be taken into account in addition to (or instead of) the monetary value. For example, it may be necessary to make a general overall evaluation of the partitioning alternatives, in which consideration is paid to the relative amount of cultivated land, forest and grazing within each share, the area of the various pieces of land, the quality of the soil, the yield from the forest, distances, roads, buildings possibilities etc. – Decision-making on the basis of such diffuse criteria can be avoided by using a procedure which, in the past, was often followed in Norway and other countries. The method was to divide each of the individual patches of arable land, forest, etc. so that the sons first got a half each of the best strip of land, then a half each of the next best, etc. Obviously, this system of partitioning – especially if repeated several times – can result in unsatisfactory and inexpedient farming units. The widespread use of this method indicates that it is often found more important to be able to use specific criteria of equality than to avoid value reduction. If the man who makes the allocation wants to avoid this he can always give each of his sons neighbouring pieces of land of equal worth.

The principle of equality – as I have defined it – does not answer the question of *who* should have equal shares. Both the circle of recipients and the recipient units can be determined in many different ways. And these decisions will frequently be person-oriented. Whether a married couple is reckoned as one or as two persons when equal expenditure is being calculated on a present to be spliced between several people (married and single) may, for instance, be decided on the basis of whether or not they are both wage earners.

The *circle of recipients* to which the principle of equality is applied is often limited to those who are involved in the same allocation process, for example the guests at the same children's party, the contributors to the same joint enterprise, the heirs to the same estate, etc. Both when it is decided who is to be included in an allocation process and when it is decided whether all should have equal shares, importance is often attached to membership in some group or organization, e.g., being Peter's playfriends, children of the same family, pupils of the same class at

213

school, employees in the same enterprise, inmates of the same prison, citizens or residents of the same country, etc. Common characteristics of the recipients other than those of belonging to some joint unit can also be taken into account, for instance whether they are equal with regard to age, sex, rank, need, fitness, merit etc. Sometimes these two types of criteria are combined, for instance when the (equal) right to vote is conditioned by age and citizenship.

There are many ways in which importance can be attached to such recipient characteristics as age, sex, rank, need, fitness and merit etc. These can, as already mentioned, serve as criteria when delimiting the circle of recipients and they can also be taken into account when the recipient units are fixed. This applies regardless of which principle of distribution is used. An added significance which some of these characteristics can have is that they may serve as distribution criteria, for example in such a manner that transfers increase with the age of the recipient or with his rank, merit or need. It also happens that some of the characteristics (e.g. need or fitness) are only taken into account when evaluating what the individual recipient is to have, and that the distribution is regarded as irrelevant. All these questions are discussed in more detail in section V and what follows.

As may be seen from the various examples given, there can be big variations in the *size* of the recipient group. Only John and Peter are to share the bar of chocolate their aunt brought them, for instance, while the opportunity of influencing the composition of parliament is divided between all those having the right to vote. One question treated in moral philosophy is whether there are any values in which *all human beings* should have equal shares. For example, it has been claimed that everyone should have an equal chance of achieving the best life he is capable of (*Frankena* 1966 p. 14), that everyone has the same right to be treated as a person and not as an object (*Bodenheimer* 1967 p. 83), that in allocating rights everyone concerned is entitled to be considered (i.e. not to be ignored) (*Ginsberg* 1965 p. 79) and that all men should have a claim to an equal share in all those advantages which are commonly desired and which conduce to human well-being (*Honoré* 1968 p. 94). Other 'human rights' which should be equally divided between everyone have also been considered. The values referred to are usually highly abstract. And the criteria of equality which can be applied must necessarily be very diffuse.

Principles of *distributive justice* (see chap. 2, section V) are often given as reasons for object-oriented equality. But other reasons may also be given for dividing equally, e.g., that it simplifies the decision-making

214

process or reduces the risk of conflict between recipients. There are also specific rules which prescribe object-oriented, equal distribution, for instance legal regulations on inheritance, rationing of food during periods of shortage, the right to vote, and conscription. There is frequent interplay of the same kind as was discussed in earlier chapters between the principles of justice and such specific rules.

IV. RANDOM SELECTION

I will first examine cases where a *formalized procedure* is used to ensure a *random* selection. One example is when lots are drawn or a penny is tossed to see who will receive something or do a particular job of work ; 'one potato, two potato, three ...' and similar rhymes which children use when they allot roles during play, are another example. Such procedures are employed not only in everyday activity but also on more formal occasions, for instance when a jury is selected or when exemption from military service is determined on the basis of drawing lots.

Questions of vital importance, e.g., issues of life and death, have been decided in this manner. Drawing lots is often regarded as the right procedure when someone is to be chosen for an especially dangerous mission or if a life has to be sacrificed to save others. Sentence of death has also been decided by drawing lots or throwing dice. *Wedberg* (1935) has given a series of examples from various countries. One type of situation in which the method has been frequently used is when the number of guilty persons is so great that the authorities do not want to punish them all. For instance, from a detachment of troops who have deserted or mutinied, every 10th or 100th is executed while the remainder are released. Another instance is when it is uncertain who the (most) guilty party is. Wedberg gives examples of several Swedish and Finnish law cases from the 17th and 18th centuries in which by drawing lots it was decided who of several accused should be sentenced to death for murder. In these cases all those accused had attacked the victim but it was impossible to ascertain which of them had dealt the mortal blow.

The use of these devices in decision-making can be based on two different kinds of considerations. One is to regard random selection as a means of securing an *equal distribution of chances* for obtaining the relevant good or evil. Another possibility is to conceive the decision as being *left to a higher power* : 'the lot is cast into the lap, but the whole disposing thereof *is* of the Lord', according to Proverbs (16, 33) ; and in the Acts of the Apostles (1, 24-26) the choice of an apostle to replace Judas is described thus :

'And they prayed, and said, Thou, Lord, which knowest the hearts of all *men*, shew whether of these two thou hast chosen,

That he may take part of this ministry and apostleship, from which Judas by transgression fell, that he might go to his own place.

And they gave forth their lots; and the lot fell upon Matthias; and he was numbered with the eleven apostles.'

A decision made by God or some other celestial power is not usually regarded as random. In principle, therefore, the two points of view are incompatible, but this does not prevent elements of both views being combined. The result may, for instance, be considered random in one sense and determined in another; or one may vacillate from one way of reasoning to the other. In some cases there may be a kind of dialectic thinking which converts pure chance into its opposite, the fully determined.

In many of those instances where drawing lots, throwing dice etc. have been employed to decide important issues, it is hard to know which of the two points of view has been the decisively motivating factor. Opinions have differed in regard to the Swedish and Finnish law cases mentioned above (see Wedberg, 1935 pp. 25-26 with references). Wedberg's own opinion is that throwing dice in these cases was not (or at any rate was not primarily) believed to represent any heavenly revelation. The procedure was adopted, he says, because *lex talionis* prescribed that a life should be given for a life, but not more than one for one. When two or more persons were responsible for a murder it was necessary, and sufficient, that one of them be sentenced to death. And if there was no reason to differentiate between them they should, for the sake of equality, be given the same opportunity of saving their lives by throwing dice. In other words, there may have been a combination of notions of retribution and equal distribution lying at the bottom of the arrangement.

As pointed out by *Aubert* (1959 pp. 20-22) and *Rescher* (1961 pp. 9 ff. and 1966 pp. 93-95), drawing of lots, throwing dice etc. are frequently defended in terms of justice. This is maintained both when the result is believed to be ordained by a supernatural power and when it is attributed to pure chance. But the conception of justice involved in these two instances is not the same. In the former case God or Fate is regarded as distributor and the justice which is done may be strongly person-oriented. Because He is all-powerful the distributor can ensure that the benefits or burdens fall to the right person, for example to the person deserving or best suited to them. I will return below (section V onwards) to such criteria of distribution, and here concentrate only on those cases where the selection is believed to be random. Here, the

216

allocation is purely object-oriented since everyone has an equal chance irrespective of what kind of person he is.[2]

A common characteristic between randomness and object-oriented equality is that no personal characteristics of the recipients are taken into account. One could say that random selection is a way of providing for equal distribution, not of the good or evil itself but of the chances of getting it.[3] Because of their similarity, random allocation can serve as a substitute for equal distribution in cases where it is considered right that the recipients should be treated absolutely the same and where, therefore, one would like to give them equal shares but where this is not possible because, for instance, the benefits or burdens are indivisible.

The two principles, however, lead to very different results. In the one instance each recipient receives the same as the next. In the second instance, some get everything and others nothing. One cannot therefore expect that random selection will always be accepted as a substitute for equal distribution. The more important it is for the distributor to control the results, the less acceptable it will be for him to leave the outcome to chance. On the other hand, the greater the need to simplify decision-making and to make it impersonal and object-oriented, the stronger will be the motive to apply random devices. I will later (in Chapter 9) examine more closely the significance of these factors and the interplay between them.

If random selection is used frequently in allocations of the same kind of values among the same recipients, the difference from equal distribution will be less. The difference will completely disappear when the number of allocations becomes sufficiently great – assuming that everything which is dealt out is taken into account. But one cannot always make such an assumption because judgement about whether or not justice is done often refers to an individual allocation.

So far I have considered cases where a formal procedure (as, for instance, drawing lots) is used to ensure that selection is random. But there are also cases where allocation is *arbitrarily* decided so that chance

---

2. The delimitation of the set of values, the groups of recipients and the recipient unit can, however, be based on person-oriented criteria. What was said about this in section III also applies here.
3. In principle there is nothing to hinder other ways of allocating chances. One can, for example, arrange a lottery where the chances are allotted proportionally between the recipients, for instance according to one or another person-oriented criterion. But since such procedures are seldom used in practice, I will not go into them more deeply.

distribution may be achieved without employing any formal procedure. The reason for acting in this manner may be that distribution is considered irrelevant as, for instance, when someone throws a handful of coins to a bunch of beggars. But the intention may also be to ensure that the recipients, in the long run, receive equal treatment. As an example let us imagine a family situation where the father now and then gives a coin, an apple or something similar to the children when they have helped him. He does not think it right that the children always get a reward for the services they render, nor has he any wish to introduce a rigid system, for instance so that a reward is given every other or every third time they help him, or for fetching milk but not for fetching the newspaper. On the other hand he does not want in the long run to discriminate between the children. He therefore tries to divide both jobs and rewards incidentally so that they are evened out in the long run. Even though approximate equality may be obtained in this way, arbitrary allocation is not so easily conceived as an application of principles of justice as is the formalized method of random selection. This is probably because one has a better guarantee that the person making the allocation acts impartially – and hence that chances really are equal – when the procedure is formalized.

The idea of justice that chances (or opportunities) should be equally allotted has, however, an important field of application which has not yet been mentioned. It is often claimed that society should afford everyone the same opportunity of developing their abilities, talents and interests. The extent to which the equal opportunities are realized depends, in this case, not on pure chance but (also) on characteristics of the recipients – for example, their resolution and ability to exploit the possibilities furnished to them.

V. ALLOCATION ACCORDING TO TIME PRIORITY OR LOCATION

Queues, waiting rooms and waiting lists provide examples of allocation according to time priority. Usually it is the person who comes *first* who has the advantage, as is expressed in the sayings 'the early bird catches the worm' and 'first come, first serve' and in the legal maxim *'prior tempore, potior jure'*. But other distributions based on position in time can also be imagined, for instance that 'the first shall be last'.

Sometimes the position in time only determines *when* the different recipients receive their transfers. In such cases only the timing of the transfers is distributed according to this criterion, whilst the kind and size of the values received are determined in another way, for example by everyone receiving the same amount. But it also happens that position decides both *who* receives something and/or *what* they get. For example : 700 people stand in a cinema queue, but the cinema has only 500 seats. The last 200 therefore do not get in and, amongst those who do, the first get the best seats. Or, a person sells the same object to two different buyers : normally the man who bought first will have the right to the object while the other must be content with claiming compensation from the seller, which may not amount to very much.

Allocation is also sometimes made according to the location of recipients. One's placing at the dinner table, for instance, determines the order in which one gets food when the dishes are sent round. It can also decide *what* one gets, and *whether* one gets anything at all if there is little on the dish. Other examples which can be given are the officer who allots jobs to his men according to their position on parade, and the teacher who follows the line of desks when he puts questions to his pupils. Location also plays a role in queues but then it serves solely as an indication of position in time.

The recipients' position in time and space is sometimes incidental. In these instances a kind of random selection is made when position is the determining factor. In other instances the placing may be decided by one or another criterion of the recipients. For instance, they are placed according to rank or dignity at the dinner table. It may also be that a position is indicative of need, effort or sacrifice. The fact that someone stands first in the queue may be a sign that he has waited longer than the others and perhaps also that he has a greater interest in obtaining the values which are to be allocated.

Sometimes justice is considered to require rank order equality (cf. chap. 2, section V), so that No. 1 receives first (or, possibly, most), No. 2 next, etc. It may, for instance, be thought unjust if those at the end of the cinema queue get in first. But such ideas of equality do not always apply. The reason for allocating according to position can be the purely practical one that when everyone cannot receive at the same point in time there must be some sequence to go by, and position then appears to be a simple and easily applicable criterion.

The position of recipients is not a purely object-oriented criterion but it is *more* object-oriented than the criteria we will deal with in the following sections. The only characteristic of the recipients to which importance is attached is where they are placed in time or space on a particular occasion. Their personal qualifications, attitudes or actions are of no direct significance. The fact that such features can be of in-

219

direct importance because the placing depends on them, is another matter.

It should perhaps be stressed that, in what has been said, it is only placing on a *particular occasion* with which I have been concerned. More permanent placings as, for example, place of residence, order of birth among siblings, seniority in one's job, etc. are regarded as status criteria and discussed in section IX.

VI. ALLOCATION ACCORDING TO NEED OR ACCORDING TO SACRIFICE OR SUFFERING

When we say that a person *'needs'* something or other, we sometimes mean that he 'desires' or 'is inclined to strive for' the thing to which reference is made. In this sense a man needs everything that he likes to have whether this be, for instance, food, clothing, alcohol or drugs. But the expression is often used with a rather different meaning, describing what the person 'requires' in order to preserve or increase such values as, for example, health, knowledge or happiness. In this, partly normative, sense a child may need medicine which he does not like, while he is not considered to need sweets which he does like. The word 'need' will here be used as a common designation for the two concepts. When more precise expressions are necessary I will distinguish between 'to desire' and 'to require'.

'Sacrifice' and 'suffering' (or 'dislike') will be used as expressions for refraining from, or being prevented from satisfaction of need. The word 'sacrifice' is normally employed when the reduction in satisfaction results from one's own actions or omissions, while the word 'suffering' (or 'dislike') is generally employed when this is due to other factors. However, I will not attempt to make any sharp distinction between these concepts. In both cases, what one abstains from (or is prevented from) can be either something one 'wants' or something one 'requires'.

When I refer to allocation according to need, it is always the *recipients'* needs I have in mind. The needs of the distributor can also affect the allocation but this will not be discussed in the present connection.

The expression 'allocation according to need' is often used only to cover cases where the aim is to *increase* need satisfaction, that is to say only when benefits are allocated. Needs may, however, also be taken into account when an allocation (for instance of punishment or burdens) results in *reduced* need satisfaction. But in this context it is more natural to use expressions such as 'allocation according to suffering' (or 'sa-

220

crifice'). Reference is sometimes also made to 'allocation according to ability', for instance in connection with taxation. The word 'ability' can here be used so that 'great ability' (to carry burdens) means the same as 'small sacrifice' or, in other words, as 'small reduction in need satisfaction'. The questions which arise, however, are largely the same whether an increase or a reduction of satisfaction is being considered. These will therefore be examined together in what follows and I shall occasionally use the expression 'allocation according to need' as a joint term for the allocation criteria which have been mentioned here.

The needs of the recipients may be considered when deciding several of the issues mentioned in section II. Firstly, need may be taken into account when the *circle of recipients* is decided upon. For example, mother hands out cake only to those children who want it, and social assistance is given only to those who require it (or only to those who badly require it). Similarly, the class of tax-payers can be limited to those who can pay without making too great a sacrifice. Secondly, the *recipient units* can be delimited on the basis of need. A charity organization which distributes wireless sets to the poor, may deem it adequate to give one set to each household regardless of whether this household consists of few or many persons – on the grounds that people living together can listen to the same wireless.

Thirdly, needs are often taken into account when deciding what kind of values and how much *each individual recipient* should have. The recipients' claims and wishes are usually determined by their needs. And it may also, from the point of view of the distributor seem reasonable to pay attention, as far as is possible, to what each recipient desires or is thought to require. In the same way, it may be considered important that the person to whom a burden is allocated is able to bear it without too great a sacrifice. And as regards punishment, the attitude may be taken that the guilty party should be made to suffer to the extent that he understands that it is not worth-while to behave as he has done, but should not be made to suffer more than is necessary to achieve this aim.

Needs may be considered relevant in one of these respects without being so in another. For instance, the circle of recipients may be determined by need qualifications, while importance is not attached to differences in need when deciding how much each individual recipient should have. Conversely, the circle of recipients is sometimes determined by other criteria (for example, according to who Peter's playmates are) whereas allocation is made according to need.

When needs are taken into account in deciding what each recipient should have, this will indirectly affect the *distribution* arrived at. But

221

this may be accidental. The fact that transfers are adjusted to the individual's need often indicates that questions of distribution are considered irrelevant and this fact may be used as an argument for regarding them as irrelevant. Mother says, for instance, to the children at the birthday party, 'you can have as much as you want, so there is no need to quarrel about who has most'.

However, when questions of distribution are considered relevant needs may be taken into account, for instance in the application of certain principles of equality. One possibility is that a *rank order* is followed, so that the person who has greatest need receives most, he who has the next greatest need comes next, etc. With regard to allocation of burdens, the comparable arrangement would be that the person who has the greatest ability (in the sense mentioned above) contributes most, he who is next-best equipped contributes next most, etc. Application of this principle of distribution assumes that needs (or sacrifices) can be ranked. This is certainly not always the case, but there is sometimes a sufficiently clear conception of relative strength for this to be done. One finds, for instance, that A is hungrier than B and therefore needs more food, or that A is more impoverished than B and therefore needs greater help, or that A is richer than B and can therefore make a contribution with less sacrifice. Ranking based on the strength (or importance) of needs may be possible even if these are of different kinds. In some cases certain kinds of needs (for example, for medical assistance) are given absolute priority over others. But generally both the nature and the magnitude of different needs are taken into account when they are ranked. Even though mother and father normally consider it more important that the children are properly clad than that they have sporting equipment, it may be that they allot priority to John's need for a pair of skis rather than to Peter's need for new trousers if, for example, Peter already has 10 pairs of trousers and John has no skis at all.

Another principle of equality which can be applied is that everyone should have his needs equally well *satisfied*. This can have differing meanings. One possible interpretation is that distribution be such that the marginal utility of the transfers be the same for all recipients. Similarly, burdens can be distributed so that the marginal sacrifice is equally heavy. By 'marginal utility' I mean the utility value of the last unit which the recipient gets, and by 'marginal sacrifice' I refer to the sacrifice made with the last unit of his contribution. I will explain these concepts – borrowed from economics – in more detail in the next chapter.

On some occasions the set of values available is insufficient to raise

222

satisfaction to an equal level for all recipients. One approach towards equality, in such cases, is that he who is worst off gets so much that he is raised to the level of No. 2, that these two then get so much that they arrive on a level with No. 3, etc. and that those who are above the final level which is reached by proceeding in this manner receive nothing. (See fig. 1 in which the plain columns indicate the degree of satisfaction of each recipient before allocation and the shaded columns show the additional satisfaction resulting from allocation.) But there are also other ways of approaching equality, for example by allocating values so that each recipient receives proportionally equal amounts of what is required to reach a desired level (see fig. 2).

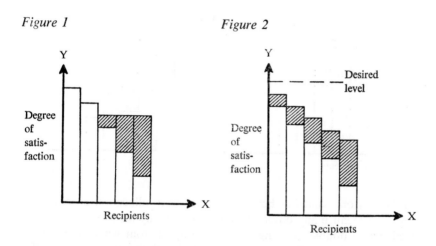

Figure 1   Figure 2

When burdens or tasks are allocated with the intention that the sacrifice involved be the same for everyone, similar questions arise if the sum of burdens is not so large that all recipients can reach the same level. Here, too, there are different ways of approaching equality. A parallel to creating equality from the bottom upwards when allocating benefits (see fig. 1) is to create equality at the top by allocating burdens according to ability to carry them (see fig. 3 where the shaded columns show the reduction in satisfaction which the burdens imposed involve). As an example we can cite the answer given by a primary school pupil (in the 5th form) when asked how the job of helping the teacher should be allocated. The answer was that the teacher should preferably choose the

223

pupil who was most able to sustain the break in teaching which the service entailed. And this principle of distribution was expressed thus : 'Take the cleverest. First the very cleverest, then the next cleverest, etc. but not the worst if they have not become clever.'[4] Another alternative is proportional distribution of a similar kind to that mentioned above (fig. 4).

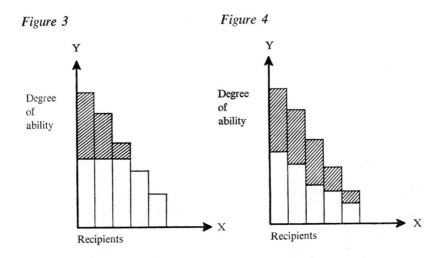

Figure 3   *Figure 4*

It follows from what has been said so far that 'allocation according to need' can mean many different things. As already mentioned, the word 'need' has a double meaning. And quite apart from whether it is used in one sense or the other ('to desire' or 'to require'), opinions may differ as to which needs a man *has*, which of them should be *taken into consideration* during an allocation process, and the *way* in which they should be considered. There are many possible variations but we can perhaps distinguish between two main tendencies. One of these, which I refer to as the tendency towards *individualization*, is characterized by a strong concern for individual features of the recipients. Here it is intended that each of them get what he needs according to his own special preferences or abilities. When the trend is in this direction importance

4. The example is taken from an investigation of school children's attitudes of justice made by Siri Naess (1969).

224

is usually attached more to what the individual recipient receives than to questions of distribution. The other main tendency is that of *levelling out*. Questions of distribution are here considered essential. One tries somehow to place the recipients on as equal a footing as possible. Individualizing and levelling tendencies can, to some extent, be compatible – but only to some extent. If one goes too far in the direction of levelling, this will be at the expense of individualization, and vice versa.

That values be allocated according to need is sometimes *claimed in the name of justice*. What is usually aimed at in such cases is a kind of allocation which levels out differences. The final goal is often a more even distribution of all kinds of benefits and burdens.

One formulation of such a principle is 'from each according to his abilities, to each according to his needs'.[5] This has been regarded both as a principle of justice and as an ideal of solidarity and brotherhood. The phrase can be interpreted in several different ways but I will here regard it as expressing a pure principle of need with more even distribution of benefits and burdens as its goal. I thus take 'according to one's abilities' to mean that contributions should come from those who can carry the burdens with least reduction in the satisfaction of their needs. Construed in this way, the two parts of the principle are in harmony with each other when considered from the angle of distribution, since both work in the direction of evening-out satisfaction of needs. If, however, ideas of balance between contributions and returns are applied, it is difficult to combine the two parts of the principle. The person who has greatest ability, and is therefore to contribute much, has as a rule relatively few unsatisfied needs and receives little. The principle is therefore hard to justify unless one gives distributive justice absolute priority over retributive justice.

The kibbutzes in Israel offer an interesting example of how attempts have been made to put the principle into practice.[6] Those who are accepted as members must give everything they own (apart from purely personal effects) to the kibbutz and what they are later allowed to accept as presents etc. from outside is very restricted. One of the main rules is

5. The principle is sometimes attributed to Marxism, but according to Tucker (1963 p. 306 et seq.) this attribution rests upon a misunderstanding. It was originally formulated by Louis Blanc (Organisation du travail, 1839). Marx has certainly quoted the phrase but Tucker (p. 318) contends that he did not attach great importance to it since he considered increased production to be more important than distribution.
6. This description of the kibbutz system is primarily based on information furnished by Weingarten (1959) and Darin-Drabkin (1963).

that hired labour not be employed in the kibbutz since they wish to have 'a society based on justice, without exploitation' (*Darin-Drabkin* loc. cit. p. 93). The work is allocated between the members by a job-coordinator on the basis of what needs to be done and the ability of the individual members to do the various jobs.[7] The members of the kibbutz do not get paid for their work but it is assumed that their needs are covered. Most of what they get is in the form of material goods (living quarters, food, clothing, theatre tickets, etc.). They are occasionally given small amounts of money – to be used in the holidays and such like – but some people regard this as a dangerous lapse from principle. Special committees decide the distributional questions which may arise, among other things, which types of need should be given priority – for instance, whether higher profits should be used to acquire better housing for the individual families, better communal buildings (for example, kitchens and dining rooms), more clothing or improved food. The members' needs dominate all decisions but ideas are frequently founded on standardized conceptions of what people require. In the case of individual benefits, for instance clothing, this tends to result in object-oriented equal distribution. One need which is given very high priority is the care and cure of sick and disabled persons. Weingarten mentions a case where a member of a kibbutz who became paralysed was flown to the United States and given hospital and convalescence treatment there at the kibbutz's expense – in spite of the fact that finances were strained and conditions in the kibbutz very spartan. Both Weingarten (loc. cit. p. 145) and Darin-Drabkin (loc. cit. p. 146 et seq.) stress that there has been development in the direction of increased individualization in the distribution of benefits since the early kibbutz period. This is probably connected with economic progress.

The desire to create a just society is obviously one of the most important ideological forces behind the kibbutz movement. The maxim 'from each according to his abilities, to each according to his needs' is frequently quoted by supporters of the movement and they claim that social justice is obtained by following this principle (see Darin-Drabkin loc. cit. p. 87 et seq., pp. 179 and 272). But other arguments are also advanced in support of the principle, inter alia that it creates a homogeneous society and prevents conflicts (loc. cit. p. 91).

7. The job-coordinator and others who have administrative duties (treasurer, secretary etc.) are elected by the assembly in which every member has the right to vote. To be job-coordinator is one of the most thankless tasks in the whole kibbutz system, writes Weingarten (loc. cit. pp. 48-49), because it often involves imposing work on people who do not want it.

226

By the expression 'fitness' I refer to how well or how badly recipients are able to use, exploit or take care of the values which are transferred. For instance, one allocates according to fitness when one gives the carpenter a hammer and saw, the tailor needle and thread, the small boy bricks to build with and the older boy an electric train. Appointment and promotion on the basis of qualifications and allocation of work according to talent and capability provide similar examples. Rights and duties are allocated according to fitness when they are given only to persons who are expected not to misuse them. A prisoner who asks for parole can, for instance, be described as unfit to receive it if it is assumed that he will misuse the occasion to escape. And a pupil may be unfit to sit at the back of the classroom because he makes a noise or cheats if the teacher does not have him under constant control.

There is usually some goal or other to be promoted when fitness is considered relevant. If, for example, work or appointments are allocated according to fitness, the aim is usually to have the work done as well as possible. And when objects are allocated, the aim may be to utilize material resources in the best possible way. In some instances it is solely in the interests of the distributor that the goal is promoted. But it also happens that recipient or broader social interests are to be taken care of. The kind of fitness required depends upon the goal which is set. One person who is fit for a job in the sense that he is capable of doing the work is perhaps not fit to encourage good relations among the employees.

The concept fitness could perhaps have been stretched to include need ('fitness to avail oneself of benefits'). However, I have found it appropriate using 'fitness' and 'need' as two separate categories. But the dividing line is not sharp and sometimes both are applicable and pull in the same direction. It can be said, for instance, that the reason for giving a hammer and saw to the carpenter is both that he needs them and that he is fit to use them. But on some occasions the two considerations pull in opposite directions. For example, it is not certain that the applicant who is best fitted for an appointment is also the one who most needs it.

Evaluation of fitness (as with evaluation of need) can vary in its degree of specificity. Importance is sometimes attached only to a few outer and easily ascertained characteristics, for instance, examination marks and age on appointment to a position, while in other cases an

227

overall evaluation will be made of all the recipient's characteristics which could possibly be of significance.

In common with need, fitness can be taken into account when delimiting the circle of recipients and/or the recipient units and also when it is decided what and how much each individual recipient should have. The distribution is often regarded as irrelevant and if it *is* thought relevant it is not certain that the criteria governing the transfers also serve as a measurement of values. For instance, some friends are on a camping holiday and divide the work between them according to fitness, so that Ann cooks the food, Mary washes up, Fred chops the wood and Dick fetches water. Perhaps they follow this division of labour without bothering to ascertain whether it entails one person having more to do than another. And if they do regard the distribution as being of importance and, for instance, try to distribute the burden evenly, it is possible that they only look at actual working hours and do not take into account the contribution each has made according to his degree of fitness.

There are also instances, however, where fitness is graded and serves as a yardstick when evaluating the distribution. This is especially pertinent when the fitness of various persons for the same job are judged. Applicants for a post, for example, are judged by their qualifications and ranked in order of fitness by the nominating authorities. Or students who sit for an exam or test receive marks according to how fit they are considered to be to carry on the activity for which the exam qualifies them.

In cases where fitness is graded the principle of *rank order equality* can be applied, for instance so that the person who is best fitted is placed first, the next best second, etc. It is also possible that notions of *relative equality* are involved – for example, when allotting marks and making other similar evaluations – but this is perhaps most relevant in instances where attention to fitness is interwoven with ideas of merit. The other ideas of equality which can be associated with distribution according to need (see section VI) are, however, unlikely to be applied in connection with fitness.

Claims for rank order equality or relative equality can in some cases be founded on notions of justice. For instance, it may be thought unfair when the most qualified person does not get the job. This is perhaps most likely when evaluation of fitness is combined with the idea that the person who is most fitted 'has a right' to the post. In such cases elements of retributive justice may enter the picture. Not only has the decision been prejudicial to the person who was most fit for the job but – in one sense – he has also been refused something to which he had

228

a claim. In most cases, however, consequence-oriented reasons for distribution according to fitness are more appropriate than reasons of justice.

VIII. ALLOCATION ACCORDING TO RIGHT, DUTY AND DESERT

Recipients sometimes have *rights* or *duties* vis-à-vis the distributor. They may be his employees whose duty it is to work and whose right it is to receive a wage. Or perhaps they are his customers who have a right to delivered goods and a duty to pay the costs of these. Or they may be inheritors of the estate which he administers and, by law, entitled to their share. Duties and rights can be more or less firmly established. They can be founded on promises or agreements or directly on legal rules or other norms, for example on principles of retributive justice.

There is no sharp distinction between the state of having a right or duty and that of having *deserved* something. These expressions are sometimes employed synonymously. We can say, for example, that a person who has performed some service 'deserves' something in return or that he has a 'right' (or 'claim') to something, and the meaning can be approximately the same in both cases. But the concept 'desert' is frequently stretched further – especially in connection with rewards, punishment and revenge. For example, we may say, 'he had really no right to a reward, but I thought he deserved it'. And we may say that a person 'deserves' to be punished although we would not say that he has a duty to submit to punishment. The expression is used in this sense in what follows. In all cases where a transfer has the character either of appreciation for something positive or reaction against something negative, I say that desert is taken into account.

Transfer from one to another of these different conceptions occurs frequently. Rewards which are regularly given on the basis of desert may (as mentioned in chap. 4, section IX) gradually give rise to the idea that the recipients are entitled to be rewarded. And the idea that punishment is deserved can give rise to the notion that one has a duty to submit to it (see chap. 7, section III).

It is characteristic of right, duty and desert criteria that they are *oriented towards the past* and are *normative*. Weight is attached to certain phenomena (promises, agreements, services, damaging actions etc.) which have occurred before the allocation is made and to which normative relevance is attached. The manner of reasoning is, in these respects, different from what it is when fitness is taken into account:

then, one mainly looks to the future – towards the expected consequences of the decision. But in order to forecast the consequences one must often build upon what has happened earlier. When a decision has to be made about an applicant's fitness for a job, attention may be paid to his training and experience and to how well he has worked previously. However, such factors can also be relevant when enquiring into a person's merit. If, for example, an employee is promoted on the grounds that he has done a good job in his previous post, it may not be clear whether this is because he has worked well and shown himself to be fit for a higher position or whether it is felt that he deserves a reward for his efforts. Often elements of both these ideas are merged.

The notion that fitness is the proper basis for some kinds of allocation, for instance promotion, may develop into the idea that those who are best fitted have a *right* to be promoted. Similar conceptions can also be associated with the idea that needs should be satisfied. For instance, it may be considered a human right that man's most vital requirements be secured. However, in what follows I will not be concerned with those ideas of rights which are based on a desire to satisfy needs or to recognize fitness.

Criteria of right, duty and desert are never completely object-oriented : importance is always attached to something that has to do with the recipients. The degree of person-orientation varies. Sometimes only overt characteristics of an event or its consequences are taken into account. In other cases, when judging what recipients have deserved or what rights and duties they have, regard may also be paid to their beliefs, attitudes and intentions and to such factors as, for example, their age, ability and education.

Rights, duties and desert, in common with need and fitness, may be taken into account in various connections – for delimitation of the circle of recipients and the recipient unit, for what the individual recipient should receive (or contribute), and for the distribution.

Existing rights and obligations are generally of decisive importance for *what the individual recipient receives* (or contributes). Sometimes a recipient renounces his right or the distributor relieves him of a duty. But if this does not happen, it is normally taken for granted that rights and duties should be complied with – even if need or fitness points in another direction. One can imagine instances where it could be said 'I admit that you have a right to this, but even so you are not going to get it because you don't need it' or '... because you are not fit to take care of it'. But, normally, priority will be given to rights and duties. This, of course, does not mean that references to alleged rights or duties

230

always make strong arguments. The contention must have a basis which is accepted by the other party or which furnishes the possibility of bringing compulsion to bear on him.

What a person has deserved – of good or evil – can also carry considerable weight when what he should receive is to be decided. But this is not normally so completely decisive as are rights and duties. Allowance for other factors – for instance, need or fitness – may suggest that one refrain from punishing or from giving a reward even if one feels that it is deserved.

In some cases the only reason for making a transfer is that this is thought to be deserved. For example, one gives something solely as a reward, or imposes an injury for the sole purpose of punishing. But notions of desert can also be taken into account when determining the type or size of transfers made primarily for other reasons. The principle aim may be, for instance, to satisfy a need but the extent to which this is done is partly determined by ideas of merit. When mother deals out the ice cream Peter gets an extra large portion because he has helped her and John gets an extra small one because he has been naughty.

When right, duty or desert determine the nature and size of individual transfers, the resulting distribution is sometimes considered irrelevant. This is most likely when established rights or duties constitute the basis of the transfers. If everyone gets what he has a right to, one seldom hears the criticism that some get unjustifiably more than others.

But in other cases distribution is often considered important. This applies both when rights and duties are not completely fulfilled and when notions of merit determine the size of the transfers. In both these cases it may be natural for the recipients to make comparisons with each other and to argue by pointing to what others have received.

It is usual in such situations to demand some kind of equality based on criteria of right, duty or desert. Such equality is often claimed for its own sake and thus comes under our concept of justice. In what follows I will look more closely at the various notions of equality which are particularly relevant in this context.

One such notion is that there should be consistency with regard to enforcement of rights and fulfilment of duties, so that either everyone or no one gets what one has a right to or does what one is under obligation to do. For example, creditor A who has not received his dues approaches his debtor and says, 'when you first paid B and C what you owed them, you could also have paid me'. Or a debtor who wants to postpone repayment argues, 'I have not managed to repay D or E yet, so you see you will have to wait as well'. Similar reasoning can be found when recipients have obligations towards the distributor. A recipient says, for instance, 'you have permitted M and N to neglect their duty, so you could also allow me to do the same'. Or perhaps it is the distributor who argues, 'P and Q have done their duty, and so must you'.

However, in many instances it is more natural to operate with *degrees* of fulfilment rather than with such an 'all or nothing' standpoint. A debtor who is unable to fulfil all his obligations will be expected, in the name of justice, to see to it that his creditors receive *proportionally* the same amount. Generally speaking, this is the procedure when someone goes bankrupt or makes a deed of arrangement with his creditors so that they receive a certain percentage of what he owes them. A similar manner of reasoning can be applied when what is involved is not rights or duties with a relatively definite content and size but vaguer ideas of desert. These calculations of proportionality cannot be exact. But, even so, one may have certain approximate ideas of the relation between the criteria of merit and the transfers. One can, for instance, feel that one crime is *a little* graver than the next and therefore deserves slightly heavier punishment, and that another criminal act is *a lot* more serious and therefore deserves a much more severe sentence. One may have similar approximate ideas on relative equality with regard to exchange payments and rewards. As already mentioned (chap. 2, section V, 3), this line of thought can be illustrated with the help of the formula

$$\frac{a_1}{p_1} = \frac{a_2}{p_2} = \frac{a_3}{p_3} \ldots \ldots = \frac{a_n}{p_n}$$

which means that the relation between the value of the allotments (a_1, a_2, etc.) and the value of the criteria of desert (p_1, p_2, etc.) are the same for each recipient.

There may also be instances where one is satisfied with rank order equality. If we use the above symbols, that which is needed to satisfy this claim can be formulated thus:

When $p_1 > p_2 > p_3 \ldots \ldots > p_n$, then
$\qquad a_1 > a_2 > a_3 \ldots \ldots > a_n$.

The difference between this and relative equality is that importance is attached only to the sequence ('more than' and 'less than') and not to the size of the intervals (whether there is 'much more' or only 'a little more'). This claim for equality is therefore a more modest one.

Demands for equality seem to occur more frequently when the

232

allocation is based on desert, than when it is based on need or fitness.[8] In a later chapter I point to several factors which may explain this difference. One such factor has to do with the relationship between retributive and distributive justice. As mentioned in section VI, it is hard to combine the principle of balance that he who contributes a lot should receive a lot, with the principle of distribution : 'from each according to his abilities, to each according to his needs'. Other principles of equality which can be tied to criteria of need or fitness are also likely to clash with notions of balance. But when desert is the basic criterion, conceptions of retributive and distributive justice harmonize well, and they can mutually support each other. The fact that one takes account of desert when deciding what the individual recipient should have, means that one – wholly or in part – regards the transfers as reward, punishment, exchange payment or the like. It then becomes natural to evaluate the transfers in terms of retributive justice : the recipient should have a suitable 'payment' for what he has done – of good or evil. And ideas of payment lead naturally to the idea that what is the 'right price' for one recipient is also the 'right price' for another. The overall size of payment should depend upon what each person has done, but the 'level of prices' must be the same for everyone, i.e., relative equality is expected. In other words, conceptions of balance between action and reaction tend to lead to the idea that there should be relative equality between recipients.

This does not mean that evaluations in terms of retributive and distributive justice always coincide. Let us take as an example a person who gets a parking fine of £ 5. He feels that, in itself, there is no disproportion between his offence and the punishment. The requirement of retributive justice is satisfied. But if other people have only been fined £ 2 for similar offences, or £ 5 for more serious ones, he will perhaps think that the requirement of relative equality (distributive justice) has not been met. Suppose that, to change the example, sentences for traffic offences are made much more rigorous : the general opinion will probably then be that there is a lack of proportion between the offence and the punishment – but this does not prevent relative equality between the individual punishments. In the long run, however, such divergences tend to be evened out because comparisons with what other people get influence the scales of measurement.

8. The trend went clearly in this direction among the school children of the Oslo district who were interviewed on distribution issues by Siri Naess (1969 pp. 79-80). My own unsystematic experience from other situations in life seems to point in the same direction.

By 'status' I refer to the placement of an individual (or collective unit) into a certain category such as, for instance, man, woman, old, young, rich, poor, student, teacher, married couple, joint-stock company, sovereign state, world power etc. Some of these categories can be rank ordered (for instance, rich-poor) whereas others are considered to be on an equal footing (for instance, man-woman).[9] In both instances, the classes can be wider or narrower. Division according to age, for example, may be a binary classification into old and young, or it may be finely graded into many age groups.

It is characteristic of status categories, as defined here, that their classification is made on the basis of *outer and comparatively easily ascertainable criteria* such as, for instance, sex, age, profession, education etc. I do not regard the more diffuse and person-oriented categories, such as those of being 'well fitted' or 'highly deserving' as status categories. A further requirement is that the classification is of *social relevance*. I do not regard groupings based on biological features (for example whether a person is tall or short, fat or thin) as status criteria – unless these features are *also* socially relevant (as the colour of one's skin can be). Finally, the characteristics must be relatively *permanent*. In this respect status differs from the kind of temporary placing in time or space discussed in section V. A person's position in a queue is an example of a temporary placing, while his placing with regard to seniority in a firm may indicate status.

Reference is often made to need, fitness or desert when justifying why importance is attached to status. Distribution of work according to sex, for instance, may be argued by saying that women are best suited to some jobs and men to others. And a higher wage for men than for women may be justified by saying that men require more because they often have dependants or that they deserve more since they are less often absent from their work. In the course of time changes can occur so that criteria of fitness (or need or desert) become more rigid and turn into status criteria. For instance, to begin with a criterion such as sex or age may serve as one of several indicators of a person's fitness. Gradually more and more stress is placed on this indicator and finally it becomes the only criterion and is considered decisive even when considerations of fitness pull in the opposite direction. The principle can still be justified by claiming that it gives *largely* the same results as

9. Some social scientists restrict the concept of 'status' to rank ordered categories.

when a free evaluation of who is best fitted is made. But a further development may take place so that references to fitness become superfluous and are replaced by the belief that it is in itself right to attach importance to status. Developments may also lead in the opposite direction : a status principle may be 'softened up', for instance if one begins to look for the real reasons behind its use. The reasons one then finds (for example, fitness, need or merit) may, in such an instance, gradually displace the original principle and be attributed significance in their own right.

Which status criteria are taken account of is largely culturally determined. Differences in sex, age and social rank are, for example, considered much more significant in some cultures than in others. The colour of one's skin and other ethnic characteristics are fundamentally important in some places while in others they are of little or no significance. In one place ascribed qualities such as inherited rank carry great weight, while in others achieved characteristics such as education or profession are thought more important. The significance attributed to status and the kinds of status criteria employed, tell us a good deal about the society involved, inter alia, about social stratification and mobility.

Status can – in common with the criteria discussed in the previous sections – be considered important in various connections. The *circle of recipients* is often decided by status. For instance, only the children get lemonade during the birthday party, generally only men are called up for compulsory military service, and only citizens or residents of a country who have reached a certain age have the right to vote. As the examples show, on some occasions it is just one status characteristic which is considered relevant, while in other cases it is a combination of characteristics. The *recipient unit* may also be decided by status. Whether one happens to be married or single, for instance, may determine whether one is reckoned as an independent unit or as a part of a recipient unit. And whether or not a group of persons working together have organized their activity as a limited company may, in certain connections, determine whether they are to be counted as one or as several units.

In addition, status can be attributed importance in what the *individual recipient* should receive. Peter's parents, for example, feel that he should have some professional training since he is a boy but that Mary would do better to employ her time looking for a husband because she is a girl.

The fact that status is taken into account when individual transfers are decided upon also affects the *distribution* of values. This does not necessarily mean that distribution issues are considered relevant to the decisions which are made. But they often are so. Generally speaking, more notice is paid to distribution when decisions are based on status criteria than when they are founded on need or fitness. In the latter cases attention is frequently focused on individual characteristics of the recipients.[10] But when status is the decisive factor, people are always placed into one or another general category. And placing people in categories constitutes, in many cases, the function of providing a design for the distribution of values.

There are several ways in which distribution can be determined by status :

In the first place, if the recipients have the *same status* this may provide grounds for treating them equally. This viewpoint comes naturally when their status indicates that the recipients 'belong together' in some way or other, for example, that they belong to the same family, are pupils at the same school, employees in the same factory, inmates in the same prison, or citizens of the same country, etc. But other kinds of status similarity can also be grounds for equal treatment. When a collective unit is a 'sovereign state' this may, for example, serve as an argument for treating it like other states. And in some connections the fact that someone is 'a human being' can be a reason for treating him as other human beings. *The kind* of equal treatment which is recommended in such cases may differ : it can be object-oriented or one of the other forms of equality mentioned earlier, for example, equal satisfaction of need. The fact that equality of status is advanced as a reason for equality of treatment, tells us nothing in itself about *what* is to be equal.

In the second place, *differences* in status can serve as a reason for *different* treatment. Whether it is right to attach such importance to differences in status and *which* differences should, in this event, be considered, has played an important role in discussions of justice down through the ages. Discriminatory treatment has been defended partly with the negative argument that 'it is not unjust' when one discriminates between R_1 and R_2 since they, for instance, are of different sexes, have different ages or different education. One also finds examples of the stronger, more positive contention that 'justice demands' there be dif-

10. This can also be the case when importance is attached to *desert*. But as was mentioned in section VIII, there are here special reasons for attaching importance to distribution.

ferent treatment. On the other hand, many different forms of discriminatory treatment, for instance, between the sexes, between rich and poor, free men and slaves, black people and white etc. have been labelled unjust. Sometimes such views have been accompanied by the tendency to class the categories involved in a more general common category such as, for example, 'citizen', 'comrade' or 'human being'.

In the third place, conceptions of *rank order equality* can be applied when the status categories are rank ordered. Ranking may come quite naturally, as when age groups are involved. But the existence of an obvious numerical series to go by does not necessarily indicate what order the size of the transfers will have. For example, distribution according to age may mean that the eldest gets most and the youngest least – or that the youngest gets most and the eldest least.

Of particular interest are those rank orders which reflect the value that is attached to belonging to the different categories. Classification by income, profession or education can be given as examples. I use the word 'rank' to describe such statuses. Differences in rank are found both in society as a whole and in smaller social systems, for example in a factory, a university institute and within the family. The scale of ranking which is used can vary from system to system. The concept of 'rank' is therefore relative in a double sense. 'High (or low) rank' is something one has in relation to a particular social system and to a particular ranking scale which is relevant within that system.

Differences in rank have a tendency to be *self-preserving*. Those who are placed high on the scale frequently have a better opportunity of acquiring more of the values which determine their ranking. The rich can get their money to multiply, while it can be expensive to be poor. The successful politician is constantly invited to sit on new committees, whilst the unknown gets nowhere. One of the factors promoting this tendency is that the distributor often has good reasons for following the principle in St. Matthew, 13, 12 : 'For whosoever hath, to him shall be given'.[11] It can, for instance, be rational for a businessman to give his most important customer the best service. And the public authority which allots licences etc. is more likely to regard an outsider with scepticism than the large and well-established firm whom they know can be relied upon. *Barton* (1954) in his study of allocation practices in the Norwegian Ministry of Industry, found clear indications pointing in this direction. It was generally easier for the large firms to get a licence than

11. This point is discussed more thoroughly by Aubert (1966 pp. 112-113) and I
shall return to it later.

for the small, among other things because they could furnish more detailed and more dependable information.

But in addition to these tendencies, which are not necessarily rooted in a wish to maintain differences in rank, there may also be *positive attitudes to the rank order* and norms which prevent change. European feudalism and – to an even greater extent – the Indian caste system are examples of such norm-bound systems of rank. Even in societies with relatively high social mobility, for example present-day Norway, one finds examples of positive attitudes to rank differences and norms which serve to preserve these differences. There are, for instance, norms of distribution to the effect that those who have most or are greatest should receive the largest allotments. These norms are often based on ideas of relative equality or rank order equality. Export and import regulation in Norway during the immediate post-war years can serve as an example. Generally speaking, the practice was to grant a quota to each firm, and the quotas were usually fixed at a percentage of what each firm had exported or imported during a certain base year (for example, 1939). This system – which was frequently defended by arguments of justice – served to preserve the ranking of the firms with regard to size.

But one also finds the opposite attitude – that *differences in rank should be levelled down or eliminated*. This can be a general attitude, or it can be limited to a definite social system and/or a definite ranking scale. One can, for instance, support democracy in society as a whole but not in one's own family, and one may encourage a more even dispersal of political influence but not of economic wealth, etc. Disapproval of rank differences can result in objections to status discrimination in allocations. For example, a person who goes in for elimination of the differences in rank between the various categories of university teaching staff may take the view that they should all bear the same title, receive the same salary, lecture the same number of hours and have the same possibility of influencing decisions, etc. There are also cases where the aim of levelling out differences does not call for object-oriented equality but for allocations in which those who are worst off receive most – or all – of the values allocated. This is the only way in which differences in cumulative values, for instance economic wealth, can be evened out. Allocations to this effect can be based on some of the principles of justice discussed in the section on need.

A third possible attitude is to accept rank differences but not the present distribution of ranks. For instance, one may want those who hold high positions in society to be replaced by others. An argument in

238

favour of such changes may be that those who rank lowest are better qualified or more worthy of taking over the higher positions than those already there. Conceptions of justice based on fitness or desert can be relevant here.

I will now turn to certain questions concerning the relationship between different rank dimensions. It can be important whether the positions on different ranking scales conform with each other – for instance, so that a person with a high income also has a good education, a profession of repute, great political influence etc. ; – or whether they vary from one scale to another. I will use the expression *rank consistency* when referring to cases where the placings on different scales are in conformity with each other.[12] It seems that rank inconsistency can lead to tension. As an example we can take a clever, young man who achieves rapid promotion in his firm so that, with regard to salary and influence, he quickly overtakes employees who have served longer in that firm and perhaps have better training than himself. The situation may lead both to dissatisfaction amongst those who have been superseded and to unpleasantness and an uncomfortable feeling for the person promoted. Similar tendencies are found in society as a whole. The person who reaches a higher rank in one respect than is thought right, taking account of his low placing in other respects, is often characterized as an 'upstart' or as a 'climber'. We have also the 'shabby-genteel', the 'genius manqué' and the 'black sheep of the family' as names for other forms of rank inconsistency.

A person who ranks high in some respects and low in others can have many motives for trying to change this state of affairs. The rank inconsistency can, as mentioned, make him feel uncomfortable and make him a target for criticism or contempt. Perhaps he also simply wishes to possess more of the values of which he has few and has the opportunity to acquire these since he is well supplied with other values. A good education, for instance, can be used to obtain a highly regarded profession, a large income and perhaps also great influence. And people who have plenty of money can utilize some of this to gain influence, for example by buying up a newspaper, financing a political party or acquiring the majority of shares in an enterprise. They can also buy social prestige, for instance by contributing money for humanitarian,

12. Several other expressions have been used for what I refer to as 'rank consistency', among others, 'status equilibrium' (Benoit-Smullyan 1944), 'status crystallization' (Lenski 1954), 'status congruence' (Adams 1953, Homans 1962 pp. 91 ff. and Sampson 1969), 'status consistency' (Goffman 1957, Hodge 1962 and Jackson 1962) and 'rank-equilibrium' (Galtung 1964).

scientific or cultural purposes. But there are limits to what can be achieved through such conversion of values. A restraint lies in the fact that one is not always at liberty to utilize the values in one's possession for what one sees fit.[13] And another limitation is that it is impossible to change certain rank positions. This is obviously so with regard to rank order based on ethnic features (for example the colour of one's skin) or on caste, ancestry, family etc. There are other placings about which it is similarly difficult to do anything : senior employees have, for instance, few chances of preventing their juniors from exceeding them in salary or influence.

Rank inconsistency to which one has oneself no possibility of adjusting may lead to dissatisfaction with the system.[14] *Galtung* (1964) takes this as the starting point for his structural theory of aggression.[15] Similar ideas are advanced by *Benoit-Smullyan* (1944 p. 160). He suggests, among other things, that the French revolution may have been a result of the rank inconsistency of the middle class which made economic progress without gaining political influence. He also believes that the appearance of Nazism in Germany was connected with the fact that broad layers of the people found their economic situation worsened while they still clung to their old social standing. In both situations the rank consistency was disturbed – in one case because of economic progress and in the other because of economic depression. An interesting investigation into the relation between rank consistency and political attitudes in the United States has been made by *Lenski* (1954). He operated with four rank criteria : income, profession, education and ethnic background and found that a higher proportion voted Republican (i.e. conservative) among those who had about the same rank (high or low) on all scales than among those who ranked high on one scale and low on another. In other words, there was a connection between rank inconsistency and political radicalism. This applied to all combinations of pairs of rank

13. See what has been said on 'exchange restrictions' in chap. 3, section II and chap. 4, section VII.
14. This and other possible effects of rank inconsistency are discussed by Homans (1962, p. 94 et seq.), Anderson and Zelditch (1964) and Himmelstrand (1969 p. 84 et seq.).
15. He advances the following hypothesis (pp. 98-99) : 'Aggression is most likely to arise in social positions in rank-disequilibrium. In a system of individuals it may take the form of crime, in a system of groups the form of revolutions, and in a system of nations the form of war. But these extreme forms of aggression are unlikely to occur unless 1) other means of equilibration towards a complete topdog configuration have been tried, and 2) the culture has some practice in violent aggression.'

criteria. The strongest tendencies towards radicalism were found amongst those who were low on the ethnic scale (i.e. coloured people or those with an East or South European background) and high on one of the scales of income, profession or education.[16]

The tensions caused by rank inconsistency help to explain the development of norms which contribute towards binding together the different rank dimensions. In certain societies there are norms against all forms of social mobility which can disturb rank consistency. Such norms are particularly prominent in caste and rigid class societies. In societies where social mobility is permitted, one finds instead norms which serve to secure covariation. Norms to the effect that promotion and increases in pay should be in accordance with seniority are an example of this. Other examples are norms which make certain demands on the education required for specific professions and norms requiring more 'responsible' work to be higher paid. The claim that there should be some degree of conformity between rank criteria, is often argued in terms of justice. *Homans* (1962 p. 97) explains this by pointing out, that certain rank criteria (e.g. education, seniority, and responsibility) can be regarded as 'investments' and others (e.g. pay) as 'rewards'. As will be further discussed in Chapter 10, sections VII and VIII, it can be a demand of justice that increased investment lead to increased reward.[17]

16. There are also other investigations which point in the same direction. Jenkins (1967 p. 49) found that participants in Danish and British 'Easter Marches' had low rank consistency; Himmelstrand (1969) suggests that the civil war in Nigeria may possibly be explained in terms of rank inconsistency; Fossum (1967) found connections between rank inconsistency of nations and the frequency of revolutions in Latin America; see also the discussion on Fossum's investigation in the Journal of Peace Research 1969 No. 1 and Wallace (1971).

17. To illustrate his point of view Homans (loc. cit.) refers to some of the results of his investigation in 'Eastern Utilities Co.'. In this connection an English study made by Jaques (1956) is also of interest. He interviewed the workers in a large concern and asked what they thought was 'fair or just' payment for the various types of work done in the factory. He then tried to discover a criterion for these jobs which could explain the views given. That which proved to fit best was 'responsibility' – measured by the frequency with which employees were checked by their superiors. (The less frequently an employee was checked, the greater responsibility he was regarded as having). It was found that there was a rather high correlation between responsibility and the actual wage received and an even higher correlation between responsibility and the wage which employees intended as being the right one (loc. cit. p. 43 et seq.).

See also Sampson (1969) on the connection between rank consistency and justice.

The norms referred to help maintain rank consistency and thereby diminish the tensions of which examples were given above. But the fact that norms do exist naturally means that when they are broken this tends to aggravate tensions.

9. Allocation strategies of distributors

I. INTRODUCTION

In this and the following chapters I will discuss the conditions under which allocation activity is likely to be regulated by, and argued in terms of, principles of justice or other norms. Some of the consequences that this can have for the system of allocation, the distributor and the recipients will also be examined.

The basic assumption here, as in Chapter 4, is that conceptions of justice are learned through interplay of different kinds of influences. One such influence consists of the transmission of conceptions of justice. Transmission can take place through general norms ('brothers should share alike' or 'all are equal before the law') and when, in actual allocation situations, it is insisted or expected that there be equal distribution and that this be accepted. Such demands and expectations may originate from someone outside of the system of allocation (for instance, from the parents of children who are dividing something between them), or they can circulate inside of the system with the distributor or recipients as source. But in addition to this, there is a form of learning which does not consist of adapting oneself to the demands and expectations of other people but stems from the fact that certain behaviour is in itself profitable or unprofitable. The recipients may find, for instance, that in the long run they get most of the allocated benefits or the greatest feeling of security when allocations are made on the basis of equal shares. Or the distributor may learn from experience that this way of allocating is the easiest way of avoiding conflict. Experience which shows the way allocation has been practised in certain kinds of situations to be ad-

243

vantageous can lead to the idea that equal distribution is right in itself – regardless of whether or not it pays in a special case. I will focus my attention on this last type of learning.

The approach must, however, be rather different from that in the chapters on reciprocation since allocation problems look different according to whether they are seen from the point of view of the distributor or the recipients. It often happens that the distributor, in order to promote his own goals, applies principles of allocation other than the one the recipients would prefer. But such discrepancy does not have to be permanent. The distributor may influence the recipients so that they gradually come to accept the allocation principles he employs, or the recipients can bring pressure to bear upon the distributor and get him to change his practices. Normally both sides influence each other.

Both the distributor's and the recipients' attitudes to allocation issues can, then, be partly determined by mutual influence and partly by other factors. Certain methodological problems arise if an attempt is made to separate these determinants of behaviour (cf. *Simon* 1957, pp. 62 ff.). The difficulties are not so great if one can assume that influence was first brought to bear after the system of allocation was established. In such an event it is possible to investigate the changes which have occurred in the recipient as a result of the behaviour of the distributor – and vice versa. But influence cannot always be registered in this way because right from the beginning both distributor and recipient may have anticipated the other's reactions and adapted their behaviour accordingly. There are also instances where the participants in an allocation system are or have been involved in many other, similar, allocation systems, and the influences to which they are exposed in the different systems may be difficult to isolate from each other.

A model which is based on the distributor and recipients each having certain 'original' conceptions of how allocation should be and on these conceptions being modified through mutual persuasion can, for these reasons, be difficult to test empirically. But, even so, I suppose that such a model (or, more correctly, an approach to it) is the most appropriate one to use when trying to explain what it is that gives rise to the use and acceptance of principles of justice.

I assume that demands for justice come, first and foremost, from recipients and that they are partly determined by the tendency to make internal comparisons and partly by the recipients' need to defend themselves. The contention that claims for justice stem from the recipients does not, of course, mean that this manner of reasoning is something they have spontaneously invented for the occasion. Conceptions of jus-

244

tice are a part of the cultural heritage passed on from generation to generation. But cultural tradition brings in its train a vast variety of ideas. Which of these are brought forth and used on specific occasions depends to a large extent on the kind of interaction situation and from which of the participants the arguments originate.

What follows of this book falls into three main parts. In this chapter I discuss the strategies which a distributor would adopt supposing he were not bound by norms and did not have to consider recipient reactions. However, these suppositions will not be consistently adhered to. Among other things, I will take into account the distributor's anticipation of recipient reaction in a few instances where this arises naturally from the text. In the next chapter, allocation problems are looked at from the point of view of the recipients. The interplay of distributor and recipient behaviour is examined in the two final chapters.

II. VARIOUS STRATEGIC CONSIDERATIONS WHICH ARE OF RELEVANCE TO THE DISTRIBUTOR

A distributor must take into consideration two types of issues. One type, which I call *substantive,* relates to the content of his decisions : what should the decisions be in order to most effectively promote the aims of the distributor ? The other type, which I call *procedural,* refers to methods of decision-making. Some procedures are better suited than others to simplify decision-making processes and protect the distributor from doubt, scruples and criticism etc. In other words the choice of procedure is of significance for the costs involved in decision-making and the distributor might – in order to reduce costs – dispense with the ideal content of his decisions. In any case he will have to weigh the relative advantages and disadvantages of substantive and procedural issues if these point in different directions.

A general survey is made in section VII of various problems of procedure. In sections VIII and IX I look at those particular procedural problems which arise when the distributor is a collective unit. However, I will first concentrate on *substantive* problems. Discussion of these will (in sections III-VI) be tied to the various *aims* which the distributor may seek to promote through his activity.

I assume that distributors normally try to accomplish something through their allocations. This may be, for example, to raise children, to earn money, to maximize the national product or simply to sow happiness and harvest gratitude. All these I call 'aims' and I presume that

245

there is a connection between the aims a distributor has and the way in which he carries through and justifies his allocations.

A distinction must be made between aims and actual effects. An allocation may not have the effects which the distributor had hoped for and it may have effects which he had not anticipated. His activity may give him values which he did not take into account. Perhaps he also gets values which he himself does not realize he is getting. Effects which the distributor has not taken into account or of which he is unaware may in the long run affect his practice. But in what follows I am referring to the aims and not to the actual results unless I state otherwise.

Sometimes the distributor's only aim is to get payment for or satisfaction from the individual transfers. For instance, he sells goods and is paid by his customers, or he gives presents or good advice and receives gratitude in return. Or perhaps he just enjoys giving or feels an urge to avenge himself. In these cases his attention will be focused on the individual transfers and the reciprocal relations of which these constitute a part. It is not necessary for him, in order to achieve his goal, to consider how values should be distributed among recipients. This can be expressed by saying that his aims make the distributor inclined to be transaction-oriented and not distribution-oriented. But quite apart from this the aims can actually affect distribution. With an eye on profits, for example, the distributor may sell most to those who pay best. It is also possible that the recipients are distribution-oriented and that pressure from them causes the distributor to examine distribution issues.

I will discuss the last mentioned possibility in the following chapters. Here we are concerned with instances where the aims which the distributor tries to promote make him interested in seeing the individual transfers in relation to each other. I will examine different types of aims which, one way or another, can influence the distributor's attitude to distribution issues. The main types of aims to be discussed are : to improve or to safeguard the recipients' living conditions (section III), to care for, cure, raise, educate or in other ways influence the recipients (section IV), to produce values with the help of recipient input (section V) and to take precautions against possible injury which the recipients represent (section VI).

The aims which a distributor tries to promote do not have to be his *highest* aims. It is possible that a person whose work it is to cure people will, when asked, reply that he does not regard health as a value in itself but rather as a means to realizing higher values, for instance well-being or happiness. But for this discussion it is of no interest which aims rank highest on the distributor's abstract scale of values. The interest here is with the aims which influence his practical activity – his decisions and the reasons given for them. These will certainly not always be the aims which he, in principle, places highest.[1] The actual behaviour of an economist, for instance, who declares that maximizing the national product is not his final goal but just a means to promote 'the greatest happiness of the greatest number' may show that he is much more devoted to the national product than to human happiness.

III. ALLOCATION WITH THE AIM OF IMPROVING OR SAFEGUARDING THE RECIPIENT'S LIVING CONDITIONS

This section is concerned with cases where the aim of distributor is to improve the lot of the recipients, for example by relieving their distress, promoting their wellbeing, giving them greater opportunities of expression and development, etc. These aims are often combined with those of sowing happiness and reaping gratitude, which were referred to in the previous section. A person engaged in welfare work, for instance, can partly be motivated by a desire to help each individual client and to receive his pay in the form of thanks. But he may also be partly interested in changing the circumstances of the client so that these accord better with what he himself believes that living conditions should be. Both aims can be realized simultaneously but they can also sometimes conflict with each other. The welfare worker perhaps encounters reluctant clients who do not want the improvements he tries to foist upon them. He gets only worry and reproach from his contacts, but the payment to which he looks forward is that, in the long run, he will be able to change conditions (for instance, hygiene, nutrition, working methods etc.) in the direction he considers desirable.

There are many kinds of undertakings where the aims with which we are concerned are of central importance, for instance aid to the developing countries, rural development, assistance to commerce and industry, social services and private charity, welfare projects of various kinds as, for example, support for house building and children's institutions, cultural activity, sport and recreational projects etc. Parents who buy food, clothes, toys and sporting equipment for their children are another example.

1. See Ross (1958 p. 305) : 'The higher we go in the levels of generalization, the more doubtful it becomes whether the declared ideals correspond to real attitudes'.

Several issues arise in connection with such activities. There can be a question of *what* should be supported, *who* should receive this support and *how much* they each should have – absolutely and in relation to each other. When it is decided who will receive support importance is often attached to whether the recipients have such a status that the distributor is considered responsible for them. Parents, for example, give help and support mainly to their own children and the state to its own citizens. But apart from this it is usually natural to rely on need and/or fitness criteria when these issues arise.

It goes without saying that criteria of *need* must play a prominent part when the aim is to improve conditions for the recipients. And usually it is need in the sense of 'to require', and not 'to desire' which counts. *What* one supports usually depends upon what needs one considers important to satisfy. And *who* should be helped (when this is not status determined) and *how much* each should have, will often be determined in accordance with the principle that those who are most in need should be helped first.

One special reason for adhering to this principle is that the distributor's resources are often best utilized by being put in where the need is greatest. This holds true if (1) the resources are considered better utilized the greater the total need-satisfaction which is achieved, and (2) the increase in satisfaction for each new unit of value which a recipient receives is less the more he already has of the value. The second requirement can also be expressed by saying that there must be decreasing marginal utility.[2] This probably does not hold true in all cases. For instance, it may be that one must have more than a certain minimum quantity of a value if it is to be of any help at all and that the marginal utility therefore increases to begin with. But usually, one soon reaches a level where it begins to decrease – assuming that the level of aspiration or preferences does not change. It means more to a hungry than a replete person, for example, to get an extra loaf of bread, and more to the poor person than to the rich to get an extra £ 1.

Under the conditions mentioned above, the distributor utilizes his resources to their maximum by allocating them in such a manner that the marginal utility of the transfers is the same for all recipients. This is illustrated in Figure 1 where the three sloping lines represent the mar-

---

2. The concept 'marginal utility' originates in economics but is – under the same or different names – finding its way into other social sciences, cf. e.g. Homans (1961, pp. 265 ff. and 1962, pp. 280-81), Blau (1964, pp. 168 ff.) and Dahlstrøm (1968, p. 112).

ginal utility curves for three recipients (R_1, R_2 and R_3). R_1's need is greatest and R_2's smallest before the transfers take place. This can either be because R_1 has the smallest amount of the value beforehand or because he altogether needs more of it. When the value is divided so that the marginal utility is the same for everyone, the total need satisfaction (i.e. the sum of the areas of the horizontally shaded polygons) is maximized. If the same set of values were allocated in any other way, the subjective loss for the person receiving less would be greater than the subjective gain for the one receiving more. This is illustrated in the figure by the diagonal shading of what R_1 would lose and R_2 would win if a part of the former's allotment was given to the latter.

Figure 1

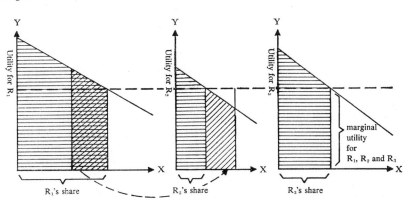

That the marginal utility is the same for all recipients can also be expressed by saying that each recipient is equally well satisfied. The resources are in other words utilized to their maximum when the distributor keeps to the principle of equality referred to in Chapter 8, section VI. If the resource total had been smaller than what is indicated in Figure 1 the result might have been that only R_1 and R_3 got something while R_2 got nothing – since, under these circumstances the resources would have been utilized fully by creating equality from 'the bottom up' (see chap. 8, section VI, fig. 1 where this type of equal distribution is illustrated in another manner).

249

In practice one can expect to find only rough approximations to the theoretical model sketched here. It may be difficult for the distributor to obtain information about the strength of the needs of the individual recipients and also about how much his transfers will contribute towards satisfying these needs. In this respect he is often dependent upon information from the recipients themselves. And this is not always reliable. In addition to this, there are many fields where no satisfactorily precise technique of measurement has yet been developed to make the necessary calculations. And last but not least, the distributor may have many reasons for not investigating and measuring as thoroughly as he is able to. Procedural considerations play a role in this connection (cf. section VII et seq.).

We must therefore expect a tendency to simplify. Attention may be paid only to *certain* differences in need, for instance those that are readily visible. Or the distributor may maintain that all recipients (or all recipients of a specific category) have the *same* need for the benefits concerned. Parents sometimes make this simplification when they reckon that children in a certain age group need the same amount of sleep and the same kind of food. As mentioned earlier (in chap. 8, section VI) a similar assumption is made in Israeli kibbutzes. When needs are believed to be uniform, equal satisfation means the same as object-oriented equality.

Moreover, we cannot assume that the distributor who is giving assistance always aims at maximizing the recipients' short term need satisfaction. In many cases more weight is laid on raising future production than present consumption. 'Help to self-help' is then considered appropriate, for example contributions towards retraining handicapped persons or assistance towards establishing industry in underdeveloped areas. Such projects are often best suited to increase satisfaction in the long run. But they presuppose that in the first instance attention is paid not only to need but also to *fitness* to make use of the assistance offered.

The person most capable of utilizing assistance is frequently not the one who has the most pressing need. When fitness is the deciding criterion the result will often be that inequalities are aggravated, since those who had relatively much beforehand will receive most through the new transfers. For example, aid to developing countries often tends to widen the gap between the least and the somewhat more developed countries and between rich and poor inside the recipient country. Measures aimed at developing the home economy often have the same effect. *Knut Dahl Jacobsen* (1964) has described how agricultural policy in Norway during the last part of the nineteenth century favoured the larger farms. Experts employed in public administration believed that the spread of information was of primary importance because this was a form of help to self-help which would, in the long run, yield the best results. And they thought that both information and other assistance should be given mainly to the owners of large farms. They were the best equipped to learn new methods of cultivation and it was they who possessed the financial resources necessary for innovation. In the second stage, large farms could serve as a model for the smaller. This line of policy met much opposition in parliament when the Liberals ('Venstre') came into power. While the public administrators relied on criteria of fitness, the majority in parliament argued in terms of need. Norwegian agriculture was on the verge of a catastrophe it was claimed. Direct financial support was therefore more important than information. And it was the small farms that most needed help.

One finds a similar conflict between fitness and need in many other fields. Should assistance to handicapped persons, for example, preferably be given to those who are worst off and therefore most need it or should help be made as productive as possible by giving it to those who can most easily be rehabilitated ? A parallel question in the field of education is that of the distribution of resources between talented and less talented students.

The importance attached to fitness is one of the reasons why allocations – even of assistance and aid – sometimes follow the principle in St. Matthew 13, 12 : 'For whosoever hath, to him shall be given'. Another factor pulling in the same direction is that the distributor – whether he puts weight on fitness or need – may depend upon the recipients for information. And those who are best off usually also have the best means of communication. They know best how to make their way to the distributor with their points of view, are most capable of stressing the factors which the distributor considers relevant, and are often most likely to be understood and believed.[3]

Desert is also sometimes taken into account. For instance, the idea that the *'deserving* poor' are those who should be helped has played a great role in charity work. And even in instances where the official aim of assistance is solely to improve human conditions, and not to reward virtue, it is difficult to completely avoid recipient merits and demerits being taken into account.

---

3. See Aubert (1966 pp. 112-113 and 1974 pp. 109-110). See also chap. 8, section II.

The inclination to pay attention to merit may be due to a lack of ability on the part of those who implement assistance programmes to free themselves from their notions of retributive justice. For example, they may find it difficult to accept unreservedly the policy that a person be given values 'for nothing' – without having shown characteristics or actions which deserve reward. And they will find it especially difficult to reconcile themselves to the idea that help should also be given to those who really deserve punishment.

IV. ALLOCATION WITH THE AIM OF TAKING CARE OF, GIVING TREATMENT TO, RAISING, EDUCATING OR INFLUENCING RECIPIENTS

As in the instances just examined, the aim here is to do something for the recipients. The difference is that the distributor does not restrict himself to improving their external conditions but also tries directly to intervene in their behaviour. There are many examples where this goal plays a central role – e.g., in parent-child relationships and in those between teachers and pupils, to a certain extent in such institutions as orphanages, homes for the aged, hospitals, military camps and correctional institutions, and in many other kinds of activity such as medical treatment, religious teaching, missionary work and political propaganda, etc.

There is no sharp border line between the aims considered here and those which were examined in the previous section. For instance, the person who tries to improve or safeguard the living conditions of his recipients through development aid will sometimes also try to re-educate the recipients so that they attain the ability and willingness to effectively utilize the material resources they receive. On the other hand, the person whose goal is education or upbringing may make sure that the recipients are equipped with the material resources (school materials, toys, sporting equipment etc.) which will give them an opportunity to develop required skills. For some distributors – for instance, parents in relation to their children – both the aim of supporting and that of influencing are of central importance. The aim of supporting the recipient was discussed in the previous section. But interplay between this and the aim of influencing the recipient gives rise to particular problems which will be examined here.

The fact that importance is attached to giving certain persons care, medical treatment, education or upbringing etc. prompts the question of *allocation of distributor tasks* in society. In most West European countries during the course of time many changes have taken place, for instance the government has assumed responsibilities which were previously the duty of the family. Where changes have been made after due consideration, it is probably a concern for *fitness* which has played the greatest role. And the evaluation of who is best fitted, for example to bring up or educate children, to cure the sick or care for old or handicapped people, etc. is again determined by what kind of influence or care the person concerned is thought to *require*. But as *Aubert* (1966 pp. 113-114) has pointed out, these kinds of considerations are not the only ones that have been at work. For instance, treatment of juvenile delinquents and mentally deranged offenders has, in part, been transferred from legal to medical authorities. This has been done not only because medical treatment is believed to be more effective but also for humanitarian reasons and because punishment is considered unjust in such cases.

Within individual social systems (the home, school, hospital etc.) where a group of recipients receive care, education, medical treatment etc., many different kinds of values are allocated. These may be material objects (food, clothing, toys, sporting equipment, educational material etc.), work and duties (help in the house, home-work, etc.), rights and privileges, punishments and rewards, etc. The recipients may also feel that the distributor's love, confidence, attention or care are values in which each should have his share. And these values can be of particular importance if the recipients are heavily dependent upon the distributor.

It is often natural for the distributor to attach decisive importance to the *needs* (in the sense of 'require') of the recipients. His aim, after all, is to do something for the recipients – for example, to bring them up, treat or improve them. What he considers they need to learn, and what aids they require for learning, will often be considered most important. What the recipients themselves desire can also carry some weight with individual distributors, but it will seem much more appropriate that they get what they require rather than what they desire. It may even be important for the distributor to *prevent* the recipients from getting some of the things they want. He may believe that this is dangerous for them or he may want to teach them restraint.

A distributor who pays attention to recipient needs, does not always try to satisfy everyone *equally well*. But if he feels the same responsibility for each recipient, he will have reason to do so. A desire to utilize his own resources as effectively as possible can also pull in the same direction. I refer to what was said on this point in the previous section. In some cases the result will be object-oriented equal distribution, because the distributor assumes that all recipients require the same amount of the value concerned. This assumption can justify equal distribution of such non-material values as, for example, affection and confidence. The need for these values may certainly vary but it is difficult to prove that there are differences and it is often not legitimate to take notice of them.

Questions of *fitness* may also be involved. Selection of students who are to receive higher education is often made on the basis of ability to profit by the education offered. There are also other examples of attention being paid to fitness in determining the circle of recipients. A person can, for instance, be exempted from military service because he is unfit. And both religious teaching and political propaganda are often (but not always) mainly directed towards people who are receptive to influence. However, in some fields (for instance, with regard to the ordinary upbringing of children and to medical treatment of people who are ill) it is felt so strongly that everyone should share the benefits that the circle of recipients is ordinarily not restricted by criteria of fitness. Nevertheless, in deciding what each recipient will receive – for example, in the way of tasks, duties and liberties – importance is often attached to fitness both in the home, at school, in hospital and in other institutions. It may very well be that concern for fitness and for need pull in opposite directions. But the possibility of conflicts between various considerations is not so obvious as in the instances which were discussed in section III.

Desert can also be of significance in determining the circle of recipients. When selecting the persons who are to receive a higher education, for instance, account may be taken of the feeling that some of the applicants deserve to be accepted because of the diligence and interest they have exhibited. Criteria of fitness and desert are sometimes combined. Both of these can, for instance, be given as the reason for selection based on exam results.

Criteria of desert, however, play a more important role in connection with the use of rewards and punishments within the allocation system. In order to rear, educate, heal or improve people, it is usually essential to be able to influence their behaviour. Enduring changes in their habits and attitudes are sometimes desirable in order to get them to actively participate in acquiring certain skills (for example, at school) or in order to secure their cooperation so that, for instance, they can receive medical treatment. Another reason for exerting influence on the recipients is that this may be necessary in order to secure peace and order, for instance in a classroom or a prison.

254

Some recipients are easy to control. If their goal is the same as the distributor's and they trust his insight as to which means are the best for achieving this purpose, they will usually follow his instructions automatically. Patients, for example, follow a doctor's instructions for such reasons. Some distributors also have other means of exerting influence. They can, for instance, restrict the recipients' freedom of movement by locking them up, or prevent violence by giving them sedatives. But in many cases the most effective – or the only available – mode of action is to influence the recipients' motivation via rewards and punishments. Through systematic use of this procedure the distributor not only has the opportunity of influencing behaviour on individual occasions but also of establishing habits and attitudes which he believes the recipients should have.

In order to appear as rewards or punishment, allocated goods and evils must be given in connection with such recipient behaviour as the distributor stamps desirable or undesirable. They must, in other words, be allocated according to merit or demerit.

There are certain limits to the feasibility of using rewards and punishment. The distributor may lack the resources and means of enforcement which are necessary if he is to reward or to punish effectively. And even if his physical power is sufficient, there may be norms, for instance concerning humane treatment and human dignity, which limit what he can use in the way of punishment (cf. chap. 7, section III). Furthermore – and this is what particularly interests us in this connection – not all methods of punishment and reward are consistent with the ends towards which the distributor's activity is directed. On the one hand there may be benefits he is reluctant to give as rewards because he believes they are not good for the recipients or that too much of them will have unfortunate effects. Parents, for instance, hesitate to reward their children with chocolate or sweets if they believe that such things are bad for children. And they will prefer not to give money if they wish to teach their children thrift and moderation. Increased freedom can also be a doubtful reward both in the home, at school and in institutions where it is important for the distributor to keep recipients under control. Although there is no harm in giving such a reward on some special occasion, it may be dangerous to institute the practice because (as mentioned in chap. 4, section IX) recipients can quickly develop the notion that they have a right to the rewards. To *deprive* recipients of benefits which they are accustomed to receiving, in order to punish them, may clash with the main purpose of the allocations. These benefits may, for example, be things which the recipients require for their health and well-being (for instance, food, clothing and sleep) or for their upbringing, medical treatment or education. The use in school of such punishments as sending a child out of the classroom or sending him home or expelling him for a shorter or longer period does, in part, run counter to consideration for his educational needs. To impose extra burdens on the recipient as a form of punishment also has its drawbacks since it gives these burdens a more definite character of being evils than they would otherwise have had. Staying in after school, extra home-work etc. as school punishment may give rise to or reinforce the idea that being at school and doing home-work are both unpleasant things. And if sending a child to bed early is used as a punishment because the child is difficult to get to bed, the child's idea that it is unpleasant to go to bed may be aggravated so that the parents' problem of getting him there at the proper time becomes worse. In the following chapters I will return to recipient reactions to the use of punishment and reward and to the further limitations on the distributor's freedom of action which these can involve.

Even though it may be impossible for the distributor to find any form of punishment or reward which does not have unfortunate side effects, he cannot completely refrain from using these means. However, he should – if he wants to act rationally – balance what he gains in using them against what he loses. And he should try to find those punishments and rewards which have the least damaging side effects. This is often best arrived at by purifying the different transfers – so that benefits and burdens other than those employed to satisfy needs are used as punishment and reward.

In many social systems criticism and praise act as suitable forms of inducement, partly because they can appear as more or less pure punishment or reward. But praise and criticism will not be conceived as reward and punishment unless the recipients attach importance to the distributor's evaluation of their behaviour. This they may do because, for instance, they are fond of the distributor or respect him or because they are dependent upon his goodwill. The extent to which this is the case varies from one allocation system to another.

In social systems where praise and criticism have little effect and where other values are not easy to manipulate, the distributor's possibilities of achieving anything via the help of punishment or reward are modest. *Sykes* (1958) believes that this applies to American prisons. The prison inmates have already been deprived of their freedom and many other benefits, and humanitarian grounds strictly limit what else can be taken from them, so that there are few remaining possibilities of operating with effective punishments. Nor does one get very far by giving rewards because they are so quickly transformed into rights. Moreover, there are limits to how many rewards can be given to a prisoner since the main purpose of imprisonment is to punish him. For these reasons Sykes believes that the prison director and his staff are often almost powerless.[4]

As mentioned in Chapter 8, section VIII (note 9), when transfers are made according to merit care is often taken to achieve *relative equality* between what the individual recipients have deserved and what they receive. The demand for equality frequently comes from the recipients (see the following chapters). But it may also be in the interest of the distributor to try to achieve this kind of equality. Inter alia, it can serve as a means of establishing a scale of values, turning punishment and reward into an intelligible 'language' which the distributor can use to inform recipients *what* is right and wrong and *how* right or wrong things are.

V. ALLOCATION WITH THE AIM OF PRODUCING VALUES
THROUGH RECIPIENT INPUT

So far instances where the recipients' well-being or development is the aim of distributor activity have been examined ; I will now look at cases where the recipients serve as a *means* of producing values. Examples of this can be found in private and public enterprises and in service institutions of different kinds. The employer or management here act as distributors by appointing their employees or by calling upon people to give their services and by allocating work, working conditions and wages etc. between them.

As long as the goal of the activity is to produce goods, services or other values, recipient *fitness* for the tasks concerned is of great importance to the distributor. It is then appropriate to take account of fitness both when recruiting people to the system (for example, when appointing employees) and when allocating work and payment etc.

Who is fitted to take part in a production process depends partly on *what* is produced and *how* this is done and partly on the *costs* of using the person concerned. For example, a person who seeks work in a factory may be unfit because he has poor qualifications, or because he is over-qualified and demands a salary which would not be economic to give him.

4. Cf. however Mathiesen (1965 pp. 9-10 and chaps. 4 and 5) for a more balanced view on the subject.

Some distributors have the power or authority to compel other people to work for them. Parents, for instance, can instruct their children to help, the slave owner can command his slaves and the government can impose conscription or direct labour. All such measures are associated with costs. These can, for example, be connected with the provision of food, board and equipment for the people given work, or they may be the costs (economic and non-economic) of giving and implementing orders. The distributor may find it appropriate to consider recipient needs when he provides for them. The least he can do is to ensure they get what they require in order to be fit to execute their job. – It may sometimes be so troublesome for the distributor to get recipients to perform work to which they object that he will find it advisable to allocate the different tasks in the manner which is most acceptable to the recipients. For such reasons duties may be made the same for everyone even if reasons of fitness indicate some differentiation. It may also be that the distributor's costs in imposing compulsory service are so great in proportion to what he achieves that he finds it better to use free manpower and to pay for this.

When the input is voluntary and contingent on compensation, exchange terms are sometimes fixed through bargaining between the employer and employees (or employee collectives or organizations). But the exchange regulating factors discussed in Chapters 3 and 4 will often intervene. The terms may, for instance, be regulated by market mechanisms or by ideas of retributive justice.

Conceptions of *desert* may be considered relevant to the size of compensation. It is usually the recipients who argue that they should be paid according to merit and that there should be relative equality. But the distributor may also tend to reason in this manner, inter alia because of his sense of justice. When, for instance, a new employee is taken on, the distributor may make comparisons with what older and experienced employees receive in the way of salary. And this may induce him to refuse to pay the new one more than he feels this person deserves in comparison with the others, in spite of the fact that it would perhaps be worth-while for him to pay more because of the shortage of manpower. Reasons of desert and of fitness do not have to contradict each other, because what a recipient is regarded as meriting may depend upon how suited he is to his work. But since merit can also depend upon other factors, the two points of view do sometimes conflict.

The distributor may make the principle of desert instrumental in influencing his employees through rewards and punishment in addition to using it because of his sense of justice. He can have long term training

258

in mind when he does this, or his intentions may be to make a more immediate impact, for example, to stimulate his employees to increased labour input or to discourage behaviour which leads to disturbances or disorder. Long term training is less significant here than in the instances examined in section IV. But much of what was said there also applies here, among other things what was said about the limitations on the distributor's opportunities of using punishment and rewards.

VI. ALLOCATION WITH THE AIM OF SAFEGUARDING AGAINST DAMAGE WHICH RECIPIENTS MAY CAUSE

In these instances, as in those mentioned above, influencing the recipients is not just an end in itself but a means of achieving something. The goal is, however, not to produce values, but to protect values against damage which the recipients may cause. One example is confinement of persons in prisons, asylums or concentration camps in order to prevent them from doing something which the distributor considers damaging or dangerous or for the purpose of deterring other people from doing the same. Putting infectious persons in quarantine and sending others to hospital or to some institution when they are considered a nuisance because of an illness or handicap are other examples. Food control, the fire brigade and various kinds of government regulation of industry and trade, also belong to this group.

The aim of safeguarding against damage is often combined with one or more of the aims we have already discussed. The reason for confining a mental patient to hospital, for instance, may partly be to place him in surroundings which are more favourable to his own well-being, partly to attempt to cure him, and partly to protect his family and the community from the trouble or the danger which his freedom might entail. And the reason, for instance, for traffic regulation can partly be to prevent accidents and partly to increase the capacity of the road network. Other control and regulation measures are also often justified both by contending that they increase production and on the grounds that they prevent damaging or useless forms of activity. In some cases the two kinds of considerations become so entwined that it seems unnatural to try to distinguish between them.

Negative criteria of fitness are of paramount importance in deciding both *who* is to be interfered with and *how* this is to be done in order to safeguard against possible harm. One limits the freedom of action of persons who in some way or other are *unfit* to decide themselves how

259

they should behave – and this is done in such a manner that one is protected against the results of their unfitness. Here, as in the cases mentioned in the previous section, the question of what fitness or unfitness depends upon must be seen in relation to what the distributor is aiming at. Although, for instance, a business man is well suited to run his own business, he may be unfit to decide for what purposes a country's exchange reserves should preferably be used, so that in a time of crisis there may be reason to impose exchange restrictions on him.

The cost factor plays the same kind of role when recipient behaviour is to be regulated or controlled as when recipient input is to be exploited for the sake of production (see section V). Whether it is worth-while intervening to avert possible damage depends not only upon how big the threat is but also upon the costs of neutralizing this threat. The size of the costs will depend, among other things, on the unwillingness or the opposition created amongst recipients when their freedom of action is restricted.[5] It will therefore be of some concern to the distributor that burdens are allocated in such a manner that opposition to them is reduced.

One factor tending to reduce resistance is that those who have their freedom restricted gain from the fact that other people are restricted in a similar way. Traffic regulations are a good example : it is the person using the roads whose freedom of action is restricted and he is also the one who gains from regulation. There are also instances where those who are subject to certain restrictions do not have any advantage from these but from other restrictions imposed on other people. They perhaps understand the advantages of living in an organized society and regard the limitations on their freedom as the price they must pay for this. In other words, ideas of exchange can be relevant here and the recipients' attitudes to restrictions may depend upon whether they find the exchange terms fair.[6]

Another instance where opposition is reduced is when restrictions are tied to criteria of guilt and responsibility. The fact that a person may cause damage does not in itself mean that he can be reproached. The insane, the infectious, the small child who has found a matchbox, the business man who follows ordinary market principles in a situation where shortage gives rise to the need for rationing and price control, and many other people, may be dangerous without being blameworthy.

5. What gives rise to opposition and how this can develop will be discussed in the following chapters.
6. Cf. Hart's (1955) point of view on 'mutuality of restrictions' as the basis for moral rights and duties. (Cited above in chap. 3, section VI, note 7).

In such cases it *may* be considered justifiable to intervene. But the easier it is to reproach a person who represents a possible danger, the more easily will intervention be accepted. It can then take on the character of retaliation which may be justified by the principle that one evil can be repaid with another.[7] As when exchange points of view apply, acceptability will increase when the principle of relative equality is applied.

The fact that a distributor mainly intervenes in instances which he considers blameworthy may also have grounds other than that he wants the intervention to be accepted. For example, he feels an urge to repay an evil with another evil or he wishes to improve the persons who are destructive. There is also often a tendency to confuse guilt and cause : it is easier for us to see that a morally wrong action can have damaging effects than that a highly moral or neutral action can have them.

VII. PROCEDURAL CONSIDERATIONS

Whichever aim the distributor has, he must take into account the difficulties inherent in making and enforcing decisions. The activity involved in collecting information, weighing the evidence, deliberating the issues, making up one's mind and carrying the decision into effect can be troublesome and unpleasant. Much depends upon the criteria on which the decisions are based. Concern for these factors, which I call 'procedural', can therefore suggest that the distributor modifies the principles of allocation which he would have preferred if he had only had to take substantive considerations into account.

If the distributor is not a single person but a group or organization, certain questions arise with regard to the internal allocation and co-ordination of tasks, authority and responsibility. However, I will not take up these issues now, but return to them for special examination in sections VIII and IX.

Let us first take a look at the different reasons for paying attention to procedure.

It is important for many distributors to *simplify the processes of decision-making.* It may take time and involve both work and money to undertake the investigations and deliberations leading up to a decision. How much it will cost depends largely upon which factors carry weight. The fewer, the more visible and the more uniform the criteria

---

7. What has been said in chap. 7, section II, on the conditions under which punishment is likely to be accepted is also relevant in this connection.

taken into consideration, the quicker and cheaper will be the process of arriving at a decision.

One factor which should have separate mention (although it could have been considered a special cost factor) is the *unpleasantness* often involved in making a decision. This unpleasantness can be due to troublesome persistence from people who are trying to achieve something, or be due to inner doubt and scruples. One can be in an agony of doubt and feel guilty knowing that the decision that has to be made will come as a hard blow to someone. One may have scruples not only about the outcome of a decision but also about the reasons which must be given for it. As pointed out in Chapter 2, section VII, the way in which a decision is justified can be important in many connections. Among other things, it may be indicative of the distributor's future practice. And for the recipients what is said by way of argumentation (for example, wounding and offensive or flattering remarks about themselves) may be more important than the outcome. Much of the unpleasantness involved in making decisions can be reduced by basing oneself upon characteristics which do not lay themselves open to discussion and by avoiding premises which may offend the recipients.

In addition it can be important for the distributor to ensure or facilitate the *implementing* of what he has decided. If, for instance, he allocates rights, duties or punishment it may be difficult to get the recipients to comply with his decisions. And even when it is easy to accomplish the allocation – it may, for example, be the dealing out of material objects over which the distributor has control – dissatisfaction, quarrelling and other trouble may arise and cause him inconvenience. The extent to which recipients are willing or unwilling to respect decisions depends partly on how just or reasonable they consider these to be. If the distributor bases his decisions on substantive premises which the recipients accept, this will make it easier to carry them through. But whether or not the recipients have confidence in the distributor and in the kind of procedure applied is also important. Inter alia, it is often important whether or not they consider him to be impartial and whether they believe that they have had a 'fair trial', i.e., a hearing which is just in the sense that everyone has had the same opportunity of presenting their arguments.

The fourth, and last, point I want to make has to do with the distributor's *responsibility*. I take 'responsibility' to mean the same as 'exposure to criticism or self-accusation' [8] and assume that the dis-

8. Cf. Eckhoff and Dahl Jacobsen (1960) where this concept of responsibility and its significance for decision-making is explained more fully.

tributor can be motivated to protect himself against this. The factors which make for responsibility are partly the same as those which give rise to such difficulties and unpleasantness as have already been mentioned. Conditions which make for doubt and reluctance when a decision is reached can be the basis of later remorse and self-accusation. And that which makes the recipients dissatisfied and disinclined to accept a decision can also result in criticism and further negative sanctions from them or others. But there are also factors additional to those already mentioned which can affect responsibility. For example, there may be instances where the distributor is in no doubt as to what the decision should be and has no problems in getting the recipients to accept it, but is still liable to receive criticism from other sources.

It is of importance in relation to all the issues discussed here whether the distributor bases his decisions on *general rules* (or principles) or whether he evaluates each individual allocation situation separately.[9]

Basing oneself on rules usually has the advantage of simplifying the decision-making process. Instead of calculating the consequences of each individual decision, the distributor can do this for several cases together if he himself makes the rules; or he can make use of other people's deliberations and experience by taking his rules from somewhere else. Rules can also reduce the unpleasantness and responsibility involved in making decisions. In particular, this will be the case when the rules are made by someone other than the distributor (or have formed themselves through practice) so that he does not feel responsible for their content. He can then push his scruples to one side and reject criticism on the grounds that it is not he personally but the rules which have determined the outcome.[10] But even if the rules have been made by the distributor himself, and he acknowledges this, they can be useful to him when someone complains that a decision is unreasonable because this gives him an opportunity to argue (to himself and other people) that it is valuable to have rules and to follow them consistently even if they lead to unsatisfactory results in a few cases. Furthermore, the application of general rules can strengthen confidence in the distributor's impartiality (cf. *Eckhoff* 1965 p. 17 et seq.). And they can make his decisions appear more just because the rules give the recipients advance infor-

9. The issues which I now examine have a certain connection with those of *act-utilitarianism* contra *rule-utilitarianism* which are mentioned in chap. 2, section III, note 1.
10. More on this point is to be found in Eckhoff and Dahl Jacobsen (1960) particularly pp. 38 ff.

mation as to what the distributor will attach weight to, so that everyone has the opportunity of adapting himself to this and of producing relevant information in support of his claims.

Some of the advantages connected with the application of rules are contingent on the recipients being acquainted with the content of these rules. This is necessary if the rules are to strengthen confidence in the distributor's impartiality and to form the basis of a 'fair trial'. The recipients' knowledge of the rules may also make it easier for the distributor to shelter behind them, thus easing the weight of responsibility. But this does not apply unconditionally if the recipients know the rules so well that they are able to criticize him for not applying them correctly. In order to simplify the decision-making process it is usually not necessary that the recipients be acquainted with the rules. In some instances this can certainly facilitate the distributor's work because the recipients then know what information he requires in order to be able to make his decisions and they will perhaps voluntarily produce this. But, on the other hand, it may also inconvenience the distributor that the recipients know the rules and use them to argue with. In activities where it is important to simplify the decision-making processes and to reduce responsibility but where no great importance is attached to creating confidence in the distributor's impartiality and justice, it will thus frequently be convenient for the distributor to apply rules which are *not* made known to the recipients. One can find numerous examples of this practice in the executive and administrative branches of government in many countries. Little effort normally goes into spreading knowledge of the regulations, instructions and the collection of precedences upon which decisions are based, and in some cases the authorities go directly in for secrecy.

Whether it is in the interests of the distributor to base himself upon rules, and whether he is best served by letting these be known or by keeping them to himself, depends not only on procedural but also on substantive considerations. The application of rules involves a certain standardization which may lead to situations where the individual decision is neither so reasonable nor so adequate as it would have been if each case had been judged on its own merits. How heavily this objection weighs naturally depends to a large extent upon the manner in which the rules are formed (see below) and applied, for example whether they are given a formalistic or a freer teleological interpretation, and whether the distributor reviews the rules from time to time with the intention of revising them in the light of the experience he has gained. But there are also substantive reasons which *favour* rules as a basis on which to

264

build. For instance, if the distributor aims at getting the recipients to adapt themselves to certain rules or principles, one way of reaching this goal is for himself to use the rules as a basis for his own decisions and to make their content known to the recipients.

Both the distributor who makes rules for his decision-making and the one who uses his discretion in each individual case are faced with the question of to *which criteria* they should attach importance. *Substantive* considerations often speak in favour of a broadening of the spectrum of relevant premises. This means that the distributor who makes discretionary decisions should try to obtain a relatively comprehensive picture of both the factual conditions and the possible consequences of his decision. And the distributor who uses rules should make these so detailed and varied, or so vague and diffuse, that a great number of factors can be taken into account. But *procedural* considerations usually speak in favour of restraint. The costs (in loss of time, expenditure, effort and opposition) of acquiring factual information and of calculating and evaluating all the long term and far-reaching consequences which the decision may have, can soon reach such proportions that it does not pay to go to this extent. I refer in this connection to *Simon's* (1959 pp. 269-270) and *Homans's* (1961 pp. 81-82) discussions of the significance of considering decision-making costs.

There can also be other procedural reasons for limiting the scope of what is taken into account. The unpleasantness involved in making decisions can, for example, be reduced if the distributor shuts his eyes to some of the damaging side effects which his decisions may have or if he refrains from making known circumstances which are wounding or offensive to the recipients. And confidence in his impartiality will be enhanced if he bases himself on rules formed in such a way that his personal influence on individual decisions is as little evident as possible.

For the reasons given, procedural considerations usually indicate that the distributor should base his decisions on more specific and object-oriented characteristics than would seem to be ideal from a substantive point of view. The result is, in many instances, a compromise between these two considerations. An employer who holds that the best fitted should be employed, and who realizes that a person's fitness can depend upon many different circumstances, restricts himself, for example, to taking account of a few, easily ascertainable criteria such as age, sex, education etc. His ideas of fitness can, in this manner, be enclosed in a set of status categories with which it is simpler to operate. Need criteria can, in the same way, be transformed into status criteria, for instance based on sex or age (see chap. 8, section IX). Other simplifications also occur. For example, it was widely accepted by the teachers and pupils of schools where *Siri Naess* (1969) investigated the prevailing conceptions of justice, that places in class should be allocated in such a manner that the special needs of individual pupils to sit in front should be satisfied. But most of the subjects mentioned only poor eyesight or hearing as examples of need criteria. Practically no one mentioned psychologically determined need. If procedural considerations carry sufficient weight, the result may turn out to be object-oriented equality or random distribution in spite of the fact that substantive considerations favour allocation according to need, fitness or desert.

The relative weight of substantive and procedural considerations depends, among other things, on how important the outcome of the decision is to distributor and recipients respectively. The more important the result is for the *recipients,* the greater amount of unpleasantness and difficulty the decision-making process will involve for the distributor and the heavier will be his responsibility. But the more important the result is for the *distributor,* the more reason there is for him to accept the unpleasantness and responsibility connected with a decision where everything relevant from a substantive point of view is taken into account. The two factors mentioned here can be combined in the ways illustrated in Figure 2.

Figure 2

Importance of result to distributor

		little	great
Importance of result to recipients	little	I	II
	great	III	IV

Where the result is of little importance to both the distributor and the recipients (cell I) neither the substantive considerations nor the procedural carry much weight except that it will then be natural to simplify decision processes. The distributor cannot be expected to make too thorough an investigation or spend long deliberating his decision. He does not need to keep to what is specific and object-oriented in order to reduce responsibility and unpleasantness – but he may do so for the sake of facility.

It is probably only seldom that the result is very important to the distributor and rather unimportant to the recipients (cell II). As an example we can imagine that there is some work to be allocated and that it is very important for the distributor to have 'the right man for the right job', but of little importance to the recipients what work they get since it is all equally difficult and equally attractive. This is an occasion for careful reflection, and the distributor does not have to be afraid of basing himself on diffuse and person-oriented criteria because he will have no difficulty in carrying his decisions through and does not risk much criticism. The process of making a decision may take time and involve some unpleasantness, but since the issue is important to the distributor he will feel that it is worth his while.

In cell III the situation is the opposite: the result is of little consequence to the distributor but very important to the recipients. As an example we can take the system previously practised in Norway where, by drawing lots, some of the men liable to compulsory military service were exempted. It was very important for those liable to conscription which of them were exempted. The authorities would therefore have shouldered a heavy responsibility if they had allocated exemption on the grounds of who was best fitted to do military service or who had the greatest need to avoid it. Basing their decisions on such criteria would also have involved a great deal of work. There was no reason to accept this responsibility and work since it was of little importance to the authorities whether Peter or Paul did military service as long as both of them answered certain minimum requirements of fitness. By using a lottery system the authorities also demonstrated – in a very conspicuous manner – that their decisions were completely impartial.

Where the result is important both to the distributor and to the recipients (cell IV) substantive and procedural considerations carry great weight and can also easily come into conflict with each other. For instance, substantive reasons may favour individual evaluation of each separate allocation on the basis of diffuse and person-oriented criteria, while procedural grounds call for adherence to fixed rules with specific and object-oriented criteria. Appointment of university professors can serve as an example. On the one hand, it is important for the university to employ those persons who, everything taken into account, are the best suited. On the other hand, the fact that the outcome is of great importance to the applicants gives grounds for using a procedure which ensures objectivity and impartiality. It is not possible to find any procedure which takes care of all these considerations. This is reflected in the fact that practices vary from country to country and that there is

267

frequent dissatisfaction with the procedure adopted – whether this goes one way or the other. The example also illustrates that different procedural considerations can pull in different directions. The practice which is followed in Norway, for example, with competent persons carefully examining the written work of all the applicants, is well suited to ensure objective and impartial treatment but not well suited to save time or energy.

VIII. ORGANIZATIONAL FACTORS

If the distributor is an organization, this may have consequences which I have so far ignored but will now examine.

In an organization where each employee has his specialized tasks, coordination is essential. And the need to coordinate activities is a reason additional to those mentioned above for having rules of action. Let us take as an example a Ministry of Supply which during a period of shortage has the job of allocating available resources throughout the country. Some of these must go to consumption, some as raw material and supplies to industry, some to emergency stocks, etc. The various decisions made will affect each other in many different ways. If, for example, coal supplies are increased to one branch of industry this may lead to a reduction in supplies to other branches, or perhaps to a reduction in personal consumption of fuel – if the ration of some other type of fuel, for instance fire wood, is not increased, which in turn would have repercussions in the paper and pulp industry, etc. The execution of an overall supply plan demands a high degree of specialization. Experts from different sectors of the industry are required, as are also economists to analyse the interplay of the various forces at work, in addition to technical, medical and legal expertise, inspection and control agencies, etc. The individual employee in such an apparatus has no chance of making rational choices of action on the basis of an overall evaluation of all the direct and indirect effects which his decisions may have for the country's supply situation. If he were to do this, he would not only need to be a specialist in all the fields mentioned and be acquainted with all the relevant data, but he would also need to possess prophetic powers to enable him to know the content of present and future decisions made by his colleagues where these affected the same fields as his own decisions.

Planning is therefore often a necessity if an organization of any size is to work effectively. By 'planning' I mean that the employees are directed to follow a set of rules which are constructed with a view to

268

promoting certain goals. With such a procedure it is primarily the rule-maker who must calculate and evaluate the consequences of the alternative courses of action. The person who is later to apply these rules in his decision-making has the – usually more simple – task of deciding how the rules will be understood and what action they recommend in individual situations. If the facts are undisputed and the rules are simple and clear, this can be done almost automatically. But if interpretation of the rules or finding of the facts is difficult, or if the rules grant discretionary powers, reflection will also be needed at this stage.

Planning can cover many or only a few of the decisions which are to be taken. And the individual rules can leave much, little, or nothing to the discretion of the decision-makers. Planning is often carried out in more than one step, for instance in such a way that the organization's highest authority fixes certain basic rules and delegates to subordinate authorities the working out of more detailed rules within the given framework. There are several examples to be found both in public administration and in private enterprise of stepwise planning with many more than two levels. – The variables which have been mentioned are connected with each other and with the size of the enterprise : the larger an organization and its field of activity and the more exhaustive and detailed the planning, the more complicated will be the system of rules and the greater the number of steps required.

How strict (i.e. how exhaustive and exact) the planning should be, depends upon a number of factors. Planning helps to coordinate decisions and the need to coordinate is greater the more interplay there is between the effects of individual decisions. In addition, planning aids in simplifying decision-making processes and reduces the unpleasantness associated with making decisions. The stricter the planning, the more automatic will be the decision-making processes. This leads to a saving of time and energy and permits the organization to employ persons who have little insight into the effects of the decisions and who do not identify themselves closely with the aims of the organization. On the other hand planning leads to a standardization of decision criteria which may result in lack of due consideration for special features of individual cases. It also means that the employees' independent judgment and initiative are inhibited. This may reduce both the pleasure they take in their work and the energy they put into it, and can make it difficult for them to handle unforeseen situations. In many kinds of activity, therefore, it is best to be content with a loose or incomplete system of rules so that room is left for the employees' own initiative and personal evaluation. Instead of furnishing the employees with rigid rules the management may find it adequate, for instance, to point out which goals they should try to realize and what strategic considerations they should take. The tasks of leadership and coordination must, in these cases, be taken care of by providing the employees with such advice and supervision that their conceptions of ends and means are brought as closely as possible into line with those of the management.[11]

The weight of the various arguments for and against strict planning varies with the nature of the activity. The fire brigade provides an example where very strict planning is desirable. In order to satisfy what is needed of coordination and speed, clear rules are necessary for what each person at the fire station should do when the alarm goes. The action which is to be taken must be planned and regulated down to the smallest detail so that everything tallies and no time is lost in deciding what to do. The actual process of putting the fire out also needs programming but of a less rigid kind since the work must be adapted to the actual conditions accompanying each fire.

But too rigid planning may be harmful in many fields of activity. *Løchen* (1966, pp. 301-303) holds this to be the case with mental hospitals. One of the points he makes is that the need for a regulated and hierarchic organization is less when the staff consists of professional men. He also notices that a strictly planned organization can create a disengaged and impersonal relationship towards its clients.

How an activity is, in fact, organized does not of course only depend on rational reflection about what is best suited to promote the distributor's aims. Among other things, the attitude of the employees may have some impact. I will look more closely at this in the next section.

IX. THE ROLE OF THE EMPLOYEE IN THE DISTRIBUTOR ORGANIZATION

Employees in an organization play a double role. They are the recipients of certain values which the management allocates, for example their own appointments, dismissal, wages and working conditions etc. At the same time they are part of the distribution apparatus which allocates values among the organization's clients. This situation is illustrated in Figure 3a where M represents management, E employees and C clients (i.e., the outsiders who receive positive or negative values from the organization). The circle represents the organization and the arrows are transfers.

11. Cf. March and Simon (1958, particularly pp. 136-171) on the conditions for and consequences of different kinds of planning.

It can also happen that an employee (as perceived by himself or someone else) acts as an independent distributor of values which he controls on behalf of the organization, see Figure 3b. The organization is depicted here as a circle with a broken circumference, illustrating that it does exist but does not appear as the distributor.

Figure 3

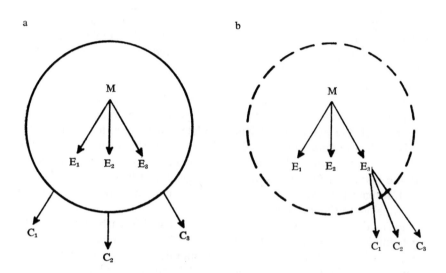

How the employees react in their capacity as recipients is not discussed here but in the next chapter. However, the question cannot be completely disregarded since the recipient attitude of the employees may affect their distributor behaviour. The main theme of this section, however, is their behaviour as distributors (or as links in a distributor apparatus).

Whether the employee's activity is perceived in one or the other of the ways shown in Figures 3a and b depends, among other things, upon whether he has personal contact with the clients, whether decisions are loosely or rigidly planned and whether several people cooperate in making the decisions. The more distant contact the employee has with the clients, the more rigidly programmed the decisions are and the greater number of people involved in making the individual decisions, the more easily will the organization be regarded as the distributor. Close contact with the client, weak planning and little cooperation over individual decisions make it more natural to regard the individual employee as the distributor. A civil servant in a governmental department is an example of the former alternative and a social worker of the latter. The distinction between the two alternatives is not clear cut. One and the same employee may make certain decisions which are perceived in one way and some decisions which are perceived in the other way. It can also happen that one and the same allocation is regarded partly as stemming from the organization and partly from the employee himself.

Whether the employee's activity is perceived in one or the other of the ways mentioned, there are important differences between him and the management.

In the first place, the management is normally more closely identified[12] with the organization than are the employees. If the organization is one over which the management has complete control (e.g. a private enterprise), the 'organization's goals' will normally be identical with the management's own goals. And even if the organization does not belong to the management but has its tasks assigned to it by others, it will first and foremost be the management which communicates with and is responsible to these others.

From the point of view of management it will often be important to get employees to identify themselves as closely as possible with the organization. This can help to raise morale and to ensure that the employees make suitable decisions. The less programmed activity is, the more important it is to have employees who identify themselves with the aims of the organization. The management can try to achieve this through its appointment policy, through its allocation of jobs and responsibility among the employees, and through various forms of direct influence. As a rule, the chances of getting an employee to put his heart into promoting the aims which the management considers to be those of the organization are greater the shorter the distance (in rank and communication) between him and the management. This means that the possibility of getting everyone to identify oneself with the organization is greater in a small organization than in a large, and that inside

12. By the expression 'identified with' something (for instance, with a person, group or idea), I mean that importance is attached to promoting the interests of the person or group involved or to realizing the idea concerned.

272

of the individual organization there can be big differences in this respect between the employees who are close to the management and those who are at a distance.

However, employee distance from management is not the only condition which is of relevance. There are also various factors which can directly counteract identification with the organization. Some of these are connected with the fact that an employee, in his capacity as recipient, may have goals which are opposed to those of the organization. For instance, he may want as high a salary as possible for the least amount of effort. Or he may need protection against exploitation or manipulation. But factors connected with the employee's role as distributor may also work in the same direction.

Planning may, among other things, have the effect of alienating employees from the aims of the organization. If the programmes consist of rules or directives which are sufficiently detailed and precise, those who follow them do not have to understand the meaning behind them. From one point of view this may be an advantage to the organization since the less reflection is needed the more automatic behaviour will be. Military training is a good illustration of systematic inculcation of readiness to obey orders without reflection : soldiers are taught to react to 'right turn' and 'left turn' automatically, without stopping to consider why the turn should be made. There are also many civil organizations, in which automatization and coordination are important, where it may be useful to employ persons who are willing to adjust themselves to rules and to obey orders without worrying too much about the reasons behind these.

However, employees who are ready to follow rules and directives soon lose sight of the goal of the activity in which they are engaged, or do not pay much attention to it in their decision-making. Strict adherence to rules is sometimes looked upon as being a value in itself.[13] In other cases references to the aims of the organization serve as rationalization for rule-worship. In bureaucracies, says *Lysgaard* (1961 p. 88), a myth often evolves around 'bureaucracy's technical/economic effectiveness. Without bureaucratic regulations and customs and forms of conduct – it is said – things just wouldn't work'.

To be guided by rules or directives in his decision-making gives the employee certain advantages. It simplifies his work, reduces his res-

---

13. See March and Simon (1958 p. 36 et seq.) with references to Merton, Selznick and Gouldner, and Berelson and Steiner (1964 p. 366 A) on the tendency to turn means into ends.

ponsibility and protects him from suspicion of bias. The fewer the objections he has to automatic and formalistic application of rules, the greater is the relative weight of these advantages.

The fact that employees can find protection in rules sometimes leads them to make rules themselves when management has failed to do so. Such rules are not formally laid down but develop gradually on the basis of precedents and analogies. Illustrative examples of such self-made rules can be found in Norwegian post war economic regulation (see *Eckhoff* 1962 pp. 67 ff.). Laws were passed, for example, on export and import regulation, exchange control and regulation of communications, which gave administrative agencies wide discretionary powers. However, a detailed system of rules quickly developed through practice, for instance to the effect that export and import licences were granted automatically on the basis of fixed quotas for individual firms, on seniority as a criterion for granting licences to taxi drivers, etc. These rules largely made use of specific and object-oriented criteria so that they were simple to apply and well suited to protect the employee. But many of them accorded poorly with the aims of the regulations.

Another important difference between management and employee is that the latter normally has more direct contact with the organization's clients. But within the employees, too, there are large variations with regard to the extent and nature of this contact. Some employees serve a large number of clients but have slight contact with each one of them. Client contact in such a case may be a factor which increases the need to shelter behind rules. The greater the pressure of work, the greater the need. Imagine, for example, the employee who sits behind his counter while the queue in front of him lengthens and irritation increases. In a situation like this it is important to be able to expedite each client quickly and without complications and to silence persistence and criticism by referring the client to the regulations or to what is customary.

On the other hand, there are employees who are occupied with fewer clients and have a deeper contact with each one of them. The psychotherapist and the welfare officer can be given as examples. The deeper contact can mean that they get to know the client as a person, develop sympathy for him and wish to help him. When an employee identifies with clients in this way, it tends to counteract his respect for rules ; but it can also mean that he becomes detached from the goals of the organization if consideration for his clients suggests this. *Løchen* (1965, pp. 188 ff.) assumes that the closer and broader contact an employee has with the clients, the more importance he will attach to their needs and the more diffuse and person-oriented will be the criteria he builds

274

upon. It seems likely that this correlation can be found when conditions are otherwise equal. But there are circumstances which make an employee less inclined to rely on diffuse and person-oriented criteria. If, for instance, the clients with whom he has to deal have strongly divergent interests, his wish to be impartial and his need to reduce the unpleasantness involved in decision-making may tend to make him base his decisions on more object-oriented and specific criteria, and he may try to avoid coming into too close personal contact with the clients.

When clients are troublesome and difficult to handle, this is also a reason for trying to keep them at a distance. But there may be conflicting motives present because the clients – at the same time as they are difficult – may appeal to the employee's compassion or his urge to help. In this case he may be inclined both to come into closer personal relationship with the client and to shy away from this. Such situations are likely to arise in mental hospitals, prisons, institutions for young offenders etc. The differences in atmosphere between one institution and another and the differences in attitude between people working in the same institution can be due to the changing predominance of these opposed tendencies.[14] *Gilbert and Levinson* (1957) have introduced the term 'custodialism' for the attitude that the task of a mental hospital is to keep and take care of the inmates and that it is impossible for the staff to have any purposeful personal relations with the psychiatric patients. The opposite attitude, which is termed 'humanism', involves a greater faith in eventual cure of the patients and the belief that there should be personal contact and a democratic relationship between personnel and patients. Research in the United States, England and Sweden suggests that the higher the rank a person holds among the nursing staff, the more 'humanistic' he will tend to be. *Johansson* (1968) gives a survey of these investigations and discusses how the findings should be explained. He points out that, among other things, those who rank lowest among the nursing personnel have closest contact with the patients (pp. 100-101). It is also easiest for them to come into conflict with the patients, and they can exert little influence (pp. 101-103). It is therefore likely that it is these people who have greatest need to protect themselves from personal engagement and contact. And this – in addition to various other factors which Johansson mentions – can perhaps help to explain their 'custodialism'.

14. The individual employee may also demonstrate ambivalent behaviour ; see Løchen (1965 p. 123 et seq., p. 131 et seq. and p. 140 et seq.) for a description of how nurses in a mental hospital vacillated between the rule-oriented and the client-oriented attitude.

We have seen that the attitude of the employee can depend upon his relationship to management on the one hand and to clients on the other. Whether or not there is frequent interaction and close contact with one or the other or both of these groups is of particular importance. The different possibilities are illustrated in Figure 4 where 'short distance' means the same as 'frequent interaction and close contact'.

In a small organization the employee may have close contact with both management and clients. As an example we can take the assistant in a country shop who is the owner's 'right hand' while he also knows all the customers personally. He will be inclined to identify himself with both parties. On the whole he follows the instructions he receives from his employer and tries to interpret them in accordance with their aims but it may well be that, out of consideration for the customers, he makes exceptions to the rules which his employer would not have done.

Figure 4

Employee's distance from management

		short	long
Employee's distance from clients	short	I	II
	long	III	IV

As an example of an employee who is close to the clients and far from management (II), we can take a person who is engaged in social work for a large and decentralized organization. He will probably have a tendency to identify himself with the clients and to attach importance to diffuse and person-oriented criteria of need, and he will be inclined to allow himself some latitude in relation to the management's rules and instructions.

A senior employee in a large organization may have close contact with the management and be at a long distance from the clients (III). In this case he is likely to identify himself with the organization and its management and to loyally follow its rules and instructions. But this does not mean that his application of the rules will be formalistic and rigid. Loyalty to management goals sometimes calls for liberal and purpose-oriented interpretations.

Junior employees in large and highly centralized organizations have

276

often a long distance both to the management and to the clients (IV). All communication with the clients, for instance, is done in writing or the number of clients is so great and communication with each so brief that the employee does not get to know any of them. Employees who belong to this category are those who are most likely to show the kind of devotion to rules described above.

10. Factors affecting recipient attitudes to allocation issues

I. INTRODUCTION

The interests of the recipients can be tied to both substantive and procedural questions. Procedural issues are of particular importance when they themselves make the allocation. This situation will be discussed in section IX. But the recipients can also be interested in the procedure adopted when a distributor makes the allocation. It may be of concern to them, for example how long it takes for the distributor to come to a decision, how indiscreet and embarrassing his investigations will be, whether they themselves will have an opportunity to argue their own interests, etc.

With regard to substantive issues, the recipient is likely to pay close attention to what *he himself* is going to receive. He can be interested in what kind of values he receives, how much he gets of them and possibly also in what he must make in return. His interest may be short term and, for example, be concerned with obtaining as many benefits or as few burdens as possible on the individual occasion. Or he may be more interested in the long term aspects of an allocation. He may pay attention not only to what he gets now but also to what he can hope to get at a later stage. – In some cases, not only the outcome but also the reasons given for it can be of interest to the recipient. This may be because he has to know the reasons before he can be sure what the transfer actually consists of, for example whether a sum of money he has received is a loan, a present or a deposit on something the distributor wishes to buy. Or the reasons may reveal something about what can be expected from the distributor in the future. It may also be that the reasons give the recipient positive or negative supplementary values by including, for example, praise or criticism.

Some recipients also take an interest in what *other recipients* receive. I am thinking now not of the interest that is involved in making comparisons, but of pure interest in how things are going with other people.

The explanation can, for example, be that the other person is a friend whom one wishes well or perhaps an enemy on whom one wishes only unhappiness and suffering.

A third substantive issue with which recipients may be concerned is that of *distribution*. Their interest can be restricted to comparing what they themselves and others have received, in order to see who has received least or most. Or there may be a more general interest in comparing what several (or perhaps all) of the persons concerned have received, in order to evaluate the *principle* of distribution which has been followed or should be followed.

And finally, the recipients may be interested in how much they all get *together*. Members of a working group, for instance, may wish to know how much work they shall accomplish as a whole and how much they are going to get for this. And children at a birthday party watch mother anxiously as she comes in with the ice cream and the cakes to see how much there is going to be all together.

Recipient interest can be evenly divided between the themes mentioned here. But often one of these is the main focus of attention. In most instances it is probably what one is to get oneself that demands the greatest attention. And it may be that interest in the set of values and the distribution is only a *derived* one : notice is taken of how large the cake is and of how it is divided because – and only because – this decides how large one's own share will be. But these interests can also be the *primary* ones. It is not unusual to see that someone considers what he gets in relation to other people as being more important than how much he gets as such. It can also happen that interest in the total set of values dominates, for instance if there is a strong feeling of solidarity between the recipients or if they want to use what they get to promote a common goal. A married couple, for instance, can be concerned with how much they together earn without attaching any importance to whether more is paid to the husband or wife. If the values are not used by the recipients for a common goal, however, it may be that the person who is primarily taken up with the total value has a derived interest in the distribution since this can be of significance to the total satisfaction (see chap. 9, section III, the text relating to fig. 1).

In what follows I will refer to a recipient as being *self-oriented* if he is interested only in what he himself gets, *distribution-oriented* if he has a primary or secondary (derived) interest in the distribution, and *collective-oriented* if he is interested in what the recipients receive as a whole.

The main subject of this chapter turns on the conditions under which

279

recipients are likely to become distribution-oriented (section III)[1] and to favour a particular type of distribution such as object-oriented equality (sections IV et seq.). But first (II) I will explain some concepts which will be made use of in what follows.

II. RECIPIENT COUPLING, VALUE COUPLING AND TRANSFER COUPLING

When a recipient reckons that what he himself receives depends upon how much the others get, I call this *recipient coupling*.[2] I would like to stress that it is the recipient's subjective notion of interdependence I have in mind. This notion can, of course, differ from the way in which an outsider views the situation and from what actually happens.

Coupling can be positive or negative. By *positive* coupling I refer to instances where the recipient conceives the correlation as being positive. Wages can serve as an example. If some people (for example, employees in private firms) receive an increase in pay (or a reduction), others (for example, civil servants) will also expect to eventually get one. An example of positive coupling of negative values is when criminals believe that if some of them get a more severe (or a milder) sentence than has so far been normal, others will receive the same. By *negative* coupling I refer to instances where the correlation is believed to be negative. The guests at a children's party, for instance, reckon that the more others get of the ice cream, the less they themselves will get. And when several people are to do a job of work together, they each realize that the more one of them does the less the others will have to do. There can also be various combinations of positive and negative coupling. For instance, R_1 may believe that what he will get is positively coupled to R_2's share, but negatively to R_3's. Or perhaps some recipients reckon that transfers will increase in step with each other until they have reached a certain level, but that if someone is to have an even greater increase this will be at the cost of others.

An important special case of negative coupling is when the quantity to be allocated is fixed so that the *total* of what the recipients receive is constant. What one person gains by increasing his share equals the others' loss. We can say that the coupling is 'stronger' in this case than in that where a large gain for one person only results in a small loss for

1. Conditions of *collective orientation* will be discussed in Chapter 12.
2. Cf. Galtung (1964 p. 101 et seq.). His concept 'coupling of units' corresponds to what I refer to as 'recipient coupling', while 'coupling of dimensions' is the same as 'value coupling' which is discussed below.

280

the others. In a similar way we can distinguish between strong and weak positive coupling. A special type of strong positive coupling is when the *ratio* between what individual recipients receive is constant, so that their gains (or losses) when the sum total of values allocated changes are proportional. As well as varying in strength, coupling can also vary in (subjective) probability. It may seem certain, rather probable, or very doubtful to a recipient that there is any such interdependence as mentioned. Opinions may also vary as to whether positive or negative coupling or no interdependence at all exists between certain transfers. Some university people, for instance, find it unfortunate that large sums are allotted to atomic and space research because they believe that there will then be less of the 'cake' left for other research projects, whereas others believe that increased allocations in one field – in the long run – will also lead to increased allocations in other fields of research.

When recipients expect negative coupling this is often because they believe that only a limited amount of values will be allocated. These beliefs may be based on reliable knowledge that the distributor has only a certain quantity at his disposal or that he has decided not to deal out more. For example, the children look at the ice cream mother is going to divide between them and know that this is all she has bought. But it can also happen that the belief rests solely on experience of what the recipients have previously received. If the transfers have so far increased evenly and relatively quickly for everyone, there is little reason to anticipate a negative coupling. But if there has been any stagnation there may be good grounds to fear this. It is understandable that in such instances recipients often keep a very sharp watch on each other because they are afraid that if one gets more than he has previously had the others will get less. *Foster* (1965) contends that certain cultures – especially what he calls 'classical peasant societies' – are permeated by such ideas. He has introduced the expression 'the Image of Limited Good' for the conception that all values in society – land, wealth, health, friendship, respect, honour etc. – are to be found only in limited quantities so that no one can expand his own shares without doing so at the cost of other people. He assumes these notions to be connected with the fact that the society is stationary and that the notions make for continued stagnation since any attempt to improve one's own situation is disapproved of.[3]

Positive coupling takes place when one reckons that the total set of

3. In American Anthropologist, vol. 68 (1966), David Kaplan and Benson Saler (pp. 202 ff.) and John W. Bennett (pp. 206 ff.) have advanced certain objections to Foster's views to which the latter replies (pp. 210 ff.).

allocated values can vary and that the variations will tend to go in the same direction for each recipient. This may be expected because, for example, one knows from experience that the distributor usually follows some principle of equality. And even if the recipients cannot base themselves on past experience, they may be so convinced that there should be equality that they, for this reason, reckon the distributor feels the same.

What the recipients expect in the way of positive or negative coupling or complete independence between transfers can have a great influence on their attitudes. Belief in *independence* tends to make the recipient self-oriented so that he is concerned only with what he himself gets and not with the distribution between himself and others nor with the total amount of values allocated. Positive and negative coupling, on the other hand, both tend to make the recipients distribution-oriented, but in different ways and to different degrees. Recipients are usually most concerned with questions of distribution when there is *negative* coupling – if the others get more, there will be less for oneself. This makes for a competitive attitude among the recipients. They will be inclined to watch what the others receive with acute interest and to oppose each other in their relationships with the distributor – if they are not able to agree on a compromise, for instance that their shares should be equal. *Positive* coupling also gives rise to an interest in what others get. The more they get, the more one can expect to get oneself. But since it is largely taken for granted what the distribution will be, this question does not arouse so much attention as when there is negative coupling. However, the recipients may take some interest in checking whether their assumption on positive coupling holds true. In their relation to the distributor they will tend to ally themselves with each other – because it is only through obtaining an increase of the total amount of values allocated that they can improve their own positions. These recipients therefore often become more collective- than distribution-oriented.

By the expression *value coupling* I mean that the value which is the direct object of allocation is – in the recipient's mind – coupled with one or more other values. The coupled values can be perceived as something the recipient *receives* in addition to the allocated value, or as something which he already *has* and of which the allocation serves as a symptom or sign.

I will first give some examples of *positive* value coupling, that is to say instances where the coupled value correlates positively with the allocated one. Mother divides a bar of chocolate between her children. The pieces of chocolate are of little importance to them but the children are still very interested in the distribution because they interpret it as an indication of mother's love. If Peter gets less than the others, he perhaps draws the conclusion – more or less consciously – that mother is not so fond of him as of the others, and is very unhappy. Or we can imagine that Smith is employed in a firm and that the boss decides how high a wage he will receive. In addition to the importance that the size of the wage has in itself, Smith also regards it as a sign of how high the boss evaluates his qualifications. If the wage is large compared with what the other employees in the firm receive, Smith gets not only more money but also increased self confidence. And if the wage is low, he is not only rather hard up but also develops a feeling of inferiority. By positive coupling of negative values I mean that one negative value is coupled to another. Punishment, for instance, is often accompanied by feelings of shame or guilt and may lead to loss of respect, esteem and confidence. And we can assume that the more severe the punishment, the greater will be these supplementary losses.

I talk about *negative* coupling of values where the allocated and the coupled values are of opposite kinds. Imagine a man who is very fond of cream cake but wants to appear modest when asked to help himself. He will then have conflicting motives. The more he takes of the cake, the less modest he will be thought. As an example where the value allocated is negative we can imagine that a dangerous or unpleasant mission is to be performed and that the person who is appointed to it (or who volunteers for it) gets sympathy, respect or admiration from the others. The more dangerous or unpleasant the mission is, the more he will probably receive of the positive supplementary values.

It may also be that the value allocated is positively coupled to some supplementary values and negatively to others. A person who is punished might receive sympathy and admiration from some people and contempt from others. He attaches importance to both, we can assume, and is perhaps in doubt as to what means the most to him.

Coupling of values usually stems from the recipient's inclination to pay attention to whether other people like or dislike him and to how they evaluate his behaviour. In lasting allocation systems where the recipients are heavily dependent upon the distributor, his opinions and attitudes are particularly important to them. What the allocation indicates with regard to the parents' love, the teacher's sympathy and recognition, the boss's confidence etc. will in such cases frequently be more important to the recipient than what is directly transferred to him.

Apart from the significance which being liked or being thought highly of by the person on whom one is dependent can have in itself, this may

283

also give rise to what we can call *transfer coupling*. By this I refer to the connection a recipient believes to exist between what he gets on one occasion and what he expects to get on later occasions. Transfer coupling is *positive* if the recipient reasons that 'since I got a lot this time, I will get plenty next time as well,' or 'since I got little this time, I probably won't get much next time'. In other words, he regards the transfer as being symptomatic – not only of the distributor's evaluation or attitude but also of his future decisions. With *negative* transfer coupling the reasoning is : 'Because I got little now, I shall probably get more next time' or 'Since I got so much this time, I will have to be content with less next time'. Here the feeling is that things will be evened out in the long run. The individual transfer is not regarded as being indicative of what the total amount will be.

The value coupling and transfer coupling which arise because the distributor's transfers are thought to be symptomatic, are largely conditioned by the recipient's tendency to compare what he receives with what other recipients get. Without such comparisons it is usually hard to know whether one gets little or much. And the more engrossed one becomes in making comparisons, the easier it is to find signs of being favoured or ignored. As already mentioned, recipient coupling – and especially negative recipient coupling – is something which makes the recipients interested in drawing comparisons. For those recipients who are dependent upon the distributor, negative recipient coupling will therefore be a factor which can give rise to positive value coupling. And where the recipients compete not only for the allocated but also for the coupled values, these latter will help to further encourage comparison-making and competitive attitudes.

To illustrate these points we can use the example of a mother who divides a bar of chocolate among her children. Because the children see the chocolate and know that mother has no more, or at any rate will not give them more than this, there is a strong negative recipient coupling : one child's gain is another child's loss. This tends to encourage the children to compare what they receive. And because of their dependency upon mother they will be inclined to regard the allocation as being indicative of where her affections lie. They may also regard their mother's affection as something in short supply for which they must compete. And the significance of the chocolate allocation can thus assume enormous proportions. I believe that this is a part of the explanation why children – and sometimes adults as well – apparently attach exaggerated importance to the distribution of values which in themselves are a mere bagatelle.

284

In the previous section we saw that, via various forms of coupling, a group of recipients can come to regard each other either as *allies* or as *competitors*. Both these attitudes – and particularly the competitive attitude – help to make the recipient distribution-oriented. If one assumes that another person's gain is one's own loss, and vice versa, there is reason to pay very close attention to whether one gets more or less or the same as he does.

Another factor which can lead in the same direction is that the other recipients often serve as 'reference group' [4] for the individual recipient – both in the sense that they are norm senders and in the sense that they are the people with whom he compares himself. What they receive can therefore serve as a measure of what he himself gets.

The yardsticks people use can be founded on experience of how different things satisfy or hinder satisfaction of primary needs. But socially determined scales of value are often more important. When, for instance, one talks about a high or a low income or living standard, severe or mild punishment etc., this would have little meaning if these descriptions were not based upon comparisons.

The people with whom one compares oneself when developing standards of measurement do not have to be the same as those with whom one is allied or has a competitive relationship. What the neighbours possess of the good things in life (for instance, whether they have TV, a car, washing machine, large or small apartment, etc.) can decide what are thought of as 'necessities' and what are regarded as 'luxuries' [5] – even though there may be absolutely no contact with the neighbours and no idea of recipient coupling. But not every one is included in the group from which yardsticks are derived. If, for instance, I read in the newspaper that Onassis has bought a new luxurious yacht, I think no worse of my little dinghy than I did before. There must be some *similarity* and/ or *proximity* before comparisons are made. I will return later to the criteria of similarity and proximity which can be relevant in allocation systems.

Other people serve not only as a basis of comparison : they also effect some influence through implantation of their norms. There are norms

4. See Merton (1957 pp. 225-386), Berelson and Steiner (1964 p. 558 and p. 661), Allardt (1965 pp. 243 ff.) and Runciman (1966 pp. 9-35 with references) on the concept 'reference group' and theories associated with it. The latter gives a detailed analysis of the concept and a good survey of research in this field.
5. See W. H. Whyte (1957 particularly chap. 24) on neighbour influence on definitions of 'luxury' and 'necessities' in an American suburban area.

which indicate standards of measurement and norms which invite comparison. These are often combined, for example, in expressions like 'everyone has a TV nowadays' or 'you really can't drive that old car any longer'. There are also norms which indicate with *whom* one should make comparisons. The circle of persons communicating norms sometimes coincides with the circle with which one is likely to make comparisons.

On the basis of what has so far been said in this and the previous sections, I present some hypotheses concerning factors connected with distribution orientation :

1. The tendency to make comparisons is stronger [6] between recipients who have the same distributor than between recipients with different distributors.

This hypothesis is partly based on the assumption that having the same distributor may be a criterion of similarity which increases the likelihood that recipients use each other's shares as a measure of how much they themselves get. There is also reason to believe that the likelihood of recipient coupling is greater when the distributor is the same. Negative coupling, at any rate, is more likely to take place because there is normally a limit to how much the individual distributor can or wants to deal out. But the same probably also applies to positive coupling since there is a greater chance that the recipients expect a proportional increase (or reduction) of transfers when they share the same distributor than when they have different distributors.

2. The tendency to make comparisons is stronger with regard to transfers made by the distributor on the same occasion than with those which he makes on different occasions.

This hypothesis also has a double foundation. When the occasion is the same there is a nearness in time and space which makes the other recipients' shares natural standards of measurement. In addition there is increased probability of mutual interdependence between the transfers (i.e. recipient coupling).

3. The smaller the increase in the set of values that the recipients expect to be able to achieve, the stronger will be their tendency to make comparisons with each other.

---

6. By the expression 'the tendency to make comparisons is stronger' (or 'increases' with this or that factor), I mean here and in what follows *both* that the *degree* of probability of finding someone making a comparison is greater *and* that there are probably relatively *more* people who make comparisons *and* that comparison probably *means more* to the individual person. All hypotheses must be read with the reservation : 'other things being equal'.

The basis of this hypothesis can be found in what was said in section II on the causes and results of negative recipient coupling. When the recipients do not have much hope of being able to enlarge the set of values allocated, they will have a tendency to perceive one person's gains as a loss to someone else and questions of distribution will become very important.

4. The tendency to make comparisons increases with the duration and comprehensiveness of the allocation system.

The more lasting and the more comprehensive relationship the recipients have with the distributor, the greater is their similarity and proximity likely to be and the more pertinent it is for them to use each others shares as yardsticks. Whether or not the probability of recipient coupling increases with the duration and comprehensiveness of the relationship is somewhat doubtful. But if negative recipient coupling takes place, distribution-orientation will tend to be strengthened through positive value coupling (see section II).

5. The tendency to make comparisons is stronger the more homogeneous are the values allocated.

This hypothesis is based on the assumption that what the other recipients receive is more suitable as a measure the more it resembles what one receives oneself. This probably applies both when the values come from the same and from different distributors. Various manners of classification can be used when making comparisons. Chocolate may be regarded as something different from toffee but they can both be allotted to the same joint category 'goodies'. There is probably no limit to the breadth of the categories with which one can operate. But common sense experience suggests that the inclination to make comparisons decreases with decreasing similarity of the values concerned. There seems as well to be a certain amount of agreement on what is *more* or what is *less* homogeneous – although it can be difficult to give any clear criteria for this.

6. The tendency to make comparisons is stronger the easier it is to find a common measure of the values.

This hypothesis has the same basis as the previous one. And the two hypotheses also partly say the same thing, since having a common measure is one of the factors which can give an impression of homogeneity. But even when there is little similarity between the objects to be evaluated it is easier to compare them if we can apply a common yardstick, for instance money. A monetary economy can, for example, increase the inclination to make comparisons within the family. Changes in this direction have, according to *Bentzon* (1963 pp. H 2-4), taken

287

place in West Greenland. As long as a subsistence economy prevailed and the family members contributed with different kinds of labour and produce, there were few possibilities of comparing individual contributions. Since a monetary economy has partially taken over there have been greater opportunities of comparing and thereby also of disagreeing on how much each member of the family with a cash income should contribute.[7]

7. Value coupling strengthens existing tendencies to make comparisons, provided that there is positive coupling of similar values, but weakens the tendencies of recipients with dissimilar couplings to make comparisons.

This hypothesis is connected with hypothesis No. 5. The fact that similar values are easiest to compare, applies not only to those that are allocated but also to those that are coupled. In the example which was mentioned earlier (section II) where mother allocates the chocolate between her children, both the allocated values (the chocolate) and the positive coupled values (mother's affection) are homogeneous. This fact helps strengthen the tendency to make comparisons. The fact that the values allocated can be measured also pulls in the same direction (see hypothesis No. 6). It is also possible that measurability increases the probability of value coupling, since recipients who feel the need to compare non-measurable values which are of great importance to them (in this example, mother's affection) may tend to look for measurable symptoms of what they receive of these values.

By the expression 'dissimilar couplings', used in hypothesis No. 7, I refer to instances where one recipient couples positively and the other negatively or not at all, and to instances where both couple positively but with different types of values. As an example we can imagine that mother divides the chocolate between her own children and some other children who are on a visit. Her own (under the conditions already mentioned) will tend to make comparisons between themselves. But whether they get more or less than the guests is of subordinate significance because they are not competing with the visitors over the coupled values which are of much greater importance than the chocolate. For the same reason, it is not so important for the visitors to make comparisons with

7. Another consequence, mentioned by Bentzon, is that those in the family who have a cash income have, because of their factual position of power in regard to spending money, obtained greater influence than those who contribute with non-monetary services. This trend towards inequality grows with the living standard because so long as the family lives at subsistence level it is more or less obvious what the money must be used for.

288

what the children belonging to the house receive. Their tendency to make such a comparison will be further reduced if they make a negative coupling, for example because they want to appear modest. There would probably have been a more marked tendency to make comparisons across family lines if it had not been mother who divided the chocolate but the children themselves.

IV. FACTORS FAVOURING OBJECT-ORIENTED EQUAL DISTRIBUTION

Distribution-orientation is a prerequisite for being interested in getting equal shares. What was said in the previous section, therefore, forms the basis of what is to be discussed below.

A distribution-oriented recipient, however, is not necessarily in favour of object-oriented equality. There are also other possibilities, for instance that he goes in for one of the other principles of equality, or that he does not want equal treatment but, for example, would like to have the largest share.

In what follows I will first (paragraphs 1-5) look at some of the factors which can get distribution-oriented recipients to favour object-oriented equal distribution, and then examine (in paragraph 6) factors which pull in the opposite direction.

1. *Equal distribution as a compromise between opposed wishes of individual recipients*

I assume that the object of allocation has a positive or negative value for the recipient. He wants therefore to have as much (or as little) as possible of it – at any rate until saturation point is reached. But, as we have seen in section II, other values may be negatively coupled to those allocated. For example, the recipient does not want to be thought greedy or immodest. Or he wants to be regarded as a 'good friend' or a 'considerate person' who does not grasp all the benefits but leaves something for other people and who accepts many of the burdens so as not to overtax others. He may also be a person to whom consideration for other people is of independent value and not only a means of retaining respect.

In such cases opposed considerations will be weighed against each other. This can be illustrated with the help of the marginal utility [8] and marginal cost concepts. I assume that the pleasure or utility which a re-

8. See concerning this concept chap. 9 III.

cipient gets from each new unit of the transferred value, varies with the size of the transfer. If it is cake which he gets, for example, a certain minimum quantity is perhaps essential if he is to taste anything at all and it is possible that the marginal utility increases with the first few bites, but it will soon begin to decrease and he will finally reach a point where he prefers not to eat any more. The unpleasant sensation of being thought greedy or immodest will also tend to vary with the size of the transfer. Our cake-eater can probably help himself to a certain amount of cake without incurring such costs. But the more he takes after this point has been reached the greedier he must expect to be considered. Let us assume that the marginal costs of being considered greedy increase and that the cost curve and utility curve intersect each other as shown in Figure 1.

Figure 1

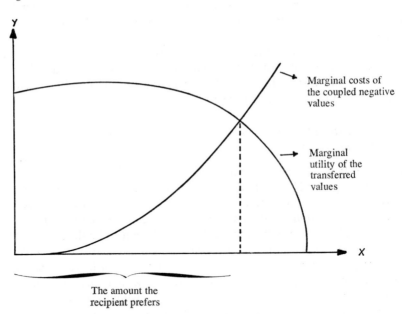

Marginal costs of the coupled negative values

Marginal utility of the transferred values

The amount the recipient prefers

The amount the recipient prefers stops short at the point where the curves intersect each other. If he gets less, he misses some gain. If he gets more, he will loose on the last units he receives because the additional burden of extra greed will be greater than the additional enjoyment of getting even more cake.

290

The curves in the figure have, of course, been chosen at random and are only meant to serve as an illustration of a viewpoint. However, the assumption that marginal utility decreases, at any rate after a certain point has been reached, is believed to apply in most cases. It may fall rapidly or more slowly. The curve, for example, is certainly flatter for money than for cake. And, naturally, there are great differences between different individuals. The assumption that marginal costs rise, that is to say that opposed considerations gather in strength more than proportionally to the transfers, certainly does not apply in all cases, but it does sometimes. And even if the marginal costs are constant or decreasing this may set a limit to how much the recipient wants.

A recipient's position will not always be the kind of compromise mentioned. On the one hand there may be cases where inhibitions dominate. The recipient, for instance, is so considerate (or so intent upon appearing considerate) that he refuses to have any of the benefits which are allocated, (that is to say, his cost curve begins higher on the y axis than the utility curve). On the other hand there are also recipients who have no compunction about acquiring as much as they can of the allocated benefits. Between these two extremes there is a continuum of cases where counter-considerations have varying influence. To prefer equal distribution as a compromise is only one of many possible solutions.

But in some cases this is a very appropriate possibility. This is especially true when the opposed considerations have their roots in concern for the other recipients (or in a desire to appear considerate). Here one must find a reasonable compromise between consideration for oneself and for the others, and equal distribution appears in such an event as the middle point which the conflicting motives can approach.

2. *Equal distribution as a compromise between competitive recipients*

Recipients often have to compromise when they themselves undertake the allocation. When there is a distributor allocating they may through negotiation or tacit understanding take a common stand on how the allocation should be made so that everyone's interests are to some extent catered for.

Compromise between the recipients presupposes a *competitive situation,* i.e. a situation in which everyone cannot be completely satisfied and in which each regards the other recipients as his competitors (negative recipient coupling). The usual reason why desires for benefits cannot be wholly satisfied is that everyone wants more than he can get. But

291

we can also imagine a situation where two or more over-considerate persons are to divide something between them. Each one of them starts negotiating by suggesting that he himself get nothing and the others have everything. But if they are to arrive at a solution they will have to modify their consideration for one another so that they each take a little. In other words, when confronted with one's competitors, this can lead to some adjustment, in either direction, of those tendencies to be considerate which already exist.

When burdens are to be allocated, the competitive situation is usually such that each person wants to get away with less than what is needed to accomplish the job. But forms of 'inverted competition' similar to those present when benefits are allocated can be imagined. There can also be competitive situations involving punishment, for instance because punishment resources are limited. There may be a shortage of prison capacity, or perhaps father's arm begins to ache before he has spanked all his children, so that increased punishment for one means that the others get off more lightly. Moreover, the shame involved in punishment tends to diminish the more people receiving punishment and the more severe the punishment that the others get. But even if there is a competitive situation the recipients' chances of reaching a compromise and of influencing the allocation are normally less when punishment is involved than when benefits or burdens are allocated.

Object-oriented equal distribution is, of course, not the only compromise solution. If, for example, the recipients find that attention should be paid to need, fitness or desert and there are great and visible differences between them with regard to the relevant characteristics, they may take this into account. It may also be that some of them are more powerful or better negotiators than others and for this reason secure themselves larger shares. The greater the similarity between the recipients with regard to both strength of interest and influence, the more likely it is that they will favour equal distribution. But even when there are certain differences between them in these respects, equal distribution may be preferred. This alternative has the special feature of being the simplest solution and also of constituting a kind of middle point between the most extreme demands. It is therefore an alternative which is likely to attract attention and which for this reason can be a 'strategic focal point' acting as a magnet for the participants' hopes and choices.[9]

9. See Schelling (1960) and what has been said of his views in Chapter 4, section III above.

3. *Equal distribution as the optimum*

So far I have only looked at recipient interest in coming to agreement and at the interests associated with individual transfers. But concern can also be tied to the allocation seen as a whole. This will especially be of interest to the distributor (see chap. 9). But the recipients, too, may be concerned with it either because they have accepted the distributor's goals or because there is a feeling of mutual solidarity between them.

As was mentioned several times in Chapter 9, the distribution can influence the realization of the goals tied to an allocation process. This applies equally as much to the recipients' goals as to the distributor's. The distribution best fitted to promote a given aim I call 'the optimum distribution'. In this section I will only be concerned with what is the optimum in relation to the aim of *maximizing the sum total of subjective values* which the recipients receive.

This question was discussed in Chapter 9, section III (the text related to fig. 1). The conclusion was reached there that with decreasing marginal utility, the optimum will be to divide the benefits in such a manner that marginal utility is the same for all recipients (in other words, so that everyone has his needs equally well satisfied). When allocating burdens the optimum – assuming a rising marginal sacrifice – must be to divide so that the marginal sacrifices are equally large. This means that if the recipients' needs (sacrifices) are the same, object-oriented equal distribution will be the optimum.

This can be illustrated by some simple examples. Let us imagine that four pieces of cake are to be divided between two children who are equally fond of cake. There will then be a larger total of satisfied need when they each receive two slices than if, for example, one of them received three pieces and the other only one. This is because when the marginal utility decreases, piece No. 2 affords more satisfaction than No. 3. The same applies when burdens are allocated. If, for example, two persons are to do a job which altogether requires four working hours, and both persons evaluate the burdens equally and feel that the sacrifice they make becomes greater with each hour, the smallest joint sacrifice will be when they each do a half of the work. But if the examples are changed so that one of the children likes cake while the other loathes it, and one worker finds the work a pleasure while the other hates it, equal distribution will not be the optimum. In such cases total satisfaction will be maximized (or the total sacrifice minimized) when one of them gets everything and the other nothing.

It is in the common interest of the recipients to arrive at an optimum distribution because they then together get most pleasure from the benefits (or least displeasure from the burdens). But for the individual recipient a distribution which gives him more can be more favourable. Concern to achieve the optimum is therefore greater in a recipient the more inclined he is to give common interest preference over his own. Concern for optimality will, as mentioned, make for a positive attitude to object-oriented equality if the needs (sacrifices) of the recipients are similar but for a negative attitude if they are sufficiently dissimilar. The conditions under which differences in need are likely to be taken into account will be discussed in paragraph 6 below.

Even when the recipients are purely egoistic, there may be forces which pull in the direction of an optimum distribution. As we have already seen, the distributor may go in for this. It is also possible that compromises between competing recipients have a tendency to approach the optimum. Some people will lose more than others win when a different solution is chosen. If, for instance, Peter and John are equally fond of cake, greater opposition will have to be overcome by persuading Peter to relinquish piece No. 2 than by getting John to give up No. 3 – since No. 2 means more to Peter than No. 3 does to John.

Recipients who wish to promote common interests can do this in two ways, *either* – as mentioned here – by trying to achieve an optimum distribution *or* by trying to increase the set of values to be allocated. The two possibilities do not exclude each other but attention is not always divided evenly between them. There may be recipients who are engrossed in getting the total amount of values increased and who attach little or no importance to the distribution. And there may be others who concentrate all or the greater part of their attention on the distribution. The last mentioned attitude is most common in recipients who reckon that there are small chances of getting the set of allocated values increased, for instance because there have been no recent signs of increase.

4. *Claims for equality as a defence of the weak and as camouflage*

A demand for equality can be a means by which recipients defend themselves against the distributor and a means by which the weaker recipients defend themselves against the stronger.

The need for a defence against the distributor is particularly strong when recipients are dependent upon him, for example because he controls benefits which they need badly and which they are not able to obtain anywhere else or because he has the power to impose burdens or

294

punishments on them. There can be different kinds of real (or imagined) threats from which the dependent recipient needs to protect himself. There may be the danger of being refused or deprived of vital values (for example, parental affection or the boss's confidence) ; or perhaps the distributor uses his control over benefits and burdens as a means of manipulating the recipients. Then again, the recipient may feel the need to protect his own self-image.

A demand for equal treatment with other recipients can be a means of defending oneself against all these dangers. If the claim is met, one is relatively well ensured against deprivation, manipulation and disillusion. Security against manipulation becomes greater the more object-oriented and specific the criteria of equality are. If everyone gets exactly the same and no account is taken of who they are or what they have done, the goods and evils allocated will not assume the character of rewards or punishment and cannot therefore be instrumental in exerting influence.

Demanding equality is not the only way in which recipients can protect themselves. In the next chapter I will give a survey of various types of defence strategies and discuss the conditions under which they are likely to be used. More detail will be payed there to the role played by demands for equality as defences.

Because of the security afforded by the principle of equality, it may be rational for a recipient to go in for this even though he otherwise would have a good chance of obtaining more of the values allocated. But those recipients who would be in a weaker position than their competitors if the principle were not adhered to are naturally most strongly motivated to support it. The principle acts for these weak recipients not only as protection against the distributor but also against the stronger recipients. We can assume therefore that if there are differences between the recipients with regard to influence, popularity etc. in their relation with the distributor, the tendency to claim equal distribution will be strongest amongst those who consider themselves least influential or popular.[10]

A recipient who feels that he gets too little may have many reasons for demanding equality instead of simply demanding more. In the first place, it is possible that equal distribution is the best that he can hope to get and that he therefore finds it most realistic to limit his demands in this manner. In the second place, his claim will bear more moral weight if it is based on the general principle of equality and is not only argued by

10. The assumption held good, but the differences were relatively small, with the primary school pupils whom Naess (1969) interviewed.

saying that he would like more himself. And thirdly, equal distribution can involve other advantages as we have already seen.

This is probably the reason why demands which in reality are aimed at getting more than other people, are sometimes camouflaged as claims for equality. In order to make it feasible to justify his demands with the principle of equality, a recipient may conceal from other people (and perhaps from himself too) how much he already has, exaggerate what the others have received, re-define the criteria of equality or in some other way give the impression that he has been treated unfairly.

Among recipients who feel insecure or who believe that they have received too little (for instance, children and institution inmates) one frequently finds a tendency to alternate between demanding equality and arguing that their own special needs should be satisfied.[11] Such ambivalent behaviour can be due to changing attitudes to the two alternative strategies. Sometimes less is gained by this wavering approach than by holding to a straight course. But a mixed strategy can also be effective since claims for satisfaction of individual needs may be best suited to gaining improvements and claims for equality may serve to consolidate one's position.

5. The procedural advantages of equal distribution

From the *distributor's* point of view, object-oriented equal distribution can have great procedural advantages : he does not have to make up his mind about individual recipient's needs, fitness, merit or other personal characteristics, and he avoids complicated calculations. In Chapter 9, section VII I discussed these and other advantages involved in using simple decision-making principles.

It is also often an advantage to the *recipients* that decisions can be made quickly and without detailed investigation. Furthermore, when the distributor follows the simple principle of equality, the recipients can more readily forecast the outcome and more easily keep check on him, than when he bases himself on person-oriented criteria. For example, it can be difficult to check whether or not the distributor is acting impartially when he attaches significance to such criteria as, for instance, need, fitness or desert. It can also lead to conflict between recipients if the distributor follows principles which make for doubt and uncertainty about what is right.

When the recipients themselves undertake the allocation, there are

11. See chap. 11, note 8 and sections VIII and IX.

other procedural factors to be taken into account. I shall examine these in section IX below.

The procedural advantages of object-oriented equality are greater the more specific the criteria of equality. When the benefits or burdens to be allocated are of such a kind that one can – without coming into conflict with other important considerations – build upon specific criteria, this is a factor which will increase the likelihood of preference for equal distribution. Some examples from *Naess's* (1969) study of school children illustrate this : there was a strong tendency to claim that the job of helping the teacher (for instance, running errands for him) should be equally devided.[12] This could be made fairly simple by letting the number of times that the individual was asked to help, serve as the criterion. There were not quite as many who supported equal distribution of the teacher's questions to pupils. The number of times could also here serve as the criterion, but it was more difficult to keep track of this because the teacher's questions were much more frequent than were the occasions on which he asked for help. And finally, with regard to how the teacher allotted places in the classroom, hardly anyone suggested equal distribution. It would have been technically possible to accomplish this, for instance if the pupils constantly changed places so that each person sat the same length of time at each desk during the school year. But this would have been a complicated solution and the frequent changes would have created confusion. These procedural considerations were certainly not the only ones that played a role (see below), but they were of some importance.

Substantive and procedural considerations can pull in different directions for the recipients as well as for the distributor (see chap. 9, section VII). And what counts most will differ. Procedural concern for simplification and speed is more likely to be a determining factor the smaller the value of what is to be allocated. But consideration for impartiality and control carry greater weight the larger the values to be allocated. Therefore, it is possible that the desire for equal distribution which springs from procedural considerations is strongest when the values are either very small or very large.

---

12. 78 % of pupils (N = 234) replied that everyone should help equally often and 50% gave this as their only reply. Corresponding figures for the teachers (N = 40) were 95 % and 23 %.

6. Factors which go against object-oriented equal distribution

When a recipient is interested both in what he himself gets and in the distribution there will normally be some connection between the standpoints he takes to the two issues. If, for instance, he is taken up by what he himself is going to get because he badly needs the allocated goods, it will be natural for him to evaluate what the others receive in the light of the need he believes *they* have for the benefit. If he finds out that their needs differ, this will be a reason for him not to favour object-oriented equality but, for instance, to suggest that everyone have his need equally well satisfied. Something similar applies when, for example, it is thought appropriate to take account of fitness, desert, right or duty, and the individual recipients are not equally placed with regard to these characteristics. I will now examine *what kind of differences* between the recipients can give rise to counter arguments against object-oriented equality.

In the first place, the differences must be regarded as *relevant*. If, for instance, everyone is agreed that weight should only be attached to merit, the fact that the recipients' needs are different is irrelevant. It does not give them grounds to reject equal distribution. *How large* the recipients consider the relevant differences to be also plays a role. Insignificant variations can easily be disregarded and the larger they become the more weighty an argument they represent against equal distribution.

How *visible* the differences are is also of some significance. There can be great individual differences which are not visible and which are therefore not taken into account. If, for instance, need (in the sense 'desire') is considered the decisive criterion it may well be that each person knows what his own wants are, but to find out how these differ from other people's is more difficult. The differences are usually most apparent when preferences go in exactly opposite directions so that one person wants something which the other person prefers to avoid. The problem is greater when trying to find degrees of difference between desires which go in the same direction. This is partly because language is poorly equipped to indicate exactly *how* well or *how* badly one regards something and partly because a recipient can exaggerate his desires, or conversely avoid stressing how strong they are because, for example, he is too proud or too modest to do so. If it is not clear that the needs are of different strengths, or if one believes that there are differences but does not know which way they go, it may be best to ignore them. The same applies to differences in fitness and merit etc.

It can happen that differences, for instance with regard to need or fitness, are both large and visible but that it is not *legitimate* to take them into account, for example because it will hurt or offend people to refer to them. In a classroom it may be clear – both to the teacher and the pupils – that certain pupils have a greater need for the teacher's time and attention. But it may be that, even so, no one supports the idea that they should have more of these values than the others because this would mean that they were identified as having little talent. Similarly, some pupils may not be so well suited to run errands for the teacher but if attention was paid to this fact, they would then be labelled untrustworthy.[13]

Differences in need for such values as affection, care and confidence are often not apparent and it may be considered less legitimate to take them into account. It is therefore difficult to find a good argument against equal distribution of such values to, for instance, children in the same family or pupils of the same class. As mentioned in section II, such values as these are frequently positively coupled to trivial benefits which parents or teachers allocate between the children. And if the children believe that everyone should have the same amount of the coupled values, this can get them to support object-oriented equal distribution of the values allocated – even if there are relevant, visible and legitimate differences in the recipients' needs. When, for example, mother is going to divide a cake between Peter and John, Peter may insist on an equal division – in spite of the fact that he is not at all interested in the cake and knows that John is very fond of it. And it may well be that John accepts this view since the values allocated are unimportant in relation to those that are coupled to them. – Positive value coupling can also partially explain the fact that helping the teacher – which nearly all pupils in the school study evaluated positively–was the value which most children said should be divided equally (see note 12). Obviously there were highly visible differences in need, fitness or merit which could have been considered relevant in allocation of help to the teacher, but almost no one attached importance to these differences. One of the reasons can have been that to be allowed to help the teacher was taken as a sign of his confidence. And it was thought that everyone should have the same amount of this value.

When there are such relevant, large, visible and legitimate differences

---

13. These examples are taken from Naess's (1969) study of teachers' and school children's attitudes to distribution issues.

between the recipients that they, for this reason, reject object-oriented equality, they may instead favour one of the different kinds of person-oriented equality. Some of the factors mentioned in the previous paragraphs (1-5) can lead in this direction when the conditions for object-oriented equal distribution are not present. I will go into this in more detail in sections VII and VIII below.

V. OBJECT-ORIENTED EQUAL DISTRIBUTION
SUMMARY AND HYPOTHESES

I will now try to draw together some of the points of view given in the previous sections and give them the form of a set of hypotheses concerning the conditions under which recipients are likely to favour object-oriented equal distribution. The term 'favour', used for the sake of brevity, indicates that the recipients will divide equally if they make the decision themselves, that they will demand equal distribution if there is a distributor, and that they may internalize the norm that it is right to divide equally. The expression 'strong (weak etc.) tendency' to favour equal distribution is used in the same sense as in section III (see note 6), so that it refers both to how likely it is that someone will favour equal distribution, how many will probably do so, and to how important they are likely to consider this to be.

A necessary condition for favouring equal distribution is that the recipients are distribution-oriented. According to the hypotheses in section III, the tendency to be distribution-oriented is encouraged by, among other things, all transfers being made by the same distributor (hypothesis 1) and on the same occasion (2), all or most recipients believing there are few chances of increasing the set of values involved (3), and the transfers taking place within a lasting and comprehensive allocation system (4). We can sum up this by saying that factors which make for similarity and proximity between the recipients and which help to provide a point of contact for their interests, will promote their leanings towards distribution-orientation. Various characteristics of the transfered values also play a role (hypotheses 5-7).

Distribution-orientation does not always lead to support of object-oriented equal distribution. Other distribution principles are sometimes preferred (see the following sections). Which distribution principle will be preferred depends to a large extent upon whether the recipients are of the opinion that the transfers should be adapted to need, fitness, desert, etc. – and on whether they find differences between themselves in

300

these respects. On the basis of what was said in section IV, the following hypothesis can be formulated :

8. The less relevance the recipients attach to person-oriented criteria (for example, need, fitness, desert, right, duty or status), the smaller and less visible the relevant differences with regard to such features, and the less legitimate it is to pay attention to them, the stronger will be the tendency to favour object-oriented equal distribution.

Similarity between the recipients with regard to their power (or lack of power) to influence the allocation, works in the same direction because it increases the likelihood of equal distribution being the most appropriate compromise between them (see section IV, 2). This gives rise to the following hypothesis :

9. The smaller the differences between individual recipients' powers of exerting influence on the allocation, the stronger will be the tendency to support object-oriented equal distribution.

What was said in section IV, 4, about equal distribution as a defence of the weak, is the basis for the hypothesis that

10. Recipients who regard themselves as being less influential or as less favoured than the others by the distributor, will tend to favour object-oriented equal distribution more than those recipients who do not have the same feeling of inferiority.

The attitudes the recipients adopt towards one another are of importance from several points of view. They affect, among other things, intra- and inter-subjective compromises which the recipients may reach (see section IV, 1 and 2) and the possibility of camouflage (4). On the basis of what was said in section IV, I advance the following hypothesis :

11. Recipients who are, or want to appear, reasonably considerate towards each other will tend to favour object-oriented equal distribution more than recipients who are inconsiderate or overconsiderate.

In other words, it is only up to a certain level that increasing (real or simulated) consideration encourages the tendency to favour equal distribution. If this level is exceeded, excessive consideration can make it difficult to reach a compromise. It may also be that the recipients' primary interest in the question of distribution will be reduced if they identify too strongly with one another.

As mentioned in section IV, 3, however, recipients with a concern for common interests can develop *secondary* interest in the distribution because total satisfaction can be increased by approaching optimum distribution. To put common interests before one's own is not the same as putting consideration for other individual persons above consideration for oneself, but there is certainly some connection between these two

301

attitudes. What has been said in section IV, 3 about optimalization gives grounds for the following hypothesis :

12. The more inclined the recipients are to promote their common interests, the stronger will be their tendency to favour object-oriented equal distribution (provided that they consider their needs for the transferred values to be the same), and the weaker this will be if there are (relevant, visible and legitimate) differences in need.

The relationship between the recipients and the distributor affects the formers' tendency to be distribution-oriented (section III, hypotheses 1 and 4) and, via this, their tendency to favour object-oriented equal distribution. But certain aspects of the relationship, especially the degree of dependence, have a more direct significance. If the recipients are dependent on the distributor this gives rise to a need for defence which can lead to demands for equality (section IV, 4). In addition, dependency often results in coupling of the allocated value with certain immaterial values (for example, the distributor's affection or confidence) in which the recipients are inclined to demand equal shares. The more lasting and the more comprehensive an allocation system is (see hypothesis 4 in section III) the greater will dependency usually be. But since there is no necessary connection between these features, I advance the following separate hypothesis :

13. The more lasting, the more comprehensive and – within certain limits – the more dependent is the relationship of recipient to distributor, the stronger will be the tendency to favour object-oriented equal distribution.

The reservation 'within certain limits' is necessary because there are cases where the recipient's dependency and subordination in relation to the distributor is *so* great that he does not dare to make any demands, not even a claim for equality, but is content to ask for favours or mercy – if he is not completely resigned to his lot. I will discuss this in more detail in the next chapter.

The procedural considerations pointing in the direction of equal distribution (see section IV, 5) give ground for the following hypothesis :

14. The more important it is for the recipients
    a. that decisions are made quickly and without detailed investigation and
    b. that they can keep a check on the distributor's decisions and have confidence in his impartiality, the stronger will be the tendence to favour object-oriented equal distribution.

Both the procedural advantages and certain of the other advantages which object-oriented equality can furnish (for example, as a means of

302

defence) depend upon it being possible to find criteria of equality which are neither too diffuse nor too complicated. And the more specific the criteria that can be built upon, the greater will be the advantages. It therefore seems reasonable to assume that :

15. The tendency to support object-oriented equal distribution will be stronger the more specific the criteria to which it can be tied.

VI. SUBSTITUTES FOR OBJECT-ORIENTED EQUALITY : WITH PARTICULAR REFERENCE TO RANDOM SELECTION

Object-oriented equal distribution cannot be achieved if the good or evil to be allocated is indivisible so that only one (or some) of the recipients can have it. Indivisibility may be due to the object's physical properties. Or it can be determined by the rules of a game or by other norms, for example the rule that only one person be the 'finder' when playing hide and seek. It may also be a matter of expediency. The system of exempting men from military training by drawing lots is an example. Theoretically it would be possible to reduce the total amount of military service by shortening every recruit's period of service. But, among other things, the fact that a certain minimum period is necessary to train a man to be a useful soldier suggests instead that the actual number of recruits be cut. And when this decision is first taken, it becomes impossible to divide equally among everyone the benefits which are to be allocated (exemption).

Moreover, even if what is to be allocated is not indivisible it may be difficult to divide it equally. The difficulties may arise because the criteria of equality are too diffuse or too complicated or because several alternative criteria of equality are available and none of these provides an obvious choice. If, for example, 3 children are to divide 4 apples between them, this can be done by taking 1 apple each and splitting the last into 3 equally big pieces. But perhaps the children find this method too complicated, or feel that they may quarrel about it, and therefore try to find another way out.

The use of *random* devices (for instance, drawing lots) is a method often chosen when the conditions indicate object-oriented equal distribution, if this were not prevented by such obstacles or difficulties as those just mentioned. Drawing of lots and similar procedures *can* also be used in other cases, for instance because one believes that the decision is then left to a higher power (see chap. 8, section IV) or because one likes the suspense involved in allowing the outcome to depend on chance. But in this section I am concerned only with instances where object-oriented equal distribution is impossible or very difficult to obtain. The question is : what, in such situations, can make random selection more attractive than either trying to overcome the difficulties of giving everyone equal shares or falling back on some other distribution principle (for example, distribution according to need, fitness or desert) ? I will approach the answer by looking at those characteristics of object-oriented equal distribution mentioned in section IV and V to see whether they are also connected with random selection and, if this is not so, what the differences are.

One important point of similarity between the two forms of distribution is that both are purely object-oriented. The desire to make an allocation without regard for personal characteristics – so that there is no discrimination on the grounds of need, fitness, desert, status etc. – is met equally satisfactorily in random distribution as in object-oriented equal distribution. In some cases this demand is met even more satisfactorily. If the criteria of equality are diffuse, an attempt to give each recipient as much as the next may leave some doubt as to whether this has actually been done. Have, perhaps, some person-oriented considerations crept in ? Such doubts are less likely to arise when a formalized random procedure is used.

Another important point of similarity is that random devices have some of the same procedural advantages as object-oriented equal distribution (see section IV, 5). They ensure that a quick decision is reached, save the participants negotiation, investigation and deliberation, afford the recipients the opportunity of keeping a check on things and protect them from bias, while at the same time the distributor is relieved of responsibility. Random selection is often more effective than any other method of decision-making when it comes to furnishing a guarantee against bias and against having to shoulder responsibility because the distributor has no opportunity to influence the result (other than by cheating).

To agree to random selection is also a possible compromise (see section IV, 1 and 2). It is sometimes the only solution, for example if recipients who are themselves making the allocation cannot manage to agree.

On the other hand, randomness is on the whole not well suited to maximize the sum of subjective values (section IV, 3). It may be that most use is made of the object when only one person receives it. But we have no guarantee that the person with the greatest need for the object will draw the lucky number.

304

Random selection is well suited to meet some of the defence needs of weak recipients (section IV, 4), but is poorly suited to meet other of these needs. The recipients avoid being manipulated by the distributor, but they have neither predictability nor security from being deprived of vital values.[14]

The factors which have been mentioned make random selection more appropriate for the recipients the more important it seems to them to avoid person-oriented decision criteria, the more heavily the above mentioned procedural considerations weigh, and the more difficult it is to reach any other compromise. And the principle becomes less suitable the more importance is attached to predictability and security, to everyone getting some of the benefits (or carrying some of the burdens) and to maximizing the sum of subjective values. The result of the interplay between these factors is that random selection is most favoured when the outcome is either of very *small* or very *great* importance to the recipients.[15]

When the outcome is of little importance, the fact that random selection involves simple techniques for arriving at a result will often be decisive. One can say, for instance, 'It's of no importance what the result will be ; we can just as well toss a penny'. If more important values are involved, less stress is put upon simplifying the decision-making and more on substantive considerations which go against leaving the result to chance. But if the value increases even more, the distributors' need to be relieved of responsibility and the recipients' need for protection against partiality become more and more urgent. For these reasons random devices are sometimes employed where the most vital values are at stake.

I have already (chap. 8, section IV) given examples of judicial proceedings where death sentences have been decided by throwing dice. There are also other situations in which a question of life or death has been decided, or where it has been recommended that it be decided in this way, for instance when a perilous mission has had to be undertaken or when someone has had to be sacrificed to save others. An American criminal case from 1841 (U.S. v. Holmes, 26 Fed. Cas. 360) deals with a situation of the latter type: A ship was wrecked and one of its lifeboats

---

14. I do not take into account here instances where so many similar transfers take place that all recipients get the same amount in the long run even though each individual result is random.
15. As mentioned above (section IV, 5), it is possible that something similar applies to object oriented equal distribution, but the tendency is much clearer with regard to random selection.

was adrift in a storm. The boat was overloaded and leaked so that eventually it was on the point of sinking. On the orders of the first mate the crew threw the male passengers, apart from two married men and a small boy (a total of 14) overboard. The following day the boat was rescued. One of the crew, Holmes, was later brought to court. (The others, in the meantime, had disappeared.) He was sentenced to 6 months imprisonment. The judge instructed the jury that the passengers were entitled to be saved before the crew apart from those of the crew who were needed to navigate the boat. If none of the crew could be dispensed with, lots should be drawn among the passengers as to who should be sacrificed. The moral aspect of the judgment is discussed by *Cahn* (1956 p. 61 et seq.). It is also referred to by *Andenaes* (1965 p. 172) who comments on this case and the English 'Mignonette'-case from 1884 in which two shipwrecked seamen were convicted for having killed and eaten a cabin-boy while they drifted about on a raft and were dying of hunger and thirst (R. v. Dudley and Stephens, 14 Q.B.D. 273, in Turner and Armitage, 1964, pp. 80-84.) Andenaes discusses whether homicide in such circumstances is punishable, and in this connection says, inter alia (p. 165) :

'And who is to determine which one is to be sacrificed ? Someone may voluntarily offer himself. ... But aside from this case, the act cannot be considered justified unless, at the very least a fair method of selection, such as the drawing of lots is employed. The strong cannot be allowed to save themselves at the expense of the weak.'

The extreme situations of which I have given examples are characterized, among other things, by the fact that it is difficult to agree that any distributor should have a right to decide over the values to be sacrificed. The first mate in the American lifeboat, who was otherwise in command both of the crew and the passengers, was not considered entitled to decide over their lives in spite of the fact that some persons probably had to be sacrificed if anyone at all was to survive and in spite of the fact that he followed the time-honoured custom of saving women and children first. And if no one is, or can be, designated as distributor, it becomes almost impossible for the recipients to find any solution through negotiation other than that of using random selection.

We can assume that random devices as a rule are more likely to be used when the recipients themselves make the decision that when a distributor makes it. This is partly because the procedural factors which favour random selection then carry greater weight and partly because it is necessary to make a compromise to which everyone can agree when there is no distributor present. But random devices *may* also be suitable when a distributor makes the decision – and even if he has the power and authority to enforce whatever he wishes. A distributor finds himself in such a dilemma when indivisible benefits (or burdens) which are of vital importance to the recipients have to be allocated. If he leaves the decision to chance he loses control of the result and if he makes the decision himself he may have to shoulder a disagreeable responsibility.

What I have called *allocation according to time priority or location* (chap. 8, section V) is also closely related to object-oriented equal distribution. It is often natural to follow this procedure when allotting time priorities – for instance, so that those who stand foremost in the queue get into the cinema first, and those who sit at the top of the table get food first as the plates are handed around. In many of these instances the reasons for letting some people be first are not particularly strong but because everyone cannot be attended to at the same time priorities have to be allotted. And by keeping to time or location placings some of the same advantages are achieved which in other situations would be found in object-oriented equality or random selection.

The procedural advantages are often the most important. The above principle is simple and is built upon specific criteria which are only slightly person-oriented. This is therefore a principle which recipients can administrate relatively easily on their own and which, when applied by a distributor, protects them from arbitrariness and partiality. The fact that the criteria are simple and readily apparent, facilitates the use of sanctions against people who deviate. Physical proximity of the recipients to one another (for instance, in queues and waiting rooms) also frequently helps to make the sanction system effective.

Substantive considerations sometimes pull in the same direction. It may be a suitable compromise between self-assertion and consideration for other people that one does not try to get in front of those at the head of the queue nor let those behind slip in front. And one approaches an equal distribution of the sacrifice of waiting by letting those who have waited the longest be the first to receive. This helps to explain why it is sometimes regarded as a principle of justice that those who come first receive first.

One condition necessary for the acceptance of allocation according to placing is usually that there are no large, visible and relevant differences between the recipients with regard to need, fitness, desert etc. In a taxi queue, for example, the person who is ill or the mother with a sobbing child in her arms might be allowed the first taxi that comes even though that person may have been at the back of the queue. But it often requires more than this before a break in order of ranking is allowed.

307

As already mentioned (chap. 8, section V) it can happen that time or location placing not only decides the time priorities that are allotted but also what the individual recipient receives of the values which are the primary object of allocation. For example, those who are first in the cinema queue are not only allowed in first but also get the best seats. And perhaps those who stand at the back do not get in at all. But it is only when the values to be allocated are relatively unimportant that 'all or nothing at all' results on the basis of location or time placing are accepted. For instance, a well-behaved queue will form in front of the ticket office even though there is a chance that the last people will not get in – but things will be very different at the exit when the public tries to escape from a cinema where fire has broken out.

On some occasions the significance of the time factor is enhanced by one or another particular circumstance, for instance by a contractual right. In such instances this can decide the allocation of large values, for example which buyer is to have preference if the same property has been sold to two different people or which mortgage holder will be best covered. A special case is that in which the time factor determines a person's status (see chap. 8, section IX) as, for example, when being firstborn is a status characteristic.

VII. FACTORS FAVOURING PRINCIPLES OF EQUALITY CONNECTED WITH NEED, FITNESS OR STATUS

In some cases the recipients consider need, fitness or status relevant when judging what they themselves ought to receive but do not pay any attention to these characteristics when questions of distribution are evaluated. But they *may* do this latter as well – and in several ways :

Firstly, the recipients may feel that some of these characteristics should be taken into account when a *circle of recipients,* whom they think should be treated equally, is determined. 'Equal treatment' can mean different things but I will only discuss here cases where object-oriented equal distribution is aimed at. In other words, I assume a situation where some of the recipients are so similar with regard to need, fitness and status that it seems natural for them to receive the same amount but where the differences between them and others are so large that the others, for this reason, are not included in the demand for equality.

Such importance is usually not attached to differences of degree as regards need or fitness. There will nearly always be some differences of degree between everyone. And it seldom comes naturally to disregard

308

the differences of some recipients while making a decisive division between these particular recipients and others. It seems more appropriate to let *qualitative* differences in need or fitness serve as the demarcation line. Some of the recipients, for example, need certain benefits which the others are completely disinterested in (or do not require). In such instances object-oriented equal distribution between the former might be a reasonable solution. The chances of equal distribution being thought reasonable (see sections IV and V) are by and large the same however the circle of recipients is delimited. The fact that need or fitness is considered important when delimiting the group may, however, make it rather more difficult to disregard these criteria when distribution issues are taken into account.

It is more common to delimit the circle of recipients by a status category, for example on the basis of the idea that certain benefits or burdens 'are suitable' for men but not for women (or the other way round) or that adults should have more (or less) of certain benefits or burdens than children. In such cases there is a tendency to separately evaluate distribution within the different sex or age groups, and it may very well be that the recipients favour object-oriented equal distribution within the individual group. Status can also be taken into account in some but not in other respects, for instance so that specific criteria of equality are used for those belonging to the same category but more diffuse criteria are applied across the categories. An example of this – which I have mentioned before – is the conception that there should be equality between the sexes in the sense that men and women should receive about the same amount, but not necessarily the same kind, of life's benefits.

As was mentioned in Chapter 8, section IX, status classification is often founded on ideas of differences in need or fitness. But there is, all the same, a considerable difference between taking direct notice of need or fitness and basing oneself on status. In the latter case one does not have to operate with small degrees of difference and vague borders. Instead, one keeps to broad categories and imagines that there are essential differences between them so that it then seems more natural to draw sharp dividing lines between recipient groups on the basis of status than on the basis of differences in need or fitness.

Secondly, need, fitness or status can also provide a *basis for special principles of equality*. Several examples of this have been given in Chapter 8. For example, there may be a demand for equal satisfaction of needs (chap. 8, section VI) or for relative equality or rank order equality based on fitness or status (chap. 8, sections VII and IX). The question now is : under which conditions are recipients likely to favour these principles of equality ?

It is obvious that these conditions differ in one respect from those of object-oriented equal distribution : differences between recipients with regard to need, fitness or status are reasons working against object-oriented equal distribution (see section IV, 6) but *not* against such principles of equality as have been mentioned here. On the contrary, there must be some differences in relevant characteristics between recipients if the conception of rank order equality or relative equality is to be applied.

But apart from this, much of what has been said above on object-oriented equality can also apply here. In the first place, the connection between distribution orientation and the tendency to favour equality is the same in both cases. And distribution orientation depends upon the same factors here as in other cases (section III). However, when importance is attached to such factors as need or fitness it may be more difficult to find a common yardstick than when the criteria are purely object-oriented, and this may weaken the tendency towards distribution orientation (section III, hypothesis 6).

Some of the properties of object-oriented equal distribution which were mentioned in section V also belong – under certain conditions – to the principles of equality which we are now discussing. Among other things, equal satisfaction of everyone's needs can just as well be a compromise (section IV, 1 and 2) and this is the best way in which to maximize total satisfaction when needs differ (section IV, 3). On the other hand, principles of equality based on either need or fitness are generally not so well suited to satisfy defence needs (section IV, 4) as is object-oriented equal distribution, nor do they have the same procedural advantages (section IV, 5).

However, in this respect, it makes a great difference how diffuse and person-oriented the criteria are. For instance, the principle of distribution that all needs be equally well satisfied may involve a high degree of individualization. Used in this way, the principle would be poorly suited to secure predictability and to afford protection against arbitrariness and bias on the part of the distributor, and it would certainly not help to simplify decision-making.

The situation will be different if more specific and less person-oriented criteria of need or fitness or if status criteria are applied. It may then be possible to find principles of equality which provide some protection against arbitrariness and partiality and which simplify decision-making. Standardized ideas on what the various categories of people need and

310

formalized criteria of fitness (for instance, education and exam marks) are examples of such criteria. Rank ordered status categories – based, for instance, on age or seniority – are especially well suited to meet the requirements of predictability and impartiality. In this respect they are not far behind object-oriented equal distribution. For example, the type of rank order equality we see when promotion occurs according to seniority is often favoured by employees and conceived as a principle of justice.

The tendency to attach importance to specific and relatively object-oriented criteria and the tendency to favour one of the principles of equality which have been mentioned are therefore closely connected. It is necessary to base oneself on such criteria if one is to reap the advantages of demanding equality. And it is partly the same factors which give rise to both tendencies, among other things the need for security and predictability and the need to protect oneself against partiality and manipulation by the distributor.

For several of the reasons which have been mentioned, it is probably easier for ideas of equality to be connected with status criteria than with need and fitness criteria. It is also possible that ideas of equality (for example rank order equality) based on status more readily take on the character of ideas of justice. The reason for this assumption is that ideas of need and fitness are consequence-oriented. As long as one builds upon these it will often be natural to justify differences and similarities by referring directly to the goals aimed at. When criteria of need or fitness are replaced by status criteria the goals are disguised and therefore one becomes more inclined to believe in equality for equality's own sake.

Rank order equality based on status presupposes that there are rank ordered status categories within the society or group concerned. The greater the number of situations in which a rank order is already considered to be relevant, the more likely it is that this will also be used as a basis when new questions of allocation arise. And if a sequence is followed when a new allocation issue is settled this contributes to its perpetuation and to promoting rank consistency (see chap. 8, section IX).

Whereas rank order equality on the basis of status helps stabilize a social system based on rank differences, the principle of distribution that everyone's need be equally well satisfied helps even out existing differences. There must be a fairly high degree of fellow-feeling between recipients if they are to support such a principle of equality. The examples one usually finds come from idealistic attempts to create a

311

new social system as, for example, the kibbutz movement in Israel (see chap. 8, section VI). The force behind the desire for equality can be that non-discrimination is regarded as a goal in itself or as a means of maximizing satisfaction (see section IV, 3, and chap. 9, section III) or avoiding conflict. But some of the other requirements mentioned above must also be met. For example, in order to carry through such a principle it seems necessary to base oneself on strictly standardized ideas of what people need so that the criteria will be sufficiently specific for practical use.

VIII. FACTORS FAVOURING PRINCIPLES OF EQUALITY CONNECTED WITH RIGHTS, DUTIES OR DESERT

If importance is attached to rights, duties or desert when individual transfers are made, this means that there is a reciprocation relationship – or at least something which closely approximates reciprocation – between the distributor and the individual recipients.[16] This makes for interplay between ideas of reciprocation and of allocation – and perhaps between ideas of retributive and distributive justice. It is on this interplay that attention is concentrated in what follows.

One important point is that recipients who are parties in reciprocal relationships with the distributor often become *more distribution oriented* than they would otherwise have been and that the likelihood that they will favour *relative equality* is great compared to, for instance, those who base their demands on need or fitness. There are several reasons for this.

In the first place, parties in reciprocal relationships need *yardsticks* with which to evaluate the values reciprocated so that they can judge whether the relation between service and counter-service, between input and compensation or between guilt and punishment is reasonable. And these yardsticks are largely taken from other reciprocal situations with which comparisons can be made. As a general rule, the need to make comparisons is greater in these cases than when values are allocated according to need or fitness. When, for instance, one's own needs serve as a basis of evaluation, the satisfaction of these needs is in itself a good measure of whether one gets sufficient. This especially applies to 'need' in the sense of 'desire'. As regards 'need' in the normative sense ('to require') external yardsticks are more frequently used but the ten-

16. In other words, the situation is the one illustrated in chap. 1, fig. 10.

dency to make comparisons is, even so, not so marked as it is in reciprocation situations.

A classic example is to be found in the parable on the labourers in the vineyard (St. Matthew 20, 1-16). Those who began their work early in the morning were originally satisfied with the agreed day's wage. But when they heard that those who began later, even those who began in the eleventh hour, got the same wage, they felt that they had been treated unjustly.

Not only reciprocation relationships but also transfers which other recipients get free, can serve as a basis for evaluation of one's own situation. Let us take as an example the situation where one child has received a shilling in reward for having helped his parents, and his brother (who has not rendered any comparable service) likewise demands a shilling. If the parents give in to this demand, the child who first received a shilling may feel badly treated. He may feel that his shilling has now lost its character of being a reward. In other words, he has been deprived of the immaterial bonus value which was associated with being rewarded by his parents and perhaps he also feels that he has worked hard for no purpose when the other gets the same without having done anything. One possible way of saving the situation is to insist that his reward was something different from what his brother received and that he must therefore get yet another shilling in order to be put on equal footing with him.

The person who is punished has the same need to look around for comparisons which can tell him how his behaviour has really been evaluated. We also find the inclination to make rapid re-evaluations here, as with the labourers in the vineyard. For example, the man who has been fined £ 5 for some small offence perhaps feels that this is reasonable until he hears that other people have only been fined £ 2 – or have been let off completely – for similar offences. Or he feels that his case has been too severely punished until he learns that other people have received fines of £ 10 for about the same offence.

Reactions – or the absence of reactions – to other people's infringements of the law are not only of interest to those who are sentenced but also to those who have been discouraged from committing similar offences because these are forbidden. When prohibited behaviour is punished, this shows that it pays to be law-abiding. And the more severe punishments are and the more consistently they are carried out, the clearer it becomes that it pays to abide by the law. The punishments awarded to other people, therefore, serve as a kind of measure of the value of one's own conformity. And when punishment is not forth-

313

coming, one can feel that adherence to the law is no longer appreciated.[17] **Law abiders** are particularly likely to resent lenient enforcement when conformity is a burden and unpunished infringement of the law yields considerable gain. They may feel it unjust that those who violate the law have advantages which the more conscientious are prevented from receiving.

When comparisons are made in order to find a yardstick for evaluation of one's own reciprocal relationships, attention is not concentrated on the absolute size of the transfers but on the *relation* between what is received and what rendered. In other words, it is the 'price level' which is of interest, for instance whether other people get free of charge what one has oneself had to pay for and whether other people pay (or receive) a higher or lower price per unit than oneself. And the equality which may be demanded will usually be a relative equality. It is not the absolute amount received but the level of prices which should be the same for everyone.

The tendency to look at other people in order to find a yardstick is stronger the poorer are the indications one's own situation provides. When, for example, the size of mutual rights and duties is determined by specific rules or agreements, it is not normally necessary to take a look at other people in order to find out whether one is getting or contributing one's share. On the other hand when, for example, ideas of retributive justice serve as bases of evaluation there is a real need for yardsticks.

I turn now to another factor which helps make the recipients distribution oriented and strengthen the tendency to demand relative equality. As mentioned in Part II, reciprocal relations (for instance, exchange, restitution and punishment) are frequently regulated by *norms* which indicate when requital is appropriate and what this should consist of. Whether these norms are specific rules or diffuse principles (for instance, such as those of retributive justice), they are usually general in the sense that they apply both to oneself and to others. This means that, when such norms are internalized, one tries to adhere to them oneself and becomes indignant when other people do not do so. Although in practice one does not always demand as much of oneself as of other people, in principle, the demands are the same. This gives rise to an interest in other people's behaviour. Attention is paid to the inter-

17. One of the primary school pupils whom Naess (1969) interviewed expressed it thus : 'The teacher must punish according to the offence. Those who have done no wrong get the reward that they have no punishment. Therefore, those who do wrong must be punished or the others will get no reward'.

314

pretation and application of norms by other people *both* in order to avoid deviation from norms, which would give grounds for criticism, *and* in order to criticize those persons who make such deviations.

When reciprocal relations are regulated by general norms of retributive justice, a basis is thereby also laid for demanding relative equality between recipients. The fact that the norms are general means that what is the 'right price' for others is also the 'right price' for oneself. When the claim for retributive justice is met for all recipients, then relative equality is established between them, and even if the claim for retributive justice is *not* satisfied it will often seem to be a natural extension of retributive ideas that there be relative equality. For instance, it may be realized that not everyone can have the *right* price because the distributor's resources are not sufficient and instead it is felt that everyone should get the *same* (reduced) price. But it also happens that claims for retributive justice and for equality of treatment conflict with each other, for instance because a recipient insists upon getting what he believes is right on the basis of retributive reasoning, while the others maintain that he must be content with proportionally as much as themselves. However, as mentioned in Chapter 8, section VIII, such discrepancies tend to level out in the long run since what other people get serves as a measure of one's own payment.

The third factor which calls for comparison is the tendency to *compete*. Firstly, in instances where the opportunity to change distributor exists (see chap. 11), both distributors and recipients may compete to establish connections with persons offering better terms. Secondly, recipients within the individual allocation system can compete even if there is no possibility of changing to another distributor. And in both instances competition gives rise to a keen interest in the terms other people get. But I will pay particular attention to competition within the individual allocation system because this involves interesting features in cases where there are reciprocal relationships between recipients and distributor.

In these instances competition can take on two quite different forms. One possibility is that the individual recipient tries to acquire a relatively *higher* payment than the others so that his profits from the individual transactions will be larger. John, for instance, tries to press his parents to give him a greater reward for his help than Peter has received for his. The other possibility is that the recipient offers *lower* prices than the others in order to increase his future turn-over at their expense. Clerks in an office, for instance, compete in their efforts to be helpful and undemanding because they reckon that the keenest among them will get most of the tasks which involve extra rewards in the way of confidence, respect, influence and the chance of promotion.

Whether it will pay a recipient to adopt any of these strategies varies with the circumstances. The more he has of exchange values in which the distributor is interested and the greater his ability compared with other recipients to deliver such values at low prices, the more he has to win by lowering his prices. The recipient who in these respects is in a weaker position but who hopes that the distributor will be especially kind or well disposed towards him will be more likely to try to secure the highest possible price for each individual transfer.

However, both forms of competition involve a certain risk. The recipient who tries to outstrip the others by making a bigger effort or demanding less payment may underestimate the others' strength and himself be the loser. It may also be that *all* recipients lose because their competition leads to a deflation of their prices without any of them increasing turn-over. The recipient who appeals to the distributor's goodwill or sympathy in order to get a higher price than the others, also risks being the loser. And even if he does not run this risk, his gain may not, after all, be any greater than the others' because he must make supplementary contributions (for instance, in the way of submission, ingratiation, future dependence etc.) if he is to get a higher price for his primary services.

A recipient who does not want any of the kinds of competition I have mentioned must be careful not to do anything which the others can *interpret* as the opening of a competitive struggle. If anyone believes that one person has started, there is the danger of everyone following suit. The safest thing for him to do therefore, is to go in for relative equality. In this way it becomes clear that he is *neither* trying to secure relatively more for himself from single transfers *nor* trying to outstrip them by selling at a lower price.

When one of their number does not toe the line this will appear as a threat to recipients who try to keep stable and uniform prices. The reaction is often one of moral indignation to those who are so 'greedy' that they secure themselves better terms than the others and to those who are 'disloyal' and press the price level down by contenting themselves with lower payment. One can find examples of this kind of reaction in business relations, in working conditions and in many other situations of everyday life. Fear of competition, in other words, is a factor helping to create sanctions against those who deviate from the principle of equality.

The more a recipient is in need of predictability and defence, the

316

more dangerous it will be for him to run the risks of competition and the more likely it is that he will favour relative equality. In addition, the need for predictability and defence also tends to strengthen a desire for relative equality in cases where competition is of little relevance, e.g. in the allocation of punishment or restitution.

A recipient who wants relative equality will often find it important that equality can be checked. This is particularly so when his attitude is motivated by a need for predictability or protection. Checking requires reliable yardsticks and this means that the relative equality must be based on specific and relatively object-oriented criteria. Some of the forces which work towards claims for equality will therefore also lead to a preference for specific and object-oriented criteria.

So far the existence of reciprocal relationships between recipients and distributor has been taken for granted. I have discussed the effects which the presence of such relationships can have on recipient attitudes to distribution. But there are also forces working in the opposite directions. The recipients' attitudes to distribution issues can determine whether or not they are interested in having reciprocal relationships with the distributor. This is particularly pertinent when there is a choice between allocation according to desert and other principles of allocation. We can take as an example the teacher's allocation among his pupils of the privilege of being allowed to help him, for instance by running errands. This benefit can be allocated in various ways : according to desert, or to fitness or need, or so that everyone goes errands equally often. If the benefit is allocated according to desert it will take on the character of a reward which, for example, is given to pupils who show good conduct. This is an advantage to pupils who usually behave well and who have no trouble in doing so. They get the benefit of running errands more often than if there had been equal distribution, while other pupils receive the same pleasure less often or at a greater sacrifice. This point of view can be given a general formulation by saying that the more a recipient has of the kind of exchange values the distributor appreciates and the less it costs him to make these available, the more he stands to gain when the distributor's benefits are allocated according to desert.[18] And correspondingly, the less disposed a recipient is to behaving in a manner which the distributor disapproves of, the more he has to gain when the burdens imposed by the distributor are

18. This does not necessarily mean that he prefers allocation according to desert. It could be, for instance, that considerations pulling in the direction of object-oriented equal distribution (see section V above) weigh more heavily than the advantages he will get if the principle of desert is adopted.

317

allocated according to desert (that is to say, become punishments). And the weaker the position of the recipient is in these respects, the more he stands to lose when the principle of desert is followed.

As mentioned above, how strong an exchange position the recipient holds in relation to the distributor is also of significance for his attitude to the question of equality. Roughly speaking, the various points of view can be summed up thus : a very strong exchange position makes for a tendency to plump for allocation according to desert without any requirement of equality (i.e. free competition). Those who have a somewhat weaker position will be more inclined to favour relative equality. And the weakest will tend to object to the principle of desert and, for example, go in for object-oriented equal distribution. This will, however, only be the case when the benefits or burdens are certain to be allocated. The situation is different with regard to benefits which can only be acquired against payment and burdens which are only imposed as punishment.

IX. PROCEDURAL CONSIDERATIONS WHEN THE RECIPIENTS THEMSELVES UNDERTAKE THE ALLOCATION

So far I have been mainly concerned with the substantive factors affecting recipient attitudes. Something has been said about procedural considerations in general (see particularly section IV, 5), but the particular questions of procedure which arise when recipients themselves undertake an allocation have still to be discussed.

I do not take into account cases where one (or some) of the recipients exercises considerably greater influence on the outcome than the others and where it therefore becomes natural to regard him (or them) as the distributor in relation to the remaining recipients. I will also disregard the possible effect of rules or orders which come from outside (for example, from parents to their children or from the government to the citizens) on how the allocations should be made.

The situation is, then, that several persons, all interested in the outcome and all more or less equally strong, are involved in a decision-making process. They may be a group of children, for example, who are to divide some sweets between them or allot roles in a game ; or they may be heirs who are to divide an inheritance between them, or some people who are to complete a job of work together and divide the various tasks among themselves.

The division will not present any problems if the recipients have no competing interests. A family consisting of mother, father, daughter and son are given, for instance, a Christmas parcel which contains one pair of nylons, a pipe, a doll and a model aeroplane. It may be that one of the parents takes on the job of distributor but this will often not be necessary because everyone immediately assumes who is to get what, and because each one of them is satisfied with what he gets and is not envious of the others. A similar situation can arise when jobs of work are to be allocated. Among a party of campers, for example, there is one who prefers to cook the food, one to wash up, one to chop wood and one to fetch water. If they are each of them best fitted to do the work they prefer, and are recognized as such by the others, the allocation will not present any problems. In a case like this, need and/or fitness criteria will usually form the basis of allocation.

If, however, the recipients have competing interests it may be difficult to reach agreement and the difficulties will tend to increase the stronger the competing interests become. Unless everyone accepts the outcome, there is the danger that no solution will be found. It is not certain that a minority will give way to the majority. And if some of the recipients manage to impose a solution on the others which the latter dislike, this can have unfortunate repercussions on future relations between the recipients. Normally the solution will be most acceptable when it constitutes a compromise treating everyone equally and making it apparent that this is done.

A special difficulty attached to decision-making here is that none of the participants is impartial since each has a personal interest in the outcome. For this reason they may hesitate to be too active during negotiations. If one of the recipients is especially keen in producing or supporting proposals, the others may think that he is trying to butter his own bread. This may lead to a situation where they also become active and support other solutions with the result that the conflict becomes more acute. Or perhaps an agreement is reached which results from the active efforts of one or a few persons. The manner in which the agreement is reached can, in such an event, leave a suspicion that not everyone has been treated equally even though there may be no other signs pointing to this. Such a thing can split the group and prejudice future allocations.

There is also another reason why great activity from one (or some) recipient(s) can arouse the suspicion of the others. Perhaps they believe (rightly or wrongly) that he aspires to become leader of the group on this particular occasion or perhaps even permanently. They may regard this as the best solution. But if they do not want any leader, or not that particular person as leader, they have an extra reason to take a sceptical view of his behaviour.

Since too much initiative can have harmful effects, the need arises for simple decision-making methods so that no one has to show any particularly great activity. It is also important that everyone participate to approximately the same extent so that the danger of biased decisions is reduced. And it is easier to check that everyone is making a similar contribution to the decision-making when little rather than a lot is done.

The need for simplification indicates that specific, highly visible and indisputable criteria of allocation should be found. From this point of view it is of no significance whether the criteria are object- or person-oriented. But the fact that there is a danger of partiality may suggest that no importance be attached to personal characteristics.

A principle of allocation which satisfies all the considerations mentioned can sometimes be found. If what is to be allocated is a homogeneous object, for example, a sum of money or a bar of chocolate, which is easily divisible into equally large portions, object-oriented equal distribution will normally be satisfactory. This is a reasonable compromise because everyone gets the same, and it is a simple manner of making a decision based on specific and easily seen criteria. But if the values are heterogeneous or not measurable it will be difficult to find sufficiently specific and indisputable criteria of equality. A way of solving the problem which is frequently used when two people are to divide something between them is that one divides and the other chooses. But even though it is perhaps theoretically possible to extend the application of this method to division among more than two people, in practice this will be too complicated.

The situation will sometimes be such that one method of allocation seems to be the best from a substantive point of view, while another principle is more suitable from a procedural standpoint. For instance, object-oriented equal distribution may appear most satisfying from a substantive point of view although specific and uncontestable criteria of equality may be lacking, while procedural considerations may in this case suggest the application of, for instance, random selection or allocation according to time priorities. Or it may be that an allocation according to need or fitness is the most suitable from a substantive standpoint while object-oriented equal distribution, or perhaps random selection or time-priority allocation, would take better care of the procedural problems.

As mentioned in Chapter 9, section VII, there may also be conflict between procedural and substantive considerations when a distributor undertakes allocations. I assumed there that the relative weight of the conflicting considerations depended upon the importance of the result to the distributor and the recipients respectively (see the comments to fig. 2). The same assumption can be made here – with the modifications following from the fact that the recipients themselves perform the work of distributor.

When the outcome is of little importance to the recipients they will be apt to simplify the procedure. There is little point in spending time and energy on deciding such matters. And there is no need to expose oneself to the disadvantages mentioned earlier of participating too actively in the decision-making process. As pointed out in section VI, this is probably one of the most important reasons why random techniques are so often used when allocating trivial values. These techniques are particularly suitable when the recipients undertake the allocation themselves because they make the role of distributor redundant.[19] We find many examples of random devices being used in such cases, for instance when determining starting positions in a game (e.g. who is to be White in chess, serve first in tennis or choose sides in football), when children allocate roles at play, etc. Allocation according to placing in time or location is also a method which is often favoured when opposed interests are relatively modest and the conditions are otherwise suited, for instance because it is only the rank order of the transfers which is to be allocated. The likelihood of any of these methods being used increases, of course, when the participants have previous experience of the methods concerned.

The greater the interests involved, the more prominent will be the substantive considerations. The likelihood is then increased that the recipients will find allocation principles which afford a better compromise between their conflicting interests but which make the decision-making process more complicated. At the same time, however, it will become more difficult to come to an agreement. It is sometimes possible to find useful solutions which are based on a combination of distribution principles. The heirs agree, for instance, that they will get equal amounts measured in economic value and that they will draw lots about particular objects. Perhaps they also introduce a sequential principle so that, for example, the one who receives the object which was most sought after does not draw lots for the next object etc. But the tension between different interests and considerations can easily lead to a situation

19. Unless the recipients suspect each other of cheating so that, for this reason, they need an outsider to arrange things for them.

where the recipients are quite unable to find a solution of their own accord.

As the interests become stronger, the need for an impartial decision also increases. If vital interests are involved this need can become so important that it completely dominates all the other considerations mentioned. Consideration for impartiality demands not only that the allocation criteria be simple but also – and perhaps most of all – that they be object-oriented. Object-oriented equality and random selection are the only principles completely satisfying these demands. If the values are indivisible, the latter procedure is the only one which can be based upon purely object-oriented criteria. It has also the advantage that no decision has to be made – other than the procedural one that a random technique be employed. This not only furnishes a guarantee against bias but is also significant in that the recipients avoid taking any responsibility for the result. The responsibility for decisions which are made jointly by recipients is lightened since several people have participated. But, even so, it can weigh too heavily when life or death are at stake. This serves to explain the use of random devices in cases such as these (see section VI). The fact that allocation according to time priorities is seldom or never used in such instances is probably partly because this is not a pure object-oriented allocation principle. It is based on specific criteria and is therefore well suited to simplify the decision-making process, but in cases where large values are involved, so that consideration for impartiality and avoidance of responsibility weigh heaviest, it is particularly important to avoid person-oriented criteria.

In what has been said above we have only been dealing with allocations in which approximately equally strong recipients have participated and where no one has tried to take over leadership of the group. Allocation issues will change if someone wishes to gain such a position for himself. Active participation when values are to be allocated is one way for an aspiring leader to demonstrate what he is made of and to find out how the others react to his aspirations. Perhaps he is willing to accept both unpleasantness and responsibility to achieve this and perhaps he demonstrates his impartiality by making sure that he himself does not get more than anyone else of the allocated values. If his active behaviour is tolerated by the others and if the solutions which he supports seem acceptable, he has then performed a service which can be repaid by the others beginning to regard him as their leader.[20]

20. In other words, we get the exchange situation which was discussed in chapter 3, section VI.

If his prestige is increased in this way, it will be easier for him to be active the next time a decision is to be reached and it will be easier to get the others to agree to his proposals. In other words, once the process is started it tends to perpetuate itself.

11. Relationship between distributor and recipients: with special reference to recipient efforts to improve or secure their position

'When man can come to grips with his needs by actually changing the environment, he does so. But when he cannot achieve such 'realistic' satisfaction, he tends to take the other path : to modify what he sees to be the case, what he thinks he wants, what he thinks others want.' Berelson and Steiner, *Human Behaviour*, 1964, p. 664.

I. THE RECIPIENTS' PROBLEM-SITUATION

There may well be recipients who are perfectly satisfied with what they have received and who feel certain that future allocations will also be fully satisfactory. But dissatisfaction with decisions already reached, the desire to improve one's position, or a dread of what the future has in store are all quite common.

Such reactions can have different causes. Among other things, distributor and recipient often have conflicting interests. Sometimes these are directly opposed, for instance in cases of punishment or when a burden is imposed upon the recipient from which he gets absolutely no advantages. In other instances distributor and recipient may have partly common and partly conflicting interests because there is a 'give and take' relationship between them. For example, the distributor divides jobs of work for which he pays, or he gives help and receives gratitude or respect as a counterservice. In such cases both parties may be interested in maintaining the connection between them but their interests clash when it comes to the terms of exchange.

Finally, there are instances where interests coincide in so far as the distributor's aim is to render some kind of support, treatment or care which the recipient wants, but where there is still not full harmony. The recipient often wants more than the distributor can or will give him. And it may also be that the recipient would prefer a kind of help other than what he receives.

324

The existence of conflicting interests does not necessarily imply recipient displeasure with the allocations. Much depends upon his expectations. But even if he gets as much or more than he had anticipated, he can still hope for future improvements or still be afraid of a future regression.

In addition to this, the inferior position of the recipient in relation to the distributor can in itself be a source of insecurity. In order to act as distributor one must have power or authority over recipients or one must dispose of resources which they require. The individual recipient is therefore usually the weaker party in the relationship. The fact that another person makes decisions which concern him can, by itself, involve an unpleasant feeling. He may dislike being controlled and manipulated. Or perhaps he is afraid of being deprived of those values on which he depends. And even if he sees no signs of such danger he can still feel a need for greater predictability. In addition to all this, his inferior and insecure situation can make it difficult for him to maintain his self-respect and preserve the image of himself he wants other people to have. The various forms of insecurity and dissatisfaction mentioned here can be present even if the recipient does not perceive any conflict between his own interests and those of the distributor.

The recipients' situation does not only depend on the internal relationship between them and the distributor but also on the attitudes and actions of outsiders. The recipients sometimes find external support. This may be spontaneous help from friends and acquaintances, moral support from like-thinkers and sympathizers or some kind of institutional protection. In our society different kinds of organizations play an important role in this connection. And in many of the cases where the interests of the distributor and recipients obviously clash and where the latter are regarded as the weaker party, society has taken steps to furnish protective measures. Labour legislation, judiciary control of public administration, and free legal aid can be given as examples. The recipient is not rid of all problems because he can obtain outside assistance. But his position is strengthened. However, such measures as I have mentioned are, as a rule, only applied when there are obviously conflicting interests. We seldom find such measures where the distributor aims to help the recipients, for instance in connection with aid to developing countries, rural development, care of the sick, old and young etc. This is one of the reasons why, as *Løchen* (1965 pp. 246-250) points out, it can be especially difficult to defend oneself against those who offer help.

Recipients' needs to improve or secure their position vary in different ways :

Firstly, there are variations in *strength* from cases where everything is already fairly satisfactory to those where the recipient's situation is intolerable. The strength of the needs depends upon several factors, on how important the value allocated is to the recipient, how dependent he is on getting it from the distributor, and what his prospects are of getting it from this source.

Secondly, a recipient's *insight* into what he wants to achieve or protect himself against can also differ. He may have a clear and realistic conception of what the distributor represents and what he himself wants. Or his behaviour can be determined by unrealistic or confused ideas of the distributor's aims and of his own needs. The degree of insight can differ, of course, from one individual to another. But it is also connected with other factors, inter alia with what kind of need is involved. For instance, most people have greater insight into their need to obtain more of the material goods which are allocated than into their need for security and self-respect.

In the third place there are variations in the dimension *specific-diffuse*. A recipient can want something which is quite specific, for example a better job or an increase in pay. But he can also want something which is highly diffuse. The degree of diffuseness is also connected with the types of need involved and with how many and how heterogeneous these are. Diffuseness is not the same as lack of insight, but they tend to go together.

Fourthly, a distinction can be made between the need to *achieve* something favourable and the need to *avoid* something unfavourable. Analytically this can be seen as two sides of the same question since when something is regarded as favourable, less favourable alternatives can also be imagined, and achieving the one means avoiding the other. But the way in which the situation is experienced and the behaviour adopted can be quite different in cases where attention is focused on the favourable alternative and activity is directed towards obtaining this than it is in cases where attention is directed towards the unfavourable alternatives and the aim of activity is defensive. As an example of these two situations we can imagine on the one hand a person who tries to get promotion to a better job and on the other a person who is accused of a crime. The manner in which the situation is viewed will to some extent, of course, be subjectively conditioned. For instance, the man who is seeking promotion may have been by-passed on several previous occasions and his attention may be concentrated on the threat of being left in his present job. But, obviously, there is also a connection between the outer features of a situation and the way in which the individual experiences it.

326

Whether a person is trying to achieve something positive or whether he is defending himself against something negative cannot always be answered in terms of either/or. Often, *both* points of view are present. During wage negotiations, for instance, workers' attitudes can be influenced both by a hope of gaining increased spending power and by the fear that their wage increase will not keep pace with rising prices.

When recipient attitudes are defensive it may be asked *whom* or *what* recipients feel the need to defend themselves against. Here, too, there will be variations. The threats which menace a recipient may come from the distributor or from other recipients ; from the allocation system as a whole or from the environment in general. The distinction made here between 'distributor' and 'allocation system' is of little relevance when the system is a product of the distributor's decisions. But this is not always the case. If, for example, a firm gets a new owner who introduces certain changes, the established allocation system and the distributor's decisions can appear as two clearly distinct things. The recipients (for example, the employees) may need to defend themselves against both of these. It can also be that they identify themselves with the system and try to defend *this* against the distributor.

I have now pointed out various features of what we can call the recipients' *problem-situation*. What follows is concerned with how the recipients, consciously or unconsciously, try to *solve* their problems. This they can do by leaving the allocation system or by having the distributor removed (section II), by exerting influence on the allocation processes (section III) or by adapting themselves to the existing situation (section IV). In later sections I will look more closely at the two latter solutions, which are often combined. I am only concerned with relatively enduring allocation systems.

II. RECIPIENT OPPORTUNITIES TO LEAVE THE ALLOCATION SYSTEM OR TO HAVE THE DISTRIBUTOR REMOVED

When a recipient is dissatisfied, this can sometimes result in his withdrawal from the allocation system in which he is involved. For instance, dissatisfied customers may transfer their custom to another shop, employees can hand in their notice and find another job, children can run away from home and prisoners can escape from prison.

It is not always easy to leave an allocation system, and sometimes it is quite impossible. Many different obstacles can bar the way. The distributor may have a monopoly of what is to be allocated so that the recipients are forced to stay with him if they are to obtain any of the values at all. And even if the values are obtainable somewhere else, it is possible that no other person than their own distributor can or will give the recipients anything (or as much). Most children, for instance, can not get as much care and love from other sources as from their own parents. It is also possible that the distributor is opposed to the idea that the recipients leave the system and that he has the power to prevent this. The costs involved in changing over to a new allocation system must also be taken into account. If you change to a new shop, you may have further to go. And if you change your job, you will have to adjust yourself to new working conditions and surroundings and perhaps even move to a new district. Making a break with your habitual distributor can in itself cost you something, for example if you respect him and feel that you owe him loyalty.

Sometimes a recipient partially withdraws from a system rather than completely desert it. For example, the customer buys less in the shop with which he is dissatisfied. The children begin to stay out in the evening, seeking social contact with their friends rather than stay at home with their parents. Gradual withdrawal can mean that the recipient is developing and that his needs change, but it can also be due to displeasure with the allocations. Partial withdrawal can also be beset with such difficulties as those mentioned above. But the difficulties are generally less acute the less complete the withdrawal.

Another possibility is that of changing the system by *removing the distributor*. For instance, a gang of boys may acquire a new leader when the previous one becomes unpopular. If the distributor is an organization, the organization itself may continue but a new management take over as, for instance, when there is a change of government or when a club elects a new committee. If dissatisfied recipients are to push through these kinds of changes they usually have to take joint action. How difficult it is to accomplish this varies from one system to another, and sometimes the difficulties are insuperable.

The problems which arise when a recipient leaves a system or manages to get a new distributor (or management) will not be discussed here. In what follows I will examine the possibilities which a recipient has of exerting influence *within* the existing allocation system. However, *threats* of partial or complete withdrawal or of demanding removal of the management still play some role in this connection since they can be effective means of achieving other changes. Recipients who are in a position to carry out these threats therefore have an advantage over recipients who are not so well placed in this respect, and they will not have the same need to utilize those other means discussed below.

III. RECIPIENT POSSIBILITIES OF INFLUENCING ALLOCATION PROCESSES

In many instances it is possible for recipients to partially avoid the distributor's control and thus *take some matters into their own hands.* Surreptitious visits to mother's cake tin or the factory stores, a few cigarette puffs in the school yard and simulated illness to avoid obligations, are examples of this. At home and in school, in military camps and at one's place of work, in prisons, hospitals etc. many such techniques tend to develop and they are used by the recipients to obtain values refused by the distributor.[1]

Recipients may also have means of *influencing distributor decisions.* The distributor is often dependent upon information furnished by the recipients, so that they may exert influence by *giving or holding back information.* If, for instance, the distributor intends to satisfy recipient needs, they may get more than they would otherwise have done by convincing him how much they need the benefit concerned or how little they have of it already. And if the distributor pays attention to fitness, for example when appointing his employees, applicants can produce exam results, references and information showing how well suited they are, at the same time repressing unfavourable information. Knowledge is not only furnished by words but also by deeds, for instance a beggar demonstrates his misery and a worker goes slow while his piece-work rate of pay is being fixed. – How much a recipient can achieve through supplying or suppressing information, depends partly on his insight into what the distributor considers relevant and his ability to appear reliable, and partly upon how dependent the distributor is upon information and what other possibilities he has of obtaining this.

A distributor can also be receptive to *arguments.* Of course, it is seldom easy to change his norms or values. At any rate this takes time. But it is sometimes possible to influence his opinions on how norms should be interpreted and applied and his ideas of what is of value in a certain situation. For instance, it may help to appeal to his sympathy, sense of

---

1. Goffman (1961) refers to this as 'secondary adjustments'. He gives a detailed description of the different kinds of such adjustments which he found in a psychiatric hospital and discusses the functions that they have (see particularly p. 54 et seq. and p. 188 et seq.). I will return later to some of his viewpoints.

justice or to a promise he has given, or it may be possible to persuade him that he will better promote his own goals by allocating values in another way than the one to which he is accustomed.

Argumentation is sometimes supported by *verbal sanctions*. The sanctions can be positive as, for example, flattery of the distributor, deference to him and expressions of gratitude. Or they can be negative sanctions such as regrets, reproaches and criticism of his unreasonability or injustice. The effects are usually strengthened if several people (recipients or outsiders) make use of the same or similar verbal sanctions. This is more likely to happen when a general principle can be appealed to (for instance, justice) than when only the recipient's own welfare can be produced as an argument.

Those recipients who have *counter-services* at their disposal have via these a means of influencing the distributor which can be very effective. In the first place, the counter-service can serve as a means of obtaining more values within the framework of current practices. A worker who is on piecework, for example, can increase his pay by working harder. A clerk may get promotion if he does his work well, and a school child good marks and praise from his teacher if he is industrious and shows good conduct. In the second place, it may also be possible to use one's control over a counter-service as a means of forcing the distributor to change his practice. Workers go on strike, for example, or they threaten to go on strike, in order to obtain higher pay or better working conditions. Irregular use of counter-services, for instance, through bribing, is another possible manner of exerting influence. What a recipient can achieve by way of his counter-services depends partly upon their value to the distributor. The more the latter is dependent upon the counter-services, the greater the chances the recipient has of being able to influence him. It is also of some importance whether the counter-services lend themselves to *manipulation* so that the recipients are themselves to some extent master over how much or how little they give. Workers' input, pupils' diligence and buyers' payments for goods they purchase are all examples of manipulable counter-services. The recovery of a patient can also be a counter-service in the sense that the therapeutist regards this as payment for his efforts. But even though there is some opportunity of manipulating this counter-service, the opportunities are on the whole fewer than in the cases mentioned above. At any rate it is seldom that planned regulation of this counter-service can be used by the patient as a means of exerting influence. And organized regulation of this counter-service – for instance, in the way some employees do with their counter-services – is almost unthinkable.

Some recipients have in addition other *resources of power* at their disposal. For example, they can threaten to withdraw completely or partially from the allocation system or they can initiate an action to get the distributor or the management of the distributor organization (see section II) removed. The use of physical force or threats of this are other possibilities.

Some of the ways and means which were referred to above (for example, to hold back a counter-service or threaten to have the distributor removed) greatly increase in effectivity when the recipients operate *collectively,* while others (e.g., appealing to the distributor's compassion and sympathy) are better suited to *individual* use. The means available can therefore determine whether the recipients operate individually or collectively. And conversely, their ability to co-operate can determine which means they use and what results they achieve. Individual as opposed to collective behaviour is also connected with the recipients' goals. When they act collectively they usually aim to promote collective interests, for instance to increase the sum total of transfers or to achieve a distribution which suits everyone. When they act individually each recipient is more inclined to further his own special interests. For example, he might try to get his own share increased or to get the allocation principle which he prefers adopted. The causal connection can go both ways here as well : the fact that the recipients have strong common interests can be one of the reasons why they act collectively. And the fact that they act collectively can result in them attaching particular importance to promoting their joint interests.

The various modes of action which have been mentioned above are not always undertaken with the intention of exerting influence. For instance, a recipient may give spontaneous expression to his displeasure or pleasure with a decision, or he may threaten in anger to withdraw from an allocation system, without giving any thought to the effects his reaction may have upon the distributor. If he does intend to exert influence his behaviour can be *calculated,* to a greater or lesser degree. There will be variations in the extent to which the recipient tries to calculate the effects of his reaction on the distributor and other people, the counter moves which may follow, and the consequences of these for himself.[2] We are interested in both calculated and uncalculated recipient behaviour – as long as it has its origin in what I referred to above (section I) as the recipient's problem-situation. Even when what a recipient

2. Mathiesen (1965 pp. 24-25) uses 'strategy' in a sense which is similar but not exactly the same as what I here refer to as 'calculated'.

says or does is only a spontaneous expression of his feelings, it does not have to be incidental that he reacts as he does in a current situation. And although he may have no intention of influencing anyone, it may very well be that the reaction makes an impression on the distributor and induces the latter to change his practice. Under certain circumstances and within certain limits it is more likely that the recipient will achieve something the more planned his behaviour is. But the most calculating attitude is not *always* the best suited. As I have already mentioned in another connection (chap. 9, section VII) the costs of calculating are a factor which must be taken into consideration. And perhaps also, by calculating too much, a person's imagination and spontaneity are restrained in a manner which hinders the realization of his goals.

Another important factor is the *sincerity* of the recipients. A recipient is 'sincere' (in the sense used here) if he himself believes what he says, i.e. if he considers the information he furnishes to be true and complete, if he has internalized the norms and values with which he pleads his case and if his promises and threats of sanction are seriously meant. Between complete sincerity and pure deception, hypocrisy and bluff, there are many intermediate cases. We can therefore talk about different degrees of sincerity.

Sincerity and calculation may very well be combined. The fact that a recipient believes what he says does not rule out the possibility that he says it in order to achieve something and has calculated the effects of doing so. On the other hand, lies and deception can certainly be completely spontaneous and uncalculated. However, it is possible that degrees of sincerity and calculation tend to correlate negatively with each other [3] – at any rate so that the very highest degrees of sincerity are seldom found in highly calculated behaviour.

Sincerity can, however, give strength. One argues with the greatest enthusiasm and conviction for what one believes to be true. And it may be difficult to get other people to believe in information, promises and threats etc. which are not seriously meant. A recipient's resources of suitable means of persuasion depend therefore not only upon what his imagination can figure out but also – to some extent – on which norms and values he has internalized and where his knowledge lies.

Which means of persuasion are considered *legitimate* also plays a role. There may be some ways and means which a recipient will refrain from using for reasons of conscience and self-respect or out of fear of being criticized. Sincerity and legitimacy are connected since it can be

3. Cf. Mathiesen loc. cit. p. 24.

thought illegitimate to give information which one knows is false and to argue with norms or values which one does not oneself accept. But legitimacy also depends upon other factors which I will touch upon later.

I have so far concentrated my attention on the resources which recipients have at their disposal. But their possibility of exerting influence also depends to a large extent on the kind of *distributor* they have to deal with. Their chances of withdrawing from the allocation system depend upon whether he has the power to oppose this ; their chances of getting him removed depend upon how strong a position he holds ; and their chances of affecting his decisions depend upon how easily influenced he is. If, for instance, the distributor knows everything, it is of no avail to withhold information. And if he has no use for the recipients' counter-services the threat of reducing these will have little effect. Whether he is receptive to the recipients' arguments depends, among other things, on the conceptions of value which he himself and his milieu have. His attitude to the recipients can also play a role, for instance if there is any question of appealing to his goodwill or sympathy.

Furthermore, it can sometimes be dangerous for a recipient to try to improve or secure his position. If the distributor is powerful and has no inhibitions against using his power, he may harshly suppress any form of opposition which he finds threatening or disagreeable. Recipient chances of achieving anything and the risk involved in attempting to do so can be combined in various ways as shown in Figure 1.

Figure 1

Recipient possibilities of achieving something

		Small	Large
Risk of trying	Small	I (The old age home)	II (The factory)
	Large	III (The concentration camp)	IV (The dictatorship)

Sometimes the possibilities are few and the risk large (cell III in fig. 1). As an example we can take a concentration camp which is well guarded and where punishment is brutal. There is very little hope of the prisoners obtaining anything from those in charge and it may be dan-

333

gerous to make an attempt. It is particularly dangerous to try any of the strategies which, in other situations, are the most effective, for example organized opposition. The recipients have few possibilities of protecting themselves if prayers for indulgence or mercy have no effect.

As an example of the opposite situation, where the chances are large and the risk relatively small (cell II, fig. 1), we can take the situation of factory employees in a society where there is a manpower shortage and worker solidarity. Because they are united and have the whole labour movement behind them and because the factory is dependent upon their input, the worker collective can operate on an equal footing with the factory management and can look after its own interests in a rational manner.

Both kinds of situations which have so far been mentioned are characterized by stability, each in its own way. The situation is unstable if both the possibilities and the risks are large or if both are small. As an example of the former (cell IV, fig. 1), we can imagine a dictatorship where widespread dissatisfaction makes a successful revolution very possible but where it is extremely dangerous to try to revolt and where the dictator – because he feels threatened – will not allow the smallest sign of opposition. In such a situation there may be vast differences in patterns of behaviour – complete resignation or strong and organized opposition – and the situation can quickly switch from one extreme to the other.

An old age home can serve as an example of a system where there are small chances of achieving anything but little risk involved in trying (cell I, fig. 1). The old people have few means of power, among other things because they can offer no counter-service of importance to the institution. But (we presume) they can criticize and present demands and desires without risking any reprisals. It may be pertinent for them to use this opportunity but since the results are few and uncertain whichever way they go about things, they will probably alternate between various patterns of persuasion. However, this will not involve sudden jumps from one extreme to another, as in the example above, but continuous switches between behaviour patterns which are comparatively similar.

IV. HOW RECIPIENTS CAN ADAPT THEMSELVES TO THE SITUATION

By the expression 'adapt themselves' I mean that recipients modify their behaviour and develop a set of beliefs and attitudes concerning themselves, the distributor and the allocation system which make it easier for them to be reconciled to existing conditions.

The dissatisfied recipient who has neither the possibility of leaving the allocation system nor of influencing it has a special need to adapt himself. The process of adaptation can, in his case, move in several different directions : sometimes he will become more inclined to accept the distributor's decisions, e.g., when he begins to identify himself with the distributor, to accept his goals and to become more confident in the latter's ability to make the right decisions. Or he may internalize the allocation principles which are applied and come to the conclusion that he and the other recipients 'are getting their due'. His acceptance of the situation can be more or less whole-hearted and there is no sharp borderline between adaptation and what we can call resignation. The resigned recipient continues to be dissatisfied or to feel insecure but he becomes reconciled to the fact that there is nothing to be done about it. Resignation can be a stage on the road to acceptance. It is possible, for instance, that the under-privileged first become resigned to their lot and then bit by bit come to accept the system and that out of this a stable class or caste society develops. But this is not the only way in which things may develop. Acceptance can also come about in other ways and resignation does not always lead in this direction. Finally there is the possibility that the recipient neither accepts the system nor becomes resigned to it but that he maintains his attitude of protest. In such a case adaptation calls for protest actions which are relatively safe and which still have some meaning for him in spite of the fact that they do not get him anywhere.

The recipient who achieves something by partially taking matters into his own hands or by influencing the distributor, also needs to adapt himself. Firstly, he does not usually achieve everything he aims at and where he falls short he, too, will either have to accept, resign or resort to symbolic protest. Secondly, problems of adaptation also arise in connection with activity which serves to improve or to secure his position. Perhaps he has to humiliate himself before the distributor in order to get what he wants. Or perhaps he has a struggle with the distributor which involves sacrifice or risk.

Whatever the circumstances, one important part of the process of adaptation is that the recipient *interpret* and *explain* what happens in such a manner that he is able to retain his self-respect and to reduce what Festinger (1957) has called 'cognitive dissonance'.

Among other things he needs to interpret and explain his own behaviour. For instance, the person who has become resigned to his lot may

335

develop a set of norms which tell him that it is wrong to oppose authority and is virtuous to show humility and submission. And the person who is still belligerent may find support in the idea that it is morally worthy to struggle for one's rights.

Explanations and interpretations can also refer to values which are the object of allocation. The recipients can adapt themselves to the situation by, for instance, belittling the benefits they do not acquire, as did Æsop's fox when he was not able to reach the grapes. Values can be discredited to different degrees and in different ways. One can be content to stress that these are values 'which I am not going to struggle for' or 'which are of no interest to me'. Or it can be claimed that they are, in principle, insignificant, for instance on the religious grounds that worldly goods are of no consequence. For those among the extremely under-privileged, religious teaching can, as *Pollan* (1962 p. 91) points out :

'communicate an overall perspective which implies resignation to the world but still upholds the group's experience of identity. The world becomes more or less worthless, and new ideals are realized within the circumscribed group.'

Instead of (or as well as) debasing the values which he does *not* get, a recipient can upgrade what he *does* receive – as is frequently done in romantic glorification of one's own country. Ideas of negative value coupling, for instance that those who are poor in property are rich in virtue, can also help to reconcile a recipient to what he receives. Or he can seek comfort in a common fate by making comparisons with other people who have received as little or less than himself.

Explanations and interpretations of the way in which allocation results have been arrived at and of who is responsible, are also very important. Recipients often tend to find an explanation which exempts them from self-reproach. One way of perceiving the allocation, which fulfils this function, is to regard the result as pre-ordained. A belief in Fate or in God can be the foundation of this kind of attitude. Or perhaps the allocation follows a status principle so that it is taken for granted that each person gets what he is entitled to according to his rank, sex, age or occupation. To regard the outcome as inevitable and acceptable comes naturally both to the person who has accepted the system and to the person who has become resigned to it. But the man who is struggling to improve or secure his position will often be inclined to protect his self-respect by criticizing other persons. For example, he may explain the result as being an outcome of the distributor's injustice or the other recipients' greed, thereby avoiding the possibility that he himself did not make the grade.

336

Optimism can also be useful. It may be founded on what *Bergler and Meerloo* (1963 pp. 155-158, cf. pp. 98-99) call 'the fantasy of poetic justice' : one believes – as if this were a kind of natural law – that 'justice will triumph in the end', for instance that one's oppressors will be struck by righteous revenge or that reinstatement will follow the wrongs one has suffered.

The interpretations and explanations of which I have given examples are best suited to fulfil their function when the recipient believes in them – or at least does not regard them as pure fabrication. And it is an advantage if he can imagine that other people also believe them. A continuous process is usually involved in building up a set of plausible interpretations and explanations, in developing these so that they can be applied to new situations, and in convincing oneself and other people that they are reliable. Much of what a recipient does and says can be regarded as (normally subconscious) efforts to develop and vindicate his explanation patterns.

The same actions, beliefs and ideologies can often serve both the aim of influencing allocation processes and the need to adapt oneself to the situation. What *Goffman* (1961) calls 'secondary adjustments' – i.e. petty thieving, slight disobedience and slyness through which the recipients acquire values which the distributor refuses them – often have this double function. The values which the recipients secure in this manner can have a certain significance for them. And the activity through which the values are obtained can help to strengthen their integrity and self confidence. It makes them feel that they have not completely succumbed to the distributor's authority but that they are independent oppositionists, capable of getting what they require. Something similar can apply to the criticism, demands and arguments which the recipients direct at the distributor. Arguments for justice, for instance, can partly help influence the distributor and partly serve as a basis for the explanation that the recipient's lack of success is not due to his own shortcomings but to the injustice of other people. Similarly, collective actions on the part of the recipients can partly help strengthen their position in relation to the distributor and partly afford them an opportunity of seeking comfort in a common fate and pleasure in unity. Which of these two effects is the most important can, of course, vary.

As mentioned earlier (section III), the recipient does not have to have any definite intentions behind his reactions and if he does, these do not necessarily lead in the same direction as the effects of his reactions. For example, it may be that recipients who continuously complain or criticize the distributor in order to influence him, achieve no more than to adapt themselves to the situation by finding an outlet for their self-assertion and aggression. Even though this effect is unintentional it may reinforce the tendency to complain and criticize.

The various features of recipient reactions referred to in sections III and IV are inter-connected. For instance, the way in which recipients argue is to some extent conditioned by what they are trying to achieve, what means of power they have at their disposal, what kind of distributor they have, and whether they operate singly or collectively, etc. In this way, certain combinations of characteristics become more likely than others. The *patterns of recipient behaviour* which I describe in what follows are examples of such likely combinations of the different forms of reaction. My aim is partly to point out connections between the various elements in a single pattern and partly to discuss why one pattern rather than another is followed.

This survey does not pretend to be complete. Attention will mainly be concentrated upon these kinds of activity which serve both to influence the distributor's decisions and to adapt the recipient to the allocation system. I will touch upon acceptation, resignation, withdrawal and attempts to remove the distributor only occasionally.

How the dividing lines between different patterns are drawn is more or less arbitrary since these gradually merge into each other. In what follows I will distinguish between cases where the recipients restrict themselves to appealing to the distributor's goodwill or compassion, cases where they argue in terms of rights and duties, and cases where they mainly rely on their own strength. Each of these three means of influencing the distributor can be used by the recipients either singly or collectively as illustrated in Figure 2.

The shaded cells of the diagram will be discussed in what follows. In section VI I deal with individual appeals to the distributor's goodwill or compassion (cell I in fig. 2). In section VII a survey is given of various types of assertions of rights (cell III). Cases where demands of this kind are argued in terms of justice are treated separately in sections VIII and IX. In the following chapter I will discuss the conditions under which recipients are likely to operate collectively and the consequences this can have for their patterns of behaviour.

338

Figure 2

Recipient strategy :   The recipients operate :

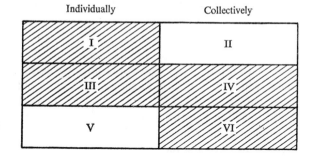

Collective appeals to the distributor's goodwill or compassion (cell II) can be assumed to be of relatively little practical importance as a means of influence and will not be examined separately. Such appeals are poorly suited to collective use. Some of the reasons for this will be pointed out in section VI and in Chapter 12. In section VII I return briefly to individual assertion of one's own power (cell V), but, for the reasons indicated there, this alternative is also not one of the most practical and will not be examined in any detail.

Figure 2 gives only a preliminary, rough illustration of different kinds of reaction. As I go along I will discuss many distinctions which cannot be seen from the diagram. The possibilities of recipients combining or alternating between behaviour which fits into the different cells (for example, alternations between I and III or III and IV and combinations of IV and VI) will also be discussed.

VI. INDIVIDUAL APPEALS TO THE DISTRIBUTOR'S GOODWILL
OR COMPASSION

The most direct manner in which a person who needs to improve or to secure his position can act is to tell the distributor what he requires and ask for it, or to say what it is that troubles him and ask to be relieved of it. Even if no other arguments are advanced and even if the recipient has nothing with which he can threaten, these kinds of requests can

339

yield results if the distributor is inclined to help or to support the recipient.

Many distributors will be so inclined. As mentioned in Chapter 9, section III, a distributor's aim may be to do just this, for example if he is occupied in charity work, with social welfare or development aid. And even when his goal is something else, satisfying a recipient's needs can be a means of promoting its realization. This is particularly so when the aim is to rear, educate or to cure the recipient (see chap. 9, section IV), but it can also apply in other cases. For instance, a distributor whose only goal is to get as much work out of a recipient as possible can be interested in ensuring that the latter does not suffer so much that his ability to work is affected. On the other hand, it is easy to find examples where realization of the distributor's goal would be impeded if he gave in to the recipient's wishes. But even when consideration for the goals does not indicate that the recipient's wishes should be granted, it may be that the distributor still gives in out of sympathy or because he feels sorry for him.

The likelihood of the distributor surrendering to the recipient's wishes thus partly depends upon the aims of the distributor and partly upon his feelings for the recipient. Of course, *what* is asked for also plays some role : is the need something which the distributor regards as worthy or unworthy, and will it be costly for him to satisfy it or not ?

It may very well be that a recipient asks for something which he does not expect to get. He may do this, for instance, because he feels the need to pour out his troubles or to air his aspirations. I assume, however, that the inclination to direct requests at the distributor is greater the more likely the recipient believes it to be that his request will be granted. The recipient's idea of what feelings the distributor nurtures for him and what the latter's attitude to the request concerned is, are therefore factors effecting *whether* a request is made, *what* is requested and *how* this is done.

There are several ways in which recipients can help arouse the distributor's sympathy for their wishes. They can ingratiate themselves with him or in some other manner evoke a more agreeable attitude from him. They can exhibit their distress in a way calculated to awaken his compassion.[4] And they can present their needs so that the distributor is more likely to regard these as honourable and to feel that their satisfac-

---

4. Goran Palm, En Orättvis Betraktelse (Stockholm 1966) has given the following description of how a beggar should behave : 'A beggar should be humble, this is the first thing we expect. He must not be aggressive, he must not scoff

tion will conform with his aims. The recipients can also appeal to norms of humanity and helpfulness. And they can give, or offer, such counter-services as loyalty, gratitude and respect. Negative sanctions, for instance reproaching of the distributor because he has not granted their wishes, may also be used.[5] Whether or not it is wise for recipients to take recourse to such measures depends upon what kind of distributor they have.

What is characteristic for all appeals to the distributor's goodwill or sympathy is that their success depends upon how well they are adapted to his range of conceptions. The recipients must in their behaviour towards him try to 'hit upon' *his* opinion of himself and his environment and *his* norms and values. Arguing with one's own norms and values is of little use if they do not coincide with those of the distributor. The recipients will often be best placed if they have actually *acquired* the distributor's views – and not only build upon these for the sake of ar-

---

note 4 (cont.)

nor threaten. It is not right to give him your mite for fear of reprisal, this taints the donor's humanitarian frame of mind. A beggar should be sympathetic in his debasement, human in his distress so that his appearance itself attracts generous fellow-feeling. Sorrow, not anger, should mark that part of his countenance which is not ravaged. It is disagreeable when he appears wholly apathetic, but rather this than that he should be arrogant and demanding. A mournful smile is also desirable ; not least for this reason, children are often excellent beggars. Occasionally a beggar may demonstrate the nature of his suffering but not so shamelessly that the audience is sickened. If the worst comes to the worst he may also be a criminal, but not so obviously that the safety of the passers-by is threatened ; his crime should be picturesque as well. It is important that the beggar be physically inferior to his well wishers. If he is bigger he should eliminate the threat which the larger person always exudes for some reason or other (why are we more afraid of bears than of bees ?) by sitting or lying down. For this reason, too, children are so often excellent beggars. Alms will be given from above otherwise there is the danger that the giver's hand will be held tight. In addition, suffering should be allocated at fitting intervals so that it does not stick in the throat ; beggars should not operate in groups. Neither should they give such a strong impression of physical power or mental despair that the passer-by *himself* risks feeling weak, powerless or threatened. Beggars must not suggest any kind of comparison of this nature. Neither must they shine with self-confidence or efficiency ; it is better that they appear resigned, uncertain, broken, pitifully amateurish in the performance of their trade.'

5. I am referring here to reproaches which are *not* based on the idea that the distributor has a *duty* to give help. If the recipient pleads that the distributor has such a duty and criticizes him for having ignored it, the situation comes under what is to be discussed in section VII. However, the distinction between these two types of cases is not a sharp one.

gumentation. Their appeals will in this event be strengthened by being imbued with conviction but, on the other hand, may be weakened by the fact that they are not so calculated.

Even if a recipient has a good chance of getting his wishes fulfilled by appealing to the distributor, he may have good reasons for not doing so. Perhaps he hesitates to ask a favour or for mercy because he does not want to reveal his own pitifulness or greed or because he dislikes the means he would have to resort to in order to have his desires satisfied. Perhaps, for example, he has norms and values which are different to those the distributor holds and prefers to respect these rather than gain the advantages concerned through flirtation or ingratiation. In other words, appeals to the distributor's goodwill or compassion can appear *illegitimate*.

In addition, the recipients may feel that it is *poor strategy* to ask for favours or mercy because this can be an admission that the distributor has a right to decide things as he sees fit. The likelihood of getting what one asks for may be increased by making such an admission, but this will not always be the case. And even if it is, this can still be a dubious procedure from a long term point of view : for example, it may then be more difficult to plead on a later occasion that one has a right to something. And if the recipient finds that he must depend upon the distributor's continued favours or mercy, this can give rise to a feeling of dependency and insecurity which more than outweighs the immediate advantages.

If the individual recipient tries to ingratiate himself with the distributor or complains to him of his distress, this may also be poor strategy from the point of view that it will be inclined to undermine recipient solidarity. Favours are a benefit in short supply and are often competed for. And competion sometimes leeds to a situation where one of the recipients employs expedients which hurt the others : perhaps he claims that he needs help more than they do or that he is more worthy of the distributor's favour ; perhaps he goes behind their backs and spread scandal as a way of ingratiating himself. It is therefore understandable that recipients who operate collectively often develop norms which forbid individual persons appealing to the distributor's goodwill or compassion.[6]

This can explain why a distributor who attaches great importance to strengthening or maintaining his position of power sometimes *invites* recipients to appeal to his goodwill or mercy. Dictators, for example,

6. See the examples given in chap. 12, section II.

tend to characterize themselves as 'magnanimous' or 'generous'. And in the days of absolute monarchy it was common to refer to the king's 'favour' or 'mercy'. For example, if a person wished to make his career in the service of his country it was important that he first win the king's 'favour' ; once 'out of favour' the situation became precarious. The king's power to grant pardon to a criminal was another aspect of the same pattern. A ruler's invitation to his subjects to come singly and plead for mercy or favours can, for several reasons, contribute to maintaining or strengthening his position of power. It stresses that he is not bound by rules and that his subjects have no right to claim anything from him, while at the same time these subjects are tempted to behave in a manner which counteracts any tendency to recipient solidarity. By getting them to compete for his favours, he prevents them from allying themselves against him.

As we have seen, recipients stand both to win and to lose by appealing to the distributor's goodwill or sympathy. What they risk *losing* is primarily the opportunity to employ other and more effective means of defence. The recipients who have no other means of persuasion are those who will have the least to lose in this respect. Other things being equal, therefore, prayers for favour or mercy are most likely to come from those recipients who do not dispose of manipulatory counter-services or other means of power and who lack an ideology which can serve as a basis for their demands. The beggar who supplicates, the sentenced criminal who asks for pardon, the small child who appeals to his parents are examples of recipients in such a situation. But, as already mentioned, there may be other reasons for not begging for favours or for mercy, e.g., because this may not be considered a legitimate way of exerting influence. Even a recipient who has no other means of persuasion at his disposal may refrain from appealing to the distributor's goodwill or sympathy for these reasons.

How much a recipient can hope to *win* by asking a favour or begging for mercy depends, among other things, on how great his need is and what chance there is of his prayer being heard. We have already seen that the goal of the allocation activity and the distributor's feelings for the recipient are of some significance in this connection. But the recipient's own position also plays a role. For instance, the fact that he has counter-services at his disposal – perhaps he is a skillful employee who may hand in his resignation if he does not obtain favourable terms – may make the distributor feel that it is wise to accommodate him. This recipient may, therefore, achieve more when demanding special terms than the other recipients. But he may also have more to

343

lose by so doing. It is not possible to make any generalization as to which alternative is the better. Whether those who have the strongest position within a group of recipients or those who have the weakest are the people who ask for favours tends, therefore, to vary.

When the distributor's aim is to help, support, raise, cure or educate the recipients, and his attitude to them is positive, there can be a great deal to win by appealing to him. And in many of these cases there is little to lose because the recipients' resources of other effective means of influence are limited. They are often unable to withdraw from the allocation system and their counter-services are difficult to manipulate or are too insignificant to be used as sanctions. In such allocation systems one can assume therefore that appeals to the distributor's goodwill or sympathy will play an important role. And since much can be gained from these appeals they will sometimes be used even though other means of defence are available. I will later return to the tendency one finds with recipients in some of these systems (for instance, with children in relation to their parents) to alternate between claims for justice and treaties for favour or mercy.

Even if a distributor is not especially well disposed towards the recipients and is not inclined to satisfy their needs so that, generally speaking, there is little to win by appealing to his goodwill or sympathy, this may still be widely resorted to. The reason for this may be that the recipients have no other means of exerting influence, or that they expose themselves to reprisals if they try to bring pressure to bear in some other way.

VII. CLAIMS AND CRITICISM ETC. FROM RECIPIENTS
OPERATING INDIVIDUALLY

In this section I will examine the behaviour of recipients who do not completely accept that the distributor can do as he pleases. Recipients may consider that the distributor is bound by norms or believe that they have power to coerce him. They may react by taking a *negative* attitude to something the distributor has done or intends to do, or they may make a *positive* demand or suggestion as to how they would prefer something to be done. In both cases the reactions can be connected with either *past* or *future* situations. By combining these characteristics we get the four types of reactions which are illustrated in Figure 3.

These four kinds of reactions frequently constitute links in the same chain of argumentation. For example, a recipient can criticize a decision

Figure 3

Recipient reactions

	Past-oriented	Future-oriented
Negative	I Criticism	II Protests to plans, refusal to obey orders, etc.
Positive	III Pointing out what should have been done	IV Demands and suggestions

which the distributor has made (I) and refuse to obey it (II) while at the same time pointing out how the problem should have been solved (III), and demanding that it should be solved in this way in future (IV). But these forms of reaction can also occur singly. For example, a recipient can criticize without pointing out what the right decision should have been and without making any demands or refusing anything. The tendency to use mainly one or another of these reactions can vary from one recipient to another and from one allocation system to the next. I assume that orientation towards the negative and the past tend to go together and that there is a corresponding connection between positive and future-oriented reactions. Those reactions which are mainly past-oriented and negative I call 'critical'; those which are mainly future-oriented and positive 'demanding'. For the sake of brevity I will occasionally use the expression 'demands and criticism' as a joint designation for all the kinds of reactions illustrated in Figure 3.

Criticism alone is seldom an effective means of influencing a distributor's decisions. A recipient who wants to exert pressure and who is strong enough to have hopes of achieving something will therefore generally produce positive and future-oriented remarks as well. But even though pure criticism does not change matters, it may still help the recipient to adapt himself to the situation. When he has something to criticize he does not have to lay all the blame for his weak position on himself, and his wants and burdens will be easier to bear. The purely critical reactions, therefore, will be most likely to occur when the recipient (1) has few chances of introducing changes and (2) has a great need to free himself from disagreeable self-reproach.

I have so far assumed that the reactions are addressed to the distributor. This is necessary if one is to talk of 'demands' and 'refusals'. However, criticism of the distributor's decisions and pointing out of what he should have done may be made to people other than the distributor himself. Reactions which are future-oriented can also be directed at other people, for instance the statement that one *intends* making a demand on the distributor. Reactions which do not have the distributor as addressee cannot serve to influence his decisions – unless they are somehow or other forwarded on to him. But they may have the function which I have already mentioned of easing adaptation and they can also help stiffen the recipient's opposition and obtain support for him in a later direct attack on the distributor. It may be a good thing to go to other people with your criticism when there is little hope of achieving anything with the distributor and when there is a risk involved in criticizing him to his face. These points of view can be summed up by saying that the weaker position the recipient has in relation to the distributor, the more negative and past-oriented his reactions will tend to be and the more likely that these will be directed to persons other than the distributor.

Critical and demanding reactions usually depend upon the recipient having something with which he can argue. Pure expressions of will can, of course, be made without any reasons being given as, for instance, when a child insists 'I *want* that' or 'I *won't* do that'. But reactions are normally more effective when they are supported by *norms or values* or by *means of power* which the recipient has at his disposal, or by both of these.

The recipients' power can, for instance, lie either in the fact that the distributor is dependent on counter-services which they can withhold or that he needs their support to maintain his position as distributor (see sections II and III above). When the recipients operate collectively, their power is sometimes sufficient to serve as the only or the most important basis for making demands on the distributor (see chap. 12). Occasionally this also applies to recipients operating singly. The customer may criticize and make demands on the shopkeeper and the latter may find that he must take this into account because he does not want to lose a client. But in allocation systems from which it is more difficult to withdraw, it seldom occurs that the individual recipient has sufficient power to coerce the distributor. He therefore needs to anchor his criticism and demands in norms or values. But the means of power which he may possess will help to support his claims. If it is difficult for him to withdraw from the allocation system, his power will primarily depend upon whether or not he disposes of any manipulatory counter-services. If he does, this is a factor which will tend to make his reactions demanding rather than only critical.

346

There are various kinds of normative arguments which may be engaged in support of recipient demands or criticism. For example, attention can be drawn to specific rules or directives which the distributor is considered to be bound by, to principles of justice or other moral norms, to the distributor's own promises, or to the purpose of the allocations. Although there are many possibilities, such arguments are not always available. It may be that no norms, promises or aims limit the distributor's freedom of action. Or perhaps such limitations do exist but the recipients are not aware of them or find no support in them. There can also be limits to what a recipient wishes to use in his arguments. Perhaps he does not like to employ norms or aims which he himself does not accept, or perhaps he does not wish to give information or make assumptions which he does not trust. And even though he is able to bring himself to use such arguments, his lack of confidence will tend to weaken his case (see section III above). They may become less suited both to influence the distributor and to adapt the recipient to his situation.

The effect of the argumentation on the distributor also depends, of course, upon whether *he* accepts the norms and values which are appealed to and whether he believes in the information and the assumptions furnished him. Whether or not the argumentation can be expected to receive ideological support from those people whose opinions the distributor respects may also play some role. The fewer means of power the recipient has at his disposal, the more important it is for him that his arguments be considered relevant by the distributor and his milieu.

Even when the recipient has useful arguments at his disposal, it is not certain that he will achieve as much by demanding and criticizing as he will by appealing to the distributor's goodwill or compassion. To oppose the distributor may involve some risk (see section III above) and even if this is not the case the distributor may be more susceptible to ingratiation and supplication than to criticism and demands. But even so, the recipient may choose the line of opposition, for example, because this seems to be more legitimate or better long-run strategy. The fact that the two patterns of behaviour each have their advantages and disadvantages, may also lead to alternations between them. This is most likely in cases where their use neither involves risk nor leads to obviously significant results.

Mathiesen's (1965) study of the relations between the inmates and staff of a Norwegian correctional institution is highly relevant to the issues discussed above. He was particularly concerned with the staff's allocation of benefits and burdens among the inmates and with inmate defensive reactions to allocation decisions. He introduces the expression 'censoriousness' to designate a defence pattern which he found to be typical for the inmates. The main characteristics of this defence pattern are that (1) reaction consists of criticism directed against the distributor's decisions and (2) that this criticism is based on norms or values which the distributor can be expected to accept.

Mathiesen stresses that recipients who operate collectively may employ 'censoriousness' as a weapon but that the likelihood of this reaction pattern being used is much greater when the recipients operate individually (loc. cit. pp. 14-15 and p. 188).[7] At any rate, the inmates of the correctional institution mainly operated individually. There was too little solidarity between them to make collective defence possible. For these reasons, Mathiesen (loc. cit. p. 16) chiefly discusses *individual* 'censoriousness'.

The arguments which the inmates produced in support of their criticism were frequently based on ideas of justice (loc. cit. p. 150 et seq.). Confinement in the institution concerned was a preventive measure which came in addition to regular imprisonment. And it was a widely held opinion that this confinement was in itself unjust. The inmates felt that they had already balanced their account with society by serving their prison sentence and were now 'serving for nothing' (pp. 152-153). These complaints were thus based on the conception of retributive justice that there ought to be balance between guilt and punishment. In addition, they often complained about injustice within the institution, for instance in connection with decisions relating to leave, release, transfer to the open section of the institution, punishment for breaches of discipline, etc. These complaints were often concerned with alleged discrimination. Here, in other words, the inmates' arguments were based on distributive justice. In some of these cases absolute equality was demanded. For instance, it was widely felt that everyone should be granted leave equally often (pp. 154-156). In other connections most of the inmates supported principles of seniority, for example with regard to transfer to the open section (pp. 156-157). Principles of merit were also applied. Mathiesen (pp. 157-160) mentions two types of such principles. One of these, which he calls 'the principle of minimum requirements', was that it was unjust to punish or reproach an inmate unless he had violated a clearly stipulated rule. The other, which Mathiesen calls 'the principle of positive achievements', was that positive behaviour and contributions on the part of the inmates should be rewarded.

7. This assumption, which I find reasonable, will be discussed in Chapter 12.

One common feature of the inmates' conception of justice was a general tendency to apply specific and object-oriented criteria. When the staff tried to give individual attention, therefore, this was often labelled unjust. But, on the other hand, the staff were frequently criticized for a lack of ability or zeal in giving any effective treatment (loc. cit. p. 166 et seq.). The inmates repeatedly pointed to the fact that the aim of their confinement was to give them treatment, that the court had promised them this, but that nothing was done to help them. The high level of recidivism was taken as a sign that the institution and its staff were not good enough. Their ideas of what 'treatment' should consist of were very vague. Some of the inmates expected pills and injections while others more or less thought of 'treatment' as being synonymous with 'sympathy'.[8] However, the fact that ideas of what *should* have been done were both vague and varying did not prevent their use as a basis for criticism.

If we apply the categories in Figure 3 to the defence pattern which has been described, we can characterize it as being largely critical. But in addition to the negative and past-oriented reactions there were also some which can be described as demanding. These were more often argued in terms of justice than of treatment – which was natural since the inmates had a much clearer conception of what was just than of what treatment should involve.

Another feature of the defence pattern was that it was not built upon threats of sanctions but upon norm and value arguments. And the norms and values which were mainly used had their origin in the law- and health-ideologies on which the institution's activity was based. In this respect, the study supports the assumption that the less power[9] the recipients have, the more likely they are to take the premises for their criticisms and demands from the distributor's own system of values. It also supports the assumption that the combination of little power and

8. The latter point of view was not only used as a basis for criticism but also for appeals to the distributor's goodwill or compassion. Such appeals were sometimes argued by claiming that one's own case was unique – which in a certain sense is the opposite of demanding equality. (Loc. cit. pp. 179-181). – Galtung (1959, 2 pp. 212-213) found a similar tendency among the prisoners he studied. They sometimes demanded that there should be no discrimination and sometimes that their own unique situation should be taken into account.
9. I presuppose that the inmates of a correctional institution are relatively powerless. They cannot threaten to withdraw from the allocation system and their counter-services (good conduct within the institution, reformation and rehabilitation) are not sufficiently manipulatory to serve as an effective means of defence.

few risks makes for a tendency to vacillate between different defence patterns (see section III, the text related to fig. 1).

It is difficult to say anything definite about the effects of the reactions which have been described. However, Mathiesen assumes that they helped the inmates to adapt to their situation, among other things because their feeling of guilt was reduced through having something which they could criticize (loc. cit. pp. 185-186). He also assumes that their criticism may have had some impact on the staff and the management by making these more inclined to base their decisions on specific and object-oriented criteria. Pressure in this direction did not meet strong resistance since the use of such criteria facilitated decision-making and also strengthened the position of the security personnel in relation to that of the treatment staff (pp. 155, 157, 158 and 194-210).

VIII. MORE ABOUT JUSTICE AS A BASIS OF INDIVIDUAL DEMANDS AND CRITICISM

The supply of arguments upon which a recipient can draw may decide *whether* or not he opposes the distributor, *what* he reacts against and the *manner* in which he does this. Among the different types of arguments which can be used, those based on justice belong to the most readily available. Most people in our culture have experienced many kinds of situations where justice is used in argumentation. And since these arguments are based on general principles having a simple structure, it is easy to transfer them from one situation where they have already been in use to new social situations which may arise.

Of course, not only whether a recipient knows that he can employ justice in his arguments but also what attitude he takes to questions of justice is important. Many variations are possible. On the one hand a recipient may be absolutely convinced of what is just. From this situation of absolute certainty a continuum can be drawn through situations where his conviction is weaker but where he considers that conceptions of justice are still applicable and natural, or at least can be used for the sake of argument, to those where it runs directly against the recipient's convictions to demand requital[10] or equal distribution. The more sin-

10. For example, because he feels bound by such exchange restrictions as I gave examples of in chap. 3 II and chap. 4 VII. A person who applies for a licence or public appointment may feel that he should not claim this as a counter-service for the personal services he has rendered or for his political loyalty.

cere the belief a recipient has in an argument, the more legitimate and appropriate it will be for him to use it. The factors which generally promote the use and internalization of conceptions of justice (see chaps. 4-7 and chap. 10) therefore also increase the chance of the recipient using them as arguments against the distributor.

There may, however, be situations in which the recipient prefers equal distribution or balanced requital, and perhaps also believes that he is entitled to claim this, but where, even so, he does not use this argument with the distributor. The reason may be that, for instance, he feels it will be useless or too risky because the distributor is a despotic prince or an authoritarian father or teacher who does not allow any recipient to insist upon his rights. Or the reason may be that the recipients have begun to operate collectively and that they refrain from advancing individual demands since they reckon that this will be detrimental to their collective interests (see chap. 12).

On the other hand there may be situations in which the recipient does not prefer equal distribution or balanced requital or perhaps does not feel that he has any right to this, but still argues for it. Perhaps he wants his own share to be as large as possible but restricts himself to asking for equality because he does not expect to get more or because he considers it more legitimate to ask for justice than for his own interests.

Generally speaking, it can be said that the recipients' problem situation (section I above) and their alternative possibilities of problem solution (section II) contribute to the formation of their pattern of argumentation. And it must be assumed that in the long run their use (or non-use) of *arguments* of justice will affect their *conceptions* of justice – because, among other reasons, people often tend to convince themselves of the validity of what they say to other people.

As we have already seen, problems can be solved partly by influencing the distributor and partly by the recipient adapting himself to the situation. As Mathiesen's study illustrates (see section VII above), arguments based on justice can fill both these functions. I will now point to a couple of factors which help to make such argumentation suitable for these purposes but which also limit the use to which it can be put.

Firstly, it is significant that conceptions of justice can give a recipient a basis for demanding his *right* and for criticizing the distributor's behaviour as being *wrong*. They thereby provide a moral foundation which helps to make the arguments more *legitimate,* i.e. make it easier for the recipient to defend his own behaviour to himself and other people. This is of significance because some demands might never have been made if the recipient had not had a basis of justice on which to build. It can also make it easier for the recipient to adapt himself, since he may need to have an image of himself as a person who never asks for more than is his due right. Conceptions of justice can also prove helpful if one's demands are not met. It is easier to preserve one's self-respect when there is another person to blame so that lack of success does not have to be attributed to one's own shortcomings. Criticizing the distributor for injustice is not the only way of defending one's own self-image, but it usually affords a stronger defence than, for example, blaming his lack of goodwill or compassion.[11]

For these reasons a recipient may base his arguments on justice even if he could have achieved more with the distributor by availing himself of other argumentation. His motive for following this line of action may, for instance, be that he would undermine the defence he has erected around his self-image if he employed alternative arguments. In many cases it weakens a person's defence to plead for mercy or to ask for favours, e.g., when a person claims that he has been unjustly sentenced for some crime.

A recipient may also become more eager to get what he demands when he believes that he has a right to it. Attitudes tend to be less coloured by compromise and behaviour less calculated with persons

11. The idea that one's own misfortune is due to other people's injustice can, however, in certain cases affect personality to such an extent that it does not make for adjustment but, on the contrary, leads into a vicious circle of protest actions and reactions, e.g. when criminals constantly return to some – perhaps genuine – injustice which they have suffered earlier during their criminal career and use this as an explanation for everything that has happened since. One example from Norwegian legal practice is to be found in *Norsk Retstidende* (Norwegian Law Reports) 1965 p. 881 et seq. where a criminal career is described as follows (p. 882):
   'The convict has explained to the expert witnesses and to the Court that he considers himself to have been unjustly treated in a case which originated in 1961 in Japan when he was dismissed from his job as seaman on board a Norwegian ship 'Sunny Lady' and sent home to Norway, and that in spite of great efforts it has not been possible for him to obtain justice from the shipping company concerned. He has stated that he commits the punishable offences – faked fire alarm and smashing of windows – in order to make the authorities aware of his claim, and he intends to continue with this.'
   Bergler and Meerloo (1963, particularly p. 20 et seq.) offer an explanation of such cases on the basis of psychoanalytical theory. They contend that a subconscious – masochistic – desire to feel offended serves as a neurotic defence for certain people. Such a person is liable to become an 'injustice collector' who looks for situations where he must suffer defeats or humiliations which he can interpret as injustices.

who are fighting for their rights than with those who only attempt to promote their interests. This can sometimes be advantageous. It may give the recipient courage to oppose the distributor even when a risk is involved, and it may give him endurance to carry the struggle through even when this is long and involves sacrifice. In addition it can make his argumentation more convincing.

But there are also disadvantages connected with this ideology. It makes for courage and enthusiasm, but reduces the ability to make realistic and cool evaluations of the available possibilities. What counts most depends upon the circumstances, among other things on the nature of the allocation system and on the power relationship between distributor and recipients. An ideology based on justice (or on other moral principles) may be essential in order to give the recipients sufficient courage to oppose the distributor. But if their strength gradually increases, the ideology may become dysfunctional in later stages of the struggle.

Another important feature of arguments based on justice is that they *set limits* to the recipient's claims. By appealing to retributive justice he demands as much as will balance his account with the distributor, but no more. And if he goes in for just distribution, this means that he will receive only as much as the others, not that they will all together have more. In this respect arguments of justice are unlike arguments based on needs or interests. The recipient's demands can, of course, be limited in such cases as well, but because needs can be insatiable this will not be due to the kind of arguments used.

The fact that justice can limit what is demanded is both a weakness and a strength. On the one hand, there is, for this reason, much which recipients cannot achieve with arguments of justice. They must find other tools of persuasion if, for instance, they want to argue that everyone should have more of a benefit than they are entitled to. And, as we shall see later (chap. 12), it may sometimes be difficult to combine demands for justice with other forms of persuasion.

On the other hand the fact that there are limits may make it easier to use arguments of justice and to get somewhere with these – as far as they go. People are usually reluctant to expose too openly their own greed. And they can to some extent conceal it – both from themselves and from other people – by not demanding more than requital or equality. In other words, the limits which are laid down help – together with the moral foundation – to make argumentation more legitimate. And from the distributor's point of view, the limitations provide some protection from a continuous increase in demands, so that for this reason he may be less hesitant to give way to the claims of the recipients.

The above-mentioned features of conceptions of justice distinguish the latter sharply from arguments to the effect that recipients' needs or interests must be met. However, several of the different types of arguments which were referred to above (section VII) as examples of what can be presented in support of individual claims and criticism resemble conceptions of justice in so far as they have a basis in morality and set limits to the claims that can be made. This applies, for example, to arguments to the effect that the distributor is bound to abide by the rules governing his activity or to keep the promises which he has made. Principles of justice and the principle that a promise should be kept have in common that they not only impose duties on the distributor but also give corresponding rights to the recipients. They are therefore well suited as arguments on which to found both criticism and demands. Some of the other 'moral' arguments which could be produced refer to distributor obligations which do not correspond with rights for recipients. Assertions to the effect that the distributor has not acted in accordance with the rules and instructions of his superiors or that he is not promoting the intended goals in a satisfactory manner, may be of this kind. Such arguments are normally better suited as a basis for criticism than for demands.

Arguments of justice and threats of sanctions are frequently used together. Although they may not carry sufficient weight separately with the distributor, they may be decisive when combined. If the recipient contends that he has some right, this will also help to make his use of power legitimate and may therefore be one of the reasons why he dares to threaten at all.

But arguments of justice can also be used by recipients who have no power resources at their disposal. Whether or not the arguments have any effect on the distributor depends, in any case, on whether they appeal to something in him. And the less power a recipient has, the more his chance of exerting influence depends on the normative appeal of his arguments. This will be strongest if the distributor has already internalized the same principle of justice as that with which the recipient makes his appeal. But even when this is not the case, arguments of justice will often find some echo in the distributor's value and norm system.

The aim of the distributor's allocation activity also plays a role. As we have seen (chap. 9), goals help to determine which allocation principles are given preference. And the more easily the promotion of these goals can be combined with recipient claims based on justice, the more

354

receptive will the distributor be to these – and the more natural it will be for the recipient to argue with them. In some cases what the distributor regards as expedient coincides completely – or nearly – with what the recipient believes is just. For example, object-oriented equality and allocation according to merit will often seem to be the right course from both points of view. And such characteristics as, for instance, age and sex can partly serve as standardized criteria of need or fitness and partly as criteria of just allocation by status. In all the various types of allocation systems mentioned in Chapter 9, there is a possibility that reasoning on the basis of justice may coincide more or less with what is considered expedient.

There will frequently, however, be some differences. For one thing, the distributor's substantive goals will often indicate a higher degree of individualization than the recipients feel is just, whereas procedural and organizational considerations (chap. 9, sections VII and VIII) may, in such instances, pull in the same direction as the recipients' claims for justice. This is because costs and unpleasantness involved in making and enforcing decisions can be reduced by building upon simple and clear criteria. When an organization acts as distributor other factors also lead in the direction of the formation of a system of rules making use of such criteria (see chap. 9, section VIII). I will later (in section IX) return to the various kinds of interplay between recipient claims for justice and the procedural and organizational factors which encourage regulation.

I have so far spoken in very general terms about 'argumentation based on justice'. But there are many different conceptions of justice. The basic idea may be that of balance in the relationship between distributor and individual recipient or it can be that of equal distribution, and in the latter case there are several competing criteria of equality. In addition, ideas of justice can vary along such dimensions as specific – diffuse and object-oriented – person-oriented.

I do not intend to go into any detail about what gives rise to the use of one rather than another type of argument for justice. Many of the factors which were mentioned above are also significant in this connection. Whether ideas of requital will be considered applicable depends largely on whether the distributor invites this, for example by establishing exchange relations with the individual recipient or by trying to influence the recipients through rewards and punishments. From the point of view of the individual recipient, justice based on requital will afford the strongest foundation for his demands. He can then claim a right which is based on his own contribution and is not conditional on what other recipients get. The fact that he has such an independent right to a benefit involves, among other things, the advantage that he does not become indebted by accepting it. On the other hand, distributive justice is better fitted to reduce the distributor's opportunities of manipulating his recipients. It may force him to defend his entire policy of allocation to the individual recipient. And because he must assume that everyone is interested in what the other recipients get and tries to find out what arguments he uses with the latter, it will be difficult for him to juggle with different types of arguments with different recipients. For these reasons one can assume that the poorer exchange possibilities a recipient possesses and the greater his need to protect himself from distributor manipulation, the more inclined he will be to prefer reasoning which is based on equality rather than on requital. And the stronger the forces which lead towards claims for equality, the more specific and object-oriented the criteria tend to be.

IX. ARGUMENTATION BASED ON JUSTICE IN RELATIONSHIPS BETWEEN CHILDREN AND PARENTS AND BETWEEN CITIZENS AND THE STATE

The general points of view developed in the last section will now be illustrated by way of examples taken from two kinds of allocation systems. A few comparisons will also be made with Mathiesen's (1965) findings from the correctional institution.

The first examples I give concern the relationship between *children and parents*. My experience – which comes from unsystematic observation of my own and my friends' children – is that children (from 5-6 years upwards) are prone to argue with conceptions of equality, retribution and requital when in contact with each other and with their parents. The word 'fair' is often used in such connections but the pattern of argumentation can also be observed in children before they have learnt the meaning of this word. The kind of justice arguments used varies a good deal, not only between different children and different families but also in such a way that one and the same child alternates between various models of justice – according to the situation.

Object-oriented equality is frequently demanded. Such arguments as, for example, '*I* want as much as him' or '*he* mustn't have more than me' or '*he* has got some, so *I* must have some too', are used. Demands for random selection and allocation by time priority are also normal. The same applies to allocation by status characteristics such as sex and age. In family discussions these various criteria of justice are often played against each other, for instance by one of the children demanding object-oriented equality while his brother or sister (or one of the parents) reasons that allocation by time priority, age or sex is the fairest. There is much switching from one principle to another. The eldest of the children, for example, refers to his age when privileges or other benefits are to be allocated, while it is the youngest who uses the difference in age and the eldest who demands object-oriented equality when duties are to be allocated. In some instances one and the same characteristic can be employed as an argument both ways. The eldest brother, for example, may argue that he should have most of some benefit because his need is greatest or because he is best-fitted, whereas the youngest claims that he should get most because his brother has already, altogether, received more. With whom the children compare themselves is also liable to differ. The comparison will probably usually be with the other children in the family but it can also be with their playfellows or with their parents ('It's not fair that I can't do that when you do it'). It seems probable that children who have brothers or sisters of approximately the same age are more inclined to argue with distributive justice than would an only child, but that the special kind of reasoning in which the child compares himself with his parents occurs more frequently with the only child.

Object-oriented equality probably is the principle on which it is normally easiest for children to reach agreement. From the parents' point of view this will often be a rational principle to adopt since it leads to simple decisions and reduces the danger of protestations and quarrels. The parents' position of power, however, is probably weakened if the practice has previously been adopted in the family that certain benefits or burdens are to be allocated according to this principle. The children have acquired a legitimate basis for claiming, for instance: 'When *he* gets some, *I* must have some too'. And the parents have reduced their opportunities of using the benefits and burdens concerned as a means of influencing their children.

But there are also other kinds of conceptions of justice within family life, e.g., that contributions be rewarded according to their merit and that in certain circumstances it is fair – or unjust – to punish. These types of claims for justice may sometimes be based on conceptions of retributive justice so that the children use what they themselves have done, what their parents have done and which reciprocal rights and duties they have towards each other to argue with. In other instances a comparison with how other people (e.g., brothers or sisters) have been rewarded or punished in similar situations can be the main argument.

357

Retributive and distributive conceptions can also be combined.

The person-oriented (and often diffuse) conceptions of justice which have been mentioned here and the object-oriented and specific which were earlier referred to, are frequently used alternately both by children and by their parents. One and the same situation is often evaluated from both these points of view. For example, one of the children may feel that he deserves a special reward while the others insist that : 'If he gets it, so shall *we*'. Or it may be that a child who has been forbidden something as a punishment claims that 'If I can't have it, neither can the others'. In other words, he insists that it is not a punishment that is involved but a limitation of his freedom which should be applied to all of them according to the principle of object-oriented equality.

Sometimes a child asks for something which the others do not get, justifying this with his need; he requires the benefit more than the others, he says, because he is older, or because he is a boy, or because he wants it very much. A claim for allocation according to need can occasionally take on the character of a claim for justice, especially when differences in need are associated with simple and clear characteristics such as age or sex. But it is probably more usual for children to appeal to their parents' goodwill, sympathy or care when their needs are pleaded rather than to their parents' sense of justice.

It is very customary to find alternating appeals to goodwill and justice. If one of the children has received something as a special reward, the others may later claim a similar benefit by appealing to principles of equality. In certain cases such alternation between the two kinds of reasons can be an effective means of securing new advantages. We can imagine a situation in which a child asks permission for something he or she wants and is warmly seconded by his or her brothers or sisters who do not have the same interests but who reckon that it will be their turn next to ask for something. On a later occasion when one of the other children makes a request, this may be supported by arguments of equality. This child may say, for example, 'John was allowed to go to the football match yesterday, so I should therefore be allowed to go to the cinema today'. Arguing need in such an instance serves to persuade the parents to increase their transfers, whilst arguments based on equality help to secure the recipient coupling on which the children's tendency to support each other's arguments of need is contingent. The two types of arguments can in this way be of mutual support. But at the same time that claims for equality can foster increased support for a recipient's arguments of need, they can also limit how much he will get. If he demands too much, his parents may refuse out of fear of the consequences of giving one child so much when the others usually demand equality.

What has been said above does not pretend to be a universally valid description of children's patterns of argumentation. There are certainly wide differences between differing cultures and milieus. The strong tendency to argue with justice to one's parents is probably conditional on a relatively democratic upbringing, the children being accepted as individuals with certain rights who are allowed to say what they think and to claim their own interests. I presume that where upbringing is more authoritarian the children will be less inclined to try to influence their parents. They will be more likely either to show resignation or to accept their parents' arrangements. And the instrument of persuasion which one first thinks of in this connection is to appeal to their parents' goodwill or sympathy. Much of what *Piaget* (1932) writes on the moral development of children indicates that the children he studied (in Geneva in the 1920's) were subject to much stricter parental authority[12] than the children (in the Oslo-area in the 1960's) from whom I gain my experience. And Piaget found little (or, at any rate, does not report having found) use of arguments of justice as a means of defence and persuasion vis-à-vis parents.

When the upbringing of children is sufficiently democratic to allow for such argumentation, I assume that it will be employed more often and lead more in the direction of object-oriented and specific equality the less secure the children feel. Children frequently tend to look upon their parents' allocation of trivial benefits as a sign of love, care and confidence. This is a factor which increases the inclination to demand equality, as has been pointed out in Chapter 10, section II. I assume that this tendency becomes stronger the more dependent the children are on their parents' affection and the less certain they are of getting this.

A comparison between what has been said above on the parent-child relationship and the results of *Mathiesen's* (1965) study of the correctional institution (see section VII above), reveals many similarities.[13] It is true that the pattern of defence adopted by the inmates of the correctional institution was characterized more by criticism and less by demands than I believe is normal among children. But the inmates

---

12. I am here referring especially to what he writes in chap. 2 (pp. 104 ff.) on 'adult constraint'. Some of his examples in chap. 3 (pp. 195 ff.) of parental methods of punishment confirm the impression of authoritarian upbringing.
13. This is also mentioned by Mathiesen (loc. cit. p. 229).

Mathiesen studied and children have in common that much of their opposition is justified with moral arguments and that they take their value premises preferably from norm systems which the distributor accepts. With both these groups of recipients, conceptions of justice play an important role in their argumentation and the models of justice most frequently employed are those based on object-oriented and specific principles of equality.

Another similarity is that, in both cases, there is a good deal of vacillation between the different types of arguments. This continuous switching from one to the other can partly be due to the fact that many different benefits and burdens are allocated in families and in correctional institutions. Here, as otherwise in life, judgments and reasons are determined by *what* is to be allocated and *why*. But in addition to this, both children and prisoners show a tendency to juggle with arguments so that justice fall in their own favour.[14]

It is possible that both the trend towards the specific and the object-oriented and the tendency to turn justice to one's own account can be taken as a sign of immaturity. Much goes to show that a sense for the diffuse and person-oriented and the ability to be considerate towards other people and to apply a more objective point of view increase with the age of the child. The fact that one finds patterns of argumentation in the inmates studied by Mathiesen similar to tohse one finds in children, may be connected with the retarded or impaired mental capacity of these inmates.[15]

I do not know whether such an assumption is justified. It is anyway most unlikely that it affords a complete explanation. It may not be due to immaturity but to the actual situation in the correctional institution that the inmates behaved like children. In any case, argumentation patterns similar to those I have described can also be found in allocation systems where there is no reason to assume that the recipients are especially immature.

We can take as an example the relationship between *state* and *citizen*. Decisions which the authorities make, for example with regard to punishment and the allocation of public burdens and benefits, are often evaluat-

14. This feature of children's argumentation for justice is stressed by Ehrenzweig (1964 pp. 162-164).
15. Most of the inmates belonged to a category of offenders which in Norwegian law is defined by the expression 'underdeveloped or permanently impaired mental capacity'. The adequacy of these terms is, however, debatable ; see Mathiesen op. cit. p. 33.

ed in terms of justice. In many of these cases, distributive justice plays the most important role. One hears such remarks as, 'It is unfair that I get no licence when N.N. got one' or 'It is not fair that we wage and salary earners are fully taxed while the self-employed have so many opportunities of tax evasion'. The conception of justice relied on can differ from one sector to another. But in many cases the tendency is to demand some kind of distributive justice based on object-oriented and specific criteria of equality, for example allocation according to seniority or in a proportional relation to fixed criteria.

The Norwegian administration of economic planning programmes offers many such examples. This trend was particularly noticeable in Norway during the first post war period when an extensive planning system with price control, rationing, export and import regulation, exchange control etc. was brought into being. Many of the laws prescribing these measures left much to the discretion of the authorities. The legislators seem to have presupposed that civil servants should make their decisions on the basis of broad evaluation of the economic effects of the measures. However, from the clients there was strong pressure to make the decisions just. And the kind of justice which was demanded most frequently was based on specific and object-oriented criteria of equality. Demands of this kind met little resistance since they harmonized well with the officials' need for simple and clear rules (see chap. 9, section IX above). We therefore experienced an escape from discretionary freedom into self-made rules which I have examined in greater detail elsewhere (*Eckhoff* 1962). With regard to export and import regulation, for example, it became normal for each firm to receive a quota which amounted to a fixed percentage of what it had exported or imported in a certain basis year (for example, 1939). In this manner both the client's demand for justice and the officials' need for clear criteria for decision-making were fairly well satisfied. But from the standpoint of social goals, this system had great disadvantages. It favoured the old and well-established firms (the 'quota aristocracy') and put obstacles in the way of initiative and adaptation to new conditions. Demands for equality which resulted in the development of specific rules occurred in other sectors as well. When it came to taxi licences, for instance, these could, according to the law, be granted by the transport authorities at their own discretion. But the principle was very soon accepted that only those people who had taxi-driving as their sole means of livelihood were granted licences. Among those who fulfilled this condition a strict principle of seniority was followed so that those who had driven a taxi longest, got a licence first. Many other examples could be given, both of demands for equality which the authorities fully or partly agreed to and of demands which were not accepted.

In many situations one also finds conceptions of retributive justice. Sometimes these are associated with specific relationships as, for example, when a punishment is thought to be unfairly hard in relation to the offence or when a business man considers it unjust that he has not been granted an export licence which he had been led to expect and for which he had accordingly made arrangements. In other instances it may be more general and vague ideas on the exchange relationship between state and citizens which enter the picture. For instance, the claim may be made that it is 'unjust that we pay so much in taxes and get so little in return', for instance in the way of road building, new schools etc. Ideas of retribution and distribution will often alternate or slide into each other in an overall conception. This is likely to happen when, for instance, punishment or taxation is evaluated. The same might be the case if someone, speaking generally, contended that, 'Norwegian economic planning legislation is unjust'. It may partly be unfair distribution (for example of quotas and licences) which the speaker has in mind, and partly an imbalance of power between state and citizen.

In the relationship between state and citizen, as in family life and the correctional institution, there is a great deal of alternation between arguments of justice and other kinds of arguments, and between different principles of justice. And what, in a particular situation, serves the interests of the individual often shows an unmistakable tendency to correspond with what he considers to be just.

The similarities between defence patterns in the three allocation systems which have been mentioned, are probably due to the fact that the systems – in spite of all their outer differences – have important features in common. They are all systems in which recipients are in a permanent state of dependence on the distributor. Normally it is impossible for the recipients to withdraw from the system, and individually they do not possess sufficient power resources to vindicate their interests. Nor does the situation usually lend itself so well to collective action (see chap. 12 below). Under these circumstances, individual demands for justice are often the strongest defence available. But if this argumentation pattern is to be used, the distributor must be sufficiently democratic to tolerate it. As mentioned in section VI, begging for favours or mercy is the citizens' typical means of defence against an authoritarian ruler. The democratization which has taken place in Norway during the 19th and 20th centuries is reflected, among other things, in the fact that demands for justice have largely replaced supplication.

It looks as if there is yet another similarity between intra-state and family relations. If the conditions are suitable for argumentation based on justice, the tendency to use such arguments will be stronger, and lead more in the direction of object-oriented and specific demands for equality, the more insecure the recipients feel. Post war economic planning in Norway was disturbing for those engaged in business and industry. Many of them felt that the economic system upon which they had based their business activity was seriously threatened. This was probably one of the factors which made them inclined to demand strict equality. But the changes which took place inside the publicly administered section of the economy may also have had some effect. There was a large increase in the number of civil servants and this probably meant that the distance between the government and the individual official was widened. And in addition to this the pressure of work increased for each individual. For reasons given earlier (chap. 9, section IX) it is understandable that these factors contributed to accentuating the employees' need for simple and clear criteria for decision-making and in this way made them more receptive to claims for object-oriented and specific equality.

12. More about the relationship between distributor and recipients

I. GENERAL COMMENTS ON WHAT GIVES RISE TO COLLECTIVE ACTION

The purest form of collective conduct is found when recipients avoid any kind of individual contact with the distributor and negotiate only as a body. But there are also less extreme forms. For example, the recipients may contact the distributor individually although their activity is coordinated through mutual arrangement or tacit understanding. Or they may *sometimes* operate as a united or coordinated body and at other times individually and independently of each other ; or *some* of them may operate in one of these ways and the rest in another. In what follows I will not distinguish between the different forms and degrees of collective conduct. However, I do assume that the nature and strength of the factors which give rise to collectivity also determine how far it goes.

The likelihood of a group of recipients operating collectively depends upon several factors. Among other things, their common and opposed interests play a role, as does also how they judge their chances of obtaining something from the distributor by the various means at their disposal. Their attitude to each other is also of some importance, i.e., whether being united in itself gives a satisfactory or an unpleasant feeling. Lastly, there may be norms which encourage or impede collective conduct. I will now discuss the significance of these factors and the way they affect each other.

Other things being equal, I assume that recipients will be more inclined to operate collectively the stronger the *common interests* they have with regard to what they hope to obtain from the distributor.[1] One thing in which they can have a joint interest is the size of the aggregate of transfers. Every recipient is interested in the distributor

1. On the other hand, common interests *with* the distributor do not provide a reason for acting collectively against him.

increasing overall transfers of positive values and reducing overall transfers of negative values. If there is any possibility of persuading the distributor to do so, this provides a motive for the recipients to unite. They have also a motive for keeping together if, in this way, they can prevent the distributor from changing the sum total of transfers to their disadvantage. These grounds for unity do not apply if the sum of transfers is unchangeable, and they carry more weight the greater are the possibilities of variation.

As observed earlier, common interests may also be tied to the distribution. This is especially true when recipient preferences differ. For example, if a brother and sister are to be given two toys, they will probably both prefer that she gets the doll and he the car, not the other way round. If the recipients have the same preferences and marginal utility is decreasing, equal distribution will give the optimum result (see chap. 10, section IV, 3). But in this case the common interest in achieving the optimum result is easily overshadowed by each recipient's desire to get as much as possible for himself.

There are also other bases for common interests. All recipients, for instance, may need predictability and security, and they may be opposed to the distributor using the transfers as a means of influencing and manipulating them.

Recipients who have certain interests in common may also have particular interests which are not shared by the other recipients or which are even directly in conflict with their interests. For example, the recipients have a common interest in the cake being as large as possible but conflicting interests in its distribution. In such cases it may be that the individual recipient *both* takes part in collective action which promotes the common goal *and* operates individually to further his particular interests. But this is often difficult. For reasons to which I will return later, adjustment to community requirements can reduce one's chances of promoting individual interests – especially those which clash with communal interests. It may therefore be a sacrifice to the individual recipient to co-operate with others in promoting a common goal. And the sacrifice is greater the stronger the particular interests which he is thus prevented from following.

Not only the strength of the interests but also the recipients' *insight* into them plays a role. One reason why recipients do not co-operate may be that they are not themselves aware what strong common interests they have – either because they do not understand their own needs sufficiently well or because they do not realize that others have the same needs.

In addition, what recipients expect to *achieve* and what they risk to lose through collective and individual action is important. If individual action appears useless, there is no sacrifice involved in not promoting one's particular interests. But the sacrifice may be large if great expectations are attached to individual action while the outcome of united action is uncertain. Perhaps the distributor makes a point of keeping them constantly aware that his goodwill is likely to disappear if they ally themselves against him.

In many cases more can be obtained by collective action than by operating individually. This is mainly due to two factors. Firstly, an individual recipient is usually considerably weaker than a distributor. And secondly, individual recipient demands tend to compete, and thus to counteract each other. Arguments also often point in different directions, so that what is maintained by one party will be contradicted by another. These weaknesses can be eliminated through collective action. But if such action is to be of any help, the recipients must *dispose of means of influence which are suited to collective use.*

Some means of influence are particularly well suited to be employed in joint action. This especially applies to threats of having the distributor (or the management of the distributor organization) removed and replaced. Attempts to accomplish such a change will not normally succeed unless many people support it. Threats of leaving the allocation system or of withholding or restricting counter-services can be effective even when they only come from an individual recipient. But these threats, too, will often be considerably more efficient if several people unite in making them. The same applies to the means of power inherent in withholding information. If the information is in the possession of several recipients, it is of little use for one of them to keep silent if others are likely to inform the distributor.

On the other hand, there are means of influence which are better suited to individual than to collective use. This applies, among other things, to appeals to the distributor's goodwill or compassion. If the aim of such an appeal is to help a single recipient, it will only be in special cases that everyone will support it. Besides this, an individual often finds it easiest to ingratiate himself and to demonstrate his need if he operates alone. This is particularly true when his tactics are to present himself as a better, more worthy or more needful recipient than the others. Collective appeals, which aim to improve the conditions of all the recipients, can also occur. But these may easily have the opposite effect to what is intended since the distributor can regard the alliance as a threat so that his goodwill disappears. And although this may not

366

happen, it is usually more difficult to arouse sympathy or response for a group than for an individual.

Claims for justice occupy an intermediate position. They have a common ideological foundation which gains in strength when all recipients give their support. But individual claims often clash with each other in a way which makes collective action difficult. For example, the recipients may agree that principles of equality should be followed but disagree as to what is equal. As we will see later, there are differences between the various principles of justice when it comes to their suitability for collective use.

It is not sufficient that the recipients dispose of means of influence which are suited to collective use. They must also have the *capacity to use these.* Firstly, they must have some understanding of the available opportunities and secondly, certain social and psychological conditions necessary for coordination must be present. The recipients must at least know of each other's existence and preferably have some means of mutual communication. It seems reasonable to assume as *Lysgaard* (1961 p. 146 et seq. and p. 203 et seq.) has done that the likelihood of collective operation increases with increased recipient interaction. But in addition to the outer circumstances being favourable to cooperation, the will to agree must also be there. The recipients must be able to reach agreement on joint strategy and must adapt themselves to the demands which this makes upon them. From the individual recipient's point of view this means that he must, to some extent, subordinate himself to the others. He must be willing to follow the collective's directives even when he personally believes that some other line of strategy would be preferable. This means that the individual recipient loses not only opportunities of negotiating special advantages for himself, but also some of his independence. How great a sacrifice this entails depends to a large extent upon his attitude to the other recipients. The more faith he has in their knowledge and judgment, the less he will lose by adapting himself.

The risk of reprisals may also be greater when recipients work in alliance than when they operate individually. Whether this is so depends, among other things, upon the distributor's attitude to the recipients and upon his power in relation to them. But whether or not the recipients can expect help and support from each other when in trouble also plays some role. If they can, there is less risk in joint action. And in addition, willingness to expose oneself to risk out of consideration for the others increases with increased helpfulness and readiness to sacrifice.

367

So far I have looked mainly at what recipients can achieve, or avoid, vis-à-vis the distributor by uniting. But what their *community in itself means to them* is also of some importance. It can be an agreeable association where companionship and cooperation create well-being and where the feeling of belonging together increases the individual's security and self-respect. Or it can be a disagreeable association where being together is a source of continuous irritation and where one either does not feel at home or considers association with the others to be degrading. The more the conditions are suited to amicable association, the greater will be the probability of collective operation.

I have now mentioned four significant aspects of recipient attitudes to each other. The likelihood of collective performance is thus increased when recipients (1) respect each other's insight and judgment, (2) are prepared to help and support each other, (3) like to be together and (4) have the feeling of belonging to a community which gives security and selfrespect. These four aspects tend to go together. In what follows I will occasionally use the expression 'mutual respect and fellow-feeling' as a joint expression for them, but they do not always appear together. For example, a recipient may respect the insight and judgment of the others but feel uncomfortable in their company. Or perhaps he may enjoy being with them but is ashamed to be thought one of their number.

The factors which promote collective activity are frequently reinforced by *reciprocal influence* and *norm formation*. For instance, the recipients may make their common interests more visible to each other ('we are all in the same boat') and strengthen one another's faith in joint action ('united we stand, divided we fall' and 'there is safety in numbers'). They can also develop norms which counteract the tendency to promote self-interest ('the common cause comes first') and norms which facilitate co-operation ('the wisest steps down'). In addition to the kind of general beliefs and principles of which I have given examples, more specific norms can develop indicating what is correct and incorrect behaviour towards one's fellow recipients and towards the distributor. I will give some examples of this below (in section II).

The different factors mentioned above are interconnected. Experience which shows that it *pays* to unite can give rise to the idea that it is *right* to do so. This also provides a motive for bringing pressure to bear on deviants. And this pressure becomes more effective the greater the mutual respect and fellow-feeling recipients have for each other. And conversely, the fact that norms of solidarity have developed and are effectively enforced will increase the possibilities of gaining advantages through collective activity. When such norms are internalized, they can also help to reinforce mutual respect and fellow-feeling.

But each of the factors can be influenced by external impulses as well. Norms which say that one should co-operate can be culturally conditioned and the same applies to whether it is regarded as an honour or a disgrace to belong to a certain category of people. For instance, in many societies, ideologies of kinship and consanguinity have contributed to unity and fellow-feeling within the family, the kinship group or tribe. Religious, political and professional ideologies often play a similar role. A working-class movement which appeals to class consciousness and unity can, for example, strengthen collectivism inside the individual factory or enterprise. In addition to ideological support, factory employees may have a powerful trade union and a Labour Party as potential allies.

The norms and values in which the recipients find support when they operate collectively, do not have to be the ones the distributor accepts. On the contrary, an ideology which is in opposition to what the distributor represents may be especially suited to strengthen their feeling of fraternity and stimulate their ability to recognize common interests. This is an important difference from recipients who operate individually. The latter are usually forced to rely on norms and values which the distributor accepts if they are to have any hope of success.

II. RECIPIENT COLLECTIVES IN DIFFERENT SOCIAL SYSTEMS

The conditions under which collective defence is likely to occur are discussed in detail in *Lysgaard's* (1961 and 1965) studies of the industrial plant and in *Mathiesen's* (1965) study of the correctional institution. In what follows I will compare some of the empirical data and theoretical points of view they offer with the assumptions made above. Material from certain other studies and my own unsystematic experience from different types of allocation systems will also be brought in to serve as illustration.

In the factory which *Lysgaard* (1961) studied, he found a clear tendency among the workers to unite in collective defence against the management. They had a strong feeling of belonging together (p. 27 et seq.) and of being in opposition to the management (p. 37 et seq.). This opposition was not based on personal dislike of the management but on a feeling that the factory's goals were in conflict with the interests of the employees.[2] There was also a well developed system of norms which helped to strengthen the unity of the workers, to secure a common strategy, and to limit the management's opportunities of exerting pressure. Among other things, the norms stated that the individual worker should not try to ingratiate himself with the management or assert himself in any way and that contact with his superiors should be limited to what was absolutely necessary (p. 41 et seq., cf. pp. 52-53). A worker must be loyal to his fellow workers. For instance, he must not communicate their shortcomings or virtues to the management and must not keep secret his own relations with the management (p. 45 et seq.). As strict an equality as possible was sought both with regard to labour input and pay. The worker who was too zealous at his job was regarded as 'making up to his superiors'. But neither should anyone be lazy; everyone should keep a reasonable tempo at work (p. 44). The workers reacted strongly to any transgression of norms. There was a chilly attitude to persons who were considered unreliable colleagues; conversation stopped when they approached and those who befriended them became themselves the object of sanctions (pp. 49-50 and p. 172).

These norms and attitudes were a defence *against* what Lysgaard calls 'the technical-economic system'. By this he refers to the system of roles and values which are erected around a factory's goals of profitability and efficiency (pp. 14-15, cf. pp. 59 ff.). The technical-economic system is 'insatiable' since its aim is not to be merely reasonably efficient and profitable but rather as efficient and profitable as possible. Emphasis is not only laid on productivity but on *increased* productivity. Furthermore, the system is 'one-sided' since it only has to do with a small part of what can be expected to interest the employees. And it is 'inexorable' in the sense that it is not in the interests of the system to keep as members those whose contribution falls short of what other persons render to the system. Even though one may not directly risk dismissal, the actual situation of competition is in itself a threat. It is a worry and a source of insecurity to be continually exposed to evaluation by one's superiors (pp. 72-73). These features of the system give rise to a feeling of stress and insecurity among the workers. But, at the same time, their benefit from membership of the technical-economic system is such that they do not want to leave it. This is their problem situation (see chap. 11, section I), and collective defence is their reaction to it.[3]

2. It was not denied that the factory and its employees *also* had certain interests in common.
3. In his study of the workers' views on professional and political issues, Lys-

If we compare this with the variables which I used earlier (section I), we can say that pressure for a steady increase in labour input and the unpleasantness and insecurity associated with being supervised are conditions against which workers have a *common interest* in defending themselves. Some of the hypotheses which Lysgaard (p. 186 et seq.) presents on 'problem conditions' for collective defence can be seen as special applications of the general proposition that the likelihood of collective behaviour – other things being equal – increases with the strength of the recipients' joint interests. This applies, inter alia, to his hypotheses (pp. 188-189) that we can expect a stronger worker collective the more unreliable and unpredictable the factory conditions are and the more illegitimate the workers consider the pressure on them to be (for example if, in the workers' opinion, the pressure is due to their superiors' personal interest in profit and their personal ambition). The hypothesis that the tendency to collective defence becomes stronger the more dependent the workers are on the factory (pp. 191-194) also coincides with this point of view. Dependence on the factory becomes less the more opportunities there are for the workers to transfer to new places of work of their own free will. This again depends upon several factors, among other things the job opportunities in the district, how specialized their skill is, their long-term obligations towards dependants, social and cultural conditions which promote or hinder mobility, etc.[4] On the other hand dependency increases with the risk of *being* dismissed. The threat of unemployment, or vivid memories of unemployment, are therefore factors which increase the need for collective defence.[5]

When discussing the dependence factor Lysgaard (pp. 192-193) also examines differences between men and women at work. He believes that women are less inclined to take refuge in collective defence because they are more strongly anchored to an actual or expected home situation and therefore feel less dependent on the factory than the men. This hypothesis finds support in studies of sex differences in occupational behaviour, see *Holter* (1970 pp. 149-150).

As mentioned above (section I) the fact that individual recipients

note 3 (cont.)
> gaard (1965 pp. 99-101 and pp. 119 ff.) has presented data which suggest that the collective may also serve as a defence against the national association of trade unions.
4. See March and Simon (1958 p. 100 et seq.) on factors which influence the workers' tendency to change job.
5. But they can also increase the *risk* involved in opposing the management, see below.

have strong *particular interests* can weaken their inclination to act collectively. In this connection *Lysgaard's* (1961 p. 196) remarks on prospects of promotion are of relevance. His hypothesis is that the greater chance employees reckon they have of moving out of the ranks of the subordinates, the less suitable will the conditions be for collective action. For this reason he expects to find weaker collectives among white-collar workers than among manual workers. This harmonizes well with the general assumption made above, because promotion is an advantage which an employee gains at the expense of others. Interest in promotion is therefore a particular interest which must be handled individually. Besides, chances of being promoted reduce the importance of joint interests by creating a feeling that 'being in the same boat' and being exposed to the same pressures is only a temporary affair.

Lysgaard (1961 p. 83 et seq.) also points to the significance of disposing of *means of influence which are suited to collective use.* In the factory where he made his study the means of power primarily used by the workers were restriction of input and withholding information which might be of importance to the management's supervision. Individual actions of these kinds would have had no effect but the strategy was effective since all workers co-operated. The same applied to the most severe threat which the workers had at their disposal, viz., to go on strike. Because of common participation, these means of power not only became more effective but also more *legitimate* and therefore easier to use. To limit one's effort at work and avoid the control of one's superiors can appear virtuous when it is done for the sake of solidarity and together with one's fellow workers, but when the individual behaves like this in order to promote his own interests it has more the appearance of laziness, slackness or unruliness. Lysgaard (p. 84) expresses this by saying that the collective not only furnishes the employee with power but also with honour.

As mentioned above (section I), it is not in itself sufficient that the recipients dispose of means of influence which are suited to collective use. They must also have the capacity to make use of these means, i.e. they must be able to *cooperate* with and *subordinate themselves* to others. I mentioned several factors which can be of significance in this connection. Some of these factors are also taken into account by Lysgaard but they are there systematized differently – into the categories 'interaction conditions' and 'identification conditions' (see especially p. 146 et seq. and p. 197 et seq.). I make no comment here on these parts of the theory, but will return later to certain aspects of them when discussing other allocation systems.

372

Lysgaard touches only lightly on the *risk* involved in opposing the factory management. He suggests (p. 195, footnote 1) that the hypothesis that the strength of the worker collective increases with the workers' feeling of insecurity applies only within certain limits of insecurity. When the limits are exceeded, the risk involved in collective action can be too great. In my opinion he should have laid more stress on the question of risk. Many of the factors Lysgaard mentions in his discussion of 'problem conditions' (see above) can work in both directions. They increase the workers' joint interest in establishing a collective defence but, at the same time, increase the risk of doing so. Obvious examples of this are arbitrariness on the part of the factory management and danger of dismissal and unemployment.

Lysgaard takes into account the fact that *external forces* can affect the factory management and its employees so that the tendency to act collectively is either encouraged or discouraged. Among other things he mentions (pp. 190-191 and p. 244 et seq.) that the ideological and political climate in the society concerned can be of importance. The stronger the social impact of technical-economic ideals, the more difficult it becomes to defend oneself against them. Nationalistic feelings of obligation to increase the country's production capacity can also help weaken worker collectives. On the other hand, factors which divide citizens, for example political controversies and class consciousness, can promote the formation of collectives. Whether or not there is a strong and united trade union movement in the country concerned is, of course, also important. Both as a source of ideological support and as a powerful ally in possible conflict, the national trade union movement can give the workers of an individual enterprise a strong basis for defending themselves collectively against the management. This is particularly true if the movement is class conscious and militant. If it has become more concerned in the promotion of common national interests (for instance, peaceful industrial relations and increased productivity) – as has been the case in Norway during the last generation – ideological support for worker collectives will be more conditional. Moreover, the *need* for collective defence inside the individual factory is less when many of the workers' interests (for instance, issues connected with wages, working hours and holidays) are taken care of by the trade unions. There are also other important institutional factors which Lysgaard does not mention as, for instance, legislation which restricts hours of work and which provides protection from arbitrary dismissal, government intervention in labour conflicts, social insurance and pension schemes etc. By mitigating the 'inflexibility' and 'insatiability' of the technical-economic system, such social measures can reduce the workers' need for collective defence. But at the same time they help to reduce the danger of opposing the factory management.

The ideological and institutional conditions of collective defence can differ widely between one country and another and from one epoch to the next. It is wise to make allowance for this when evaluating the results of research in different countries. *Lysgaard* (1961 pp. 228-230) gives as an example an American and a Norwegian study which indicate that the trend to collective defence was stronger among the Norwegian workers than among their American counterparts.[6]

We have no study of white-collar workers comparable to that made by Lysgaard of manual workers, but data are available which suggest that the trend towards collective defence – at any rate in Norway – is not so strong among them. *Holter* (1970) found in her study of sex, age and professional differences for 1000 employees in various Oslo enterprises, that the white-collar workers were more inclined than the manual workers to identify themselves with the enterprise (tables 6.28 and 34) and were less inclined to act collectively (table 6.37). Nor is membership of trade unions so high among white-collar workers as among manual workers, see *Fivelsdal* (1964).

These differences are probably connected with the fact that white-collar workers have largely lacked the politically based class consciousness and ideology of solidarity from which workers' collectives have derived their strenght. But differences in the manual workers' andt he white-collar workers' duties and placing in the structure of the enterprise certainly also play a role. As a rule the chances of promotion from a low to a higher position are much greater for office staff than for manual workers (see *Aubert* 1974, pp. 120-121). This means that the individual interests are stronger (see earlier in this section and *Lysgaard* 1961 p. 196). A white-collar worker can gain more than a manual worker by ingratiating himself with his superiors, by trying to appear more skillful than his colleagues, and by generally adopting a more competitive attitude, which impedes collectivization. Furthermore, white-collar workers constitute a less homogeneous group than other workers since there is greater differentiation between them with regard to salary, status and kinds of work. No simple dichotomy can be made between

6. L. Coch and J.R.P. French, jr., Overcoming Resistance to Change (Human Relations, 1948, 1, pp. 512-532) and J.R.P. French, jr., Joachim Israel and Dagfinn Ås, Samarbeid i industribedriften – et eksperiment med øket medvirkning fra arbeidernes side (Oslo 1957). See also Lipset, Political Man, p. 267 et seq. on the differences between European and American workers.

superiors and subordinates. This helps to make their common interests weaker and less visible and it can impede the development of fellow feeling (see Lysgaard pp. 201-202). The office staff have also less opportunity of undisturbed mutual communication at their place of work than have manual workers, and they have fewer chances of avoiding contact with the management since the density of superiors is usually higher in an office than in a workshop (Lysgaard p. 205).

Another factor of importance is that many white-collar workers play a double role, as was pointed out in chap. 9, section IX. At the same time as they themselves are recipients in an allocation system, they make decisions on behalf of the distributor and therefore tend to identify themselves with his goals.[7] This tendency becomes greater, the higher their position in the enterprise. Nevertheless, they may have a need to protect themselves against the technical-economic system's 'insatiability' and 'exorability' (see *Lysgaard* p. 85 et seq.). But it is difficult for them to base their defence on norms and values which conflict with the distributor's aims. Even so, certain forms of collective defence may take place, but white-collar workers must employ other means of influence and do not have the same strength as manual workers. I will return to this in section III.

In some of the allocation systems which were earlier discussed, there is little or no tendency among the recipients to operate collectively against the distributor.

In the correctional institution which *Mathiesen* (1965) studied (see chap. 11, section VII) there was little unity among the inmates (loc. cit. p. 122 et seq.). In spite of the fact that they were free to associate with each other, it was remarkable how many kept to themselves. And the groups which did form where not stable. There were norms that they should be loyal and fair towards each other, for example that they should not inform on fellow inmates, that they should not steal from each other, not cheat etc. But these norms were often broken. And the inmates did not trust each other and suspected illoyalty more frequently

7. Norwegian Gallup Polls – cited by Aubert, 1974, pp. 138-139 – shows that white-collar workers are more inclined than manual workers to regard their job as a satisfying occupation rather than just an opportunity of making money, and that good relations with the management are more important to them than good comradeship with their fellow employees. There are also a greater number of supporters of wage differentiation and promotion according to qualifications among white-collar workers than among manual workers. – American investigations show similar differences, see Berelson and Steiner (1964 pp. 411-412).

than was justified. Homosexuality and other types of sexual deviance, which most of the inmates despised but often suspected each other of, helped to increase disruption.[8]

The lack of unity among the inmates also affected their relationship to the institution (loc. cit. p. 136 et seq.). They had no leader who could speak on behalf of all of them. And there were no generally accepted norms as to how to behave towards the staff. Among other things, there was no norm which forbade inmates from having personal contact with the guards – as there is in some American prisons which have been investigated ('never talk to a screw !').[9] Nor had the inmates any common ideology which could be pitted against that of the institution.

How can this lack of unity and lack of ability to operate collectively be explained ? There is no doubt that the inmates had strong *common interests*. They were all dependent on the institution and could not leave it of their own free will. And they complained about largely the same things, viz., lack of predictability, the (in their opinion) arbitrary decisions that were taken, and the illegitimate pressure to which they felt exposed in the institution. Their problem situation, then, had much in common with that of the workers in *Lysgaard's* (1961) study. The inmates certainly had a subordinate status in the system and there was hardly any identification with the distributor's aims. In addition, they had every opportunity for unimpeded interaction and they belonged to a category which was outwardly homogeneous and clearly different from the staff. It would seem, therefore, that what *Lysgaard* (1961 pp. 197 ff.) calls interaction and identification conditions for formation of collectives must have been present.[10]

---

8. Nor did there seem to be much unity between the inmates in the Oslo County Jail investigated by Galtung (1959, 2). Galtung (pp. 133-135) mentions, among other things, that if anyone was suspected of being an informant, this could result in dramatic conflict. 3/5 of the inmates compared with only 1/4 of the staff, claimed that there were informants – something which perhaps indicates that these inmates also suspected each other of illoyalty more often than was justified.

   With regard to psychiatric hospitals, both Løchen's (1965) Norwegian investigation and Goffman's (1961) American study indicate relatively little solidarity between the patients, see especially Goffman, p. 60 et seq. and p. 299 et seq.
9. See Mathiesen (1965 p. 137) and the investigations mentioned there.
10. It is true that Lysgaard only claims to explain formation of workers' collectives (loc. cit. p. 122 et seq.). But it is still interesting to note the characteristics which the industrial plant and the correctional institution have in common, cf. Mathiesen (1965 pp. 218-219).

However, the inmates did not have such a good supply of *means of influence suited to collective use* as did the workers. In particular, they were not in a position to exert power by regulating their counter-services (*Mathiesen* pp. 142-145 and pp. 220-221). The inmates could achieve nothing by restricting their labour input. The institution was not dependent upon their production. The counter-services which really meant something to the institution were the conduct, improvement and rehabilitation of the inmates. But *these* counter-services did not so easily lend themselves to planned regulation by the inmates. This particularly applies to rehabilitation. It is difficult to imagine that the inmates would be able to develop norms as to how much they should be willing to allow themselves to be rehabilitated or that they would be able, jointly, to threaten retention of this counter-service if they were not given what they demanded.[11] The inmates may to a larger extent be able to control their own conduct in the institution, but neither is this easy to regulate collectively and strategically.[12]

Regulation of counter-services is not the only means of power which can be employed collectively. But some of the other possibilities (for example, to revolt) involve great risk and give small hope of gain. And other alternatives (for example, to withhold information or renounce individual advantages) demand a degree of self-discipline and ability to adapt oneself to a collective which the inmates in the correctional institution did not possess. The individual inmate there saw no reason why he should sacrifice any of his special interests out of consideration for his fellow prisoners, because he did not trust their loyalty and had little respect for their judgment. And unity in itself had no positive value to them since they did not get along well together and each one regarded it as more or less degrading to be classed together with the others. In other words, they lacked mutual respect and fellow-feeling.

---

11. That they threaten to do this *individually*, is more likely. An inmate could, for example, say : 'I have been so wrongly treated that I no longer care when I get out', or 'I will at least make sure that I come here for a *good reason* next time'. But it is seldom that such threats are taken seriously.
12. The fact that the inmates' contribution to the system is of this nature does not, in itself, exclude the possibility of a united community within the institution. But this would have to be a 'therapeutic community' in which the staff and the inmates *together* tried to realize a common goal. In other words, it would have to be an allocation system in which the recipients accepted the goals of the distributor and trusted in his ability to realize these. What I have tried to make clear is that the inmates' contribution to the system does not provide any useful basis for solidarity directed *against* the institution.

Mathiesen (pp. 129-136 and pp. 221-227) points to several possible causes of this. Among other things, he stresses that criminals are regarded as a category to which it is shameful to belong. Criminals themselves can produce nothing in defence of this. They have no common ideology and largely accept society's conception of what it means to be a criminal. It is therefore natural for the individual offender to try to protect his self-respect by denying that he has anything in common with the others. This, for instance, can lead to strong condemnation of other categories of criminals than the one to which he belongs or to attempts to convince himself and other people that he is no 'real' or 'typical' criminal.

The importance of these factors becomes clear when ordinary prisons are compared with *political prisons and concentration camps,* where the prisoners' ability to protect themselves through collective behaviour can be considerably greater. This does not apply, of course, under all circumstances. The pressure which the individual is exposed to in a concentration camp can be so overwhelming that all opposition is broken. But, other things being equal, the possibilities of defence will be much greater when the prisoners bring a common ideology with them from outside which is in opposition to the prison's. This provides a basis for mutual respect and fellow feeling so that the individual is willing to sacrifice and to risk something for the common good. And it will be possible to employ effectively such means of defence as, for instance, withholding information and the division of benefits and burdens in a manner which reduces total stress.

Differences between the personality of political prisoners and of other prisoners can, of course, play some role. But the kind of person who is drawn into an activity also depends on the ideologies which form the basis of this activity.

The ideology which prisoners bring with them does not have to be a very worthy one, from the point of view of outsiders, in order that it be a source of strength. If, within a criminal milieu, there is a well developed system of anti-social norms and values, this might be sufficient basis for collective defence in a prison. Various investigations (a.o., *Sykes* 1958) indicate that there is a more marked tendency to formation of collectives in American than in Norwegian prisons. As *Mathiesen* (1965 p. 142, cf. p. 223) suggests, this may be because the criminal milieu outside prison in the USA is better organized and probably has a clearer anti-social value orientation than in Norway.

Let us, finally, take a quick look at some of the other allocation systems which were discussed in Chapter 11, section IX.

378

Collective defence plays only an insignificant role in the relationship between *children and parents*. Children can, in certain situations, behave in collective opposition to their parents, for example by refraining from telling tales about each other or by mutually supporting each other's claims and wishes. But my experience, as far as it goes,[13] shows that brothers and sisters tend to regard one another as competitors for their parents' favours rather than as allies in opposition to them. This applies especially when the children are small. The inclination to be allies often increases with the age of children, but even with older children it is comparatively easy to break down their solidarity.

This fits well with the theoretical points of view outlined in section I above. Children have certainly a great need for defence because of their helplessness and dependency on their parents. And although the children in a family partly have competitive interests, they are in many ways 'in the same boat'. But solidarity in opposition to their parents is not likely to afford any effective protection, because the means of influence available to children are by and large better suited to individual than to collective use. For instance, children can achieve quite a lot by individually appealing to their parents' compassion or goodwill or to their sense of justice. But they have few possibilities of regulating their counter-services collectively, as can workers in a factory. The counter-services of children – e.g., to please their parents and to make progress – are very important but hard to manipulate collectively. And besides this, at least as long as they are small, children have no independent ideology on which they can base their opposition. Attempts at collective defence will therefore be most likely to occur when parents ask their children to break some norm which they have themselves taught the children (for instance, 'Don't tell tales !').

Concerted opposition from the *citizens of a country vis-à-vis the government* is difficult to imagine other than in special situations, such as when a foreign power has taken over control. In normal circumstances it is difficult to imagine anything which could bind together all interest groups in a manner which would incite them to make a common stand against the government.

It is more likely that a particular group or category of citizens act collectively in order to promote their interests – perhaps in competition with other groups having opposing interests. Certain forms of this kind of collective action are very normal. For example, we have political

---

13. As already explained, I base myself here on unsystematic observation and have no systematic study to support my views.

parties and industrial federations which represent their own interest groups. But collectivity is seldom so well established that the individual considers it illoyal to his fellow class or party members to go directly to the authorities if he believes he can achieve something for himself in this way. In such cases, too, there may be some sign of collectivism inasmuch as the group may have a common ideology which will influence individual argumentation. For example, an individual may argue with ideas of justice which do not refer to his own situation but to the distribution of values between the different social classes. By stressing such ideological points of view, individual recipients can to some extent support each other even though they make separate claims.

However, those forms of collective action which presuppose that the individual is willing to renounce important interests of his own for the sake of a common goal are rare, at any rate in Western society. Even in those sectors where political views are strongly opposed to each other, for example with regard to economic regulation of commerce and industry, there is often little solidarity between those who are affected by government measures. For instance, it is seldom that a businessman does not snap up some advantage which the authorities offer him (for example, a licence, a permit, an increased export quota etc.) out of concern that this will undermine solidarity in the private sector. Individual groups in the private sector in Norway, among these the farmers, have occasionally tried to employ collective means of power (for example, delivery strikes in order to influence public decisions on prices and subsidies) but these have so far had little effect. Many reasons can be found why those in the private sector have not formed such strong collectives in their relations to the government as, for instance, workers have done in their relationship to industrial concerns. One important factor is that they have relatively highly competitive individual interests and have looked for support to an ideology where conceptions of private ownership and free competition emphasize the significance of individual interests. In addition to this, the external circumstances do not favour co-operation to the same extent as they do at the manual worker's place of work.

III. CONNECTIONS BETWEEN CONCEPTIONS OF JUSTICE AND
TENDENCIES TO OPERATE COLLECTIVELY

I will first look at the significance of justice as a basis for recipient solidarity and opposition to the distributor. After this I will discuss some of the consequences which collective action can have for conceptions of justice and for the tendency to argue in terms of justice.

Attitudes to questions of distribution tell something of the feeling which the persons concerned have towards each other. Some attitudes to such issues indicate strong positive feelings, for example if someone says : 'It doesn't matter how things are divided between us since everything of mine is yours and all of your things are mine' ; or if someone supports the idea that the others should have as much as possible even when this is to his disadvantage. On the other hand, there are individuals wo try to get as much as they can at the expense of other people. Those who support the idea of equal distribution lie somewhere between these two extremes. They have arrived at a compromise between consideration for themselves and for others. Similarly, balance in an exchange relationship represents the middle way between the pursuit of gain and what is philanthropical (see chap. 4, section V, the text relating to notes 15 and 16), and retributive justice in a punishment relationship represents the middle way between unrestrained revenge and forgiveness.

Because justice occupies this middle position, it can, as a stage in a development process, represent a station on the line from inner dissension to fraternal feelings within a group of people. Those who are prepared to base their dealings with each other on distributive and retributive justice have reached a certain stage of mutual understanding. Although there may be many conflicts between them about what is balanced and what is equal, they have at least reached a kind of abstract consensus of opinion on how they should adapt to each other. They are thereby in a better position to operate collectively in order to promote joint interests than if a purely competitive spirit had prevailed between them.

At the same time as the ideology of justice provides some basis for unity inwards, it supplies arguments which can be used outwards – for instance, with the distributor. And there are many ways in which these arguments can be used collectively. Several recipients can support each other's claims for retributive justice, or they can collectively demand equal distribution. They can also claim justice for the group or category of individuals to which they belong. They can, for example, demand that it be treated equally with other recipient groups or that balance be established in their joint relationship to the distributor. There is no necessary connection between favouring just distribution within a group and supporting justice in the relationship between that group and others. But if one is accustomed to argue in terms of justice within the group the likelihood is thereby increased of similar argumentation being used outwards.

As mentioned in section I, conceptions of justice are not among the means of influence which are best suited to collective use. But when, over a period of time, the recipients gradually change from individual to collective defence it may come naturally to them to keep to the manner of argument with which they are familiar. In this respect the ideology of justice fits well ; and it is sufficiently flexible for the point of reference to be easily shifted from the individual to the group. Also, it makes only moderate demands on the individual's spirit of self-sacrifice and unselfishness. It is therefore an ideology on the basis of which it is possible to co-operate, even when the conditions for co-operation are not the best.

Moreover, the fact that arguments of justice have a moral basis (see chap. 11, section VIII) is important. It helps to make demands more legitimate, to provide the necessary courage to oppose the distributor even when this involves a risk, and to furnish the endurance to carry through a prolonged struggle.

Hägerström has written an essay (1939 p. 121 et seq.) in which he strongly emphasizes the significance to the underprivileged of being able to base their struggle for better living conditions on a foundation of justice. 'How can it be possible for a revolutionary party to work up the necessary enthusiasm for its struggle if it does not believe in the justice of this ?' he asks (p. 138). It is true that the suffering of the under-privileged is in itself a basis for desires and demands. But this is not sufficient, Hägerström maintains, and he accounts for this by saying (pp. 139-140) :

'The explanation is this, that pure exploitation of other people, even those who are slaves, is not possible in the long run without the help of the idea of the ruling class's own absolute right. Only through impregnation of their own divine superiority into the consciousness of the downtrodden is the opposition of the latter so moulded that there is no longer need to fear any revolt. Who will fight against the Gods when he feels himself just a feeble human being ? When an under-privileged class revolts, it is first essential that it get rid of these psychological chains which weigh more heavily than all other fetters. This takes place through acceptance of the idea that everyone, in some respect, has the same divine dignity.'

I am not sure how much these ideas are worth. But it is often at least a sign of increased courage that someone changes from entreating a favour to demanding his right. And in many instances this can be the introduction to greater unity within a group and more effective vindication of its interests. Among the many examples which can be

382

mentioned are the human rights declaration of the French Revolution and the American Declaration of Independence and the civil rights campaign in the United States.

When a number of recipients – for some reason or other – are gradually welded closer together, this may have certain *effects* on their conceptions of justice.

It seems reasonable to assume that ideas of what is just in inter-recipient relations will gradually be less influenced by self-assertion and egoism as the feeling of fellowship increases. For instance, the centre of gravity in conceptions of equality may shift from the idea that one should *oneself* have (at least) as much as the others, to the idea that the *others* should also not be treated unfairly, to the idea that one should oneself not have *more* than the others. And as regards retribution, the emphasis may change from getting what one has a right to oneself, to other people also getting what they are entitled to, and to being sure that one fulfils one's own obligations.

Other changes can also take place. Benefits and burdens, which before were regarded as individual, can gradually come to be accepted as belonging to the group. And this may mean that allocation points of view replace views of exchange. If the recipients attach great importance to avoiding internal conflict, they may also tend to use more object-oriented and specific criteria of equality. And finally, there is the possibility of more frequent use of those types of conceptions of justice which do not have the individual as their point of reference but rather the recipient group. However, whether this is likely to happen depends upon the recipients' problem situation. If the most important thing is for them all to get as much as possible, it will be natural for them to base themselves on comparisons between their own and other groups. But if it is more important to find security and to avoid arbitrary decisions on the part of the distributor, it is more likely that equality between individuals will be demanded.

As the degree of recipient solidarity increases, new features will appear. Among other things, there will be forces which *counteract the use of arguments of justice*. The result may be that such arguments are partially replaced by other means of influence.

Firstly, increased unity among the recipients will make it possible for them to employ means of power which require a greater degree of self-discipline and individual sacrifice than argumentation based on justice. For instance, they can collaborate in regulating the extent of their counter-services and can control what the distributor obtains in the way of information. They have perhaps other possibilities – for example, through political action – of putting pressure on the distributor. These means of power are often more effective than arguments based on justice and even though they may not completely replace this they can reduce its importance.

Secondly, there is not only power but also honour in being united. The fact that recipients support a common cause helps to make their demands more legitimate. And their feeling of belonging to a fellow-ship from which they obtain security and self-respect makes it easier for them to adjust to the conflict situation they find themselves in when they oppose the distributor. In other words, the ideology of solidarity can take over some of the moral functions of the ideology of justice. Even though the two ideologies do not exclude each other, they can make each other more or less superfluous.

Thirdly, development towards solidarity can bring in its train norms and values which directly counteract the recipients' use of certain types of arguments based on justice. *Lysgaard's* (1961) study of the workers' collective affords illustrative examples. The collective reacted strongly against individual workers who tried to 'curry favour' with the manage-ment. The worker should not in any way attract attention to himself ; nor should he give the impression that he does more than his fellow workers or that he is at all better than they (op. cit. pp. 41 ff.). The col-lective also reacted to those who aspired to higher jobs (op. cit. pp. 21-23). It has already been pointed out that such norms help strengthen the collective since they inhibit the individual's inclination to promote his own special interests. But at the same time they make it difficult to appeal to retributive justice in the relationship between factory and in-dividual worker. When the value of the individual's services is not to be emphasized, it is not possible to argue that the counter-services rendered him should be relative to his own services. In Lysgaard's study, the same complex of norms helped to make less relevant the question of distributive justice among individual workers. For instance, one of the demands made on the management was that praise for good work was not to be given to the individual worker but to the whole body of work-ers. This value, in other words, should not be distributed. The fact that workers were expected to restrict their contact with superiors to the absolute minimum, helped to uphold this norm (op. cit. pp. 41 ff. and pp. 52-53). Generally speaking, the management was unable to allocate such values as praise, encouragement and warnings to the individual worker. And there was therefore no question of just distribution of these values.

The workers preferred as strict an equality as possible when it came

384

to the values which were to be distributed, for instance wages and effort. As already mentioned, the informal rules were that everyone should keep a suitable tempo at work, not do too much nor too little; there should be the same pay for the same work (op. cit. p. 50), and the wage should be adjusted to the average and not to the cleverest worker (p. 42). These claims for equality were sometimes argued in terms of justice but one gets the impression that consequence-oriented arguments played a more important part. One of the workers said, for example (p. 50): 'A few rates of pay are best. That is the most just'. But immediately he added: 'It's the best way to avoid jealousy'. The fact that he attached importance to this was obviously because envy weakens the worker unity which the collective aims to maintain. Other considerations of collective utility were also advanced in support of claims for equality. Among other things it was argued that wage differentiation according to input would push the tempo of work up to a disagreeable extent: 'The one who is over-zealous should not receive more pay – or people will vie with each other to the point of exhaustion' (p. 50). The fact that ideas of utility completely or partially take over from ideas based on justice as reasons for equal distribution is a natural consequence of collectivism. It has a more obvious utility value for the collective than for the individual that everything be divided equally among recipients. And the collective advantages would not be fully realized if equality was made a right for the individual because there would then be more room for conflict over what is equal.

Holter's (1970 pp. 147-150) study of sex differences in occupational behaviour also provides some support for the assumption that orientation towards justice becomes weaker when the collective is strong. She found that with both manual and white-collar workers there was a greater tendency among the men than the women to prefer collective conduct in relation to the employer and that the men were less justice oriented than the women.

Demanding justice for the collective, e.g., claiming that the group or category to which one belongs should receive as good treatment as other groups or categories, is more in harmony with solidarity than demanding justice for the individual. But all kinds of arguments of justice can be made more or less unnecessary when recipients who are united are able to use other means of influence and seek strength in other ideologies. Furthermore, the inclination to use or to avoid using the one type of argument of justice can spread to a use or avoidance of the other.

In this and the previous chapter I have suggested the possibility of a

385

development which can be summarized as follows : a group of recipients[14] at first operate individually in their relations with the distributor and restrict themselves to appealing to his goodwill or compassion. Gradually they begin to criticize him and to make demands on
him which they argue, among other things, with ideas of justice. Their
operations gradually change from being individual to being collective.
An ideology of justice can help to initiate this process but by the time
solidarity between the recipients has reached a certain stage, arguments
based on justice tend to be replaced by other means of influence. Seen
as a whole, a main feature of this development is that the strength of
the recipients (in relation to the distributor) gradually increases as a
result of increased unity. Another feature is that the recipients change
from seeking their support in norms and values which the distributor
(and perhaps only he) accepts, to basing themselves on a more generally
accepted normative foundation (as, for instance, justice), and from there
adopting an ideology which is their own (and which is perhaps unacceptable to the distributor). These two features of the development
are connected because the weaker the position of the recipients the more
dependent they are on finding a basis in norms and values which the
distributor accepts. Even when they obtain more power they may still
need ideological support but they no longer have to stick to the distributor's system of values. In Figure 1 the connection between these features
is suggested by the shading of the likely combinations. The line of
development which has been described above is illustrated by an arrow.

I do not claim that this development from 'weak' to 'strong' forms of
defence will always take place. The opposite can also occur. And whichever direction development takes, it may follow paths other than those
sketched above. It is also possible that the system becomes stabilized at
one or other of the stages mentioned.

Among other things, there is a possibility that collective use of arguments based on justice will become consolidated as a permanent pattern
of recipient behaviour. According to what has been said earlier, this is
most likely in allocation systems where recipient solidarity lies on a
moderate level – one which is higher than that found by *Mathiesen*
(1965) in the correctional institution but lower than that of *Lysgaard's*
(1961) workers. This will often apply to *white-collar workers*. I have

14. I do not assume that the same individuals are recipients throughout the
    period of development. Such a period of development can very well last for
    several generations. But the *system* of allocation is assumed to be the same.

Figure 1

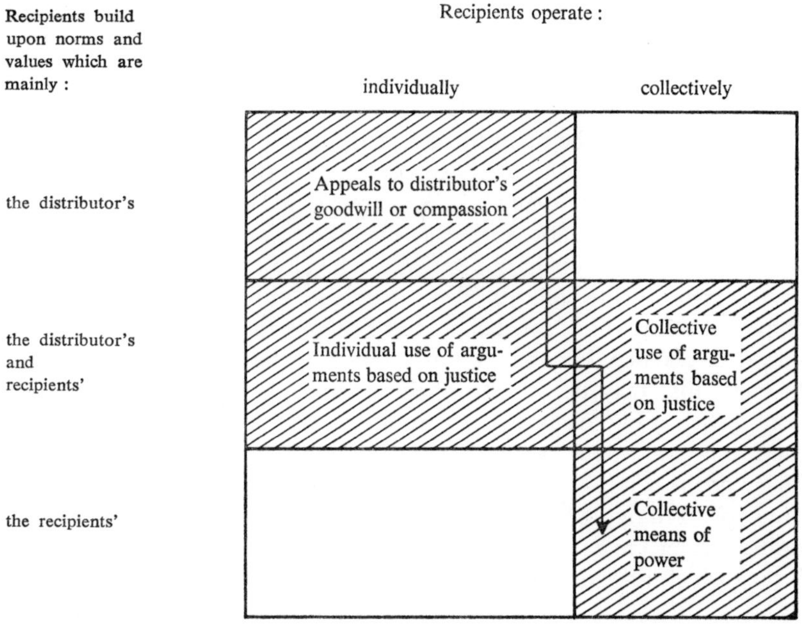

Recipients build upon norms and values which are mainly :	Recipients operate :	
	individually	collectively
the distributor's	Appeals to distributor's goodwill or compassion	
the distributor's and recipients'	Individual use of arguments based on justice	Collective use of arguments based on justice
the recipients'		Collective means of power

above (II) mentioned some reasons why there is usually not such a strong tendency among white-collar workers to fortify themselves in collective defence against the employer as there is among manual workers. Among other things, I mentioned that the white-collar workers are more inclined to identify themselves with the enterprise. It is therefore difficult for them to base their defence on norms and values which conflict with the enterprise's goals. However, their problem situation has much in common with that of manual workers. White-collar workers also need protection from arbitrary treatment and too high pressure of work. And their common interests may be strong enough to give rise to some degree of collective activity. Under these circumstances it becomes appropriate to take recourse to an ideology of justice. This can furnish some of the protection which is needed without the office workers being obliged to oppose the aims of the enterprise. In fact, of course, demands for justice can impede realization of the goals of increased production and maximum profits, for example, but because the values involved lie on different levels both sets can be supported without any evident self-contradiction.

Many white-collar workers play the double role mentioned in Chapter 9, section IX : they are recipients in the 'internal' allocation system (which includes their own pay and working conditions) but they operate on behalf of the distributor in the 'external' system (towards clients or customers). In such instances it is possible that the manner of reasoning used in one allocation system can spread to the other. For this reason, office workers may be more liable to base their defence on principles of justice when the external system is justice-oriented than when, for example, it is profit-oriented. When the external system is imbued with ideas of justice it is also very easy for office workers to combine their own defence based on justice with their loyalty to the distributor.

As regards white-collar workers in private enterprises, I know of no empirical data which can tell us much about their use of justice as a means of defence. For the reasons which have been given I am inclined to guess that they use it extensively but that there can be large variations between one occupational sector and another. On the other hand, there is a good deal of information about Norwegian civil servants to be found in committee reports, reports from wage negotiations, discussions concerning appointments and discharges etc. These indicate a rather strong tendency to argue collectively in terms of conceptions of justice which are based on object-oriented and specific criteria of equality.

This tendency can be seen in connection with appointments and dismissals. If the authorities appoint an applicant whom they consider (on the basis of diffuse and person-oriented criteria) best for the position, this will often be criticized if another applicant who ranks higher with regard to such specific criteria as seniority and exams is by-passed. To have a person removed from his post on the grounds of a diffuse and person-oriented evaluation which suggests that he is poorly suited to the work, is even more difficult. This is partly due to statute regulations, which go a long way to meet civil servants' demands for protection from arbitrary and unjust discharge or dismissal. But in addition, it has also proved to be difficult in practice to make use of the opportunities of removing civil servants which the law has left open.

Similar conditions apply with regard to the settlement of salaries. The government has not been able to follow a flexible wage and salary policy which could be aimed at attracting skilled persons to sectors where there is especial need for them. Nearly all wages and salaries are fixed by wage regulations, and comparisons between the different types of positions are the centre of attention during most discussions and negotiations over these regulations. These comparisons – which are frequently based on conceptions of justice – mean that changes in one section of the regulations will quickly escalate a series of other changes, so that great care has to be taken when making any alteration.

As regards promotion within the civil service, the principle of seniority dominates. Advocates of efficiency have often objected to this principle and have maintained that greater weight should be attached to qualifications. Several government committees which have discussed the matter have adopted the same point of view. Statements to the effect that, in future, promotions should be made on the basis of qualifications, occur in, among other places, a report of 1949 from a committee on which several government Ministers sat. But on each occasion, the result has been hardly more than a declaration of principle. The authorities responsible for appointments have either made no serious attempt to break with the principle of seniority or they have had to give in to strong opposition.

IV. DISTRIBUTOR REACTION TO RECIPIENT BEHAVIOUR

When recipients try to improve or secure their position in any of the ways mentioned in this and the previous chapter, realization of the distributor's goals may be impeded. It is therefore likely that he will then make some counter-moves.

One course the distributor can follow is to try to *remove recipient motives* for opposition.[15] He can work upon the recipients in an attempt to make them identify themselves with his goals and to get them to have confidence in his ability to make the right decisions. He can also try to convince them that what happens within the allocation system is to their own good and that there is no reason for them to feel hard-pressed or threatened. The chances of implanting an attitude of acceptance into the recipients depend, among other things, on the distributor's goals. It seems reasonable to believe, for instance, that these chances are greater if his aim is to help, support, raise or educate them than if, for instance, it is to punish them. It is also of some importance how permanent and comprehensive the allocation system is, but there are here two factors which pull in different directions. On the one hand the distributor's possibilities of exerting influence will be greater the broader

15. See Whyte (1957) who gives a detailed description of those social and cultural factors in the United States which help create attitudes of acceptance to organized distributors.

and more enduring the contact he has with the recipients ; but, on the other hand, this increases the recipients' subordination and dependency and can thus give rise to a need for defence which is difficult to remove.

Another possibility is for the distributor to furnish the recipients with *counter-motives which make for resignation.* For instance, he may threaten reprisals if they dare to oppose him. Or he may try to get them to believe that it is wrong to attempt to improve their lot, because 'each has his proper place in life', or that it is useless to try because they will get nothing out of *him.* Anticipation of future reward – in this or the next life – for those who suffer now, can also encourage resignation.

In the third place, the distributor – instead of or as well as influencing the motives of the recipients – can try to limit their *opportunities* of exerting influence. There are counter-moves that the distributor can make to each of the means of influence that the recipients have at their disposal (see chap. 11, sections II and III).

If the recipients threaten to leave the allocation system, the distributor has several ways in which he can try to hinder this : walls around prisons, punishment for running away, desertion or truancy, restrictions preventing emigration, agreements dividing the market between competitors are all different examples. If the recipients ally themselves against the distributor, the latter can try to reinforce his position of power by, for example, seeking support elsewhere. For instance, an employers' organization may be established as a counter-weight to a trade union. And if the recipients threaten to withdraw their counter-services, the distributor can attempt to make himself independent of them by, for example, finding substitutes or by trying to establish a relationship with other recipients who offer their services at more reasonable terms.

Recipient attempts to regulate the supply of information can be met in various ways. The distributor can try to create the myth that it is no good keeping things a secret because 'father knows everything' and 'God is omni-present'. Or he can argue that honesty is a virtue and that it pays in the end. He can try to make himself independent of recipient information through instituting inspection and investigation or by using allocation principles which only require easily ascertained criteria.

Argumentation from the recipients can, of course, be met with counter-arguments but there are also other ways of safeguarding oneself. One possibility is to forbid argumentation as is sometimes done in the home, school or institution ('Don't answer back !') and in countries with an authoritarian government. A more subtle approach is to slant the discussion onto a track which is not dangerous to the distributor and is perhaps, simultaneously, disagreeable for the other party. *Løchen* (1965 p. 211 et seq.) gives some good illustrations of this in his description of 'the diagnostic culture' in the psychiatric hospital which he studied. Diagnoses and diagnostic categories were used in discussions about all kinds of questions both within the staff and between the staff and the patients. Demands, criticism and objections relating to conditions in the hospital were often – instead of taking the matter up for discussion – met by keeping to the person concerned and diagnosing him or her. The doctor, for instance, was 'authoritarian' when making decisions, the matron was 'rigid' and 'hysterical' when she demanded to know what use there could be in new projects, and the psychologist was 'sub-paranoid' when he doubted that the doctor was capable of understanding and utilizing his test results. Diagnosis was often used as a diversionary manoeuvre with the patient who protested against something. For example, he might get the answer that his protest was connected with his illness, that 'he was in a phase where it was difficult for him to accept his infantile impulses' etc. (pp. 220-221). In this way it was possible to avoid a discussion of the conditions which were the object of protest. It had the effect of social control because it became difficult for the patients to make any claim. They ran the risk of their demands and protests being turned against them, which would only contribute to further emphasizing how ill they were.

The distributor may also be able to avoid certain types of argumentation by preventing recipients from acquiring the necessary basis for it. An example which is of especial interest to us is when the distributor *limits the possibilities of internal contact and comparison between the recipients.* In this way he prevents them from obtaining material for argumentation in terms of justice and at the same time makes it more difficult for them to ally themselves against him.

The distributor can to some extent limit internal contact between recipients by negotiating separately with each of them. It is very usual for distributors to do this. When, for instance, the Norwegian Ministry of Finance prepares the fiscal budget, it has separate meetings with each of the other ministries. Similarly, banks, insurance companies and other commercial enterprises normally negotiate individually with each of their clients. And some parents have perhaps discovered that if they want to give something to one of their children which the others are not going to get, it is easiest to do this when the others are not present. Separate dealings with each individual recipient *can,* of course, have the purely practical aim of simplifying negotiations. But one often gets

391

the impression that *this* is not the only reason for splitting up negotiations : it can also have the purpose (or at any rate effect) of preventing criticism and claims based on comparisons and of discouraging alliances.

In many instances the distributor does not restrict himself to splitting up the negotiations but also takes good care that no person other than the recipient directly concerned is present and that as little information as possible leaks out about what has taken place. The obligation to maintain secrecy which the distributor imposes on himself, or which is imposed on him, plays a great role in government service, private enterprise and in professional practice, e.g., in the medical and juridical professions. This obligation is usually justified by saying that it protects the recipients (patients, clients and customers). And, of course, it does often do this. But the zeal and vigilance which are shown by many distributors with regard to their own secrecy suggest that it also serves to protect themselves.

In many cases it is impossible for the distributor to prevent the individual recipient from getting to know what others have received, because he often does not have the power to prevent them communicating with each other. Even so, he may have opportunities of counteracting their tendency to make comparisons – among other things by the way in which he describes and justifies the transfers. The objects which a distributor offers can often be characterized in several different ways. For example, crayons, drawing books, paints etc. given by parents to their children can sometimes be 'toys' and sometimes 'school things' ; edible things can sometimes be 'goodies' and sometimes 'food' or 'medicine'. In other fields, too, there are possibilities of differentiating and varying the description of what is offered so that comparisons become less relevant. And in the arguments which are provided, the special nature of the transfer in question or the special needs or qualifications of the recipient concerned can be stressed. The more individualization there is and the more the arguments vary from one time to another, the less comparable the transfers will be. But the distributor is often restricted in how far he can go because recipients will not always accept any differentiation or variation which he sees fit to make. And if the recipients first find some basis on which to make a comparison, individualization will then appear rather capricious.

Whilst comparability is of special importance as a basis for ideas of distributive justice, *predictability* can promote the formation of conceptions of retributive justice. If the recipients find that benefits are regularly transferred to them in certain types of situations, they will soon tend to believe that they have a *right* to these benefits when such situations crop up. For instance, a child to whom is given something each time he runs an errand will soon regard this as his right. If evils or burdens arrive regularly on certain occasions, this can similarly give rise to the idea that the distributor has no right to impose them on other occasions. One way, therefore, in which the distributor can maintain his freedom of action is to make his decisions unpredictable.[16]

But, for the distributor, individualization and unpredictability can be two-edged swords. Realization of his own aims sometimes recommends that to the distributor he base his transfers on general rules or principles and that he acquaint the recipients with these. This may be necessary if one of his goals is to teach the recipients how they should behave. Following rules or principles also helps to simplify decision processes and to reduce the unpleasantness and responsibility often involved in making decisions (see chap. 9, section VII). Furthermore, the recipients may need to look ahead and to have the opportunity to make comparisons. And their reactions to the distributor's attempts to refuse them this may cause him trouble.

However, there is another way in which the distributor can guard himself against the development of conceptions of justice which limit his freedom of decision. He can go to the other extreme of what has been mentioned and fix specific rules for his activity which meet the recipients' need for predictability but which, at the same time, are adapted to realization of his own goals. In this way he forestalls the recipients. Instead of waiting for *them* (or perhaps his own employees, see chap. 9, section IX) to develop a set of allocation norms which are poorly suited to promote his goals, he himself makes the rules beforehand. By satisfying the recipients' need for predictability in this manner (and his employees' need for simple decision-making criteria and reduced responsibility) he protects himself from the mobilization of defence attitudes which might be difficult for him to control. As mentioned earlier (chap. 9, section VIII) there may also be other advantages – particularly for organizations which act as distributors – in programming activity. But there can also be disadvantages due to reduced flexibility and adaptability in decision-making.

Even though there are many possibilities of counter-moves on the part

16. Unpredictability can in other connections also serve as a means of maintaining control. If, for instance, the distributor carries out inspection in order to obtain information on conditions which the recipients want to keep secret from him, it is important that the recipients do not have prior knowledge of when the inspection is to be made.

of the distributor, the result can be that he *wholly or partially gives in* to pressure from the recipients. Counter-moves are not always sufficiently effective. And even when they could be so if the distributor did everything in his power to get his own way, he may have reasons for showing moderation.

Firstly, a rational distributor will pay attention to the costs. The fact that the recipients are dissatisfied can, in itself, be a burden. It may give rise to friction and to conflict and sometimes also to an undermining of the distributor's authority (see *Homans* 1961, p. 293 et seq.). And by opposing his decisions, the recipients can also put other obstacles in his way. The counter-moves of which I have given examples above also cost something. They may cost time, trouble and money and may help to increase recipient dissatisfaction.

Secondly, when recipients defend their interests in a certain way this is not always a disadvantage to the distributor but may even have certain advantages. As *Lysgaard* (1961) points out, the workers' collective has that positive value for the industrial enterprise that the employees adapt themselves to the labour situation. Besides this, the collective helps to make conditions in the factory both clear-cut and predictable :

'A whole category of employees are socially organized through the workers' collective and one knows where one has them and can make one's arrangements accordingly. Even if one had free hands to plan an effective factory administration, one would want to treat people alike within certain categories. We have here a category which *wishes* to be treated alike and which behaves in accordance with this administratively clear-cut principle.' (Pp. 248-249.)

When the recipients support decision-making on the basis of principles of justice, this can also have its advantages for the distributor. If, for example, the recipients normally demand equality, the argument that one person cannot have individual attention can be useful to the distributor when he refuses requests for special favours.

Even when the advantages that the distributor has from recipient defence measures do not balance the disadvantages, they constitute items in the balance sheet which must be taken into account when evaluating whether or not it pays to neglect recipient claims. If the distributor is an organization, there may also be special advantages for the organization's employees in adapting their decision-making to recipient conceptions of justice (see chap. 9, section IX).

In the third place, pressure from the recipients may result in the distributor acquiring new knowledge or changing his norms or conceptions of value. A distributor who at first was only concerned to increase his own profits may, for instance, gradually begin to feel that it is a goal in itself to promote the comfort and well-being of his recipients, and for this reason may review his allocation principles. Or perhaps the distributor has always been concerned for the well-being of his recipients but gradually becomes better acquainted with what they need most and how help should be given to be as effective as possible. It is also possible that the distributor internalizes the allocation norms which the recipients support, for instance certain principles of distributive justice, and bases himself on these regardless of whether or not they conform with his own goals.

The factors which have been mentioned often go together, so that a distributor may partly absorb the ideas of the recipients and partly pay attention to them in order to avoid displeasure and conflict. Let us take as an example an employer who, because he is to cut down production or because he is rationalizing production, finds he must dismiss a number of his employees. From the point of view of efficiency he would prefer to dismiss those whom he considers the least qualified but, nevertheless, he chooses to follow the principle of seniority and dismiss first those who were most recently employed – without regard to qualifications. The reason why he does this may be partly because he knows that his employees are strongly in favour of the principle of seniority and that it would lead to disagreeable conflict if he did not follow their wishes. But as well as this, he may himself feel that it would be unfair to his old and deserving workers to show them the door. It is often impossible to know which of these motives plays the greater role.

As we have already seen, recipient argumentation based on justice has a good chance of evoking a response from the distributor since he too normally has conceptions of justice. It may well be that, in the beginning, he did not judge the allocation issues involved from the point of view of justice, or that *his* views differed from those of the recipients. But the joint ideological basis still affords a chance of reciprocal *rapprochement*. From the distributor's side this can mean that he partly adjusts the principles which he considers the most suitable for his purpose so that consideration for justice is to some extent met without completely losing sight of his goals. For example, an employer who would have preferred to make appointments on the basis of diffuse, overall ideas as to who was best suited, may fall back upon specific criteria of fitness (for instance age, education and experience) which are more in accordance with the recipients' conceptions of justice. Similarly, rewards and punishment which a distributor allocates with the intention of improving or educating the recipients, can to some extent be adapted to claims for justice without renouncing too much in terms of what serves the distributor's purpose.

I have so far mainly considered cases where there is some unity between the recipients – either because they operate collectively or because they maintain similar points of view. Together, they then constitute a power factor which the distributor cannot afford to ignore. If the recipients each pull in different directions, the situation is something else. Their activity can still affect the distributor's decisions, but then in different ways. In some instances the distributor may find that it pays to aggravate differences between the recipients. Perhaps he wants to play them off against each other in order to strengthen his own position of power. In other cases his efforts may be directed at finding a compromise. If, for instance, he is exposed to pressure from several recipients, each of whom separately demands as much as possible of the benefits he deals out, it may be that he takes the middle way and introduces one or another form of equal treatment. Although none of the recipients may be completely satisfied with this, it is perhaps the line of least resistance for the distributor. It is also a solution which may help cut down competition between the recipients, inter alia because it can then be argued that it is fair. In other words, in such instances the ideology of justice serves to protect the distributor from recipient cross pressures.

Bibliography

Adams, J. Stacy, Toward an Understanding of Inequity, *Journal of Abnormal and Social Psychology*, Vol. 67, 1963, pp. 422-436.

Adams, Stuart, Status Congruency as a Variable in Small Group Performance, *Social Forces*, Vol. 32, 1953, pp. 16-22.

Allardt, Erik, Grundläggande dimensioner i ett samhälles struktur (Basic dimensions of a society's structure), *Tidsskrift for samfunnsforskning*, 1965, pp. 235 ff.

Allen, Carleton Kemp, Justice and Expediency, in *Interpretations of Modern Legal Philosophies, Essays in Honor of Roscoe Pound*, N.Y. 1947, pp. 15 ff.

Andenaes, Johannes, *The General Part of the Criminal Law of Norway* (Engl. transl. by Thomas P. Ogle, S. Hackensack, N.J. 1965).

– General Prevention – Illusion or Reality, *Journal of Criminal Law and Criminology and Police Science*, Vol. 43, 1952, pp. 176-196.

– The General Preventive Effects of Punishment, *University of Pennsylvania Law Review*, Vol. 114, 1966, pp. 949-983.

– The Moral or Educative Influence of Criminal Law, *Journal of Social Issues*, Vol. 27, 1971, pp. 17-31.

Anderson, Bo and Zelditch, Morris jr., Rank Equilibration and Politics, *Archives Européennes de Sociologie*, 1964, pp. 112 ff.

Anners, Erik, *Äganderätt och handelsintresse* (Ownership and trade interests), Uppsala 1960.

Aristotle, *The Nicomachean Ethics*, with an English translation by H. Rackham, The Loeb Classical Library, London & N.Y. 1926.

Aubert, Vilhelm, *Priskontroll og rasjonering* (Price Control and Rationing), Oslo 1950.

– Chance in Social Affairs, *Inquiry*, 1959, No 1, pp. 1 ff., also in : *The Hidden Society*, Totowa, N.J. 1965.

– Competition and dissensus : two types of conflict and of conflict resolution, *The Journal of Conflict Resolution*, Vol. 7, 1963, pp. 26 ff.

– Rettferdighet i sosiologisk belysning (Justice in the light of sociology), *Tidsskrift for samfunnsforskning*, 1966, pp. 101 ff.

– Justice as a Problem of Social Psychology, *Archiv für Rechts- und Sozialphilosophie*, Vol. LVI, 1970, pp. 465 ff.

– Stratification, in : Natalie Rogoff Ramsöy, ed., *Norwegian Society*, forthcoming, Oslo 1974.

Barnard, Chester I., *The Function of the Executive*, Cambridge, Mass. 1938, 16th ed. 1964.

Barth, Fredrik, The Role of the Entrepreneur in Social Change in Northern Norway, *Årbok for Universitetet i Bergen, Humanistisk serie*, 1963, No. 3.
- *Models of Social Organization*, Royal Anthropological Occasional Paper No. 23, Glasgow 1966.
Barton, Allen, *Sociological and Psychological Problems of Economic Planning in Norway*, unpublished Ph. D. dissertation, N.Y. 1954.
Barton, Allen, and Mendlovitz, Saul, The Experience of Injustice as a Research Problem, *Journal of Legal Education*, Vol. 13, 1960, pp. 24 ff.
Bayerschmidt, Carl F., and Hollander, Lee M., *Njáls Saga*, English translation with introduction and notes, N.Y. 1955.
Bedau, Hugo A., Justice and Classical Utilitarianism, in Friedrich and Chapman, *Nomos VI, Justice*. 1963, pp. 284 ff.
Benoit-Smullyan, Emilie, Status, Status Types, and Status Interrelations, *American Sociological Review*, Vol. 9, 1944, pp. 151-161.
Bentham, Jeremy, *An Introduction to the Principles of Morals and Legislation*, Oxford 1789.
Bentzon, Agnete Weis, *Familie og aegteskab i Vestgrønland II* (Family and marriage in Western Greenland), mimeographed, Copenhagen 1963.
Bentzon, Fridolin Weis, *Den sardiske haevn* (The Sardinian revenge), mimeographed, Copenhagen 1967.
Berelson, Bernard, and Steiner, Gary A., *Human Behavior, An Inventory of Scientific Findings*, N.Y. 1964.
Bergler, Edmund, and Meerloo, Joost A.M., *Justice and Injustice*, N.Y. and London 1963.
Bergmann, Gustav, Purpose, Function, Scientific Explanation, *Acta Sociologica*, Vol. 5, 1961, pp. 225 ff.
Berlin, Isaiah, Equality as an Ideal, *Proceedings of the Aristotelian Society*, Vol. 56, 1955-56, pp. 301 ff., also in Olafson, 1961.
Bienenfeld, F.R., Justice, Aggression and Eros, *The International Journal of Psycho-analysis*, 1957, pp. 419 ff.
Blau, Peter M., *The Dynamics of Bureaucracy*, Chicago 1955.
- *Exchange and Power in Social Life*, N.Y. 1964.
Blaug, Mark, *Economic Theory in Retrospect*, Revised ed., Homewood, Ill. 1968.
Blegvad, Mogens, Equality, Utility, and Moral Rules, *Danish Yearbook of Philosophy*, 1964, pp. 23 ff.
Bodenheimer, Edgar, *Treatise on Justice*, N.Y. 1967.
Bohannan, Paul, Some Principles of Exchange and Investment among the Tiv, *American Anthropologist*, Vol. 57, 1955, pp. 60 ff.
- *Justice and Judgment among the Tiv*, London 1957.
Boulding, Kenneth E., *Conflict and Defence*, N.Y. 1962.
Brøgger, Jan, Conflict Resolution and the Role of the Bandit in Peasant Society, *Anthropological Quarterly*, 1968, pp. 228 ff.
- *Ressurser og status i en ungdomsgjeng* (Resources and status in a gang of youths), *Tidsskrift for samfunnsforskning*, 1968, pp. 19 ff.
Brunner, Emil, *Gerechtigkeit*, Zürich 1943.
Buchanan, James M., and Tullock, Gordon, *The Calculus of Consent*, Ann Arbor 1965.

Cahn, Edmond, *The Sense of Injustice*, N.Y. and London 1949.
- *The Moral Decision*, Bloomington, Indiana 1956.

Carlsson, Gøsta, Reflections on Functionalism, *Acta Sociologica*, Vol. 5, 1962, pp. 201 ff.

Caruso, Igor H., La notion de responsabilité et de justice immanente chez l'enfant, *Archives de psychologie*, Vol. XXIX, Neuchâtel 1943, pp. 113 ff.

Castberg, Frede, *Problems of Legal Philosophy*, Revised ed., Oslo and London 1957.

Chapman, John W., Justice and Fairness, in Friedrich and Chapman, *Nomos VI, Justice*, 1963.

Christie, Nils, Changes in Penal Values, *Scandinavian Studies in Criminology*, Vol. 2, Oslo and London 1968, pp. 161 ff.

Cohen, John, *Chance, Skill, and Luck*, Penguin Books, London 1960.

Coleman, James S., *The Adolescent Society*, N.Y. 1961.

Dahlstrøm, Edmund, Exchange, Influence and Power, in Torben Agersnap (ed.), *Contributions to the Theory of Organizations*, 1968, I pp. 107 ff.

Darin-Drabkin, H., *The Other Society*, N.Y. 1963.

Del Vecchio, Giorgio, *Justice*, English translation, Edinburgh 1952.

Dowrick, F.E., *Justice according to the English Common Lawyers*, London 1961.

Dror, Yehezkel, Organizational Functions of a Domestic Tribunal : A Case Study of the Administrative Tribunal of the United Nations, *British Journal of Industrial Relations*, Vol. II, 1964, pp. 42 ff.

Durkheim, Emile, *De la division du travail social*, 1893, English translation by George Simpson, *The Division of Labor In Society*, 1933, Free Press, Paperback ed., N.Y. 1964.

Eckhoff, Torstein & Jacobsen, Knut Dahl, *Rationality and Responsibility in Administrative and Judicial Decision-making*, Interdisciplinary Studies from the Scandinavian Summer University, Copenhagen 1960.

Eckhoff, Torstein, Justice, Efficiency, and Self-Made Rules in Public Administration, *New York University Institute of Comparative Law, First Conference Copenhagen 1960*, Copenhagen 1962, pp. 52 ff., also in Torstein Eckhoff, *Justice and the Rule of Law*, Oslo 1966, pp. 66 ff.

– Justice and Social Utility, *Legal Essays, Festskrift for Frede Castberg*, Oslo 1963, pp. 74 ff., also in Torstein Eckhoff, *Justice and the Rule of Law*, Oslo 1966, pp. 43 ff.

– Impartiality, Separation of Powers, and Judicial Independence, *Scandinavian Studies in Law*, Vol. 9, 1965, also in Torstein Eckhoff, *Justice and the Rule of Law*, Oslo 1966, pp. 110 ff.

– The Mediator, the Judge and the Administrator in Conflict-resolution, *Acta Sociologica*, Vol. 10, 1966, pp. 148 ff.

Ehrenzweig, Albert A., Toward a Psychoanalysis of Law and Justice, *Festskrift tillägnad Karl Olivecrona*, Stockholm 1964, pp. 148 ff.

– Psychoanalytical Jurisprudence : A Common Language for Babylon, *Columbia Law Review*, Vol. 65, 1965, pp. 1331 ff.

Emge, C.A., Sicherheit und Gerechtigkeit, *Abhandlungen der Preussischen Akademie der Wissenschaften 1940*, Berlin 1941.

Exner, Franz, *Gerechtigkeit und Richteramt*, two inaugural orations, Leipzig, 1922.

Feinberg, Joel, Justice and Personal Desert, in Friedrich and Chapman, eds., *Nomos VI, Justice,* N.Y. 1963.

Festinger, Leon, A Theory of Social Comparison Processes, in : Hare, Borgatta and Bales, *Small Groups,* N.Y. 1955, pp. 163 ff.

– *A Theory of Cognitive Dissonance,* Evanston 1957.

Fivelsdal, Egil, *Funksjonaerenes syn på faglige og politiske spørsmål* (White collar workers' view on professional and political questions), Oslo 1964.

Flugel, J.C., *Man, Morals and Society,* London 1945.

Foa, Uriel G., Interpersonal and Economic Resources, *Science,* Vol. 171, 1971, pp. 345 ff.

Fock, Niels, Mataco Law, XXXVI Congreso internacional de americanistas, Sevilla 1966.

– Regulation of Conflicts in Amerindian Societies, in : Höglund and Ulrich, eds., *Conflict Control and Conflict Resolution,* Interdisciplinary Studies from the Scandinavian Summer University, Vol. 17, 1972.

Fossum, Egil, Factors influencing the Occurrence of Military Coups d'Etat in Latin America, *Journal of Peace Research,* 1967, pp. 228 ff.

Foster, George M., Peasant Society and the Image of Limited Good, *American Anthropologist,* Vol. 67, 1965, pp. 293 ff.

Frankena, William K., *Some Beliefs About Justice,* The Lindley Lecture, University of Kansas, 1966.

Friedrich, Carl J. and Chapman, John W. (eds.), *Nomos VI, Justice,* N.Y. 1963.

Galtung, Johan, Expectations and Interaction Processes, *Inquiry,* 1959, pp. 213 ff.

– *Fengselssamfunnet* (The prison society), Oslo 1959.

– A Structural Theory of Aggression, *Journal of Peace Research,* 1964, pp. 95 ff.

– Institutionalized Conflict Resolution, *Journal of Peace Research,* 1965, pp. 348 ff.

Gilbert, Doris C., and Levinson, Daniel J., 'Custodialism' and 'Humanism' in Staff Ideology, in : Greenblatt, Levinson and Williams, eds., *The Patient and the Mental Hospital,* Glencoe, Ill., 1957.

Ginsberg, Morris, *On Justice in Society,* Pelican Books, 1965.

Glass, David C., Changes in liking as a means of reducing cognitive discrepancies between self-esteem and aggression, *Journal of Personality,* Vol. 32, 1964, pp. 531-549.

Gluckman, Max, *The Judicial Process among the Barotse of Northern Rhodesia,* Glencoe, Ill., 1955.

– *The Ideas in Barotse Jurisprudence,* New Haven, 1965.

Goffman, Erving, *The Presentation of Self in Everyday Life,* Anchor Books ed., N.Y. 1959.

– *Asylums,* Anchors Books ed., N.Y. 1961.

Goffman, I.W., Status Consistency and Preference for Change in Power Distribution, *American Sociological Review,* Vol. 32, 1957, pp. 275 ff.

Goldschmidt, Verner, *Retlig Adfaerd* (Legal behaviour), Copenhagen 1957.

Goodhart, A.L., *English Law and The Moral Law,* London 1955.

Gouldner, Alvin W., The Norm of Reciprocity, *American Sociological Review,* Vol. 25, 1960, pp. 161-178.

Graf, Richard G., and Green, Duane, The equity restoring components of retaliation, *Journal of Personality*, Vol. 39, 1971, pp. 581 ff.

Gurvitch, Georges, Justice, *Encyclopaedia of the Social Sciences*, Vol. 8, N.Y. 1932, pp. 509 ff.

Hägerström, Axel, Om social rättvisa (On social justice), *Socialfilosofiska uppsatser*, Stockholm 1939, pp. 121 ff.

Harrison, Jonathan, Utilitarianism, Universalisation, and Our Duty to Be Just, *Proceedings of the Aristotelian Society*, Vol. 52, 1952-53, pp. 105 ff., also in Olafson, 1961.

Harrod, R.F., Utilitarianism Revised, *Mind*, Vol. 45, 1936, pp. 137 ff.

Hart, H.L.A., Are there any Natural Rights ?, *The Philosophical Review*, Vol. LXIV, No. 2, April 1955.

– Prolegomenon to the Principles of Punishment, *Proceedings of the Aristotelian Society*, 1959.

– *The Concept of Law*, Oxford 1961.

Heider, Fritz, *The Psychology of Interpersonal Relations*, N.Y. 1958.

Himmelstrand, Ulf, Tribalism, Nationalism, Rank-Equilibration and Social Structure, *Journal of Peace Research*, 1969, pp. 81 ff.

Hocking, William Ernest, Justice, Law, and the Cases, in *Interpretations of Modern Legal Philosophies, Essays in Honor of Roscoe Pound*, N.Y. 1947, pp. 332 ff.

Hodge, Robert W., The Status Consistency of Occupational Groups, *American Sociological Review*, 1962, pp. 336 ff.

Hoebel, E. Adamson, *The Law of Primitive Man*, Cambridge, Mass., 1954.

Holter, Harriet, *Sex Roles and Social Structure*, Oslo 1970.

Homans, George Caspar, *The Human Group*, N.Y. 1950.

– *Social Behavior, Its Elementary Forms*, N.Y. and London 1961.

– *Sentiments and Activities, Essays in Social Science*, Glencoe Ill. and London 1962.

Honoré, A.M., Social Justice, in : Robert S. Summers, ed., *Essays in Legal Philosophy*, Berkeley and Los Angeles 1968, pp. 61 ff.

Hospers, John, *Human Conduct, An introduction to the problems of ethics*, N.Y. 1961.

Jackson, Elton F., Status Consistency and Symptoms of Stress, *American Sociological Review*, Vol. 27, 1962, pp. 469-479.

Jacobsen, Knut Dahl, *Teknisk hjelp og politisk struktur* (Technical assistance and political structure), Oslo 1964.

Jaques, Elliott, *Measurement of Responsibility*, London 1956.

Jenkins, Robin, Who Are These Marchers ?, *Journal of Peace Research*, 1967, pp. 46 ff.

Johansson, Sten, Custodialism Among Mental Hospital Personnel, in : Agersnap, ed., *Contributions to the Theory of Organizations I*, Copenhagen 1968.

Johnson, Ronald C., A Study of Children's Moral Judgments, *Child Development*, Vol. 33, 1962, pp. 327 ff.

Kant, Immanuel, *Metaphysik der Sitten*, Königsberg 1797.

Kelsen, Hans, *What is Justice ?, Collection of essays*, Berkeley and Los Angeles 1957.

Kohlberg, Lawrence, The Development of Children's Orientations Toward a Moral Order, *Vita humana*, 1963, pp. 11 ff.
- Development of Moral Character and Moral Ideology, *Review of Child Development Research I*, N.Y. 1964.
Köhler, Wolfgang, *The Place of Value in a World of Facts*, N.Y. 1938.
Kolsrud, Knut, *Primitive relasjoner* (Elementary relations), mimeographed, Oslo 1958.
Kristol, Irving, Equality as an Ideal, *International Encyclopedia of the Social Sciences*, N.Y. 1968, V.
Kutschinsky, Berl, Law and Education : Some Aspects of Scandinavian Studies into 'The General Sense of Justice', *Acta Sociologica*, 1966, pp. 21 ff.
- Knowledge and Attitudes Regarding Legal Phenomena in Denmark, *Scandinavian Studies in Criminology*, Vol. 2, 1968, pp. 125 ff.

Langholm, Sivert, Violent Conflict Resolution and the Loser's Reaction, *Journal of Peace Research*, 1965, pp. 324 ff.
Lenski, Gerhard E., Status Crystallization : A Non-vertical Dimension of Social Status, *American Sociological Review*, Vol. 19, 1954, pp. 405-413.
Løchen, Yngvar, *Idealer og realiteter i et psykiatrisk sykehus* (Ideals and realities in a psychiatric hospital), Oslo 1965.
- Komparativ organisasjonsanalyse (Comparative Analysis of organizations), *Tidsskrift for samfunnsforskning*, 1966, pp. 295 ff.
Luce, R. Duncan and Raiffa, Howard, *Games and Decisions*, N.Y. 1957.
Lyons, David, *Forms and Limits of Utilitarianism*, Oxford 1965.
Lysgaard, Sverre, *Arbeiderkollektivet* (The workers' collectivity), Oslo 1961.
- *Arbeidernes syn på faglige og politiske spørsmål* (The workers' view on professional and political issues), Oslo 1965.

Mabbott, J.D., Punishment, *Mind*, Vol. 49, 1939, also in Olafson, 1961.
Macaulay, Steward, Non-Contractual Relations in Business : A Preliminary Study, *American Sociological Review*, Vol. 28, 1963, pp. 55 ff.
Malinowski, Bronislaw, *Argonauts of the Western Pacific*, London 1922.
- *Crime and Custom in Savage Society*, London 1926.
Mandelbaum, Maurice, *The Phenomenology of Moral Experience*, Glencoe, Ill., 1955.
March, James G. and Simon, Herbert A., *Organizations*, N.Y. 1958.
Mathiesen, Thomas, *The Defences of the Weak, A Sociological Study of a Norwegian Correctional Institution*, London 1965.
Mauss, Marcel, *Essai sur le don*, Paris 1950, English translation, *The Gift*, London 1954.
Medinnus, Gene R., Immanent Justice in Children : A Review of the Literature and Additional Data, *The Journal of Genetic Psychology*, 1959, pp. 253 ff.
Merton, Robert K., *Social Theory and Social Structure*, Glencoe, Ill., 1949, revised ed. 1957.
Monberg, Torben, *The Religion of Bellona Island*, Copenhagen 1966.

Naess, Siri, *Rettferdighetsholdninger. En undersøkelse av skolebarn og lærere* (Attitudes of justice. An investigation of school children and teachers), mimeographed, Oslo 1969.

Ofstad, Harald, *An Inquiry into the Freedom of Decision*, Oslo 1961.

Olafson, Frederick A. (ed.), *Justice and Social Policy,* Spectrum Book, N.Y. 1961.

Oppenheim, Felix, The Concept of Equality, *International Encyclopedia of the Social Sciences,* N.Y. 1968.

Osgood, Charles E., Suggestions for winning the real war with communism, *The Journal of Conflict Resolution,* Vol. 3, 1959, pp. 295-325.

Perelman, Ch., *The Idea of Justice and the Problem of Argument,* English translation, London 1963.

Piaget, Jean, *Le jugement moral chez l'enfant,* Alcan 1926, English translation, *The Moral Judgment of the Child,* London 1932, 5th ed. 1968.

Pollan, Sonja, Prestetradisjon og presterekruttering 1720-1955 (Traditions and recruitment of priests 1720-1955), *Tidsskrift for samfunnsforskning,* 1962, pp. 83 ff.

Rapoport, Anatol, *Fights, Games, and Debates,* Ann Arbor, Mich. 1960.

Rasmussen, Knud, *Across Arctic America,* N.Y. and London 1927.

Rawls, John, Two Concepts of Rules, *The Philosophical Review,* LXIV, 1955, pp. 3-32.

– *A Theory of Justice,* Cambridge, Mass., 1971.

Reiss, Hans (ed.), *Kant's Political Writings,* Cambridge 1970.

Rescher, Nicholas, The Concept of Randomness, *Theoria,* 1961, pp. 1 ff.

– *Distributive Justice,* Indianapolis and N.Y. 1966.

Rhenman, Eric, Organizational Goals, in : Torben Agersnap, ed., *Contributions to the Theory of Organizations I,* Copenhagen 1968, pp. 75 ff.

Riesman, David, *The Lonely Crowd,* New Haven 1950.

Roethlisberger, F.J. and Dickson, W.J., *Management and the Worker,* Cambridge, Mass. 1939, 7th ed. 1946.

Ross, Alf, *On Law and Justice,* London 1958.

Runciman, W.G., *Relative Deprivation and Social Justice,* London 1966.

Russett, Cynthia Eagle, *The Concept of Equilibrium in American Social Thought,* New Haven, 1966.

Salin, Edgar, Just Price, *Encyclopaedia of the Social Sciences,* Vol. 8, N.Y. 1932, pp. 504 ff.

Sampson, Edward E., Studies of Status Congruence, in : L. Berkowitz, ed., *Advances in Experimental Social Psychology,* Vol. 4, N.Y. and London 1969.

Schelling, Thomas C., *The Strategy of Conflict,* Cambridge, Mass. 1960.

Selznick, Philip, *Law, Society and Industrial Justice,* Russell Sage Foundation, 1969.

Sidgwick, Henry, *The Methods of Ethics,* 5th ed. London 1893, the chapters on justice also in Olafson, 1961, pp. 3 ff. and 29 ff.

Simon, Herbert A., *Models of Man, Social and Rational,* N.Y. 1957.

– Theories of Decision-Making in Economics and Behavioral Science, *The American Economic Review,* Vol. XLIX, 1959, pp. 253 ff.

Simpson, Richard L., *Theories of Social Exchange,* General Learning Press, Morristown, 1972.

Skolnick, Jerome H., *Justice Without Trial, Law Enforcement in Democratic Society,* N.Y. 1967.

Sobel, J. Howard, Generalization Arguments, *Theoria*, 1965, pp. 32 ff.
Spencer, Herbert, *Principles of Ethics*, Part IV Justice, London 1891.
Sykes, Gresham M., *The Society of Captives*, Princeton, N.J. 1958.

Thibaut, John W., and Kelley, Harold H., *The Social Psychology of Groups*, N.Y. 1959.
Thurnwald, Richard, *Economics in Primitive Communities*, London 1932.
Torgersen, Ulf, *Programutforming og partifasade* (Elaboration of the program of political parties and the presentation of the party profile), mimeographed, Oslo 1967.
Tucker, Robert C., Marx and Distributive Justice, in : Friedrich and Chapman, *Nomos VI, Justice*, N.Y. 1963, pp. 306 ff.
Turner, J.W. Cecil, and Armitage, A.L.L., *Cases on Criminal Law*, Cambridge 1964.
Turner, Jim L., Foa, Edna B., and Foa, Uriel G., Interpersonal Reinforcers, *Journal of Personality and Social Psychology*, Vol. 19, No. 2, August 1971.

Wallace, Michael D., Power, Status, and International War, *Journal of Peace Research*, 1971, pp. 23-35.
Walster, Elaine, and Prestholdt, Perry, The Effect of Misjudging Another, Over-Compensation or Dissonance Reduction ?, *Journal of Experimental Social Psychology*, Vol. 2, 1966, pp. 85-97.
Weber, Max, Wirtschaft und Gesellschaft, *Grundriss der Sozialökonomik*, III, 2nd ed. Tübingen 1925.
 – *Max Weber on Law in Economy and Society*, ed. Max Rheinstein, Cambridge, Mass., 1954.
Wedberg, Birger, *Tärningkast om liv och död* (Throwing dice with life and death at stake), Stockholm 1935.
Weingarten, Murray, *Life in a Kibbutz*, Jerusalem 1959.
Westermarck, Edward, *The Origin and Development of the Moral Ideas*, I and II, London 1906 and 1908.
Whyte, W.F., *Street Corner Society*, Chicago 1943.
Whyte, William H. Jr., *The Organization Man*, London 1957.
Wollheim, Richard, Equality and Equal Rights, *Proceedings of the Aristotelian Society*, Vol. 56, 1955-56, also in Olafson 1961.
Wright, Georg Henrik von, *The Varieties of Goodness*, London 1963.

Indices

405

Schelling, T.C., 88, 91 n, 95 f, 292
Selznick, P., 182, 273 n
Sidgwick, H., 19, 29 f, 34 n, 35 n
Simon, H.A., 11 n, 45 n, 64 n, 244, 265, 270 n, 273 n, 371 n
Skolnick, J.H., 67, 77
Sobel, J.H., 27 n
Spencer, H., 34 n
Spinoza, B., 150 n
Steiner, G.A., 18, 73 n, 74 n, 130, 153 n, 169 n, 273 n, 285 n, 324, 375 n
Sykes, G.M., 256 f

Thibaut, J.W., 12 n, 56, 169 n
Thurnwald, R., 84
Torgersen, U., 66
Tucker, R.C., 225 n

Tullock, G., 10 n, 66
Turner, J.L., 54 n, 58 n

U.S. v. Holmes, 305 f

Wallace, M.D., 241 n
Walster, E., 200 n
Weber, M., 11 n, 59, 111 n, 112
Wedberg, B., 215, 216
Weingarten, M., 225 n, 226
Westermarck, E., 68 n, 84, 155 n, 161 n, 186 n, 188 n, 189, 193 n
Whyte, W.F., 72 n, 73, 105 n
Whyte, W.H., 285 n, 389 n
Wright, G.H. von, 72 n, 136 n

Zelditch, M., Jr., 240 n

407

Diagnostic culture, 391 f
Dictators, 333 f, 342 f
Diffuse reasons, 43 f
Distribution, defined, 205, relation to allocation, 205 f, problems connected with, 209 ff, effects of retributive justice on, 98 f. See also Allocation
Distribution-orientation, defined, 279, factors giving rise to, 285 ff, effects of, 300 ff
Distributive justice, defined, 31 f, different kinds of, 34 ff, relation to retributive justice, 233, 315, 355 f. See also Justice
Distributor, defined, 5 ff, 32, allocation strategies, 243 ff, organization, 268 ff, relationship to recipients, 324 ff, removal of, 327, different kinds of, 333 f, reactions to recipient behaviour, 389 ff
Drawing lots, 37, 215 ff, 267, 303 ff, 321
Duels, 160 f
Duty, allocation according to, 229 ff, 312 ff

Economic planning, 361 f
Employees, helping each other, 64 f, in the distributor organization, 270 ff, finding protection in rules, 274. See also Labour relations.
Enforcement, of obligations, 109 f, of decisions, 262
Equality, and balance, 31, and distribution, 31 f, different principles of, 34 ff, object oriented, 35 f, 211 ff, 289 ff, 320, subjective, 36, 38 f, 40, relative, 36 f, 38 f, 232 f, 312 f, rank order, 37, 237, 311, equal chances, 37 f, 215 ff, 303 ff, equal satisfaction of needs, 36, 222 f, 309 f, 311 f
Equilibrium, 31, 64 n
Eskimos, revenge, 155, 160
Exactness, in exchange relationships, advantages and disadvantages of, 107 ff, 110 ff
Exchange, defined, 3 f, 53 ff, economic and social, 54, specialized and unspecialized, 55 f, objects of, 55, 58 ff, of material things, 58 ff, of services, 63 ff, of abstention from harming, of compliance with norms, 70 ff, of exemption from norm-compliance, 76 ff, of positive attitudes, 79 ff, regulation of, 56 ff, 83 ff, restrictions, 57, 123, motivation and obstacles to, 86 ff, as norm-creating factor, 69 f, 71 f, 83 ff, as peace-securing factor, 97 f, in conflict resolution, 164 f, and power, 71, and restitution, 133 f, 143 f, and punishment, 175, 176
Expiatory punishment, 175 ff

Factual premises, 19 ff
Fire brigade, 270
Fitness, defined, 38, 227, allocation according to, 227 ff, 250 f, 254, 259 f, 308 ff, and status, 234 f
Formalized hostilities, 160 f
Free will, and moral responsibility, 188 n
French revolution, 240
Frustration and aggression, 153 n
Functional theories, 93, 99 ff

Game theory, 91 n, 94 n, 95 f
Glossy pictures, exchange of, 62
God, the jealous, 189, decisions made by, 215 f
Gods, exchange with, 68
Goodwill, payment for, 81 f, appeals to, 338 ff, 358, 366 f
Government, interference in economic affairs, 75 f, 361 f. See also Citizen and state
Gratitude, as payment, 64 f, 79 ff, 98
Greenland, punishment in, 183 n, family relations, 287 f. See also Eskimos
Group interests, with regard to exchange, 96 ff, restitution, 139 ff, revenge, 157, allocation, 364 ff

Help, exchange of, 63 ff, allocation of, 247 ff, to self-help, 250

tion, 146 f, punishment, 185, justice, 111 f, 117 f, 128, conditions of, 112 ff
Market places, 112
Marxism, 225 n
Mataco-Indians, 160 n
Material things, exchange of, 58 ff
Matthew effect, 237 f, 250 f
Measurement, of values, 114, 146 f, of responsibility, 241 n, developing standards of, 285, 312 ff
Mental hospitals, 270, 275, 329 n, 376 n, 391 f
Mercy. See Compassion and Pardoning
Middle ages, trade, 59, 112
Military service, exemption from, 215, 267
Minimax principle, 91 n, 94 n
Mixed-motive games, 91 n, 95 f
Monarchy, absolute, 343
Monetary system, and market formation, 112 f, 114
Monopolization, effects of, 63 f, 90 f, 328
Moral responsibility, 188 n
Mosaic law, 189 f, 193
Moscow trials, 179
Mutual respect and fellow-feeling, 368
Mutuality of restrictions, 72, 260

Nazism, 240
Need, defined, 38, 220, allocation according to, 220 ff, 248 ff, 253 f, 308 ff, 358, equal satisfaction of, 222 ff, 253 f, connections with status, 234 f
Negotiation. See Bargaining and International relations
Nordic societies, revenge in Viking times, 155, 158 f, 163 ff
Normative reasons, 23, 25 ff, for punishment, 196 ff
Norms, relations to strategies, 10 ff, regulating argumentation, 45 f, 195, regulating exchange, 56 ff, compliance as object of exchange, 70 ff, exemption from norm-compliance, 76 ff, of competence, 119, forbidding injury, 69 f, 72 f, 135 f, demanding restitution, 136 ff, demanding revenge, 155, regulating revenge, 158 ff, regulating the use of punishment, 178 ff, norm violation as a requirement of punishment, 180 f, normative justification of punishment, 196, norms against social mobility, 241, demanding relative equality, 314 f, promoting collective activity, 368, 384 f. See also Principles and Rules
Norway, organizational development in, 122 f, law of torts, 143, 147, agricultural policy, 250 f, public administration, 361 f, political controversies, 380
Nulla poena sine lege, 181 n

Object oriented, equality, 35 f, 38 f, 211 ff, 289 ff, 348, 357, reasons, 43 f, conceptions of justice, 192, allocation principles, 210 f, 304
Opinion, support of, 66
Opportunity, equal, 37 f, 38 f
Optimum distribution, 248 f, 293 f
Organization, defined, 118 f, formation of, 120 f, significance for exchange, 118 ff, relation to agreements and market mechanisms, 122 f, as vehicle of new forms of exchange, 123, making older forms of exchange superfluous, 122 f, redressing damage and covering losses, 144 ff, and revenge, 166, and punishment, 184 f, as distributor, 268 ff

Pardoning, criminals, 187, 343
Parents. See Children
Party, defined, 5, 32
Peasant societies, 281
Person oriented, reasons, 43 f, conceptions of justice, 192, allocation principles, 210 f, 230
Personal exchange, 115 f
Personality traits, and conceptions of justice, 85 f, and revenge, 154 f, their strategic value, 155 f

Planning, allocation, 268 ff, 273 f, 361 f

Plea bargaining, 77

Poetic justice, the fantasy of, 337

Police, 67, 77

Political prisons, 378

Position, defined, 38, allocation according to, 218 ff, 307 f

Power, recipients' assertion of, 331, 338 f, 346

Power-conferring norms, 118 f

Predictability, recipients' need for, 294 f, 325, advantages and disadvantages for the distributor, 269 f, 392 f

Price determination, 89 ff, based on justice, 59, 92, 93 f, 98, on specific rules, 101 ff, on market mechanisms, 111 ff

Primitive societies, exchange in, 59 ff, 103 f, revenge in, 153 ff

Principles, defined, 26, inferences from, 25 ff, of justice, 29 ff

Prisons, 191 f, 256 f, 347 ff, 359 f, 375 ff

Procedural problems, connected with allocation, 208 f, 245, 261 ff, importance for recipients, 278, 296 f, 302 f, when recipients undertake the allocation, 318 ff

Proportionality, in retributive justice, 71, in relative equality, 36 f, 232 f, of rewards, 132

Public administration, 361 f

Public peace arrangements, 112

Public service organization, 144

Punisher, need to defend his action, 170 f, 195, legitimacy, 174 f, 179 f, 189, exchange as basis of legitimacy, 175, avoiding responsibility, 182

Punishment, defined, 148 ff, 167, difference from revenge, 149 f, alternative to revenge, 162, as means of exerting influence, 167 ff, 195, 255 ff, compared with reward, 169, consequences for future relationship, 170, acceptance of, 170 ff, importance of being warned, 173 f, 182, 184, 199, by reciprocity,

175 f, expiatory, 177, norms regulating the use of, 178 ff, laws against corporal, 183, amount of, 184, 189 ff, significance of organization, 184 f, principles of justice connected with, 185 ff, relation to restitution, 188, collective, 188, reasons for and against, 194 ff, allocation of, 313 f, 357 f

Queues, 218 ff, 234, 307

Random selection, 37 ff, 215 ff, 267, 303 ff, 321 f, as a principle of justice, 31 f, 216 f

Rank consistency, 239 ff, and political attitudes, 240 f, and justice, 241, tensions caused by inconsistency, 241

Rank differences, in exchange relationships, 80 f, 103 f, and punishment, 192 f, and distribution, 236 ff, self-preserving, 237 f, attitudes to, 238 f

Rank dimensions, 238 ff

Rank equilibrium, 239 n

Rank order equality, 38 f, 219, 222, 228, 237, 311, 312 ff

Reasons, defined, 13 ff, different types of, 19 ff, consequence oriented, 19 f, 20 ff, non-consequence oriented, 23 ff, rule oriented, 26, diffuse, 43 f, determinants and effects of, 44 ff, 194 ff, as means of influencing attitudes, 47, informative effects of, 47 f, significance for evaluation, 48, for and against punishment, 194 ff

Recipient coupling, 280 ff, 286 f

Recipients, defined, 5 ff, 32, relevant characteristics of, 38 f, units and circle of, 208, 210, 221, 228, 235, attitudes to allocation issues, 278 ff, need to protect themselves, 294 f, 302, 316 ff, 324 ff, efforts to improve or secure their position, 324 ff, ways of influencing allocation, 329 ff, adaptation, 334 ff, 351, collective actions, 364 ff

Reciprocation, defined, 3 ff, different

kinds of, 3 ff, 7 ff, 51 ff, of negative values, 148 ff
Reciprocity norms, 103 ff. See also Retributive justice
Reference group, 285
Relative equality, 36 f, 38 f, 232 f, 312 ff
Reprisals, risk of, 333 f, 367 f
Resources, of argument, 45, 195
Respect, as exchange value, 64 f, 115
Responsibility, protection against, 48, 78, 182, 262, 305, as a factor in exchange, 78 f, moral, 188 n, measurement of, 241 n
Restitution, defined, 4, 133 f, connections with exchange, 134 f, regulating factors, 134 ff, norms, 136 ff, justice 141 ff, agreements, 143 f, organization, 144 ff, market mechanism, 146 f, alternative to revenge, 162 ff
Retributive justice, defined, 30 f, ideas of equality involved in, 39 ff, relation to distributive justice, 233, 315, 355 f. See also Justice
Retroactive laws, prohibition against, 181 f
Revenge, defined, 148 ff, relation to punishment, 149 f, 162, revenge-promoting strategies and norms, 153 ff, normful effects of, 156 f, norms against, 157 ff, techniques against, 160 ff, restitution as an alternative to, 162 ff
Reward, defined, 93 n, motives for giving, 129, as means of exerting influence, 129 ff, 255 ff, connections with retributive justice, 129 ff, allocation of, 313, 357 f
Right, allocation according to, 229 ff, 312 ff, fighting for one's, 352 f, 382 f
Role-differentiation, in criminal procedure, 199
Rule-utilitarianism, 27
Rules, defined, 26, inferences from, 25 ff, regulating exchange, 101 ff, relation to principles of justice, 102 f, deliberate making of, 120 f, regulating restitution, 142 f, as justification of punishment, 198, procedural advantages of following, 263 ff, effects on employees, 275 ff. See also Principles and Norms
Rural development, 247 ff

Sacrifice, allocation according to, 220 ff
Sacrifices, to gods, 68
Sadism, 152 f
Sanctions. See Punishment, Reward, and Verbal sanctions
Sardinia, revenge in, 155
Secondary adjustments, 329 n, 337
Self-oriented recipients, 278 f
Seniority, 239, 389
Services, exchange of, 63 ff
Sex differences, in occupational behaviour, 371, 385
Sincerity, recipients', 322, 350 f
Social mobility, 241
Social services, 247 ff
Solidarity, 368
Specific, reasons, 43 f, conceptions of justice, 192, allocation criteria, 265 f, 297, 303, 320, 395
Standpoints, 13 ff
Status defined, 38, 234, duties, 65 allocation according to 234 ff, 308 ff, and equality, 236, rank ordered, 237 ff, connections with need, fitness and desert, 234 f. See also Rank
Status congruence, 239 n
Status consistency, 239 n
Status equilibrium, 239 n
Strategies, relation to norms, 10 ff, of argumentation, 46 ff, 195, of exchange, 57 f, giving rise to exchange norms, 85, 92 ff with regard to restitution, 137 f, promoting revenge, 153 ff, to restrict the use of revenge, 160 ff, of punishment, 168 ff, of allocation, 243 ff, recipients', 338 f
Stratification. See Rank differences
Street-gangs, exchange of information, 67, reciprocity-norms, 104 f
Subjective equality, 35, 38 f, 40

413

Suffering, allocation according to, 220 ff

Talionic principle, 159, 176 f, 189 f, 192, 193
Third party, taking over revenge, 161 f, in conflict resolution, 165 f
Time priority, allocation according to, 38 f, 218 ff, 307 f
Tiv tribe, 104 n
Torts, development of the law of, 142, 145 f, 147

United Nations, declaration of human rights, 181 n
University professors, appointment of, 267 f

Utilitarian reasons, for punishment, 196 ff. See also Consequence oriented reasons

Vacillation, between different types of arguments, 334, 350 f, 366
Value, transfer of, 3 ff, premises, 19 ff, conversion of, 57, measurement of, 114, 146 f, coupling, 282 f, 288
Verbal sanctions, 330
Vikings, revenge practices, 155, 158 f, conflict resolution, 163 ff

Welfare work, 247 ff
White collar workers, 374 f, 387 f
Work, exchange of, 63 ff
Workers' collective, 393 f